D0804364

RUSSIAN FEDERATION

MONGOLIA

Beijing

BO HAI

NORTH KOREA

SOUTH KOREA

YELLOW SEA

Shanghai

EAST CHINA SEA

VIETNAM

SOUTH CHINA SEA

LAOS

SHANGHAI
See pp120–67
Street Finder maps
pp168–73

EYEWITNESS TRAVEL

BEIJING &
SHANGHAI

EYEWITNESS TRAVEL

BEIJING & SHANGHAI

MAIN CONTRIBUTOR: PETER NEVILLE-HADLEY

DK

LONDON, NEW YORK,
MELBOURNE, MUNICH AND DELHI
www.dk.com

PRODUCED BY BRAZIL STREET
PROJECT EDITOR Andrew Humphreys
ART EDITOR Gadi Farfour

DORLING KINDERSLEY
SENIOR EDITOR Hugh Thompson
DTP DESIGNER Natasha Lu
PICTURE RESEARCHERS Ellen Root
PRODUCTION Linda Dare

CONTRIBUTORS
Peter Neville-Hadley, Donald Bedford, Christopher Knowles

PHOTOGRAPHERS
Chen Chao, Colin Sinclair, Linda Whitwam

ILLUSTRATORS
Gary Cross, Richard Draper, Paul Guest,
Chapel Design & Marketing, John Mullany

Printed in Malaysia by Vivar Printing Sdn Bhd.

First American Edition 2007
14 15 16 10 9 8 7 6 5 4 3 2

Published in the United States by DK Publishing,
345 Hudson Street, New York, New York 10014

Reprinted with revisions 2009, 2011, 2013

Copyright 2007, 2013 © Dorling Kindersley Limited, London
A Penguin Company

Published in the UK by Dorling Kindersley Limited.

A CATALOG RECORD FOR THIS BOOK IS
AVAILABLE FROM THE LIBRARY OF CONGRESS.

ISSN 1542-1554
ISBN: 978-0-75669-518-7

FLOORS ARE REFERRED TO THROUGHOUT IN ACCORDANCE WITH
US USAGE; IE THE "FIRST FLOOR" IS AT GROUND LEVEL.

Front cover main image: Qinan Hall, Temple of Heaven, Beijing

MIX
Paper from
responsible sources
FSC
www.fsc.org   FSC™ C018179

CONTENTS

Gateway, Lama Temple, Beijing

INTRODUCING BEIJING AND SHANGHAI

**A colonial-era lion guarding a
doorway on the Bund, Shanghai**

◁ **Inner Court gateway, the Forbidden City, Beijing**

Antiques in the Dongtai Road market, Shanghai

Players and spectators at a game of
mah jong, Hou Hai, Beijing

The Hall of Prayer of Good
Harvests, centerpiece of the
Temple of Heaven, Beijing

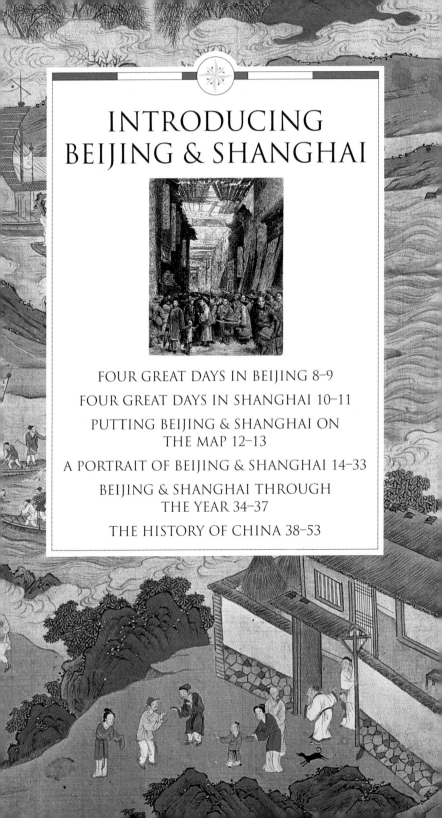

INTRODUCING
BEIJING & SHANGHAI

FOUR GREAT DAYS IN BEIJING

Rapidly redeveloping Beijing changes on an almost weekly basis, so here are four days largely dedicated to giving a flavor of an older China before it vanishes. Famous sights like the Temple of Heaven and the Forbidden City, are safe from the bulldozers, but traditional *hutong* life is certainly under threat, as are the old open-air markets visited here, such as Guanyuan and

Practicing
tai ji quan

Panjiayuan. There's also a day spent away from the city at the Great Wall, a must for all visitors to Beijing. Energetic sightseers should manage everything on these itineraries, but this selection can also be dipped into for ideas. All walks are reachable by public transport. Price guides are for two adults or for a family of two adults and two children, excluding meals.

EMPIRE TO REPUBLIC

- The imperial splendor of the Forbidden City
- Stand on the spot where modern China began
- Pay your respects to the embalmed Chairman Mao

TWO ADULTS allow ¥300

Morning

Start early at **Jing Shan Park** (*see p68*) at the east side where the last Ming emperor hanged himself on a tree known as the Guilty Sophora. Climb to the top of the hill for a spectacular view south across the roofscape of the **Forbidden City** (*see pp62–7*). Just below is the northern entrance to the palace. It would be easy to spend a day here, but for a first taste rent an audio guide and travel south along the main axis, through the emperors' private quarters, and past the great halls of audience and administration. Just a simple walk through such as this will still take up much of the morning. There are snack restaurants dotted around the interior, marked on maps.

Heroic Socialist sculptures in front of Mao's Mausoleum

Afternoon

Leaving the palace by the main entrance you pass through the **Tian'an Men** (*see p59*); buy a ticket that allows you to mount the Ming-era gate and stand where Mao stood to announce the formation of the People's Republic on October 1, 1949. The Chairman's embalmed body lies in his **mausoleum** (*see p58*), which is straight ahead (not open every day), but first deposit bags to the south of the **National Museum of China** (*see p59*). The museum presents a manipulated history of China through some of the

most famous treasures of the imperial era as well as photos and installations chronicling the Communist rule since 1949. Finish the day by walking to the southern end of Tian'an Men Square and ascending the **Qian Men** (*see p58*), one of the last relics of the Ming city walls. The views back across the square to the Forbidden City are the stuff of memories.

FAMILY BEIJING – INSECTS TO ACROBATS

- To market, for flowers, birds, fish, and insects
- Let the children run wild in the park
- Partake in a tea ceremony
- See an acrobatic show

FAMILY OF FOUR allow ¥1,000

Morning

There has been a revival of Beijing's traditional pastimes: *hua, niao, yu, chong* – flowers, birds, fish, and insects. Take a taxi to the **Guanyuan Market** to see the revived popularity of all four, especially the insect vendors in the alley at the rear. Jump on the subway at nearby Fucheng Men and ride four stops north to Jishuitan. This is the beginning of the Hou Hai walk (*see pp100–101*), which you can follow as far as the restored **Mei Lanfang Memorial Hall**. At this point taxi south for lunch at **Lao Beijing Zhajiang Mian Da Wang** (*see p198*).

Tian'an Men, the imposing gate from which the square takes its name

◁ Emperor Hui Tsung (r.110–26) transporting pierced stones, from *A History of the Emperors of China* (color on silk)

Afternoon

From the restaurant it is a short walk to the magnificent **Temple of Heaven** (see pp74–7), where you can see locals enjoying the green spaces, playing board games, and exercising. Plus of course there are the many and varied historical buildings. Then back north to the **Purple Vine Teahouse** (see p108), just outside the Forbidden City's west gate, for tea in a traditional setting. In the evening, you have the option of **Beijing Opera** or **traditional acrobatic performances** in historic surroundings at either the Huguang Guildhall or Zhengyici Theater (see p107). Children will definitely prefer the latter.

Practicing *tai ji quan* at the Temple of Heaven

ANCIENT ARCHITECTURE AND MODERN ART

- Walk the Great Wall
- Visit the resting place of Ming emperors
- View cutting-edge art in a former factory compound

TWO ADULTS allow ¥600

Morning

Arrange an early start with your taxi – hired in advance – for a trip to the **Great Wall at Badaling** (see p92). Once there, head off along the right hand section of wall for a longer hike – once you clear the crowds you can better enjoy the expansive views and fresh air without being

The Great Wall – the great unmissable daytrip from Beijing

jostled for space. If you haven't brought your own packed lunch you can eat at one of the restaurants at the site, but they are touristy and fairly expensive.

Afternoon

Most organized tours head off to the **Ming Tombs** (see pp88–9) but these are not especially compelling unless you're really interested in Ming funerary architecture or are enjoying your break from the city. Keep the visit short then, and have the driver head back to central Beijing via the **798 Art District** (see p85) for a former industrial compound now busy with artists' studios, galleries, and a handful of suitably cool cafés in which to observe Beijing's boho scene.

DISCOUNT SHOPPING

- Explore Beijing's biggest flea market
- Hunt clothing bargains
- Lunch on Chinese dumplings

TWO ADULTS ¥200 plus shopping

Morning

Make an early morning start – the earlier the better – for a trip to **Panjiayuan Market** (see p103), best at weekends but still busy on other days, too. Here you'll find just about any and every kind of souvenir imaginable at prices far lower than tourist shops. From the market take a short taxi ride to nearby **Hong Qiao Market** (see p103) to browse the shoes and clothes in the

main market, pearls upstairs (beware the low quality, though), or everything from PlayStations to jigsaws and radio-controlled models in Toy City, which is in an annexe to the rear. If you can haul yourself away, aim to grab lunch on **Qian Men Dajie**, which is just a short ride west and is lined with boutiques and restaurants, some specializing in *jiaozi* (dumplings).

Afternoon

After dining, stroll to the **Beijing Silk Store** (see p104), which is just off Qian Men. From here, take a taxi on to **Bai Nao Hui** (see p104) for computer accessories and other electronics, then further east to **Yaxiu Market** for cheap clothing (see p104). This is a good place to finish up as you are now in the heart of Sanlitun, with its vast array of bars and restaurants in which to help you recover.

A seller of bead, coral and stone necklaces at Hong Qiao Market

FOUR GREAT DAYS IN SHANGHAI

One of the greatest pleasures of a visit to Shanghai lies in observing the contrast between the solid civic worthiness of the foreign buildings on one side of the Huangpu, and the newly erected glitzy towers that face them across the water. The first day out samples both, while the second focuses on the city's excellent art collections. The third returns to the contrast of old and new, but tells the story through retail, after which, take a break from the bustle with an expedition out of town to the so-called "Venice of the East," the canal town of Suzhou. Price guides are for two adults or for a family of two adults and two children, excluding meals.

Fan dancer on the Bund

The Shanghai skyline, as seen from the Bund

OLD AND NEW SHANGHAI

- Colonial architecture on the Bund
- Lunch on the waterfront
- The skyscrapers of Pudong
- Tunnel rides, express elevators, and ferry trips

FAMILY OF FOUR allow ¥1,000 plus meals

Morning
Start at the south of the **Bund** *(see pp122–3)* around the Fangbang Middle Road junction. Get there early to watch locals perform their morning exercises of *tai ji quan* or sword play on the promenade. Spend a few hours wandering the grand riverfront sweep, enjoying the early 20th-century foreign architecture, or take the elevated riverside walkway for striking views of the Pudong skyline. Some riverfront buildings can be entered to view original murals and period fittings. Reaching Suzhou Creek, double back via **Huangpu**

Park to browse the many boutiques. For lunch with views, dine at **M on the Bund** *(see p206)* or **Sir Elly's** at the Peninsula Hotel *(see p186)*.

Afternoon
The well-signposted **Bund Sightseeing Tunnel** *(see p136)* offers a ride beneath the river in electric gondolas. You emerge near the base of the **Oriental Pearl TV Tower** *(see p136)*. Here, you can either buy a ticket for the **Shanghai History Museum** or visit the **Shanghai Ocean Aquarium** *(see p136)* next door, which is one of the best of its kind. Take the elevator to the top of China's tallest building, **Shanghai World Financial Center** *(see p137)* and enjoy the lofty views over the city from the observatory. There is a food court in the basement of nearby **Jinmao Tower** *(see p137)*, or stay for dinner at one of the Grand Hyatt's restaurants, all with staggering views. Walk back to the riverside and the ferry terminal and pay ¥2 for a brief ride across the river back to where you started.

ALL ABOUT ART

- **Fabulous artifacts at the Shanghai Museum**
- **Lunch in contemporary style at MOCA**
- **Shop for arts and crafts**

TWO ADULTS allow ¥200 plus meals and show tickets

Morning
The former race course, now **People's Park** (subway: People's Square) has become the center of Shanghai's cultural life. Start with the **Shanghai Museum** *(see pp126–9)*, which is one of the best in China. How you divide your visit depends on your preferences for ancient artifacts or modern art. Opt to spend the morning here enjoying delicate Chinese calligraphy, pottery, and paintings. Afterwards cross the park to the **Shanghai Urban Planning Exhibition Hall** *(see pp124–5)*, which traces the structural history and future of this fast expanding megacity.

People's Park with the Shanghai Grand Theater in the background

Afternoon

For lunch and a further dose of modern Chinese art there's the nearby **MOCA (Museum of Contemporary Art)** *(see p124)*, which is worth visiting for the architecture alone. Pass the strikingly modern **Shanghai Grand Theater** *(see p125)* and check what's on during your stay; your hotel can help make a booking if necessary. For a terrific view of the places you have just visited, cross the road to the Tomorrow Square building and take the elevator up to the reception of the **J.W. Marriott** *(see p186)* on the 38th floor for panoramic views. Finally, take a short taxi ride south to the **Taikang Road** *(see p161)* a center known for its contemporary art galleries, cafés, small boutiques, and craft workshops.

Taikang Road, the place to pick up paintings and applied art

ALLEYWAYS AND AVENUES

• Shop on Nanjing Road
• Compare the old Chinese and foreigner quarters
• Visit a colonial villa

TWO ADULTS allow ¥500.

Morning

The pedestrianized part of **Nanjing Road** (Henan Road to Xizang Road) was once known as the best shopping street in China. It may no longer be cutting-edge, but it still remains the city's most atmospheric avenue for shopping and street

Monks at the City Temple in the Yu Gardens Bazaar

entertainment. From here you can walk or take a taxi to the Old City and the busy **Yu Gardens Bazaar** *(see p130)*. Most of the flying-eaved buildings here are of recent construction but there is the working City Temple, the Yu Gardens, and the very picturesque Huxinting Teahouse as well as lots of shops. Enjoy lunch in one of the dumpling restaurants around the teahouse but aim to be there early as these places get very busy.

Afternoon

Walk west from the bazaar among the winding alleyways of the Old City to get a taste of the past – old people sitting outside their homes playing *mah jong* while the washing billows overhead and bicycles cut through the narrow paths. Pass old temples, mosques, and markets, before cutting north to **Huaihai Middle Road**, once the grand Avenue Joffre and now where the chic department stores and malls reside. This isn't the place for bargains but it is fun window-shopping alongside the Chinese.

Finish the day by taking a taxi to **Sinan Mansions** *(see p159)*, which is located at the corner of Sinan Road and Fuxing Road. This area of 1930s villas has been redeveloped as a hip dining, drinking, and shopping district in the heart of the former French Concession.

GARDENS OF SUZHOU

• Enjoy a canal boat ride
• Dine on Suzhou specialties
• Stroll around gardens designed over generations

TWO ADULTS allow ¥350.

Morning

Suzhou *(see pp144–9)* is close to Shanghai but an early start by train, which will take around 30 minutes, is still recommended (you can also join an organized tour). This is one of many canal towns around Shanghai nicknamed the "Venice of the East." Visits begin with a ride in the local equivalent of a gondola, taken from across the road from the railway station, to alight at the **Pan Men Scenic Area** *(see p149)*. This is where you find the double gate and climb the Ruiguang Pagoda. Then head by cab to the stunning **Suzhou Museum** *(see p144)*, designed by I M Pei, which focus on the area's rich cultural and archaeological history. Next, visit the sprawling **Humble Administrator's Garden** beside the museum *(see pp146–7)*.

Afternoon

Take a taxi north to Guanqian Street for lunch at **Deyue Lou** *(see p207)* before visiting Suzhou's gardens, such as the quieter and more intimate **Ou Yuan** *(see p144)* or the **Master of the Nets Garden**, considered the most satisfying for its balanced *feng shui*.

Tour boats awaiting passengers for a canal cruise

Putting Beijing & Shanghai on the Map

Beijing sits on a plain 25 miles (40 kilometers) east of the mountains that once offered protection from the war-like tribes of the provinces beyond. It is one of very few capitals not sited on a major river system. By contrast, Shanghai sits on the banks of the Huangpu River, on silt carried down in the muddy waters of the Yangzi and washed up the Huangpu with the tide. Since rapid development began in the 19th century, constant dredging has been necessary.

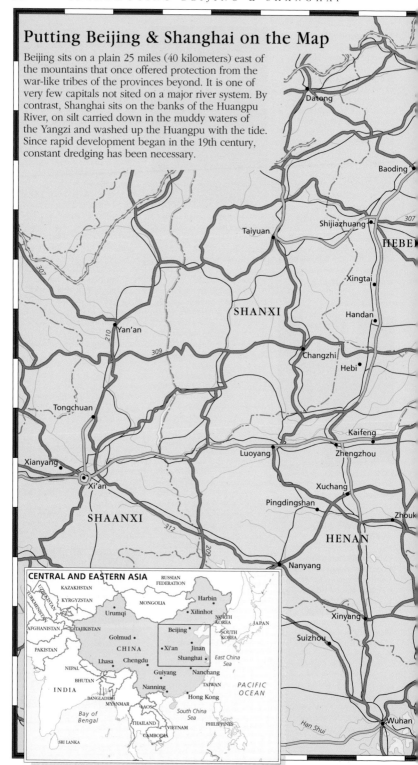

Datong

Baoding

307

Taiyuan   Shijiazhuang

HEBEI

Xingtai

SHANXI   Handan

Yan'an

210

309   Changzhi

Hebi

Tongchuan

Kaifeng

Xianyang   Luoyang   Zhengzhou

Xi'an   Xuchang

Pingdingshan   Zhouk

SHAANXI   312

209   HENAN

Nanyang

Xinyang

Suizhou

Han Shui   Wuhan

CENTRAL AND EASTERN ASIA

RUSSIAN FEDERATION

KAZAKHSTAN

UZBEKISTAN   KYRGYZSTAN   MONGOLIA   Harbin

TURKMENISTAN   Urumqi   Xilinhot

AFGHANISTAN   TAJIKISTAN   NORTH KOREA   JAPAN

Golmud   Beijing   SOUTH KOREA

PAKISTAN   CHINA   Xi'an   Jinan

Lhasa   Chengdu   Shanghai   East China Sea

NEPAL

BHUTAN   Guiyang   Nanchang   PACIFIC OCEAN

INDIA   Nanning   TAIWAN

BANGLADESH   Hong Kong

MYANMAR   LAOS   South China Sea

Bay of Bengal   THAILAND   VIETNAM   PHILIPPINES

CAMBODIA

SRI LANKA

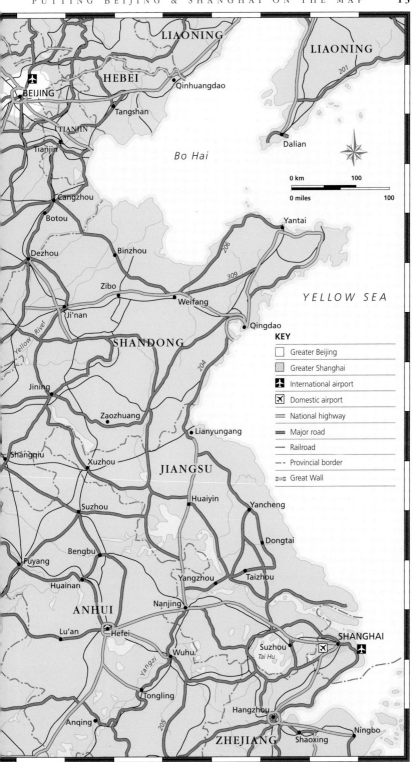

A PORTRAIT OF
BEIJING & SHANGHAI

The two cities of Beijing and Shanghai have long loomed large in the Western imagination, one as the capital of an ancient and cultured civilization, all temples and ceremony, and the other as a legendarily louche colonial-era collision of Western and Eastern cultures, famed as the "Paris of the East."

The modern-day realities are rather different. Standing in the shadow of towering glassy skyscrapers and partly obscured by clouds of construction dust and traffic pollution, the two cities seem to be rapidly converging towards a culturally unspecific modernity that already sees Shanghai appearing as an anonymous urban landscape of the future in Western science fiction films. In both cities, boulevards have been driven through narrow alleys, and ancient courtyard housing is disappearing beneath shopping malls and tower blocks. Rapid regeneration of the infrastructure of both Beijing and

Tile relief from the Forbidden City

Shanghai was judged necessary for the Beijing Olympics 2008 and 2010 Shanghai World Expo. Change and growth are common to all developing cities, but here they seem to be happening much faster and on a much larger scale than anywhere else. Beyond the similarities are some profound regional differences and historic rivalries – the citizens of Beijing and Shanghai are particularly well-known for needling each other, each with a sense of pride based on their home cities' fundamentally different histories and cultural traditions. Despite the long periods spent under foreign rule, Beijingers see themselves as the truly Chinese

Crowded Bin Jiang Avenue, the Bund, Shanghai

◁ Red flags flying next to Qian Men on Tian'an Men Square

Early morning exercises along the waterfront promenade of The Bund, Shanghai

inheritors of a rich imperial culture, while Shanghainese are perhaps more future-oriented, and see themselves as the open-minded absorbers and interpreters of foreign culture and commerce to the rest of China. The Shanghainese inevitably look east from the Bund across the river to the gleaming towers of Pudong, a mini-Manhattan, where the 101-floor Shanghai World Financial Center surpasses the 88-story Jinmao Tower. Pudong is a three-dimensional advertisement for Shanghai's booming economy, designed to increase the confidence of foreign investors. Shanghai has the highest average income per household in China, and leads the emergence of a middle class, tiny as a percentage of the overall population of China, but still larger than the populations of many a European nation.

THE POLITICAL CAPITAL

Beijing's response to Pudong has been to embark on a concerted building program of its own, with a roster of spectacular architecture. There is the Central Business District to either side of the East Third Ring Road, which features the flamboyant CCTV Tower by Holland's Rem Koolhaas, and the 1,000-ft (330-meter) China World Trade Center Summit tower, Beijing's tallest building. Elsewhere, Frenchman Paul Andreu's startling egg-shaped National Theater for the Performing Arts rises immediately west of Tian'an Men Square, and Briton Norman Foster's dragon-shaped Terminal 3 increases capacity at the international airport. Herzog & de Meuron's Olympic Stadium in the shape of a giant bird's nest located on the city's historic north–south axis, directly north of the Forbidden City, was home to the Beijing Olympic Games in 2008.

And while Shanghai may be the country's commercial center, political shifts register on Beijing's seismometer first. Word-of-mouth from within the government's high-security Zhong Nan Hai compound, the modern equivalent of the Forbidden City, typically fuels whispered debate amongst the city's inhabitants, who see themselves as the closest to power.

On a more personal level, Beijing-ers consider themselves cultured but laid-back, and both admire and resent the notorious business acumen of their big-city rivals to the south. The former consider the latter *jinjinjijiaode* or calculating. In return, the Shanghainese consider Beijingers to be no less calculating – it's just that they hide it behind a smoothly political exterior. The Shanghainese are proud of their familiarity with foreign things, and foreigners on the street attract less attention there than they do in Beijing. Quentin Tarantino's visit to Beijing for *Kill Bill* caused considerable buzz amongst the class tuned in to foreign culture. In contrast, Tom Cruise's visit to Shanghai for *Mission: Impossible III* produced only a studied yawn. The 2012 James Bond film *Skyfall* features scenes shot in Shanghai.

Shanghainese often consider Beijingers, and especially any still speaking the outmoded language of politics, as country bumpkins.

Praying at the Lama Temple, Beijing

CITY TALK

Beijingers often regard Mandarin, the official national language of China, of administration, and of a classical education, as their own dialect. But the local habit of adding a retroflex "r" suffix to many words gives their pronunciation a non-standard growl, and makes it sound as if they are rolling the language around their mouths like wine-tasters, before spitting it out.

Shanghainese is a language incomprehensible to all other Chinese except some from neighboring Zhejiang and Jiangsu Provinces (the original homes of most Shanghai people or their forebears).

In anticipation of a larger than usual influx of visitors for internationally high-profile events, the government has been calling for increased levels of culture and civilization, sometimes despairing of the citizens of both cities. Some Beijing men have a habit of taking off their shirts and rolling up their trousers above the knee in hot weather, while Shanghainese of both sexes wear Western-style pajamas in the street. Campaigns against such behavior have joined those against spitting and swearing.

But, however much the government strives to dress up both populations and skylines into a uniform readiness to receive visitors, no one should regard either city as representing any more than itself, each with a distinctly different spirit.

Window shopping on Shanghai's Nanjing West Road

Language and Script

The Chinese script can be traced back to the oracle bones of the Shang dynasty (16th–11th centuries BC) that were inscribed with symbols representing words and used for divination. Despite changes brought about by different writing materials, Chinese characters have remained remarkably consistent. It is said that to read a newspaper takes knowledge of at least 3,000 characters but an educated person would be expected to know over 5,000. Since 1913 the official spoken language has been *Putonghua* (Mandarin) but there are many regional dialects. Although people from different parts of China may not be able to understand each other, they can use a shared written script.

Cang Jie, *minister of the legendary Yellow Emperor, was supposedly inspired to invent the Chinese script one morning after seeing bird and animal tracks in the snow.*

A BEAUTIFUL SCRIPT

Writing was elevated to an art form considered on a par with painting as a visual aesthetic *(see pp26–7)*. As the process changed from inscribing bone, brass or stone to using a brush on silk and paper, a more fluid writing style became possible.

Seal, in red cinnabar – this may be a name seal, or inscribed with other characters.

Oracle bones *display China's first examples of seal script. Questions were inscribed on the bones, which were then burnt – the way cracks divided the inscriptions was deemed significant.*

Bamboo slats *were used from around the 5th century BC. These were tied together to make the earliest type of books. Used for administrative and philosophical texts, the script runs from top to bottom.*

Writing materials were silk, stone, or paper, which was first invented around the 2nd century BC.

Cursive script *(cao shu)* has strokes that run into each other. Fluid and dynamic, it allows for great expressiveness.

The Diamond Sutra (AD 868) *is the world's first block-printed book to bear a date. Printing was probably invented about a century earlier. Movable block printing was developed in the 11th century but had less social impact than in Europe because of the thousands of symbols required.*

CHINESE CHARACTERS

May be composed of pictographic, ideographic and phonetic elements. The radical (or root), an element that appears on the left or at the top of a character, usually gives a clue as to sense. Here, in the character for "good," pronounced *"hao,"* the radical combines with another meaning element "child." The concept, therefore, is that "woman" plus "child" equals "good."

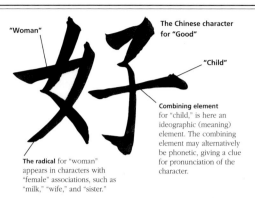

"Woman"

The Chinese character for "Good"

"Child"

Combining element for "child," is here an ideographic (meaning) element. The combining element may alternatively be phonetic, giving a clue for pronunciation of the character.

The radical for "woman" appears in characters with "female" associations, such as "milk," "wife," and "sister."

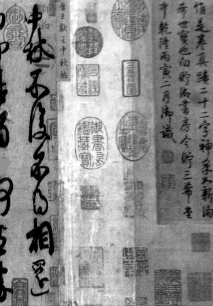

Pinyin is a Romanization system that was introduced in 1956. While Pinyin will never replace the character forms, it is an easier method for children to start learning the language and useful for input to computers.

Chinese typewriters were very difficult to use. The typist had to find each character in a tray of thousands. Computers have made typing Simplified script much easier – the user types in the Pinyin and gets a sub-menu of several possible characters.

STYLES OF CALLIGRAPHY

Zhuanshu, or seal script, was developed during the Zhou era and used for engraved inscriptions.

Lishu, or clerical script, probably evolved during the Han era and was used for stone inscriptions.

Kaishu, or regular script, developed from Lishu after the Han era, is the basis of modern type.

Cao shu, or cursive script, literally grass script, has strokes that are reduced to abstract curves or dots.

Xingshu, or running script, has strokes that run together, and is a semicursive script.

Simplified script was introduced in 1956 to make it easier for peasants to learn to read.

Chinese Literature

Dating back to the sixth century BC, the earliest Chinese texts were primarily philosophic, such as the Confucian *Analects* and Daoist *Daode Jing*. History as a literary genre was not established until the Han period (206 BC–AD 220) with Sima Qian's *Historical Records*: thereafter each dynasty wrote a history of the preceding one. As for the novel, a fully fledged Chinese example did not appear until the Ming period (1368–1644) and was developed during the Qing dynasty until it was eventually stifled by Communism. Since the 1980s Chinese authors have been allowed greater freedom of expression, although, in 2000, news of exiled writer Gao Xingjian's Nobel Prize for Literature was suppressed.

Confucius, author of the *Analects*, and his disciples

CLASSICS

Post-Qin dynasty, once Confucianism had become the state orthodoxy, five early works were canonized as the Five Classics: *the Book of Changes, Book of Documents, Book of Songs, Spring and Autumn Annals* and *Book of Ritual*. These books were established as the basis for Chinese education.

The scholar class or literati *achieved the status of government official through success in the civil service examinations, based on detailed knowledge of the Classics and accomplishment in writing.*

TANG POETS

With early beginnings in the *Book of Songs* and *Elegies of Chu*, Chinese poetry reached its height more than twelve hundred years later in the Tang period (618–907). The two greatest Tang poets are considered to be Du Fu and Li Bai. Others include the Buddhist Wang Wei, also 8th-century, and slightly later Bai Juyi (772–846).

Baoyu prefers to flirt with the women rather than obey his father and study hard to advance his career.

Du Fu *(AD c.712–770) wrote of suffering in war, as well as of family life. His keynote is compassion, considered a Confucian virtue. His poems display enormous erudition.*

Li Bai *(AD c.701–761) was a more ebullient figure. A prolific poet, his favorite subjects were moon gazing and carousing. The theme of freedom from constraint is a Daoist one.*

EPIC NOVELS

In the Ming era, the novel developed from folk tales and myths into classics such as *Journey to the West, Romance of the Three Kingdoms* and *The Water Margin* – a tale of the heroic fight against corruption. Later, the Qing novels used a more elevated language and subtle characterization, culminating in the romantic novel, *Dream of the Red Chamber*. These novels contain many characters that reoccur in other cultural contexts from Beijing Opera to popular television serials and films.

Guandi, God of War, *derives from Guan Yu, a general of the state of Shu, portrayed in* Romance of the Three Kingdoms. *This novel was based on historical figures from the Three Kingdoms Era (AD 220–80). A symbol for justice, honesty, and integrity, his figurines are found in temples throughout China.*

Journey to the West *is a comic fantasy based on the pilgrimage to India of the Buddhist monk Xuanzang. The late Ming novel centers on Monkey, one of the monk's companions who represents carefree genius, bravery, and loyalty.*

DREAM OF THE RED CHAMBER

Perhaps the greatest Chinese novel, this portrays the decline of an aristocratic Qing household. Infused with a Daoist sense of transcendence, it focuses on the life and loves of the idle Baoyu and twelve perceptively drawn female characters.

20TH CENTURY

In the early 20th century, fiction writers and playwrights addressed social issues in a new realist style. However Communism demanded revolutionary themes. After the persecution of writers during the Cultural Revolution *(see pp50–51)*, experimental forms and styles gradually emerged. However, the books of Chinese authors may still be banned if they are openly critical of the government or are "spiritual pollutants"; nevertheless pirated versions are often widely available.

Mo Yan *is a post-Cultural Revolution fiction writer. Best known for his novel* Red Sorghum *(1986), made into a major film, he writes in a rich style, often graphic, fantastic, and violent.*

Lu Xun, *early 20th-century writer of short stories and novellas, is known as the father of modern Chinese literature. His realist, satirical style is indebted to such writers as Dickens. He is renowned for his humorous depiction of Ah Q, an illiterate but enthusiastic peasant, done down by the forces of convention.*

Religion and Philosophy

Traditionally, the three strands in Chinese religion and philosophy are Confucianism, Daoism, and Buddhism. An eclectic approach to religion allows the three to coexist, often within a single temple. Confucianism, the first to gain real influence, can be seen as a manifestation of the public, socially responsible self. Daoism represents a personal and wilder side; its emphasis on the relativity of things contrasts with Confucian concern for approved roles. Buddhism, a foreign import, is spiritual and otherworldly, offering an alternative to Chinese pragmatism. During the Cultural Revolution, religion was outlawed as contrary to Communist ideas. Today, people are largely able to express their beliefs.

Laozi, Buddha, and Confucius

CONFUCIANISM

Originated by Confucius (551–479 BC) and developed by later thinkers, Confucianism advocates a structured society in which people are bound to each other by the moral ties of the five familial relationships: parent-child, ruler-subject, brother-brother, husband-wife, and friend-friend. In Imperial China, Confucianism was the philosophy of the elite scholar-gentleman class. For much of the Communist era, it was reviled as a reactionary philosophy linked to the former ruling aristocracy.

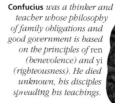
Confucius *was a thinker and teacher whose philosophy of family obligations and good government is based on the principles of* ren *(benevolence) and* yi *(righteousness). He died unknown, his disciples spreading his teachings.*

Filial piety, *or* xiao, *another Confucian precept, consists of obedience to and reverence for one's parents, and by extension respect for other family members and one's ruler.*

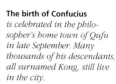
The birth of Confucius *is celebrated in the philosopher's home town of Qufu in late September. Many thousands of his descendants, all surnamed Kong, still live in the city.*

The paying of respects *to one's ancestors is based on filial piety and runs throughout Chinese culture. During the Qing Ming festival in April, Chinese traditionally clean and upkeep their ancestors' tombs.*

Scholars *collated the Confucian Classics including the* Lunyu *(Analects), a series of Confucius's sayings, well after his death. The Classics were the basis of education until 1912.*

DAOISM

Strongly linked with early folk beliefs, Daoism incorporates the traditional concepts of an ordered universe, *yin* and *yang*, and directed energy, *qi*. Over time, Daoism developed into a complex religion with an extensive pantheon. Daoist philosophy encourages following one's intuition and following the grain of the universe by living in accordance with the Dao.

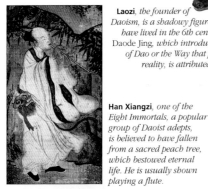

Laozi, *the founder of Daoism, is a shadowy figure, who may have lived in the 6th century BC. The* Daode Jing, *which introduces the idea of Dao or the Way that permeates reality, is attributed to him.*

Han Xiangzi, *one of the Eight Immortals, a popular group of Daoist adepts, is believed to have fallen from a sacred peach tree, which bestowed eternal life. He is usually shown playing a flute.*

Daoist alchemists *aimed to find an elixir for eternal life, winning influence with emperors. Daoism influenced scientific development, and contributed to the discovery of gunpowder in the 9th century.*

In "Peach Blossom Spring" *by Daoist poet Tao Qian, a fisherman chances upon a lost idyllic world and encounters Immortals. Daoist reverence for nature led to the creation of numerous paradises.*

BUDDHISM

In China the Mahayana school of Buddhism, which promises salvation to anyone who seeks it, is followed. Enlightened ones, *bodhisattvas*, remain in this world to help enlighten others. Through deeds and devotion believers gain merit and maintain their connections with the *bodhisattvas*, bringing them closer to nirvana.

The Laughing Buddha, *or Milefo, is an adaptation of the Maitreya, the Future Buddha. His large belly and laughing face are signs of abundance and he is worshiped in the hopes of a happy, affluent life.*

The Guardian King *of the South (left) is coiled by a snake; the King of the North holds a parasol. Kings of the four directions guard the entrance to many temples protecting the main deity from evil influences.*

Luohans *or arhats are the Buddha's disciples and often appear in temples in groups of 18. Their holiness is thought to enable them to achieve extinction (nirvana) on death.*

A Buddhist supplicant *burns sticks of incense in aid of prayer. Buddhist temples throb with spiritual energy, as worshipers pray and make offerings to gain merit.*

Architecture

Tiled imperial dragon

For over two thousand years, the Chinese have used the same architectural model for both imperial and religious buildings. This has three elements: a platform, post-and-beam timber frames, and non-loadbearing walls. Standard features of building complexes include a front gate, four-sided enclosures or courtyards, and a series of halls in a linear formation running north. Most Chinese buildings were built of wood, but because wooden buildings tend to catch fire, only a few structures remain; the earliest date from the Tang period.

Aerial view of the Forbidden City, showing the traditional linear layout

HALL

In every context, the Chinese hall or *tang* follows the same pattern: a platform of rammed earth or stone, and timber columns arranged in a grid. The front of the hall always has an odd number of bays. Between the columns and beams are brackets *(dougong)*, cantilevers that support the structure, allowing the eaves to overhang. The timber is brightly painted, the roof aesthetically curved, and tiled or thatched.

Gate of Heavenly Purity (see p64)
An archetypal Chinese hall, the central doorway and uneven number of bays emphasize the processional element.

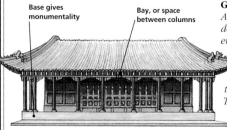

Base gives monumentality

Bay, or space between columns

Standard Hall
Buildings in China conformed to a set of rules about proportions. This uniform architecture created a sense of identity – useful in a large and disparate country.

STORIED BUILDING (LOU) AND STORIED PAVILION (GE)

Multi-story buildings in China predate pagodas and varied from two-storied private homes to huge seven- or more story towers built to enjoy the scenery. Storied pavilions were used for storage and had doors and windows only at the front. Both types of building kept the standard elements of base, columns, and hanging walls.

Storied Pavilion
These were used for storing important items, such as libraries of Buddhist sutras or colossal statues.

Characteristic "flying eave"

Symmetrical façade

Storied Building
The construction of tall buildings relied heavily on the dougong bracket.

PAGODA

Based on the Indian stupa, the Chinese pagoda, or *ta*, was developed in the first century AD along with the arrival of Buddhism. Multi-storied pagodas appeared in Buddhist temple complexes (although later they often stood on their own) and were originally intended to house a religious relic. They were built of brick, stone, or wood.

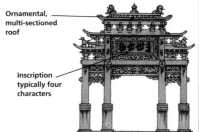

Top resembles Indian stupa

Base, usually with an underground chamber

ORNAMENTAL ARCHWAY

The *pailou*, or *paifang*, is a memorial or decorative archway. Made of wood, brick, or stone, and sometimes with glazed tiles, it often bears an edifying inscription. *Pailou* were erected at crossroads, temples, bridges, government offices, parks, and tombs.

Ornamental, multi-sectioned roof

Inscription typically four characters

CITY WALLS

Early defensive walls, like other early architectural forms, were made of earth – either pounded hard by pestles or moistened to make a clay and pressed around reed frames. Later walls were often built using brick. City walls were traditionally square, with the main gate to the south. The Chinese for "city" *(cheng)* also means "wall."

Easy to defend with a bow

Gate tower, often a two-story *lou*

City wall and gate
The towers on top of walls can vary from small buildings to palatial multi-story structures.

City Walls
Typically made of rammed earth and brick, ramparts and watchtowers were an effective defense. Both Beijing and Shanghai were originally surrounded by such walls.

ARCHITECTURAL DETAILS

It is interesting to interpret the architectural detail on Chinese buildings. The use of yellow tiles, for example, was reserved for the emperor. The Nine-Dragon Screen, which occurs in the Forbidden City and elsewhere, is also imperial since the dragon symbolizes the *yang*, or male principle, and by extension the emperor.

Chiwen
Able to douse flames with water, the Chiwen often appears at the end of a roof ridge (see p63) as a protection against fire.

Dougong
A bracket (dougong), transmits the load from roof to column. It's a traditionally complex, nail-free, and ornamental construction method.

Traditional Arts

Funerary bronze bell

The earliest Chinese artifacts were found in royal tombs. These include bronzes, ceramics, and jades from the Shang and Zhou period, as well as terracotta warriors from the Qin period. Of the many rich art forms that subsequently developed in China, painting and pottery are perhaps the most important, and have reached the highest aesthetic level. Other significant art forms include sculpture, notably the Buddhist sculpture of Western China. There are also many distinctive and popular forms of Chinese decorative art.

Buddhist sculpture in the Gandharan style

Ritual bronze tripod *from an early royal tomb, decorated with a mythical animal design known as a* taotie.

Wet and dry ink used to give the detail of the trees.

POTTERY

Since inventing porcelain, China developed a huge range of potting, decorating, and glazing techniques that were imitated from Europe to Japan. Chinese ceramics led the world in aesthetic taste and technique up until the demise of the Qing dynasty.

Tang earthenware tomb figure *representing a fierce warrior, with typical rough* sancai *(three-color) drip glaze. This was a lead-based glaze, fired at a low temperature.*

Textured strokes give the rocks depth.

Song celadon bowl, *with incised floral design. Celadon was the European name given to the refined gray-green glaze of this type of stoneware and porcelain.*

Ming vase *in the blue-and-white style known and imitated internationally. The technique involves underglaze painting in cobalt blue before the pot is fired.*

Qing famille-rose vase, *a delicate porcelain in a distinctive palette. The name comes from the use of bright pink enamel.*

Bird-and-flower painting *(including the depiction of fruit and insects) reveals the Chinese Daoist interest in observing the natural world. Despite the lightness of subject, the paintings have an intense, quasi-scientific depth.*

CHINESE PAINTING

Considered the highest traditional art form, Chinese painting is executed on silk or paper using a brush and inks or watercolors. **Landscape painting**, associated with the scholar class, reached a highpoint in the Northern Song and Yuan periods. Huang Gongwang *(see below)*, a master of the Yuan, was admired for his simple calligraphic style.

Religious painting *first appeared along the Silk Road with the arrival of Buddhism from India. The Chinese soon developed an individual style.*

Ink wash is used for the hills in the distance.

Bamboo painting *was a genre of the scholar class. Bamboo symbolized the scholar-gentleman who would bend but not break in the face of adversity.*

TRADITIONAL CRAFTS

As well as the traditional high art forms of painting and pottery, China has a wealth of beautiful decorative arts. Delicate carvings in lacquer, ivory and jade are popular, as are colorful cloisonné items, decorated inksticks (or cakes), snuff bottles, and fans.

Snuff bottles *were produced in large numbers during the Qing period. Made of glass, jade, mother-of-pearl, or semi-precious stones, they were delicately carved or painted on the inside in exquisite detail.*

Lacquer carving *is distinctive for its deep red color and floral designs, and is often used on boxes.*

Cloisonné *is a style of enameling. Individual metal cloisons, usually made of copper, are soldered together and inlaid with different colored enamels. The object is then fired and polished.*

Traditional Chinese Gardens

Lotus, a favorite symbolic flower

The Chinese garden developed as a synthesis of two concepts linked in Daoist philosophy *(see p23)* – scenery and serenity: the contemplation of nature in isolated meditation led to enlightenment. Therefore, the educated and wealthy built natural-looking retreats for themselves within an urban environment. The garden creates poetic and painterly concepts, and aims to improve on nature by creating a picture that looks natural but is in fact entirely artificial. For this the Chinese garden designer used four main elements: rocks, water, plants, and architecture.

Classical Chinese garden design *was considered a type of three-dimensional landscape painting or solid poetry.*

Rocks: *There were two main kinds of rock – the eroded limestones from lakes, often used as sculptures, or the yellow rock piled up to recall mountains and caves to the mind of the viewer. The beauty and realism of the rockery usually determined the success or failure of the garden.*

Water: *An essential element of life, water also could be used in the garden as a mirror and so appear to increase the size of the garden. Water also serves as a contrasting partner and therefore a balance to the hard stone. Finally it is a home for goldfish, symbols of good fortune.*

Corridors, paths, and bridges *link the different areas and give the artist control over how the views are presented to the visitor.*

Interiors *of pavilions were important as the venues for creativity. A lot of care was taken to select an appropriate and poetic name for each building.*

Patterns and mosaics *brighten up the garden and are also symbolic. Cranes represent longevity, while the yin and yang symbol often appears where a path forks in two.*

GARDEN VIEWS

Using these four elements the garden is like a series of tableaux painted onto a roll of silk. One by one they come before your eyes just as the artist intended them to. As you follow the paths, you see just what he wanted you to see. These may be borrowed views, where the scenery from somewhere else is made to look part of the picture; hidden views, where you round a corner to come upon an unexpected scene; or contrasting views where leafy bamboo softens the view of rock, or opposite views as the *yin* element water balances the *yang* element rock.

A moon gate *is a round door that neatly frames a view as though it were a picture. Gates can be square-, jar-, or even book-shaped.*

Patterned screens *allow in a certain amount of light and may be used to cast patterned shadows on white walls. They are also sometimes used to give tempting partial views through to other areas of the garden.*

Plants: *Plants were used sparingly and usually for their symbolic qualities. Thus the lotus is purity, as it flowers from the mud; bamboo is resolve, it is difficult to break; plum is vigor, as it blooms in winter; the pine is longevity, for it is an evergreen; the imperial peony, is wealth.*

Buildings: *An intrinsic part of the garden, these pavilions and waterside halls provide a place for contemplation and more importantly a specific viewpoint, as well as shelter from the sun and rain. They could range from open kiosks to multi-story halls and meeting rooms.*

PENJING

Dating as far back as the Tang dynasty (618–907), *penjing* is the art of creating a miniature landscape in a container. Not limited to small trees, the artist may use rocks and specially cultivated plants to portray a scene of natural beauty, as though it were a landscape painting. As well as being beautiful, the harmony in these creations is seen as the spiritual expression of man's relationship with nature, the meeting of the temporal with the omnipresent. Often part of a Chinese garden will be devoted to the display or cultivation of this delicate art.

The Chinese art of *penjing*, the forerunner to Japanese bonsai

Beijing Opera

Emperor Qianlong, credited with starting Beijing Opera

One among many hundreds of local operas across China, Beijing Opera began in the Qing dynasty. It is said that Emperor Qianlong (r.1736–96), on a tour of the south, was rather taken by the operas of Anhui and Hebei and brought these troupes back to Beijing, where a new form of opera was established. The Guangxu emperor and Dowager Empress Cixi were also keen devotees and helped develop the art form. Beijing Opera has proved remarkably resilient, surviving the persecution of actors and the banning of most of the plays during the Cultural Revolution.

Souvenir mask

BEIJING OPERA
Visually stunning and with a distinct musical style, the plays are based on Chinese history and literature. Beijing Opera is a form of "total theater" with singing, speech, mime, acrobatics, and symbolic visual effects.

Monkey *is one of the favorite characters – clever, resourceful, and brave. He appears in Chinese classic literature (see p21).*

The colors of the painted faces *symbolize the individual character's qualities. Red, for example, represents loyalty and courage; purple, solemnity and a sense of justice; green, bravery and irascibility.*

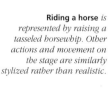

Riding a horse *is represented by raising a tasseled horsewhip. Other actions and movement on the stage are similarly stylized rather than realistic.*

The acrobatics *of Beijing Opera combine graceful gymnastics and movements from the martial arts. Training is notoriously hard. The costumes are designed to make the jumps seem more spectacular by billowing out as they spin.*

MUSICAL INSTRUMENTS

Despite the dramatic visual elements of Beijing Opera, the Chinese say that they go to "listen" to opera, not to see it. The importance of the musical elements should not therefore be underestimated. Typically six or seven instrumentalists accompany the opera. The stringed instruments usually include the *erhu* or Chinese two-stringed violin, *sanxian* or three-stringed lute, and moon guitar, or possibly *pipa* (traditional lute). The main function of the instruments is to accompany the singing. Percussion instruments include clappers, gongs, and drums. These are used largely to punctuate the action; movement and sound are intimately linked. Wind instruments also sometimes feature, such as the Chinese horn, flute, and *suona*.

Gong

Suona　　**Pipa**　　**Erhu**

Mei Lanfang *was the foremost interpreter of the female role type or* dan *during the opera's heyday in the 1920s and 1930s. Traditionally all female roles were played by male actors, although that has now changed.*

THE FOUR MAIN ROLES

There are four main role types in Beijing Opera: the *sheng* (male) and *dan* (female) roles have naturalistic make-up. The *jing* or "painted faces," in contrast, have stylized patterned, colored faces, while the *chou* are comic characters.

Sheng: these may be young or old, with beard or without.

Chou: with a white patch on his face, the *chou* is usually dim but amusing.

Dan: there are six parts within this role from virtuous girl to old woman.

Jing: the most striking looking, they also have the most forceful personality.

Modern Arts

The birth of modern art in China at the start of the 20th century coincided with greater contact with the West. Experiments with new materials and styles in the visual arts, Western-style music, "spoken drama" (*huaju*), cinema, and modern literary forms such as free verse all took root at this time. However, after 1949, this creativity was stifled by Soviet-influenced Socialist Realism. During the Cultural Revolution many artists were even persecuted on the grounds that their works were "reactionary." Since the 1980s there has been some liberalization in the arts and new, exciting forms have developed.

The Oriental Pearl TV Tower, *Pudong, Shanghai is among the buildings that reflect China's high-rise architecture boom since the early 1990s.*

This example of performance art *is by Cang Xin, a Beijing-based conceptual artist, active since the mid-1990s. The title of this piece,* Unification of Heaven and Man, *alludes to classical Chinese philosophical concepts.*

Shaven-headed man

MODERN ART

This painting, *Series 2 No. 2,* is by Fang Lijun, leader of the Cynical Realism school, which came about as a reaction to the demise of the pro-democracy movement in 1989. Rejecting idealism, these artists make fun of the problems of life in China.

Sculpture *entitled* Torso, *by Zhan Wang, a Shanghai-based conceptual artist. Zhan uses reflective steel sheets to give the illusion of solidity.*

Orchestral and chamber music *has been popular in China since the early 20th century. There are many schools specializing in Western-style music, and several high-quality ensembles and artists on the world scene.*

CHINESE CINEMA

From early classics such as *Street Angel* (1937), Chinese cinema has scaled new heights of international success, with the work of such directors as Zhang Yimou, who produced the 2008 Beijing Olympics opening ceremony.

Farewell My Concubine *(1993), directed by Chen Kaige, a post-Cultural Revolution filmmaker, who gave expression to new moral uncertainties, is set in the world of traditional Beijing Opera.*

The Hong Kong film industry *followed its own path and became primarily famous for its action movies. Renowned martial arts star Jackie Chan, seen above in an early acting and directorial debut,* Fearless Hyena, *made many films and successfully crossed over from Hong Kong to Hollywood.*

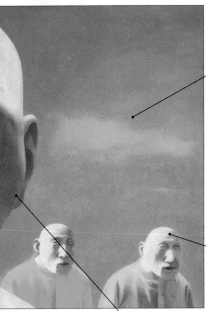

Background is a hazy blue, making it appear dream-like

Wei Wei *is one of the bestselling pop stars in China today, along with Jay Chou, who also stars in adverts and movies. Rock music only took off in the 1980s: Cui Jian, the "grandad" of Chinese rock, is seen as a rebel by the authorities. Hong Kong's less controversial Canto-pop singers enjoy more freedom.*

Anonymous figures seem threatening

Main figure is yelling or yawning – is he angry or just bored?

Ballet *in contemporary China mixes traditional Chinese and Western influences. Here, the ballet version of Zhang Yimou's film* Raise the Red Lantern *is performed by members of the National Ballet.*

Modern theater *provides an expression of Chinese life in the 21st century. Here, a scene from* Toilet *(2004), a black comedy, is performed by the National Theater company in Beijing. The play broke taboos with its frank portrayal of urban life and treatment of homosexuality.*

THROUGH THE YEAR

The dates of traditional Chinese festivals are tied to a lunar calendar, which has 29.5 days a month. This means that festival dates move around in the same manner as the Christian Easter does. Public holidays associated with Communism – National Day and International Labor Day, for example – are fixed on the familiar Gregorian (Western) calendar. Some

Chinese New Year banner

celebrations of Western origin, such as Christmas, are also observed. Very few Chinese have any sort of discretionary holiday from work, so on the longer public holidays a large proportion of the population takes to the road all at the same time. At such times it is unwise to attempt much travel, and many tourist attractions may be shut for a day or two (*see p37*).

SPRING

The four seasons are far more clearly marked in Beijing than in Shanghai, which tends to be either cool and humid, or hot and humid, year round. Spring in Beijing sees seeds from the many scholar trees blown into drifts by winds that clear away the pollution. However, those same winds also sometimes bring scouring clouds of sand from the arid northwest, turning the skies dark and yellow.

A red lantern – lucky symbol

Festival, which is also known as Chinese New Year, is a time when wage packets contain bonuses, debts must be settled, and everyone who can heads for their family home. Many temple fairs take place at this time, especially in Beijing, and these often feature stilt-walkers, acrobats, opera singers, and other traditional entertainments. Museums and most offices are shut for at least three days, many for longer, although a great deal of shopping goes on, commonly encouraged by department store sales.

Lion dancing, performed as part of Spring Festival celebrations

everywhere. It is also a time for eating the sticky rice balls known as *yuanxiao*.

JANUARY–FEBRUARY

Spring Festival (Chun Jie)
Beijing, Shanghai. This occurs with the first new moon after January 21, which will be January 31 in 2014, February 19 in 2015, February 8 in 2016, and January 28 in 2017. Spring

FEBRUARY–MARCH

Lantern Festival Beijing, Shanghai. Coinciding with a full moon, this festival marks the end of the 15-day Spring Festival period. Lanterns bearing auspicious characters or in animal shapes are hung

MARCH

International Women's Day (*March 8*), Beijing, Shanghai. A holiday, or half-day holiday, for the female part of the population; men go to work as usual.

MARCH–APRIL

Peach Blossom Festival
Shanghai. This festival takes place among more than 6,175 acres (2,500 hectares) of peach orchards in the Nanhui District outside Shanghai over a two-week period in late March and early April, depending on the progress of the blossom. Visitors come to admire the trees and to eat at local

Red lanterns form a tunnel in a Beijing park during the Lantern Festival

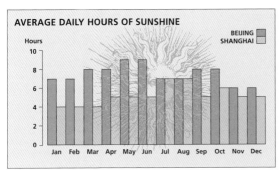

AVERAGE DAILY HOURS OF SUNSHINE

BEIJING
SHANGHAI

Sunshine Chart
Although Beijing appears to receive a generous number of hours of sunshine throughout the whole year, the reality is that air pollution often creates a haze over the city that prevents the sun getting through. Shanghai has similar problems with smog.

homes that have temporarily become cafés, restaurants, and guesthouses, in a tradition called *nongjia le*.

APRIL

Clear Brightness Festival (Qing Ming Jie) *(April 5)*, Beijing, Shanghai. Also known as the Tomb-Sweeping Festival, this takes place two weeks after the vernal equinox, usually April 5, but April 4 in leap years. People visit their ancestors' graves to make offerings of snacks and alcohol. Around this time, *qingtuan*, which are green sticky rice balls, are eaten.
Shanghai Formula One Grand Prix Shanghai. This is an entirely foreign event with no Chinese competitors. The 56-lap race takes place around a 3.3-mile (5.5-km) circuit.

SUMMER

Shanghai steams and drips as the heat steadily rises, and the increased usage of air-conditioning units causes electricity shortages and black-outs. On a more northerly latitude, Beijing is washed clean by intermittent showers, but it is otherwise hot and sticky.

MAY

International Labor Day *(May 1)*, Beijing, Shanghai. This was shortened from a three-day to a one-day holiday in 2008. It marks the start of the domestic travel season. This is the time of year when all Chinese

A dragon boat, with the drummer setting the rhythm for the rowers

people visit their families.
Meet in Beijing Beijing. This is a cultural festival running throughout all of May with an unpredictable mix of Chinese and foreign elements at a variety of venues around the city.
Art Beijing Beijing. China's biggest contemporary art fair is held in May each year.

JUNE

Dragon Boat Festival (Duanwu Jie) Beijing, Shanghai. Held on the fifth day of the fifth lunar month (usually June), this popular festival features races between colorful dragon-headed boats. On-board drummers set the tempo and keep the twin rows of paddlers in unison. The festival honors the honest official, Qu Yuan, who drowned himself after banishment from the court of the Duke of Chu

nearly 2,500 years ago. Shocked citizens threw rice cakes into the water to distract the fish from his body. Rice cakes are eaten today in the form of *zongzi*, pyramids of glutinous rice wrapped in river reeds and tied up with string. Races and pageantry can be seen at Qinglong Hu near the Ming Tombs outside Beijing, and on various lakes and rivers around Shanghai.
Shanghai International Film Festival Shanghai. Held over one week in mid-June, this celebration of celluloid showcases plenty of Chinese cinema unlikely to be seen much in the West – but don't expect anything beyond officially approved projects – along with a selection of unchallenging foreign fare. However, the festival is still important enough for international stars to put in an appearance.

Shanghai International Film Festival poster

AVERAGE MONTHLY RAINFALL

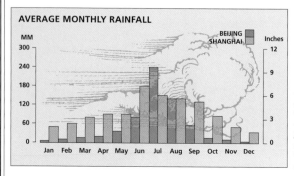

BEIJING
SHANGHAI

MM
300
240
180
120
60
0

Inches
12
9
6
3
0

Jan Feb Mar Apr May Jun Jul Aug Sep Oct Nov Dec

Rainfall Chart
Typically for a coastal city, Shanghai is wet throughout the year. Beijing receives its greatest rainfall during the height of summer, when the prolonged and heavy downpours provide a welcome release from the seasonal heat.

Exercising with a spinning top in a Beijing park in fall

FALL

The months of September and October are easily the best time to visit Beijing. The summer heat has gone and in its place are warm, dry days, with frequent cool breezes that clear the smog-laden skies. Farther south, the baking temperatures and humidity associated with summers in Shanghai have also dropped to more comfortable levels.

JULY–AUGUST

Qi Xi Beijing, Shanghai. Taking place on the seventh day of the seventh lunar month, which is usually August, Qi Xi celebrates the story of the earthly cowherd and celestial weaving girl who were separated by the gods but who are annually reunited in the heavens by a bridge of magpies. It is the Chinese equivalent of Valentine's Day, and it's going through something of a modern revival, especially in Shanghai, where it involves much shopping for gifts and fully-booked restaurants.

Mooncake

AUGUST–SEPTEMBER

Mid-Autumn Festival (Zhong Qiu Jie) Beijing, Shanghai. On the 15th day of the eighth lunar month (usually in September), this festival, also known as the Harvest or Moon Festival, is traditionally a time for family reunions. Shops fill with boxes of mooncakes *(yuebing)*, extremely fattening pies filled with bean paste. As of 2008, China has a one-day national holiday on the closest working day to the Mid-Autumn festival.

OCTOBER

National Day *(October 1)*, Beijing, Shanghai. Marking the anniversary of Mao's speech in which he declared

National Day's massed military parades – a throwback to the days of Communist-era China

AVERAGE MONTHLY TEMPERATURE

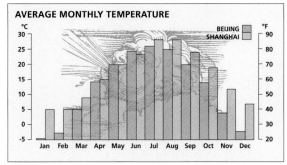

BEIJING
SHANGHAI

Jan Feb Mar Apr May Jun Jul Aug Sep Oct Nov Dec

Temperature Chart
Beijing annually endures extremes of temperature, with the thermometer often dropping below zero in winter and then threatening to blow in the heat of summer. Shanghai ranges from sultry to sweaty, with the heat exacerbated by humidity.

the foundation of the People's Republic. Crowds turn out to watch massive parades, particularly at Beijing's Tian'an Men Square. This is another three-day holiday that for most people and businesses expands into a full week. Every city sight and scenic rural tourist destination is crowded to its limits and beyond.

Rolex Shanghai Masters Tennis *(two weeks in October)*, Shanghai. Asia's flagship tennis event takes place at the Qizhong Tennis Center in Shanghai. Established in 2009, the tournament is one of nine ATP Masters 1000 events and the only tennis Masters to take place in Asia. More than 100 tennis professionals, including the world's best players, participate in 99 matches over a nine day period. Information on court schedules, order of play, and ticket prices is available at www.shanghai rolexmasters.com.

WINTER

Beijing winters are not only bitterly cold but the briefest exposure to the arid atmosphere desiccates the face instantly. The dry air and cool temperatures also accentuate the creation of static electricity so be wary reaching for taxi and hotel door handles. By contrast, Shanghai is traditionally deemed to be warm enough year-round for private homes

Typical Beijing winter weather – heavy snow and icy roads

not to be heated, but although temperatures do not drop as low of those of Beijing, the humidity makes the cold more penetrating. Occasional strong winds make viewing Shanghai panoramas from a cosy room in your hotel seem far more attractive than actually venturing out.

DECEMBER

Christmas Day *(December 25)*, Beijing, Shanghai. Although not a traditional holiday in China, this day has been adopted via Hong Kong, which means, of course, that there is a stress on the commercial aspect. Shopping malls and foreign-run hotels have conspired to press this idea upon the Chinese in major cities to the point that it is now rare for a high-street store not to acknowledge the holiday with images of *Shengdan Laoren*, the Chinese version of Father Christmas.

JANUARY

New Year's Day *(January 1)*, Beijing, Shanghai. Although overshadowed by the Spring Festival (Chinese New Year) celebrations that take place soon after *(see p34)*, Western New Year is still a public holiday, celebrated with gusto by the large number of expatriate foreigners living in Beijing and Shanghai.

PUBLIC HOLIDAYS

New Year's Day (Jan 1)
Spring Festival or Chinese New Year (Jan 31, 2014; Feb 19, 2015; Feb 8, 2016; Jan 28, 2017)
Tomb-Sweeping Day Apr 5, 2014; Apr 5, 2015; Apr 4, 2016
International Labor Day (May 1)
Dragon Boat Festival Jun 2, 2014; Jun 20, 2015; Jun 9, 2016
Mid-Autumn Festival Sep 19, 2013; Sep 8, 2014; Sep 27, 2015; Sep 15, 2016
National Day (Oct 1–3)

Avoid traveling during Spring Festival and the first weeks of May and October. At these times everyone who can afford to takes to the road, either on holiday or to visit relatives. Prices rise, and it is impossible to get a bus or train ticket, or an internal flight. However, traffic in Beijing and Shanghai thins and it can be a pleasant time to spend in either place.

THE HISTORY OF CHINA

*C*hina boasts one of the longest single unified civilizations in the world. Its history is characterized by dramatic shifts in power between rival factions, periods of peace and prosperity when foreign ideas were assimilated and absorbed, the disintegration of empire through corruption and political subterfuge, and the cyclical rise of ambitious leaders to found each new empire.

FIRST SETTLERS

From around 8000 BC, settlements of populations based on a primitive agricultural economy began to emerge in the eastern coastal regions and along the rich river deltas of the Huang He (Yellow River), the Yangzi, and the Wei. These civilizations focused on hunting, gathering, and fishing, and the cultivation of millet in the north and rice in the south. Each civilization is notable for its own distinct style of pottery, such as the bold earthenware of the Yangshao (5000–3000 BC) and the black ceramics of the Longshan (3000–1700 BC).

Yangshao pottery amphora

BRONZE AGE CHINA AND THE FIRST KINGDOMS

The first dynasty in China was founded by the Shang around 1600 BC. The Shang lived in large, complex societies and were the first to mass-produce cast bronze. Power centered on the ruling elite who acted as shamans of a sort, communicating with their ancestors and gods through diviners.

Elaborate bronze food and wine vessels were used both for banqueting and for making ancestral offerings. Inscriptions on oracle bones provide the first evidence of writing, dating from around 1300 BC.

In 1066 BC, the Zhou seized power, establishing their western capital at present-day Xi'an. The Western Zhou initially sustained many of the traditions of the Shang, but later reorganized the political system, and replaced the use of oracle bones with inscriptions on bronze and, later, writing on silk and strips of bamboo.

The Eastern Zhou (770–221 BC) is divided into the Spring and Autumn period (770–476 BC) and the Warring States period (475–221 BC). The Eastern Zhou period was dominated by political conflict and social unrest, as rival factions jockeyed for power. It also saw economic expansion and development as the use of iron revolutionized agriculture. It was in this climate of unrest that the philosophical ideologies of Confucianism, Daoism, and Legalism emerged.

TIMELINE

		5000–3000 BC Yangshao culture based around the Wei river	**2200–1600 BC** Existence of semimythical first dynasty, the Xia	**1300 BC** First writing on oracle bones	
8000– 6500 BC Neolithic period				**c. 551–479 BC** Life of Confucius	**475–221 BC** Eastern Zhou: Warring States
8000 BC	**6000 BC**	**4000 BC**	**2000 BC**	**1000 BC**	**500 BC**
	6500–5000 BC Earliest settlements in northern China		**1600–1050 BC** Shang dynasty	**770–476 BC** Eastern Zhou: Spring and Autumn period	**513 BC** First mention of iron casting
		Bronze food vessel, Shang	**1066 –771 BC** Power seized by Zhou		

◁ **Detail from "The first Emperor of the Han Dynasty Entering Guandong" by Song painter Chao Pochu**

Dynasty Timeline

China was ruled by a succession of dynasties, broken by periods of fragmentation and civil war. The emperor's authority was divinely granted through a mandate of heaven and was thus unlimited. Leaders of succeeding dynasties claimed that the previous leadership had displeased the gods and had therefore had its heavenly mandate withdrawn.

SHANG DYNASTY

1600–1050 BC

The Shang dynasty marked the emergence of Bronze Age China and palace culture. A semi-divine king acted as a shaman and communicated with the gods.

Bronze tripod food vessel, Shang

WESTERN HAN

206 BC–AD 9

Gaozu	206–195 BC
Huidi	195–188 BC
Shaodi	188–180 BC
Wendi	180–157 BC
Jingdi	157–141 BC
Wudi	141–87 BC
Zhaodi	87–74 BC
Xuandi	74–49 BC
Yuandi	49–33 BC
Chengdi	33–7 BC
Aidi	7–1 BC
Pingdi	1 BC–AD 6
Ruzi	AD 7–9

Broken terracotta heads found at Jingdi's tomb

EASTERN HAN

AD 25–220

Guang Wudi	25–57	Chongdi	144–145
Mingdi	57–75	Zhidi	145–146
Zhangdi	75–88	Huandi	146–168
Hedi	88–105	Lingdi	168–189
Shangdi	106	Xiandi	189–220
Andi	106–125		
Shundi	125–144		

TANG

618–907

Gaozu	618–626	Jingzong	824–827
Taizong	626–649	Wenzong	827–840
Gaozong	649–683	Wuzong	840–846
Zhongzong	684 & 705–710	Xuanzong	846–859
Ruizong	684–690	Yizong	859–873
	& 710–712	Xizong	873–888
Wu Zetian	690–705	Zhaozong	888–904
Xuanzong	712–756	Aidi	904–907
Suzong	756–762		
Daizong	762–779		
Dezong	779–805		
Shunzong	805		
Xianzong	805–820		
Muzong	820–824		

Sancai-glazed dancing tomb figures

FIVE DYNASTIES & TEN KINGDOMS

907–960

Based north of the Yangzi, five successive dynasties swiftly usurped one another, with no dynasty lasting for more than three reigns. The Ten Kingdoms to the south went through a similarly turbulent period.

Throughout this period and most of the Song dynasty, the northern frontiers were dominated by the semi-nomadic Liao dynasty (907–1125) in the east, and by the Western Xia (990–1227) in the west. In 1115, the Liao were overthrown by the Jin (1115–1234), who forced the Song southwards in 1127.

YUAN

1279–1368

Genghis Khan (1162–1227) united numerous Mongol speaking tribes and captured Beijing in 1215. His grandson, Kublai, completed the conquest of China by finally defeating the Southern Song in 1279.

Kublai Khan	1279–1294
Temur Oljeitu	1294–1307
Khaishan	1308–1311

Ayurbarwada	1311–1320
Shidebala	1321–1323
Yesun Temur	1323–1328
Tugh Temur	1328–1329,
	1329–1333
Khoshila	1329
Toghon Temur	1333–1368

MING

1368–1644

Hongwu	1368–1398	Longqing	1567–1572
Jianwen	1399–1402	Wanli	1573–1620
Yongle	1403–1424	Taichang	1620
Hongxi	1425	Tianqi	1621–1627
Xuande	1426–1435	Chongzhen	1628–1644
Zhengtong	1436–1449		
Jingtai	1450–1457		
Tianshun	1457–1464		
(Zhengtong restored)			
Chenghua	1465–1487		
Hongzhi	1488–1505		
Zhengde	1506–1521		
Jiajing	1522–1567		

WESTERN ZHOU DYNASTY

1066–771 BC

The Zhou founded their capital at Chang'an (Xi'an). They continued some Shang traditions, but reorganized the political system, dividing the nobility into grades. The feudal system of the Western Zhou broke down after the capital was sacked and the king slain.

EASTERN ZHOU DYNASTY

770–221 BC

Spring and Autumn
770–475 BC

Warring States
475–221 BC

The Zhou dynasty ruled at its eastern capital of Luoyang alongside numerous rival states. This long period of almost constant warfare was brought to an end when the Qin emerged victorious.

QIN DYNASTY

221–206 BC

Qin Shi Huangdi	221–210 BC
Er Shi	210–207 BC

Statue of attendant from the tomb of Qin Shi Huangdi

PERIOD OF DISUNITY

220–589

China was divided into the warring Wei, Wu, and Shu kingdoms. The Wei briefly re-united China under the Western Jin (280–316), the first of the six Southern Dynasties (280–589), with their capital at Jiankang (Nanjing). The north was ruled by a succession of ruling houses – the 16 Kingdoms (304–439). The nomadic Toba Wei set up the Northern Wei dynasty, the first of five Northern Dynasties (386–581) with a capital first at Datong, then at Luoyang.

SUI

581–618

China was once more united by the short and decisive rule of the Sui.

Wendi	581–604
Yangdi	604–617
Gongdi	617–618

Emperor Wendi's flotilla on the Grand Canal

NORTHERN SONG

960–1126

Taizu	960–976	Shenzong	1068–1085
Taizong	976–997	Zhezong	1086–1101
Zhenzong	998–1022	Huizong	1101–1125
Renzong	1022–1063	Qinzong	1126–1127
Yingzong	1064–1067		

Painting by Emperor Huizong

SOUTHERN SONG

1127–1279

Gaozong	1127–1162
Xiaozong	1163–1190
Guangzong	1190–1194
Ningzong	1195–1224
Lizong	1225–1264
Duzong	1265–1274
Gongdi	1275
Duanzong	1276–1278
Di Bing	1279

QING

1644–1911

Shunzhi	1644–1661
Kangxi	1661–1722
Yongzheng	1723–1735
Qianlong	1736–1795
Jiaqing	1796–1820
Daoguang	1821–1850
Xianfeng	1851–1861
Tongzhi	1862–1874
Guangxu	1875–1908
Pu Yi	1909–1912

Emperor Zhengde's love of leisure led to a relaxation of imperial control

Imperial dragon detail on the back of a eunuch's official court robe

FOUNDATION OF IMPERIAL CHINA

The Warring States Period was finally brought to an end as the Qin emerged victorious. In 221 BC, Qin Shi Huangdi pronounced himself the first emperor of China and ruled over a short yet decisive period of history. The Qin state was based on the political theories of Legalism, which established the role of the ruler as paramount and espoused a system of collective responsibility. Following unification, Qin Shi Huangdi conscripted thousands of workers to join together the defensive walls to the north, creating the Great Wall. He standardized the system of money, and weights and measures, and laid the foundations for a legal system. A ruthless ruler, Qin Shi Huangdi died in the belief that his famous terracotta army would protect him in the afterlife from his numerous enemies.

Lance soldier from Qin terracotta army

The founding of the Han dynasty (206 BC–AD 220) heralded a "golden age" in Chinese history. Emperor Gaodi (r. 206–195 BC) established the capital of the Western Han (206 BC–AD 9) at Chang'an (Xi'an), and retained much of the centralized administration established by the Qin. Subsequent emperors developed the civil service examination to select able men for state office. Han society was founded on the principles propounded by Confucius, and the Confucian classics formed the basis of the civil service examination. Daoism and *yin-yang* theory coexisted with ancestor worship and would form the basis of indigenous Chinese belief *(see pp22–3)*.

The Han empire expanded with regions of Central Asia, Vietnam, and Korea being brought under Chinese control. In 138 BC, General Zhang Qian was sent to establish diplomatic links with Central Asia and returned with tales of rich pastures and "heavenly horses." The fine thoroughbreds of Ferghana (in modern Uzbekistan) were traded in exchange for Chinese silk, starting the flow of goods along the fabled Silk Road.

Han rule was briefly interrupted as Wang Mang seized power in AD 9, only to be restored by Guang Wudi (r. AD 25–57), who established the Eastern Han capital in Luoyang. Once more, the Han expanded Chinese territory. Paper was by now in use for much official documentation and the first Chinese dictionary was produced. Buddhism began its spread to China with the first Buddhist communities being established in Jiangsu province.

Chariot and footmen, impressed into a tomb's brick, Han

TIMELINE

213 BC Burning of the books as part of process of "unification"	206 BC–AD 9 Western Han capital established at Chang'an (Xi'an)	c. 139–126 BC Official envoy Zhang Qian establishes first diplomatic and trading links of Silk Road		c. 100 First dictionary Shuo Wen produced with more than 9,000 characters
		AD 2 First known census: 57,671,400 individuals	Bronze horse and rider, Han	

200 BC	100 BC	1	AD 100

221–206 BC Qin dynasty under first emperor, Qin Shi Huangdi	165 BC First official examinations for the selection of civil servants	25–220 Eastern Han dynasty capital at Luoyang	65 First mention of Buddhist community established at court of Prince Ying of Chu
	Tomb figure, Qin		

Sui emperors Yangdi and Wendi in a detail from "Portraits of the 13 Emperors" by Tang painter Yen Li Pen

PERIOD OF DIVISION

From the rule of Hedi (r. AD 88–105), the Eastern Han declined. Civil war finally split the country in 220. The next 350 years were characterized by almost constant warfare as China was ruled by over 14 short-lived dynasties and 16 "kingdoms."

China was divided into the Northern and Southern dynasties (265–581), each region taking on its own distinct character. Foreign peoples took control of the North, such as the Toba branch of the Xianbei, who founded the Northern Wei in 386. These rulers were receptive to foreign ideas and religions, creating some of the finest Buddhist cave complexes first at Yungang, near their capital in Datong, and from 494, at Longmen, when they moved their capital to Luoyang.

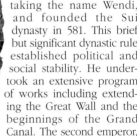

Apsara from Buddhist cave, Northern Wei

As foreign invaders took control of the North, the Han Chinese retreated south to establish their new capital at Jiankang (Nanjing). In a climate of relative stability, the south became the economic and cultural center as the population shifted to the Yangzi delta. Philosophy and the arts flourished alongside a renewed interest in Daoism and a growing interest in Buddhism.

UNIFICATION AND STABILITY

Following military successes against the Liang and the Chen, the Northern Zhou general Yang Jian (541–604) pronounced himself emperor, taking the name Wendi, and founded the Sui dynasty in 581. This brief but significant dynastic rule established political and social stability. He undertook an extensive program of works including extending the Great Wall and the beginnings of the Grand Canal. The second emperor, Yangdi (569–617), restored diplomatic relations with Japan and Taiwan and extended trade to Central Asia.

190 Communications with central Asia are cut

AD 2 First known census: 57,671,400 individuals

Colossal Buddha at Yungang Caves, Northern Wei

310 Massive exodus of Chinese upper classes to South

581–618 Sui dynasty, initiated by Wendi's reunification of China

200 | **300** | **400** | **500** | **600**

220 Civil war breaks out between the kingdoms of Wei, Shu, and Wu

265–581 China divided into Northern and Southern dynasties

386–535 Northern Wei, first of the ruling houses to adopt Buddhism

c. 6th C First true porcelain produced

c. 7th C Woodblock printing first used in China

GLORY OF THE TANG

The Tang dynasty (AD 618–907) marks a high point in Chinese history. During this golden age, China enjoyed an extended period of peace and prosperity. The arts flourished and were enriched by foreign styles, motifs, and techniques such as silver-working. Foreign religions, such as Nestorian Christianity, were tolerated and co-existed alongside native Daoism and Confucianism. Woodblock printing was invented by the Chinese some time during the 7th century and hastened the spread of Buddhism.

Sancai glazed horse, Tang

Following the An Lushan rebellion of 755, the Tang became increasingly inward looking. The great Buddhist persecution of 841–46 was symptomatic of a dynasty in decline, which finally fell in 907.

THE LIAO DYNASTY (907–1125)

The Liao dynasty, which at its largest covered much of Mongolia, Manchuria, and northern China, was ruled by semi-nomadic and pastoral people, the Qidan. The Liao maintained a dual administration, Qidan and Chinese, and even a prime-ministership, to ensure the survival of their own customs and traditions whilst utilizing the efficiency of Tang structures of government. In 1115, the Qidan were overthrown by another semi-nomadic people, the Ruzhen (Jurchen).

With the support of the Northern Song, the Ruzhen took control of the north and founded the Jin dynasty. The Liao were forced westwards to the region of the Tian mountain range in present-day Xinjiang, where they established the Western Liao (1125–1211). The rest of northwest China was dominated by the Western Xia, a Tibetan related people who recognized the Liao as their overlords.

FIVE DYNASTIES AND TEN KINGDOMS (907–960)

While the north of China was dominated by the insurgence of semi-nomadic peoples from the steppe regions, the south was ruled by a series of short military dictatorships. The Song dynasty was founded in 960 by Zhao Kuangyin, a military commander of the later Zhou (951–960), whose imperial name became Shizong. In the Yangzi delta and regions to the south, the Ten Kingdoms existed in relative peace and stability and were reunited by the Song in 979.

Painting of an official celebrating, Five Dynasties (923–938)

TIMELINE

618–907 Tang heralds new golden age	690–705 Empress Wu Zetian rules as first empress of China	755–763 An Lushan rebellion drives emperor and court from Chang'an to Sichuan		806 Earliest dated printed manuscript, the Diamond Sutra		907–60 Period of division known as Five Dynasties and Ten Kingdoms	10th c. Gunpowd and fire ar first used
	700	**750**		**800**	**850**	**900**	
661 Chinese administration in Kashmir, Bokhara, and the borders of eastern Iran	705 Famous poet Li Bai born	*Tang silver*		806–820 First bankers' bill 770 Death of great poet Du Fu		907–1125 Qidan people rule northeastern China as the Liao dynasty, making Beijing their southern capital	

THE SONG DYNASTY (960–1279)

The Song presided over a period of cultural brilliance and unprecedented growth in urban life during which the social makeup of China fundamentally changed. Less territorially ambitious than the Tang, the Song stimulated economic development through improved communications and transport. New industries based on mass production began to emerge, notably the porcelain industry based in Jiangxi province. During the Southern Song, China underwent an industrial revolution producing quantities of raw materials such as salt and iron on a scale that would not be seen in Europe until the 18th century.

In this buoyant economic climate a new middle-class emerged, stimulating demand for the new range of consumer goods. Power shifted from the aristocratic elite to government bureaucrats, who spent their spare time practising the arts of poetry, calligraphy, and painting. Collecting and connoisseurship led to an artistic renaissance and the founding of the first Imperial collections. Emperor Huizong was a great patron of the arts who used ancient precedents and values to buttress his own position. Neo-Confucianism and a renewed interest in Daoism marked a return to indigenous beliefs and traditional structures of power.

The Northern Song repeatedly came under attack from the Western Xia in the northwest and the Jin in the northeast. Only 12 years after joining forces with the Song against the Liao, the Jin invaded the

Illustration of Song Emperor Huizong, r. 1101–1125

Northern Song capital at Bianliang (Kaifeng), capturing emperor Qinzong and forcing the court to flee southwards. The capital of the Southern Song (1127–1279) was established at Lin'an (Hangzhou) south of the Yangzi.

JIN DYNASTY (1115–1234)

The Jin were a semi-nomadic Tungusic people originating from Manchuria. War with the Song and persistent attacks from the Mongols resulted in a weakening of the Jin state which by the early 13th century formed a buffer state between the Song in the south and the Mongols in the north. In 1227, Mongol and Chinese allied forces defeated the Jin and in 1234 the Jin emperor committed suicide. The Jin state was integrated into the rapidly expanding Mongol empire.

Early movable type, Song

960–1126 Northern Song reunites China and bases capital at Bianliang (Kaifeng)

Detail of painting by Emperor Huizong

1127–1279 Southern Song dynasty with capital at Hangzhou, after being forced south by the Jin

1154 First issue of paper money (Jin)

1206–1208 Song and Jin at war

950	1000	1050	1100	1150	1200

990–1227 Western Xia people establish kingdom dominating northwest China

1041–8 First attempts at printing with movable type

1090 First attested use of compass on Chinese ships

1115–1234 Jin dynasty founded in northeast China forcing Liao westwards

1214 Jin move capital from Beijing to Kaifeng in Henan province

MONGOL RULE (1279–1368)

The Mongol leader Genghis Khan united the various Mongol-speaking tribes of the steppes and in 1215 conquered northern China. He divided his empire into four kingdoms, each ruled by one of his sons. His grandson Kublai Khan (r. 1260–94), ruler of the eastern Great Khanate, finally defeated the Southern Song in 1279 and proclaimed himself emperor of the Yuan dynasty. China now became part of a vast empire which stretched from the East China Sea across Asia as far as Russia, the Ukraine, and Baghdad. Two capitals were maintained at Dadu or Khanbalik (present-day Beijing) and Yuanshangdu (Xanadu). The Silk Routes opened once more, connecting China to the Middle East and Medieval Europe. Direct contact was now made for the first time between the Mongol court and European diplomats, Franciscan missionaries, and merchants. According to the writings of Marco Polo, the

Buddhist deity, Yuan

Italian merchant spent 21 years in the service of Kublai and his court.

The Mongols ruled through a form of military government, in contrast to the bureaucratic civil service established by the Chinese. Although Chinese and Mongol languages were both used for official business, the Chinese were not encouraged to take up official posts. Muslims from Central and Western Asia took their place, and the Chinese increasingly retreated from official life.

As there were no clear rules for succession, civil war broke out in 1328 between Mongol nobles.

The secret societies of the Red Turbans and the White Lotus led peasant rebellions and in 1368 General Zhu Yuanzhang forced the Mongols out of China, becoming the first emperor of the Ming dynasty.

MING DYNASTY (1368–1644)

The Ming (literally "brilliant") dynasty was one of the longest and most stable periods in China's history. The founder of the Ming, Zhu Yuanzhang, rose from humble beginnings to become a general, ruling as emperor Hongwu ("vast military accomplishment"). During his reign, Hongwu introduced radical changes to both central and local government, which he made binding on his successors. The emperor's role became more autocratic as Hongwu dispensed with the position of Prime Minister, taking direct responsibility for overseeing all six ministries himself.

Hongwu appointed his grandson to be his successor. Upon his death, his son the Prince of Yan, who controlled the region around Beijing, led an army

Genghis Khan (c.1162–1227), Persian miniature

TIMELINE

1215 Mongols capture Beijing	1234 Jin emperor commits suicide and Jin integrated into Mongol empire	*Mongol on horseback*	1368–1644 Ming dynasty, founded by rebel leader General Zhu Yuanzhang	1403 Construction of Great Walls in North China
	1250	1300	1350	1400
1227 Genghis Khan dies, having united various Mongol speaking tribes of the steppe	1279–1368 Kublai Khan defeats Southern Song and rules China as emperor of the Yuan dynasty	1328 Civil war breaks out between Mongol nobles		*Jade elephant, Ming*

The existing battlements of the Great Wall, reinforced and joined together during the Ming dynasty

against his nephew, taking Nanjing and proclaiming himself emperor Yongle ("Eternal Joy"). Yongle (r. 1403–24) moved the capital to his power base in Beijing, where he created a new city based on traditional principles of Chinese city planning. At its core lay the Forbidden City (see pp62–7), the imperial palace and offices of government, surrounded by a grid system of streets, with four imperial altars at the cardinal points. The entire city was walled to provide both protection and enclosure. In 1421, Beijing became the official capital and, bar a short interlude during the Nationalist era in the early 20th century, would remain so until the present day.

By the 15th century, China had become a significant maritime power, its ships dwarfing those of contemporary Europe. Blue and white porcelain, silk, and other luxury items were in high demand in the foreign markets of Japan, Southeast Asia, and the Middle East. Yongle sent six maritime expeditions under the Muslim eunuch admiral Zheng He, which

Wedding jewelry, Ming

reached as far as the east coast of Africa. In 1514 Portuguese traders first landed in China, purchasing tea which then became a fashionable drink in European society. Porcelain provided ballast for the ships, and other luxury items were brought back along with the cargo. Trade was dominated by the Dutch in the 17th century, only to be surpassed by the British a hundred years later. Jesuit missionaries, who arrived in the 16th century, claimed few converts but gained access to the emperor and the inner court.

The arts thrived under emperor Xuande (r. 1426–35), an artist and poet, who patronized the arts, notably the porcelain industry at Jingdezhen. In literature, the late Ming is noted for its great dramas and classical novels, such as Journey to the West (see p21). Philosophy of the time reinforced the Neo-Confucianism of the Song.

The late Ming was dominated by peasant uprisings, incursions by Japanese pirates and Mongolian tribes, and excessive eunuch power. Rebellions within China eventually joined with external forces to end Ming rule.

Gilt bronze bowl, Ming

1426–35 Xuande emperor becomes first Ming emperor to patronize the arts extensively	1514 Portuguese land in China, becoming the first Europeans to trade in tea and porcelain	1573–1620 Wanli reign begins well but dynasty declines as emperor takes little interest in duties	1620 Emperor Taichang poisoned by eunuchs
1450	**1500**	**1550**	**1600**
1420 Construction of the Forbidden City in Beijing completed	Early 16th century Later Ming monarchs neglect duties of government and eunuch power increases	1538 Jesuit Father Matteo Ricci enters southern China and begins missionary duties	1570 Popular novel Xi Yu Ji (Journey to the West) published	1600s Dutch dominate European trade with China	1601 Jesuit missionary Matteo Ricci allowed to enter Beijing

QING RULE (1644–1911)

The Manchu leader Nurhachi established the Later Jin in 1616, organizing the scattered tribes of the north into eight banner units. In 1636, the Manchu ruler Abahai changed the name to Qing, literally "pure," and prepared the way for the capture of Beijing in 1644. Under Manchu control, China was once more ruled by a foreign people. The Manchus were keen to adopt the Chinese method of rule, encouraging Chinese scholars into the service of the new empire. Dual administration at national and provincial levels meant Manchu and Chinese bureaucrats worked side by side using first Manchu and later Chinese as the official languages of government. However, despite the close interaction of Manchu and Chinese, the ruling Manchus were careful to maintain a distinct separation in order to protect their own privileges and cultural traditions.

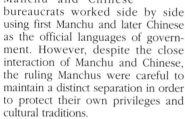

Emperor Kangxi, r. 1661–1722

The first emperors of the Qing were enlightened rulers who presided over one of largest and most populous countries in the world. The territorial aspirations of Emperor Kangxi brought the regions of Central Asia and southern Siberia once more under Chinese control. Kangxi was succeeded by Emperor Yongzheng. It was his fourth son, Emperor Qianlong, "Lasting Eminence," (r. 1736–96) who heralded another golden age. An ambitious ruler, Qianlong was determined to extend China's borders beyond those of the Tang, personally leading campaigns to Burma, Vietnam, and Central Asia.

During the 18th century, contact with the west increased through Jesuit missionaries and trade. By the mid-18th century, the Chinese sought to control trade by refusing all official contact with Westerners and opening only Canton to foreign merchants. Pressure from European embassies increased as the British sent Lord Macartney in 1792–94 to establish diplomatic relations and open China to trade. China refused to grant a single concession to the British.

THE DECLINE OF THE EMPIRE

The 19th century is one of the most turbulent periods of Chinese history, as internal uprisings, natural disasters, and the relentless encroachment of the West culminated in the end of the empire. A succession of weak rulers were manipulated and controlled by

Lord Macartney's massive entourage arriving at Qianlong's tent

TIMELINE

		1644–1800 Military expansion into Central Asia and Siberia; colonization of new territories Yunnan and Xinjiang		**1723–1735** Kangxi's son Yin Zhen seizes power ruling under name of emperor Yongzheng		*Emperor Shunzhi, r. 1644–61* **1747** Qianlong builds Yuanming Yuan *(see p84)* in western style	
	1650		**1675**	**1700**	**1725**	**1750**	
1644–1911 Manchus establish Qing dynasty	**1650** First Catholic church in Beijing	**1661–1722** Rule of Kangxi emperor. Appoints Jesuits to run Board of Astronomy		**1736–1795** Qianlong, a great patron of the arts, rules over another golden age			**1757** Chinese restrict all foreign trade to Canton

A merchant testing tea quality in a Cantonese warehouse

the Dowager Empress Cixi, who ruled for much of the late Qing from "behind the curtain." The Taiping Rebellion of 1850–64 devastated south and central China.

Western powers, frustrated by the reluctance of the Chinese to open to foreign trade, brought the Chinese under increasing pressure. Keen to protect the trade of opium from their colonies in India, the British engaged in the First Opium War (1840–42), which culminated in the Treaty of Nanjing, resulting in the opening of four new ports to trade, the payment of huge indemnities, and the ceding of Hong Kong to Britain. Following the Arrow War (Second Opium War) with Britain and France (1856), the European forces divided China into "spheres of influence" – the British strongest along the Yangzi and in Shanghai, the Germans controlling Shandong province, and the French controlling the borders with Vietnam.

In 1900 the Boxers allied with imperial troops and attacked the foreign legations in Beijing. An eight-nation army defeated the onslaught, and Cixi fled to Xi'an, blaming everything on the emperor. The Chinese government paid once more for the loss of life and Cixi returned to Beijing until her death in 1908. The child emperor Pu Yi lived in the Forbidden City as the last emperor until his abdication. On 1 January 1912 the Republican leader Sun Yat Sen inaugurated the Chinese Republic.

FROM EMPIRE TO REPUBLIC

In the final years of the empire, many Chinese intellectuals recognized the need to modernize. Supporters of the Reform Movement of 1898 propounded the adoption of western technology and education, and, following the Boxer Rebellion, a number of reforms were adopted. Elected regional assemblies were set up, further undermining the power of the Qing. In 1911 the empire collapsed completely. Sun Yat Sen was elected provisional President of China, but was soon forced to resign in favor of general Yuan Shikai, who sought to become emperor. Yuan was forced to back down when governors revolted and he died soon after in 1916. China then came under the control of a series of regional warlords until it was united once more with the founding of the People's Republic of China in 1949.

Sun Yat Sen, 1866–1925

The Cultural Revolution

In 1965, Mao Zedong set in motion a chain of events that were to unleash the turmoil now known as the Cultural Revolution. Having socialized industry and agriculture, Mao called on the masses to transform society itself – all distinctions between manual

Actor in opera

and intellectual work were to be abolished and class distinction disappear. The revolution reached its violent peak in 1967, with the Red Guards spreading social unrest. The People's Liberation Army (PLA) finally restored order, but the subsequent years were characterized by fear, violence, and mistrust.

Children were encouraged *to take part in the Revolution. Their enthusiasm led to the destruction of family photographs and posses- sions. In some cases, children denounced their own parents.*

THE RED GUARD

Mao appealed to students to form the Red Guard, in whom he entrusted the fate of the revolution. The movement rapidly gathered momentum and the Red Guard, who raised Mao to godly status, traveled China spreading Mao Zedong "Thoughts," smashing remnants of the past, vandalizing temples, and wreaking havoc.

Mass public meetings *were held as part of the Socialist Education Movement, a precursor of the Cultural Revolution intended to reverse "capitalist" and "revisionist" tendencies perceived in social and economic life. Everyone was required to attend.*

An injured cadre *is carried away after being denounced. Shamings became the bench mark of public meetings. Many politicians and teachers were paraded and accused, leading to job loss and, in some cases, suicide.*

The *Little Red Book* was essential to the Red Guard and issued to every soldier under Lin Biao's command.

Demonstrating their opposition *to Soviet-style communism and their support for Maoism, Red Guards change a Beijing street sign in front of the Soviet Embassy from East Yangwei to Fanxiu Lu (Anti-revisionism Road).*

Lin Biao spread the study *of the "Thoughts of Mao" and compiled the* Little Red Book *which became obligatory reading for his army recruits. As head of the PLA, Lin Biao provided essential military backing and was Mao's named successor. He died in a plane crash over Siberia in 1971 amid rumors of an imminent usurpation.*

Model operas *were the pet project of Mao's third wife, Jiang Qing. She set about creating a politically correct revolutionary culture. Many artists and intellectuals were sent to the countryside for re-education.*

May 7 Cadre Schools *were set up by the central government in 1968. 100,000 officials plus 30,000 family members were sent to perform manual labor and undergo ideological re-education. An unknown number of lower-ranking cadres were sent to thousands of other cadre schools.*

Liu Shaoqi *(right), president from 1959–66, was one of a number of high officials to be denounced, imprisoned, and paraded in "struggle rallies." He died from his experiences.*

GANG OF FOUR

The Gang of Four, as they became known, orchestrated attacks on intellectuals and writers, high officials, the party, and the state and were responsible for some of the worst excesses of the Cultural Revolution. Zhang Chunqiao, critic and propagandist, Yao Wenyuan, editor-in-chief of *Shanghai Liberation Army Daily*, Wang Hongwen, a young worker, and Mao's third wife Jiang Qing, an ex-film star, dominated the political center unchallenged until Mao's death in 1976. Millions of Chinese citizens watched their televized trial in 1980–81. Jiang Qing, who was singled out by propagandists and became one of the most hated figures in China, was defiant until the end, railing against her prosecutors throughout the trial. She took her own life in 1991, while serving her life sentence.

Lynched effigies of members of the Gang of Four hanging from a tree

Chiang Kai Shek (1887–1975), leader of the KMT

COMMUNISTS AND NATIONALISTS

After the fall of the empire, the political landscape changed dramatically and became dominated by two forces, the Nationalist Party or Kuomintang (KMT) and the Communist Party, founded in 1921. The Nationalists were led first by Sun Yat Sen from his power base in Guangzhou, then by General Chiang Kai Shek who seized power in 1926. In 1923 the two Parties formed a "united front" against the warlords, but in 1926 the Communists were expelled from the KMT. Chiang Kai Shek led his army to Nanjing where he tried to establish a Nationalist capital, and betrayed the Communist-led workers of Shanghai who were massacred by underworld gangsters. The Communists were driven underground and Mao Zedong retreated to the countryside.

High in the mountains of Jiangxi province, Mao and Zhu De founded the Jiangxi Soviet in 1930. From this inaccessible base, the communists began to redistribute land to the peasants and institute new marriage laws. In 1934, Chiang Kai Shek drove the communists from the area, forcing Mao to embark on the legendary Long March. Yan'an, where the march ended, became the new Communist Party headquarters and would remain so until 1945.

JAPANESE ATTACK

Domestic turmoil laid China open to attack, and in 1931 the Japanese occupied Manchuria, founding the puppet state of Manchukuo and placing the last Qing emperor, Pu Yi, at its head. By 1937 the Japanese had occupied much of northern China, Shanghai, and the Yangzi valley ruthlessly taking cities, wreaking death and devastation. The Japanese were finally driven from Chinese soil in 1945, and China was plunged into civil war.

THE EAST IS RED

By 1947, the Communist policy of land reform was reaping rewards and gaining the support of people in the countryside. In 1948–9, the Communists gained decisive victories over the KMT. On 1 October 1949 Chairman Mao pronounced the founding of the People's Republic of China. Chiang Kai Shek fled to Taiwan, establishing a Nationalist government and taking with him many Imperial treasures.

毛主席革命路线胜利万岁

Communist poster depicting Mao surrounded by the masses

TIMELINE

1912 Abdication of emperor Pu Yi marks the end of Imperial China	**1921** Founding of the Chinese Communist Party	**1945** End of World War II; Japan defeated	**1958** Radical reform of the Great Leap Forward	**1965** Mao launches Cultural Revolution
		1937 Japanese take much of northern China	**1947** Civil War breaks out in China	
1910	**1920**	**1930**	**1940**	**1950**	**1960**
	1926 Chiang Kai Shek seizes leadership of National Party	**1934** Mao leads the Red Army on Long March	**1951–2** Rural co-ops established	
	Last Emperor Pu Yi	**1931** Japanese invasion of Manchuria	**1949** Mao proclaims founding of People's Republic of China	

In the early years of the People's Republic, the Chinese worked hard to rebuild a country devastated by 100 years of tumoil. New laws sought to redress inequities of the past, redistributing land and outlawing arranged marriages.

Zhou Enlai with President Nixon

The Party promptly branded intellectuals as "rightists" and sent them to the countryside for re-education. Frustrated with the slow rate of change, Mao launched the Great Leap Forward in 1958. Large communes providing food and childcare replaced the family, releasing manual labor and improving productivity. But unrealistic productivity targets and the falsification of statistics concealed the disastrous effect of Mao's experiment. Agricultural failure coupled with natural disasters resulted in the starvation of millions

Having reformed agriculture and industry, Mao sought to transform society and launched the Cultural Revolution in 1965 *(see pp50–51)*. The greatest excesses of the period were over by 1971, but the country was tightly controlled and directed until Mao's death in 1976. Deng Xiaoping emerged as leader, implementing economic reforms which returned land to the peasants and encouraged greater economic freedom.

The economic liberalization of the 1980s stimulated the economy but was unmatched by political freedom. On 4 June 1989 the democracy movement called for political reform and an end to corruption, but was brutally suppressed in Tian'an Men Square. Whilst many students and intellectuals fled abroad, others remain incarcerated in China's jails. Deng Xiaoping pressed on with economic reform, and the 1990s saw the opening of Special Economic Zones and stock exchanges in most major cities. By 1992, China's economy had become one of the largest in the world.

The unprecedented rate of economic growth in the 1990s was matched by the transformation of the landscape as traditional buildings made way for modern highrises. The former colonies of Hong Kong and Macau were returned to China and foreign investment flooded in. Entrepreneurs prospered, and the Communist Party has been keen to attract this new class into its ranks. Disbanding the state economy has also spawned inequity, and the gap between rich and poor grows ever wider. How the most populous nation on earth resolves the many issues it faces remains to be seen. The handover of power at

Chinese traders on the Stock Exchange

the top of the Communist Party in late 2012 saw President Hu Jintao and Premier Wen Jiabao pass the reins to a new generation of leaders whose task will be to achieve economic growth while maintaining national unity.

1970	1980	1990	2000	2010	2020

Little Red Book

1976 Mao dies

1978 Deng Xiaoping emerges as leader

1989 Democracy movement suppressed in Tian'an Men Square

1972 President Nixon is first American president to visit China

1993 Jiang Zemin becomes president; construction of Three Gorges Dam begins

1997 Hong Kong handed back to China; Macau, two years later

2003 Chinese launch first manned spacecraft; Hu Jintao becomes president

2001 China admitted as member of World Trade Organization

2008 Beijing hosts the 2008 Olympic Games

2012 President Hu Jintao and Premier Wen Jiabao step down and hand over power to Xi Jinping and Li Keqiang

2010 Shanghai hosts the 2010 World Expo

BEIJING

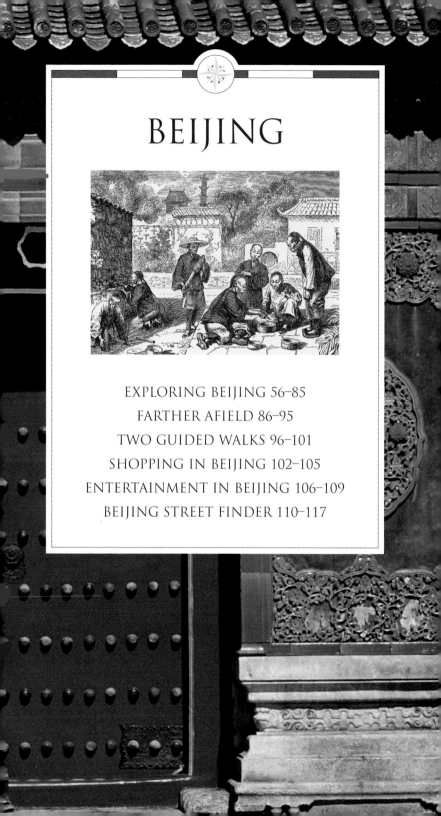

Exploring Beijing

Beijing's most significant sights and districts are
marked on this map. At the core is the Forbidden
City, with Tian'an Men Square and Qian Men to the
south, and the shopping district of Wangfujing to its
east. North of the Forbidden City stand the Drum and
Bell Towers, and farther northeast is the Buddhist
Lama Temple. North of Bei Hai Park, the Mansion of
Prince Gong stands in an historic district of *hutongs*,
the old alleyways that riddle the city. To the south,
Tian Tan, known as the Temple of Heaven, is a
majestic example of Ming dynasty design. Beijing's
suburbs are also dotted with sites including the
magnificent Summer Palace complex.

LOCATOR MAP

KEY

▨	Street-by-Street area: see pp58–9
✈	International airport
🚇	Train station
🚌	Long-distance bus station
M	Subway station
🚌	City bus station
🛕	Temple
✝	Church
━	National highway
━	Major road

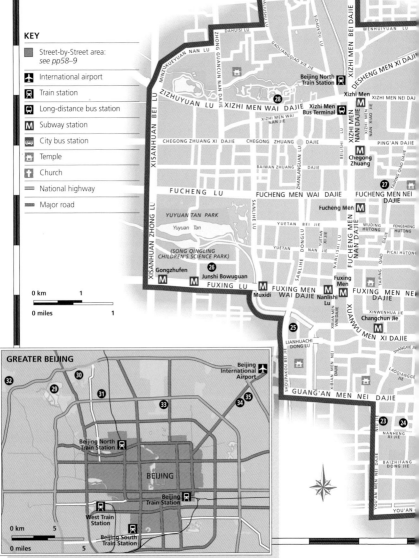

SIGHTS AT A GLANCE

Historic Buildings, Sites, and Neighborhoods
Ancient Observatory ⓲
Beijing Urban Planning Exhibition Hall ❸
Dazhalan & Liulichang ❹
Drum & Bell Towers ⓫
Forbidden City pp62–7 ❻
Legation Quarter ❼
Mansion of Prince Gong ⓾
National Olympic Stadium ㉝
Qian Men ❷
Summer Palace pp80–83 ㉙
Tian'an Men Square pp58–9 ❶
Yuanming Yuan ㉚

Shops and Markets
Wangfujing Street ⓱

Museums and Galleries
798 Art District ㉞
Beijing Natural History Museum ⓴
China Railway Museum ㉟
Military Museum of the Chinese People's Revolution ㉖
National Art Museum of China ⓰

Southeast Corner Watchtower (Dongbian Men) ⓳

Temples, Churches, and Mosques
Confucius Temple ⓭
Cow Street Mosque ㉓
Dong Yue Miao ⓯
Fayuan Temple ㉔
Great Bell Temple ㉛
Lama Temple ⓬
Miaoying Temple White Dagoba ㉗
South Cathedral ❺
Temple of Heaven pp74–7 ㉑
White Clouds Temple ㉕
Xiannong Tan ㉒

Parks and Zoos
Bei Hai Park ❾
Beijing Zoo ㉘
Di Tan Park ⓮
Jing Shan Park ❽
Xiang Shan Park ㉜

SEE ALSO

• *Street Finder* pp110–17

• *Where to Stay* pp178–82

• *Where to Eat* pp198–202

GETTING AROUND

A system of ring roads encircles the city center, and the best way to explore this area is by taxi, by subway, or by bicycle (see pp226–7). The bus service, though extensive, is generally slow and overcrowded. Organized tours are another option for a quick overview of the sights. Most hotels and agencies operate tour buses for visiting sights outside Beijing, although hiring a taxi for the day allows for greater flexibility.

Street-by-Street: Tian'an Men Square ❶

天安门广场

Chairman Mao

Tian'an Men Guangchang – the Square of the Gate of Heavenly Peace – is a vast open concrete expanse at the heart of modern Beijing. With Mao's Mausoleum at its focal point, and bordered by 1950s Communist-style buildings and ancient gates from Beijing's now leveled city walls, the square is usually filled with visitors strolling about as kites flit overhead. The square has also traditionally served as a stage for popular demonstrations and is most indelibly associated with the student protests of 1989 and their gory climax.

Cyclists along Chang'an Jie

Great Hall of the People
Seat of the Chinese legislature, the vast auditorium and banqueting halls are open for part of the day except when the National People's Congress is in session.

★ Zhengyang Men
Along with the Arrow Tower this tower formed a double gate known as the Qian Men. It now houses a museum on the history of Beijing.

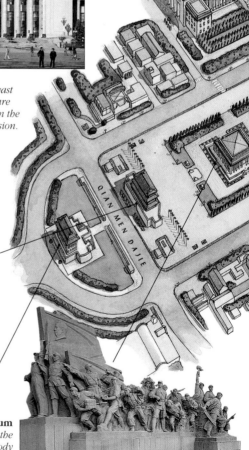

The Arrow Tower or Jian Lou, like Zhengyang Men, was first built in the Ming dynasty.

★ Mao's Mausoleum
Flanked by revolutionary statues, the building contains the embalmed body of Chairman Mao. His casket, raised from its refrigerated chamber, is on view mornings and afternoons.

★ **Tian'an Men**
Mao proclaimed the founding of the People's Republic of China on October 1, 1949 from this Ming dynasty gate, where his huge portrait still remains.

LOCATOR MAP
See p114 Street Finder Map 4 C1

| 0 meters | 20 |
| 0 yards | 20 |

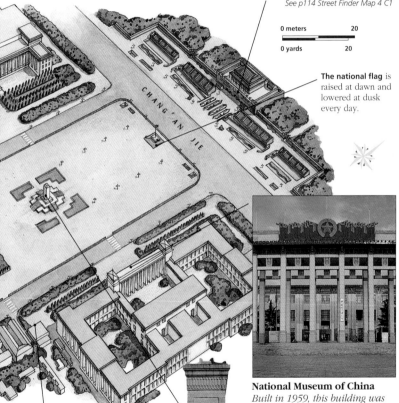

CHANG'AN JIE

The national flag is raised at dawn and lowered at dusk every day.

National Museum of China
Built in 1959, this building was originally home to the Museum of Chinese History and the Museum of the Revolution, now merged. The displays include items from both museums, among them propaganda from the history of the Communist party.

Bags, coats, and cameras
must be left here before visiting Mao's Mausoleum.

Monument to the People's Heroes
Erected in 1958, the granite monument is decorated with bas-reliefs of episodes from China's revolutionary history and calligraphy from Communist veterans Mao Zedong and Zhou Enlai.

STAR SIGHTS

★ Mao's Mausoleum

★ Zhengyang Men

★ Tian'an Men

Zhengyang Men, Qian Men – part of Beijing's central fortifications

Qian Men ❷
前门

Qian Men Dajie. **Map** *4 C2.* Ⓜ *Qian Men.* ◯ *8:30am–4pm daily.* 📷

Qian Men or the Front Gate consists of two towers, the **Zhengyang Men**, on the southern edge of Tian'an Men Square, and the **Jian Lou Arrow Tower** just to the south. Zhengyang Men (Facing the Sun Gate) was the most imposing of the nine gates of the inner city wall that divided Beijing's imperial quarters in the Forbidden City from the "Chinese City," where, during the Manchu Qing dynasty, the Chinese inhabitants lived.

Rising 131 ft (40 m), the gate stands on the north-south axis that runs through the Tian'an Men and the Forbidden City. Its museum has dioramas of the old city walls, and photographs of Beijing's old streets.

The 125-ft (38-m) high Jian Lou (Arrow Tower), originally built in 1439, has 94 windows that were used for shooting arrows. Both the Jian Lou and Zhengyang Men were badly damaged by fire during the Boxer Rebellion. In 1916, the enceinte, a semi-circular wall that connected the two towers, was demolished to make way for a road. Jian Lou is now closed to the public. Across the road to the east, the Old Railway Station was built by the British and now houses a number of shops. The area around Qian Men, originally the city's old shopping district, has received a radical make-over. Qian Men Dajie is now a broad, pedestrianised street flanked by brand boutiques and mini shopping malls, as well as cafés and restaurants housed in ancient Beijing-themed buildings. A 1930s-style tram runs up and down the street, ferrying shoppers and tourists.

🚇 **Zhengyang Men**
Tel *(010) 6511 8110.* ◯ *daily.* 📷

Beijing Urban Planning Exhibition Hall ❸
北京市规划展览馆

20 Qian Men Dong Dajie. **Map** 5 D2.
Ⓜ *Qian Men.* **Tel** *(010) 6701 7074.*
◯ *9am–5pm Tue–Sun.* 📷 🖥

Just east of the historic Qian Men area, this four-story building traces the history of Beijing's urban development through photographs, old maps, and models. It also offers a glimpse into what the architecture and urban landscape of Beijing will look like in the future. This is dramatically represented through two short 3-D films, as well as a huge scale model of what the city should look like in 2020. A highlight of the exhibition, the 3,200-sq-ft (300-sq-m) model covers most of the third floor and is also viewable from a gallery above.

Large scale model at the Beijing Urban Planning Exhibition Hall

BEIJING'S CITY WALLS

The earliest defensive walls around Beijing (then called Yanjing, later Zhongdu) were erected in the Jin dynasty (1115–1234) and modeled on the wall around Kaifeng. The Mongol Kublai Khan rebuilt Zhongdu, naming it Dadu, and encompassed it with a 19-mile (30-km) wall. It was only during the Ming era (1368–1644) that the walls took on their final shape of an Outer Wall with seven gates, and an Inner Wall with nine gates. The magnificent Inner Wall was 38 ft (11.5 m) high and 64 ft (19.5 m) wide. The walls and most of their gates were unfortunately demolished in the 1950s and 60s to make way for roads. Of the inner wall, only Qian Men and Desheng Men survive, while the outer wall retains only Dongbian Men *(see p73)*. The old gates live on as place names on the second ring road, and as the names of stations on the Beijing Underground Loop line.

Arrow Tower of Qian Men

Shop selling Communist memorabilia, Dazhalan Jie

Dazhalan & Liulichang ❹
栅栏和琉璃厂

Map 4 C2. Ⓜ Qian Men.

South of Qian Men are the narrow and lively *hutongs (see p69)* of the old Chinese quarter. The inner city wall and its gates separated the "Inner City" containing the imperial quarters of the Manchu emperors from the "Chinese City," where the Chinese lived apart from their Qing overlords. Today, the district buzzes with shops, cinemas, and restaurants. Running west off the northern end of Qian Men Dajie is Dazhalan Jie (also known locally as Dashilan), whose name "Big Barrier Street" refers to the

Cyclists on restored Liulichang Jie

now-demolished gates that were closed every night to fence off the residents from Qian Men and the Inner City. The area was damaged during the Boxer Rebellion and later restored. There are *hutong* tours by rickshaw – drivers just wait in the street in Dazhalan.

The area is a great place for browsing, and has several quaint Qing-era specialty shops. Located down the first alley on the left from Dazhalan Jie is the century-old pickle shop **Liubiju**, selling a vast array of

pungent pickles. **Ruifuxiang**, on the right-hand side of Dazhalan, dates from 1893 and is renowned for its silks and traditional Chinese garments. On the south side of Dazhalan Jie is the Chinese medicine shop **Tongrentang Pharmacy**, which has been in business since 1669 and enjoyed imperial patronage. On the same side of the road, the **Zhangyiyuan Chazhuang** or Zhangyiyuan Teashop has been supplying fine teas since the early 20th century. To the west of Dazhalan Jie, Liulichang Jie, with its restored buildings and many stores, is a fascinating place to wander around. It has everything from ceramics, bric-à-brac, paintings, lacquerware, and antique Chinese books to Cultural Revolution-era memorabilia. However, beware of so-called "antiques" which should be judiciously examined before buying.

South Cathedral ❺
南堂

141 Qian Men Xi Dajie. **Map** 4 A2.
Ⓜ Xuanwu Men.

The first Catholic church to be built in Beijing, South Cathedral (Nan Tang) stands close to the Xuanwu Men

underground station, on the site of Jesuit Matteo Ricci's former residence. Ricci was the first Jesuit missionary to reach Beijing. Arriving in 1601, he sent gifts of European curiosities such as clocks, mathematical instruments, and a world map to the Wanli emperor, thus gaining his goodwill, and was eventually given permission to establish a church.

Like many of China's churches, this restored building has suffered much devastation. Construction first began in 1605, and it subsequently burned down in 1775. It was rebuilt a century later, only to be destroyed once again during the Boxer Rebellion of 1900. The cathedral was rebuilt in 1904. Also known as St. Mary's Church, it is the city's largest functioning Catholic cathedral, and has regular services in a variety of languages including Chinese, English, and Latin. Service timings are posted on the noticeboard. A small gift shop is located near the south gate.

Stained glass at the South Cathedral (Nan Tang)

Forbidden City
故宫

Decorative wall relief

Forming the very heart of Beijing, the Forbidden City, officially known as the Palace Museum (Gugong), is China's most magnificent architectural complex and was completed in 1420. The huge palace is a compendium of imperial architecture and a lasting monument of dynastic China from which 24 emperors ruled for nearly 500 years. The symbolic center of the Chinese universe, the palace was the exclusive domain of the imperial court and dignitaries until the abdication in 1912. It was opened to the public in 1949.

Chinese Lions
Pairs of lions guard the entrances of halls. The male is portrayed with a ball under his paw, while the female has a lion cub.

Storehouses

Offices of the imperial secretariat

★ Golden Water
Five marble bridges, symbolizing the five cardinal virtues of Confucianism, cross the Golden Water, which flows from west to east in a course designed to resemble the jade belt worn by officials.

OUTER COURT
At the center of the Forbidden City, the Outer Court is easily its most impressive part. Most of the other buildings in the complex were there to service this city within a city.

Meridian Gate (Wu Men)
From the balcony the emperor would review his armies and perform ceremonies marking the start of a new calendar.

Gate of Supreme Harmony
Originally used for receiving visitors, the 78-ft (24-m) high, double-eaved hall was later used for banquets during the Qing dynasty (1644–1912).

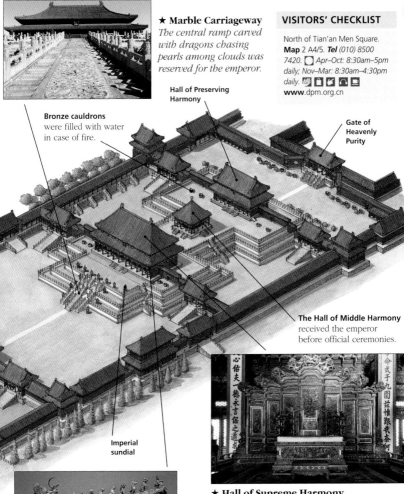

★ Marble Carriageway
The central ramp carved with dragons chasing pearls among clouds was reserved for the emperor.

VISITORS' CHECKLIST

North of Tian'an Men Square.
Map 2 A4/5. **Tel** (010) 8500 7420. ⬜ Apr–Oct: 8:30am–5pm daily; Nov–Mar: 8:30am–4:30pm daily. 🈁 🚻 🍴 📷 💺 📖
www.dpm.org.cn

Hall of Preserving Harmony

Bronze cauldrons were filled with water in case of fire.

Gate of Heavenly Purity

The Hall of Middle Harmony received the emperor before official ceremonies.

Imperial sundial

★ Hall of Supreme Harmony
The largest hall in the palace, this was used for major occasions such as the enthronement of an emperor. Inside the hall, the ornate throne sits beneath a fabulously colored ceiling.

Roof Guardians
An odd number of these figures, all associated with water, are supposed to protect the building from fire.

STAR FEATURES

★ Golden Water

★ Marble Carriageway

★ Hall of Supreme Harmony

DESIGN BY NUMBERS

The harmonious principle of *yin* and *yang* is the key to Chinese design. As odd numbers represent *yang* (the preferred masculine element associated with the emperor), the numbers three, five, seven, and the ultimate odd number – nine, recur in architectural details. It is said that the Forbidden City has 9,999 rooms and, as nine times nine is especially fortunate, the doors for imperial use usually contain 81 brass studs.

Palace door with a lucky number of studs

Exploring the Forbidden City

Magnificent though the Outer Court is, there is still a great deal more to see. A short distance north through the Gate of Heavenly Purity lies the Inner Court with three impressive palaces and the private living quarters of the emperor. Farther on, beyond the Imperial Flower Garden stands the northern Gate of Divine Prowess and exit into Jing Shan Park *(see p68)*. On the western and eastern flanks of the Inner Court, it is also possible to explore numerous halls, some of which house museum collections (entry fee payable).

The Pavilion of a Thousand Autumns in the Imperial Gardens

🌸 Inner Court

Beyond the Hall of Preserving Harmony *(see pp62–3)* lies a narrow courtyard with gates leading to the open areas east and west of the Outer Court and a main gate, the **Gate of Heavenly Purity**, leading to the Inner Court. Tradition has this gate to be the only building in the whole palace not to have been burned down at least once, and thus the oldest hall of all. The walls to either side that form a boundary between the Outer and Inner Courts only date from the early days of the republic, when the last emperor, Pu Yi *(see p65)* was confined to the rear of the palace until ejected by the Christian warlord Feng Yuxiang in 1924.

To either side of the gate are groups of smaller halls, built on a more human scale, separated by narrow alleys; this area was once the residence of concubines and imperial offspring.

Straight ahead, back on the main axis, stand three splendid palaces, mirroring those of the Outer Court

but on a smaller scale. The double-eaved **Palace of Heavenly Purity** was used as the imperial sleeping quarters. It was here that the last Ming emperor, Chongzhen, wrote his final missive in blood, before getting drunk, killing his 15-year-old daughter and his concubines, and then hanging himself on Jing Shan *(see p68)*, just north of the palace, as peasant rebels swarmed through the capital. In the late Qing era it was used for the reception of

officials, and after 1900, even foreign ones, who previously had not been allowed inside the palace. The last emperor's wedding ceremony was also held here. Beyond lies the **Hall of Union**, used as a throne room by the empress, and to house the jade seals of imperial authority. Then comes the **Palace of Earthly Tranquility**, living quarters of the Ming empresses.

🌸 Imperial Gardens

The **Imperial Flower Garden**, north of the three inner palaces and the Gate of Earthly Tranquility, dates from the reign of the Ming Yongle emperor. It is symmetrically laid out with pavilions, temples, and halls, as well as a rock garden. On the west and east sides of the garden are the charming **Pavilion of a Thousand Autumns** and **Pavilion of Ten Thousand Springs**, each topped with a circular roof. One of these was the site of the school-room used by Sir Reginald Johnston, tutor to the last emperor. Johnston, Pu Yi, and the empress would sometimes have picnics in the gardens.

Positioned centrally in the north of the garden, the **Hall of Imperial Peace** formerly served as a temple, while on top of the lofty rockery in the northeast of the garden the **Imperial View Pavilion** boasts views over the gardens and beyond. During the Qing dynasty, sacrifices were performed in the gardens on Qi Xi, the seventh day of the seventh lunar month, and

The intricately carved and painted ceiling in the Hall of Union

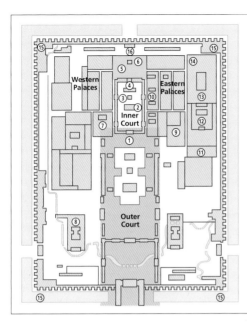

THE FORBIDDEN CITY

① Gate of Heavenly Purity
② Palace of Heavenly Purity
③ Hall of Union
④ Palace of Earthly Tranquility
⑤ Imperial Flower Garden
⑥ Hall of Imperial Peace
⑦ Hall of Mental Cultivation
⑧ Hall of Martial Valor
⑨ Hall for Worshiping Ancestors
⑩ Palace of Abstinence
⑪ Nine Dragon Screen
⑫ Hall of Imperial Zenith
⑬ Palace of Peaceful Longevity
⑭ Flower Garden of the Palace of Peaceful Longevity
⑮ Arrow Tower
⑯ Gate of Divine Prowess

| 0 meters | 300 |
| 0 yards | 300 |

KEY

▨ Area illustrated *(see pp62–3)*

the Chinese equivalent of Valentine's Day *(see p36)*. The sacrifices were made by the emperor and empress, and directed to a pair of stars that represent lovers.

⚏ Western Palaces

Much of the western flank of the Forbidden City remains closed to visitors, but the halls west of the three inner palaces are accessible. South of these, a network of high-walled alleys links a labyrinth of smaller halls that were the residences of imperial concubines. Particularly fine is the **Palace of Eternal Spring**, where *trompe-l'oeil* paintings at the ends of the passageways make them appear to extend to infinity.

The southernmost accessible hall, the **Hall of Mental Cultivation**, was used by the Yongzheng emperor *(see p93)* for his residence, rather than the Hall of Heavenly Purity, where his father, the Kangxi emperor, had lived for 60 years. The East Warm Chamber of the Hall of Mental Cultivation was the site of the formal abdication of Pu Yi, the last emperor. The document was signed by his father, who was regent.

There are also further exhibitions in some of the buildings lining the western side of the Outer Court; these include occasionally changing displays of court insignia, and ancient weapons and musical instruments. Before returning to the main Meridian Gate it is possible to venture farther west to the **Hall of Martial Valor** (still shown as off-limits on palace maps). The hall was the home of the palace's printing work-shop and censors. It now contains a model illustrating the layout of the key central halls in miniature. Other exhibits make much of the Manchu emperors' acceptance of Chinese culture, using the Confucian classics to guide their governance.

THE LAST EMPEROR

Aisin Gioro Pu Yi, ascended the Qing throne at the age of three in 1908 after the death of his uncle, the Guangxu emperor. His brief reign as the Xuantong emperor was brought to an end on February 12, 1912, when he abdicated the throne in the Forbidden City to make way for the new Republican government. The powerless Pu Yi continued

to live in the palace until 1924, before being ejected by a warlord and escaping to the Legation Quarter. He was later installed as the Japanese puppet emperor of Manchukuo, residing in his palace in Changchun. At the end of World War II, he was arrested and handed over to the Chinese Communists, who imprisoned him in 1950. In 1959, Mao granted him amnesty. Pu Yi never returned to the Forbidden City, and he died of cancer, childless, and anonymous in 1967, after working for seven years as a gardener at the Beijing Botanical Gardens.

Pu Yi (1905–67), China's "Last Emperor"

🏯 Eastern Palaces

On the east side of the Inner Court lies a much closer knit series of smaller palaces and courtyards, formerly used as the residences of imperial concubines. Nowadays, some of these areas serve as museums of jade, paintings, enamels, and other antique collectibles. Among them is the impressive **Clock and Watch Exhibition**, housed in the **Hall for Worshiping Ancestors**, which once held memorial tablets to Qing ancestors. You can walk among the vast pillars, which have now been replaced, the water-damaged coffer ceiling high above revealing why this was necessary. The sizeable and fascinating display of clocks includes elaborate Chinese, British, and French timepieces collected by Qing emperors, from a clumsy giant multi-bucket clepsydra to fragile bejeweled replicas of balloons and steamships, and delicate automata. One piece is topped by a robotic figure that dips his brush in ink and writes eight Chinese characters, as can be seen on an accompanying video. A limited number of the clocks are gently wound and set off at 11am and 2pm daily.

Decorative gate in the Eastern Palaces quarter

On the east side of the Inner Court is the **Palace of Abstinence**, where the emperor would fast before sacrificial ceremonies. Next to it is the **Palace of Prolonging Happiness**, a bizarre and incomplete structure of rusting steel and carved stone, designed to be surrounded by water, begun only two years before the fall of the Qing dynasty. Wings to either side of the palace, which were once the home of some of the museum's research departments, now house regularly changing exhibitions usually involving calligraphy, painting, and ceramics.

A little further southeast of the exhibition halls stands a beautiful **Nine Dragon Screen**, a 100-ft (31-m) long spirit wall made from richly glazed tiles and similar to the screen in Bei Hai Park *(see p68)*. Chinese ghosts only travel in straight lines, and this screen blocked the straight route north through the Gate of Imperial Zenith and the Gate of Peaceful Longevity. Displays of jewelry and other treasures begin in a long passage up the west side of the courtyard, and continue in the **Hall of Imperial Zenith**, the **Palace of Peaceful Longevity**, and farther halls to the north. These halls are where the venerable Qianlong emperor (reigned 1736–95) lived out his retirement.

The infamous Empress Dowager Cixi *(p81)* also retired to these same northern halls a century later during the brief period she allowed the Guangxu emperor to take the throne. Their interiors are in striking contrast to other halls, displaying a taste for dark paneling inset with mother-of-pearl, which is also to be seen at Cixi's complex at the Eastern Qing Tombs *(p93)*. Treasures on display here include scroll paintings and calligraphy, as well as everything from magnificent imperial headdresses with golden dragons disporting themselves among clouds of azure enamel, to vast boulders of jade carved into mountain scenes.

Imperial five-clawed dragons on a glazed Nine Dragon Screen

CHINESE DRAGONS

The Chinese dragon is a curious hybrid of sometimes many animal parts – snake's body, deer horns, bull's ears, hawk's claws and fish scales. Endowed with magical characteristics, it can fly, swim, change into other animals, bring rainfall and ward off evil spirits. The five-clawed dragon represented the power of the emperor, and therefore could only adorn his imperial buildings. The Chinese dragon is a beneficent beast offering protection and good luck, hence its depiction on screens and marble carriageways, and its significance, even today, in festivals such as Chinese New Year.

🏯 Pleasure Gardens

Both Qianlong and Cixi kept their keenest pleasures to hand. The retired emperor's was the secluded **Flower Garden of the Palace of Peaceful Longevity** (also known as the Qianlong Garden), which is graced with rockeries, a small theater stage, and, most strikingly, the **Pavilion for Bestowing Wine**. This is where Qianlong and companions would play intellectual drinking games, floating cups of wine along a writhing 88-ft (27-m) long channel in the stone floor, and composing poems.

Cixi's passion was opera, and just to the east of the garden is the three-story **Pavilion of Pleasant Sounds**, a gaudy stage and fly-tower, fully equipped with hoists and trap-doors, its ceiling painted with fluffy clouds. In celebration of her 60th birthday the empress watched some ten consecutive days of performances here. The building opposite, which is where she would sit, contains costumes and scripts used by the imperial troupes.

The less gentle side of Cixi is remembered just to the north at the **Well of the Pearl Concubine**. In 1900, as foreign armies approached to lift the siege of the Legation Quarter *(see p49)*, Cixi prepared to flee for Xi'an, intending that the Guangxu emperor should accompany her. His favorite

The four corners of the palace walls are guarded by Arrow Towers

concubine dared to protest, and was thrown down the well for her temerity.

🏯 Palace Walls and Gates

The fortified wall around the Forbidden City was originally enclosed within a moat. Another wall ran around the grounds of the Imperial City, including what are now Bei Hai Park and Zhong Nan Hai government compound, the "new Forbidden City." The palace's walls are marked at each of its four corners by elaborate **Arrow Towers**, notable for their many eaves. Of the four palace gates, the horseshoe-shaped **Meridian Gate** or **Wu Men** *(see p62)*, which is the southern entrance to the Forbidden City, can be climbed to visit the temporary exhibitions displayed in the central pavilion. This was the home of some of the first displays of palace treasures during the Nationalist era. It also affords views down into the bustle surrounding the ticket offices, and along the walls.

The northern gate of the palace is called the **Gate of Divine Prowess** or **Shenwu Men**, and originally served as a combined bell and drum tower. It now hosts an exhibition of old photographs and drawings related to the architecture and construction of the palaces and other buildings. Unfortunately the labeling of all items is in Chinese only.

Glazed tile panel from palace gate

The former City Bank of New York, now Beijing Police Museum

Legation Quarter ❼
东交民巷

Map 5 D1. Ⓜ *Qian Men.* **Beijing Police Museum** *Tel* (010) 8522 5018. ⬭ 9am–4pm Tue–Sun.

When the Conventions of Peking ended the Second Opium War in 1860, foreign delegations were permitted to take up residence in a quarter southeast of the Forbidden City. Here, the first modern foreign buildings took root.

On the southeast corner of Tian'an Men Square, the distinctive stripey brick building was the first railway station built within the walls of Beijing, constructed by the British in 1901. It is now a shopping mall and theater for Beijing Opera. East of the station, along Dong Jiao Min Xiang, is the former City Bank of New York, now the **Beijing Police Museum**. Displays on the suppression of counter-revolutionaries and drug dealers share space with early tokens of authority from the Jin and Ming eras. There are also live transmissions from a roadside traffic camera.

East again is the Catholic church of **St. Michael's**, built in 1902, and opposite the church, the **former Belgian Legation**, modeled after a villa that belonged to King Leopold II. A rear entrance leads into a square fringed by mock European buildings. Most are now offices, but you can enter the lobby and see traces of the original fittings.

Bei Hai with Jing Shan's summit in the background

Jing Shan Park ⑧
景山

44 Jingshan Xi Jie, Xicheng. **Map** 2
A3. Ⓜ️ Tian'an Men West. **Tel** (010)
6404 4071. ⏰ 6am–9pm daily. 🎫

Situated on Beijing's north-
south axis, Jing Shan Park has
its origins in the Yuan dynasty
(1279–1368). Its hill was
created from earth that was
excavated while building the
palace moat during the reign
of the Ming Yongle emperor.
In the early years of the
Ming dynasty it was known
as Wansui Shan (Long Life
Hill), but was renamed
Jing Shan (View or
Prospect Hill) in the
Qing era. Foreign
residents also referred
to it as Coal Hill (Mei
Shan), supposedly
because coal was
stored at the foot of
the hill although
other theories exist.
    Until the fall of the
Qing, Jing Shan was linked to
the Forbidden City and was
restricted to imperial use. The
hill's purpose was to protect
the imperial palaces within
the Forbidden City from
malign northern influences,
which brought death and
destruction according to
classical *feng shui*. However,
it failed to save the last Ming
emperor Chongzhen, who
hanged himself from a locust
tree (*huaishu*) in the park in
1644, when rebel troops
forced their way into Beijing.
Another tree, planted after the
original tree was cut down,
marks the spot in the park's
southeast. The park is dotted

with several pavilions and
halls, but the highlight of
any visit is the superb view
of the Forbidden City from
the hill's Wanchun Ting
(Wanchun Pavilion).

Bei Hai Park ⑨
北海公园

1 Wenjin Jie, Xicheng. **Map** 1 F3.
Ⓜ️ Tian'an Men West. **Tel** (010)
6403 3225. ⏰ 6am–9pm daily. 🎫

An imperial garden for more
than 1,000 years, Bei Hai
Park was opened to the
public in 1925. Filled with
artificial hills, pavilions,
and temples, it is
associated with Kublai
Khan, who redesigned
it during the Mongol
Yuan dynasty. The
Tuancheng (Round
City), near the south
entrance, has a huge,
decorated jade urn
belonging to him.
    The park is named
after its extensive lake, **Bei
Hai**, whose southern end is
bordered by the inaccessible
Zhong Nan Hai, Communist
Party Headquarters. In the
middle of Bei Hai, Jade Island
was supposedly made from
the earth excavated while
creating the lake. It is topped
by the 118-ft (36-m) high
White Dagoba, a Tibetan-style
stupa built to honor the visit
of the fifth Dalai Lama in
1651. Beneath the huge
dagoba, **Yongan Si** comprises
a series of ascending halls.
The lake's northern shore has
several sights, including the
massive **Nine Dragon Screen**,
an 89-ft (27-m) long spirit

**White Dagoba, Bei
Hai Park**

wall made of colorful glazed
tiles. Depicting nine
intertwining dragons, it was
designed to obstruct evil
spirits. The Xiaoxitian Temple
lies to the west.

Mansion of
Prince Gong ⑩
恭王府

17 Qianhai Xi Jie, Xicheng. **Map** 1 F2.
Ⓜ️ Ping'Anli. **Tel** (010) 6620 6599.
⏰ 7:30am–4:30pm daily. 🎫

Beijing's most complete
example of a historic mansion
is situated in a charming
hutong district west of Qian
Hai. It was supposedly the
inspiration behind the
residence portrayed by Cao
Xueqin in his classic 18th-
century novel *Dream of the
Red Chamber (see pp20–21)*.
Built during the reign of the
Qianlong emperor, the house
is extensive and its charming
garden is a pattern of open
corridors and pavilions, dotted
with pools and gateways.
Originally built for Heshun,
a Manchu official and the
emperor's favorite, the
residence was appropriated
by the imperial household after
he was found guilty of using
regal motifs in his mansion
design. It was later bequeathed
to Prince Gong in the Xianfeng
emperor's reign (r.1851–61).
The house is popular with
tour groups, so early morning
is the best time to visit and
afterwards, the local *hutongs*
can be explored. In summer,
Beijing Opera is performed in
its Grand Opera House.

**Elaborate arched gateway, Mansion
of Prince Gong**

Beijing's Courtyard Houses

At first glance, Beijing seems a thoroughly modern city, but a stroll through the city's alleyways *(hutongs)* reveals the charm of old Beijing. These *hutongs* – weaving across much of central Beijing – are where many Beijing residents *(Beijingren)* still live. Typically running east to west, *hutongs* are created by the walls of courtyard houses *(siheyuan)*. Formerly the homes of officials and the well-to-do,

Washing the laundry in public

most are now state-owned. The *hutongs* are very easy to find, try the alleyways between the main streets south of Qian Men, or around Hou Hai and Qian Hai. The modernization of Beijing has destroyed many traditional *siheyuan*, but some have been cleaned up and have again become homes. A few have been converted into hotels *(see pp178–82)*, allowing the visitor a closer look at this disappearing world.

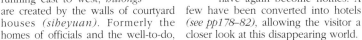

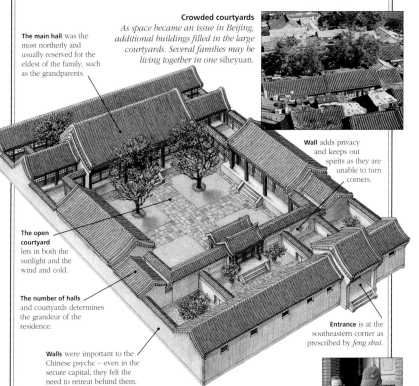

Crowded courtyards
As space became an issue in Beijing, additional buildings filled in the large courtyards. Several families may be living together in one siheyuan.

The main hall was the most northerly and usually reserved for the eldest of the family, such as the grandparents.

Wall adds privacy and keeps out spirits as they are unable to turn corners.

The open courtyard lets in both the sunlight and the wind and cold.

The number of halls and courtyards determines the grandeur of the residence.

Entrance is at the southeastern corner as prescribed by *feng shui.*

Walls were important to the Chinese psyche – even in the secure capital, they felt the need to retreat behind them.

Social housing
With several families living together, a strong community spirit is fostered, while the hutong *outside becomes an extension of the home.*

Typical Beijing *hutong*
You can take organized rickshaw tours of the hutong, *sometimes with a visit to the Mansion of Prince Gong (see p68), but it can be more fun to explore them by yourself.*

A view of the Bell Tower from Beijing's Drum Tower

Drum & Bell Towers ⓫
鼓楼

Northern end of Di'an Men Wai Dajie, Dongcheng. **Map** 2 A2. Ⓜ *Gulou Dajie*. **Tel** *(010) 8403 6706.* ◯ *daily.*

Located on the north-south meridian that bisects the Forbidden City and Tian'an Men Square, the Drum Tower (Gu Lou) rises up from a historic Beijing *hutong* district (*see p69*). The squat structure seen today was originally built in 1420 during the reign of the Ming Yongle emperor. Visitors can clamber up the steep stairs to look out over the city and

inspect the 25 drums there. The one large and 24 smaller drums were beaten to mark the hours of the day. According to the official Chinese accounts, the original drums were destroyed by the foreign soldiers of the international army that relieved Beijing during the Boxer Rebellion.

A short walk north of the Drum Tower, the Bell Tower (Zhong Lou) is an edifice from 1745, which replaced an earlier tower that had burnt down. Suspended within the tower is a 15-ft (4.5-m) high and 42-ton (42,674-kg) bell, that was cast in 1420. During Spring Festival (*see pp34–5*), visitors can pay to ring the bell for good luck.

Lama Temple ⓬
雍和宫

12 Yonghe Gong Dajie, Dongcheng. **Map** 2 C1. Ⓜ *Yonghe Gong.* **Tel** *(010) 6404 4499.* ◯ *9am–4pm daily.*

Beijing's most beautiful temple complex, the Lama Temple (Yonghegong) was constructed during the 17th century and converted into a Tibetan lamasery in 1744. Its five main halls are a stylistic blend of Han, Mongol, and Tibetan motifs. The first hall has a traditional display – the plump laughing Buddha, Milefo, is back-to-back with Wei Tuo, the Protector of Buddhist Doctrine, and flanked by the Four Heavenly Kings. **Yonghe Hall** beyond has three manifestations of Buddha, flanked by 18 *luohan* – those freed from the cycle of rebirth. Even farther back, the Tibetan-styled **Falun Hall** or Hall of the Wheel of Law has a statue of Tsongkhapa, the founder of the Yellow Hat sect of Tibetan Buddhism.

The highlight, however, is encapsulated within the towering **Wanfu Pavilion** (Wanfu Ge) – a vast 55-ft (17-m) high statue of Maitreya (the Future Buddha), carved

The striking main gateway of the colorful Lama Temple

For hotels and restaurants in Beijing see pp178–82 and pp198–202

Statue of Confucius at the main entrance, Confucius Temple

from a single block of sandalwood. The splendid exhibition of Tibetan Buddhist objects at the temple's rear includes statues of the deities Padmasambhava (Guru Rinpoche), and the Tibetan equivalent of Guanyin, Chenresig, alongside ritual objects such as the scepter-like *dorje* (thunderbolt) and *dril bu* (bell), symbols of the male and female energies.

Confucius Temple ⓭
孔庙

13 Guozijian Jie, Dongcheng. **Map** 2 C1. Ⓜ *Yonghe Gong.* **Tel** (010) 8402 7224. ◯ 7:30am–6pm daily. 📷

The Confucius Temple is the largest in China outside Qufu, the philosopher's birthplace in Shandong province. The alley leading to the temple has a fine *pailou* (decorative archway), few of which survive in Beijing. First built in 1302 during the Mongol Yuan dynasty, the temple was expanded in 1906 in the reign of Emperor Guangxu. It is a tranquil place that offers respite from the city's bustle. Around 200 ancient stelae stand in the silent courtyard in front of the main hall (Dacheng Dian), inscribed with the names of those who successfully passed the

imperial civil service exams. Additional stelae are propped up on the backs of *bixi* (mythical cross between a tortoise and a dragon), within pavilions surrounded by cypress trees. On a marble terrace in the main hall are statues of Confucius and some of his disciples.

Di Tan Park ⓮
地坛公园

N of the Lama Temple, Dongcheng. **Map** 2 C1. Ⓜ *Yonghe Gong.* **Tel** (010) 6421 4657. ◯ daily. 📷

An ideal place to stroll amidst trees, Di Tan Park was named after the Temple of Earth (Di Tan), which was the venue for imperial sacrifices. The park's altar (Fangze Tan) dates to the Ming dynasty and its square shape represents the earth. Under the Ming, five main altars were established at the city's cardinal points – Tian Tan (Temple of Heaven) in the south, Di Tan in the north, Ri Tan (Temple of the Sun) in the east, Yue Tan (Temple of the Moon) in the west, and Sheji Tan (Temple of Land and Grain) in the center. Mirroring ancient ceremonies, a lively temple fair *(miaohui)* is held during the Chinese New Year *(see pp34–5)*, to welcome the spring planting season and appease the gods.

Guardian at entrance, Dong Yue Miao

Dong Yue Miao ⓯
东岳庙

141 Chaoyang Men Wai Dajie, Chaoyang. **Map** 3 E4. Ⓜ *Chaoyang Men.* **Tel** (010) 6551 0151. ◯ 8am–4:30pm Tue–Sun. 📷

On Beijing's eastern side near Chaoyang's Workers' Stadium, the mesmerizing Dong Yue Miao takes its name from the Daoist Eastern Peak, Dong Yue, also known as Tai Shan. It is fronted by a fabulous glazed Ming dynasty *paifang* inscribed with the characters "Zhisi Daizong," meaning "offer sacrifices to Mount Tai (Tai Shan) in good order."

This colorful and active temple, dating to the early 14th century, was restored at considerable cost in 1999, and is tended by Daoist monks. The main courtyard leads into the Hall of Tai Shan, where there are statues of the God of Tai Shan and his attendants. The greatest attractions here are over 70 "Departments," filled with vivid Daoist gods and demons, whose functions are explained in English captions. In Daoist lore, the spirits of the dead go to Tai Shan, and many Departments dwell on the afterlife. The Department for Increasing Wealth and Longevity, for example, offers cheerful advice.

Corn laid out to form Chinese characters, temple festival, Di Tan Park

National Art Museum of China ⑯
中国美术馆

1 Wusi Dajie, Dongcheng. **Map** 2 B4.
Ⓜ *Dong Si Shi Tiao.* **Tel** *(010) 6400
6326.* ◯ *9am–5pm daily, last entry
4pm.* ▨ www.namoc.org/en

Hosting a number of
exhibitions of Chinese and
international art, as well as
occasional photographic
displays, the National Art
Museum of China (Zhongguo
Meishuguan) has 14 halls
spread over three levels. This
quite ordinary building holds
an exciting range of Chinese
modern art, which suffers less
censorship than other media,
such as film or literature.
Magazines such as *Time Out
Beijing* and *The Beijinger*
carry details of exhibitions.

Wangfujing Street ⑰
王府井

Map 2 B5. Ⓜ *Wangfujing.* **Night
Food Market** ◯ *5:30pm–10pm
daily.* **St. Joseph's Church** 74 Wangfujing Dajie. ◯ *early morning
during services.*

Bustling Wangfujing Street
(Wangfujing Dajie), Beijing's
main shopping street, has
been undergoing significant
redevelopment since 2008.
The street is now lined with
malls and plazas filled with
high fashion and other retail
outlets. Everything from
curios, *objets d'art*, antiques,

**The imposing façade of St. Joseph's
Church, Wangfujing Street**

clothes, and books can be
found here. The huge **Foreign
Language Bookstore** is a good
place to buy a more detailed
map of Beijing. The street has
a lively mixture of
pharmacies, laundry
and dyeing shops, as
well as stores
selling silk, tea,
and shoes.
  However, the
street's highlight
is the **Night Food
Market**, with its
endless variety of
traditional Chinese
snacks, including
skewers of beef,
and more exotic
morsels such as
scorpions. Other
offerings include
pancakes, fruit,
shrimps, squid, flat bread, and
more. The Wangfujing Snack
Street, south of the Night
Market, also has a range
of colorful restaurants.

The impressive triple-domed
St. Joseph's Church, known
as the East Cathedral, is at 74
Wangfujing Dajie and is one
of the city's most important
churches. It was built on the
site of the former residence
of Jesuit Adam Schall von Bell
(1591–1669) in 1655, and has
been rebuilt a number of
times after being successively
destroyed by earthquake, fire,
and then during the Boxer
Rebellion. It is fronted by
an open courtyard and an
arched gateway.

Ancient Observatory ⑱
古观象台

Map 5 F1. Ⓜ *Jianguo Men.* **Tel** *(010)*
6524 2202. ◯ *9am–4pm daily.* ▨

Beijing's ancient
observatory (Gu
Guanxiangtai) stands
on a platform
alongside a flyover
off Jianguo Men
Nei Dajie. Dating to
1442, it is one of
the oldest in the
world. A Yuan
dynasty (1279–
1368) observatory
was also located
here, but the
structure that
survives today
was built after the
Ming emperors
relocated their capital from
Nanjing to Beijing. In the
early 17th century, the Jesuits,
led by Matteo Ricci (1552–
1610) and followed by Adam
Schall von Bell, impressed
the emperor and the imperial
astronomers with their
scientific knowledge,
particularly the accuracy of
their predictions of eclipses.
  The Belgian Jesuit Father
Verbiest (1623–88) was
appointed to the Imperial
Astronomical Bureau,
where he designed a set of
astronomical instruments in
1674. Several of these were
appropriated by German
soldiers during the Boxer
Rebellion of 1900, and were
only returned after World
War I. A collection of reproduction astronomical devices

**Ecliptic armillary sphere,
Ancient Observatory**

Delicious street food at the Night Food Market, just off Wangfujing Street

For hotels and restaurants in Beijing see pp178–82 and pp198–202

The atmospheric Red Gate Gallery, Southeast Corner Watchtower

lies in the courtyard on the ground floor, some decorated with fantastic Chinese designs including dragons. Steps lead to the roof, where there are impressive bronze instruments, including an azimuth theodolite, used to measure the altitude of celestial bodies, and an armillary sphere, for measuring the coordinates of planets and stars.

Southeast Corner Watchtower (Dongbian Men)

Southeast Corner Watchtower ⓳
东边门箭楼

Off Jianguo Men Nan Dajie, Chongwen. **Map** 5 F2. M *Beijing Zhan*. **Red Gate Gallery** *Tel (010) 6525 1005.* ⬜ *10am–5pm daily.* 🖼 *for exhibition details visit* **www**.redgategallery.com

A short distance south of the Ancient Observatory, an imposing chunk of the Beijing City Walls *(see p60)* survives in the form of the 15th-century Southeast Corner Watchtower (Dongbian Men).

After climbing onto the Ming dynasty battlements, visitors can walk along the short but impressive stretch of attached wall to admire the towering bastion, pitted with archers' windows, and look down on the city below. The walls of the tower are engraved with graffiti left by soldiers of the international army that marched into the city to liberate the Foreign Legations during the Boxer Rebellion in 1900.

Within its splendid, cavernous interior, accessed from the battlements, the rooms reveal enormous red wooden columns and pillars, crossed with beams. The **Red Gate Gallery**, one of Beijing's most appealing art galleries, is situated within this superb setting on levels 1 and 4. Originally founded in 1991 by an Australian who came to Beijing to learn Chinese, the gallery exhibits works in a wide variety of media by up-and-coming contemporary Chinese artists. Forthcoming exhibitions are listed on the gallery's website *(see above)*.

Beijing Natural History Museum ⓴
自然历史博物馆

126 Tianqiao Nan Dajie, Chongwen. **Map** 4 C3. M *Qian Men, then taxi.* **Tel** *(010) 6702 4431.* ⬜ *9am–5pm Tue–Sat.* 🖼 **www**.bmnh.org.cn

Housed in an enormous 1950s building covered in creepers, this museum is the largest of its type in China, with about 5,000 specimens arranged into three collections: zoology, paleontology, and botany. The most interesting collection is found in the Paleontology Hall which displays a selection of the dinosaurs and prehistoric animals that populated China between 500 million and one million years ago. Exhibits to look out for include the large-handed Lufengosaurus from the early Jurassic period, and a skeleton of the spine-nosed Qingdaosaurus (*Tsintaosaurus spinorhinus*), from the late Cretaceous period, whose skull sported a horn-like crest. The zoology section displays an abundance of marine, bird, and plant life to explain and illustrate the course of evolution from simple aquatic to far more complicated land-based forms. There is a also a display devoted to human evolution, however, many of the braver visitors head for the basement that houses a macabre display of cross-sections of human cadavers, pickled corpses, limbs, and organs. The botany collection is less impressive but also much less disturbing.

Dinosaur skeletons in the Paleontology Hall, Natural History Museum

Temple of Heaven ㉑

天坛

Gate to the Round Altar

Completed during the Ming dynasty, the Temple of Heaven, more correctly known as Tian Tan, is one of the largest temple complexes in China and a paradigm of Chinese architectural balance and symbolism. It was here that the emperor would make sacrifices and pray to heaven and his ancestors at the winter solstice. As the Son of Heaven, the emperor could intercede with the gods, represented by their spirit tablets, on behalf of his people and pray for a good harvest. Off-limits to the common people during the Ming and Qing dynasties, the Temple of Heaven is situated in a large and pleasant park that now attracts thousands of visitors daily.

Qinian Dian, where the emperor prayed for a good harvest

Name plaques are often written in the calligraphy of an emperor.

The circular roof symbolizes the sky.

THE TEMPLE OF HEAVEN COMPLEX

The main parts of the temple complex are all connected on the favored north-south axis by the Red Step Bridge (an elevated pathway) to form the focal point of the park. The Round Altar is made up of concentric rings of stone slabs in multiples of nine, the most auspicious number. The circular Echo Wall is famed for its supposed ability to carry a whisper from one side of the wall to the other.

① Hall of August Heaven
② Qinian Dian (Hall of Prayer for Good Harvests)
③ Red Step Bridge
④ Echo Wall
⑤ Imperial Vault of Heaven
⑥ Round Altar
⑦ Seven Star Rock
⑧ Hall of Abstinence

| 0 meters | 250 |
| 0 yards | 250 |

KEY

☐ Area illustrated

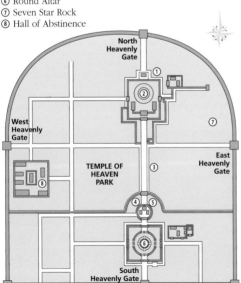

North Heavenly Gate

West Heavenly Gate

TEMPLE OF HEAVEN PARK

East Heavenly Gate

South Heavenly Gate

Red is an imperial color.

Dragon and phoenix motifs inside and out represent the emperor and empress.

STAR FEATURES

★ Caisson ceiling

★ Dragon Well pillars

The golden finial is 125 ft (38 m) high and prone to lightning strikes.

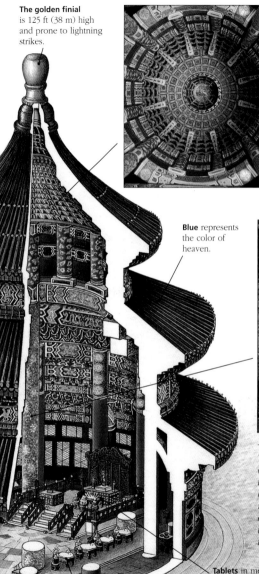

VISITORS' CHECKLIST

Tian Tan Dong Lu, Chongwen.
Map 5 D4. **Tel** (010) 6702 8866.
Ⓜ *Qian Men, then taxi.* 🚌 *34, 6, 35.* **Park** ⬜ *6am–10pm daily.* **Temple Buildings** ⬜ *8am–5pm daily.*

★ Caisson ceiling

The splendid circular caisson ceiling has a gilded dragon and phoenix at its center. The hall is entirely built of wood without using a single nail.

Blue represents the color of heaven.

★ Dragon Well pillars

The roofs of the hall are supported on 28 highly decorated pillars. At the center, the four huge columns, known as Dragon Well pillars, represent the seasons, while the other 24 smaller pillars symbolize the months in a year plus the 12 two-hour time periods in a day.

Tablets in memory of his ancestors were worshiped by the emperor.

Symbolic offerings

Marble platform

Three tiers of marble form a circle 300 ft (90 m) in diameter and 20 ft (6 m) high. The balusters on the upper tier are decorated with dragon carvings to signify the imperial nature of the structure.

QINIAN DIAN

Originally built in 1420, the Qinian Dian, or Hall of Prayer for Good Harvests, is often incorrectly called the Temple of Heaven. There is in fact no single temple building as such at Tian Tan, a more literal translation of which is Altar of Heaven – referring to the whole complex.

Exploring the Temple of Heaven

The Temple of Heaven complex (or Tian Tan, which is more correctly translated as Altar of Heaven) is set in one of Beijing's most impressive parks. The temple was the place where earth, signified by square shapes including the bases of the enclosures, communicated with heaven, signified by the rounded top. This motif of square and rounded shapes is repeated in the layout of the park. Today, local retired people, inured both to the magnificence of the buildings and their hordes of visitors, use the site as a public recreational space, practising *tai ji quan (tai chi)*, various martial arts, and other exercises, flying kites, and rehearsing Beijing Opera, all of which add to the charm.

Triple gates for emperor (east), officials (west), and gods (center)

🏯 The Tian Tan Complex

Entering through the North Heavenly Gate, the first building encountered is the **Hall of August Heaven**. This once held wooden spirit tablets representing imperial ancestors. It is also where preliminary ceremonies would take place.

But the Hall of August Heaven is dwarfed by the **Qinian Dian**, or **Hall of Prayer for Good Harvests**, which has come to symbolize Beijing almost as much as the Tian'an Men. This circular tower, topped by a conical roof of dark blue tiles and a gold knob, is perhaps the most beautiful building in the entire city, standing on a great triple-layered, circular, marble plinth, and painted in blue, green, and gold, with red latticed doors at ground level. One of its many claims to fame is that it was constructed without the use of a single nail. Visitors should lean inside for a view of the dragon and phoenix, which form the centerpiece of the

caisson ceiling. This central roundel is mirrored by a natural marble slab in the center of the floor, which is where the emperor would make his prayers for good harvest in the autumn.

The emperor would spend the night before the rituals fasting at the **Hall of Abstinence**, southwest of the Qinian Dian. Prior to this

he would have been carried in a yellow palanquin through the shuttered streets of the city in almost complete silence, accompanied by as many as 500 officials and ceremonially dressed eunuchs. The foreign legations, who settled in Beijing after 1860, were sent notice to keep away and not disturb the procession. Services to the British-built railway station at Qian Men had to be halted for the duration of the ceremonies. The Abstinence Hall itself is the Forbidden City in miniature, walled and moated, entered by two great gates accessed by bridges.

Running south from the Qinian Dian, the **Red Step Bridge** is the central axis of the whole complex, an elevated walkway of stone and marble leading to the main altar. Before the altar is the **Imperial Vault of Heaven**, a lower round building used for storing ceremonial equipment. This is surrounded by the perfectly circular **Echo Wall**, with the same sonic effects found in some European cathedrals, where even a whisper travels round to a listener on the other side. A handclap made while standing on different stones at the center produces a different number of echoes. However, since this is one of the most-visited sights in Beijing, it's rarely possible to test either effect amongst the hubbub of everybody else's efforts.

Imperial Vault of Heaven, store for ceremonial equipment

For hotels and restaurants in Beijing see pp178–82 and pp198–202

The Round Altar, site of the annual winter solstice sacrifice

Although the Qinian Dian is regarded as the star, in fact the focus of the Tian Tan complex is the vast triple-tiered **Round Altar** that dominates the southern part of the site. The altar is made up of marble slabs laid in nine concentric circles with each circle containing a multiple of nine pieces. The center of the altar represents the center of the world. Supposedly, the extraordinary acoustics of the construction magnify the sound made by anyone speaking at the center. This is where the emperor would perform the annual winter solstice sacrifice of a young bullock.

Various minor buildings around the site were for the use of musicians and other attendants, and for preparation and cremation of the sacrifice.

The park's venerable cypresses were important enough to be the subject of poems, while the seeds of the park's elms were traditionally made into cakes. These cakes, along with a certain "dragon-whisker" vegetable from the grounds, were regarded as delicacies, believed to have added spiritual or medicinal qualities. However, the park's flora has not always been so respected – many of the trees were cut down for firewood during the Nationalist era.

Although the original temple enclosure was off-limits to ordinary people, by the 18th century there were merchants' stalls along both the inside and outside of the north wall, some of which reappeared in the late 1980s, only to be cleared away again in recent times.

Xiannong Tan ❷
先农坛

West of the Temple of Heaven.
Map 4 C4. Ⓜ️ *Qian Men, then taxi.*
🚌 ⭕ *9am–4pm daily.*

As late as the 1930s almost half of the land within the southern part of the city walls was still green space, and the Xiannong Tan complex, which was immediately west of Tian Tan, was nearly the same size. Tan is more correctly translated as altar than temple, and as with its better-known neighbor, the emperor came here annually to perform vital ceremonies. On the vernal equinox he would perform various sacrifices then dress as a farmer and, with various officials guiding the oxen, would plough three furrows. This ritual was performed here from 1420, when some of the remaining halls were constructed, until 1906.

The World Monuments Fund has restored several halls, some of which now house an exhibition on the rituals, while the **Hall of Jupiter**, second in size only to the Forbidden City's Hall of Middle Harmony, is now home to the **Museum of Ancient Architecture**. This museum provides an excellent introduction to the construction techniques of so much that has been lost, helpfully illuminated with detailed models. A fascinating three-dimensional plan shows the Beijing of 1949, with the magnificent city walls and gates largely intact.

YUAN SHIKAI

So important were the ceremonies at the Temple of Heaven in demonstrating the right to rule that not long after the founding of the republic in 1912, first president Yuan Shikai insisted that he should use them to reaffirm his unstable authority. His trip to the Temple of Heaven to perform the rites in 1915 was widely viewed as his first step to becoming emperor, although the solemnity of the occasion was some-what ruined by his decision to travel in an armored car, and by the presence of cameras there to record the events. Shortly afterwards he organized a petition demanding that he ascend the throne, and began the process of installing himself as the first emperor of a new dynasty. Protest from overseas and revolt amongst his supporters brought this to a halt in March 1916, and by June an exhausted Yuan was dead, leaving China to decades of civil war and Japanese occupation.

Yuan Shikai, 1859–1916

A decorative ceiling roundel at the Museum of Ancient Architecture

Cow Street Mosque ㉓
牛街清真寺

88 Niu Jie, Xuanwu. **Map** 4 A3.
Ⓜ *Xuanwu Men, then taxi.* **Tel**
(010) 6353 2564. 🕐 *8am–4pm
daily. Avoid Fri (holy day).* 📷

Beijing's oldest and largest
mosque dates back to the
10th century. It is located in
the city's Hui district, near
numerous Muslim restaurants
and shops. The Hui, a
Chinese Muslim minority
group mainly from Ningxia
province, are now scattered
throughout China and number
around 200,000 in Beijing.
The men are easily identified
by their beards and
characteristic white hats.

The Cow Street Mosque
is an attractive edifice, with
Islamic motifs and Arabic
verses decorating its halls
and stelae. Its most prized
possession is a 300-year-old,
hand-written copy of the
Koran *(Gulanjing)*.

Astronomical observations
and lunar calculations were
made from the tower-like
Wangyue Lou. The graves
of two Yuan dynasty Arab
missionaries engraved with
Arabic inscriptions can be
seen here. The courtyard is
lush with greenery, making it
an idyllic escape from Beijing's
busy streets. Visitors are
advised to dress conservatively.
Non-Muslims are not allowed
to enter the prayer hall.

Buddhist statuary in the main hall, Fayuan Temple

Fayuan Temple ㉔
法源寺

7 Fayuan Si Qian Jie, Xuanwu. **Map**
4 A3. Ⓜ *Xuanwu Men.* 🕐 *8:30am–
4pm Mon, Tue & Thu–Sun.* 📷

A short walk east from Cow
Street Mosque, the Fayuan
Temple dates to AD 696 and
is probably the oldest temple
in Beijing. It was consecrated
by the Tang Taizong emperor
(r. 626–49), to commemorate
the soldiers who perished in
an expedition against the
northern tribes. The original
Tang era buildings were
destroyed by a succession
of natural disasters, and the
current structures date from
the Qing era.

The temple's layout is
typical of Buddhist temples.
Near the gate, the incense
burner *(lu)* is flanked by the
Drum and Bell Towers to the
east and west. Beyond, the

Hall of the Heavenly Kings
(Tianwang Dian) is guarded
by a pair of bronze lions, and
has statues of Milefo (the
Laughing Buddha) and his
attendant Heavenly Kings.
Ancient stelae stand in front
of the main hall, where a
gilded statue of Sakyamuni
(the Historical Buddha) is
flanked by bodhisattvas and
luohan – those freed from
the cycle of rebirth.

At the temple's rear, the
Scripture Hall stores *sutras*,
while another hall contains
a 16-ft (5-m) Buddha statue.
The grounds are busy with
monks who attend the
temple's Buddhist College.

White Clouds Temple ㉕
白云寺

6 Baiyuanguan Jie, Xuanwu. Ⓜ
Nanlishi Lu, then taxi. **Tel** *(010) 6346
3531.* 🕐 *8am–5pm daily.* 📷

Home to the China Daoist
Association, the White Clouds
Temple (Baiyun Guan) was
founded in AD 739 and is
Beijing's largest Daoist shrine.
Known as the Temple of
Heavenly Eternity, it was one
of the three ancestral halls of
the Quanzhen School of
Daoism, which focused on
right action and the benefits
of good karma. Built largely
of wood, the temple burnt to
the ground in 1166, and since
then has been repeatedly
destroyed and rebuilt. The
structures that survive date
largely from the Ming and Qing
dynasties. A triple-gated Ming
pailou (decorative archway)

Resplendent interior of the Cow Street Mosque

stands at the entrance. It is believed that rubbing the carved monkey on the main gate brings good luck. The major halls are arranged along the central axis, with more halls on either side. The Hall of the Tutelary God has images of four marshals who act as temple guardians, while the Hall of Ancient Disciplines is dedicated to the Seven Perfect Ones, disciples of Wang Chongyang, the founder of the Quanzhen School. The Hall of Wealth is popular with pilgrims who seek blessings from the three spirits of wealth, while the infirm patronize the Hall of the King of Medicine.

The temple grounds are full of Daoist monks with their distinctive topknots. It is most lively during the Chinese New Year (*see pp34–5*), when a temple fair (*miaohui*) is held.

Buddhist monks, Miaoying Temple White Dagoba

Military Museum of the Chinese People's Revolution 26

军事博物馆

9 Fuxing Lu, Haidian. Ⓜ *Military Museum.* **Tel** *(010) 6686 6244.* ◯ *8:30am–4:30pm Tue–Sun.* 🖼 **www**.jb.mil.cn

Topped by a gilded emblem of the People's Liberation Army, the Chinese Military History Museum is devoted to weaponry and revolutionary heroism. It is close to Muxidi, where the People's Liberation Army killed scores of civilians in 1989. Visitors are greeted by paintings of Mao, Marx, Lenin, and Stalin. The ground floor exhibits defunct F-5 and

F-7 jet fighter planes, tanks, and surface-to-air missiles. The top floor gallery chronicles many of China's military campaigns.

Miaoying Temple White Dagoba 27

妙应寺

Fucheng Men Nei Dajie, Xicheng. **Map** 1 D3. Ⓜ *Fucheng Men.* **Tel** *(010) 6616 6099.* ◯ *9am–4pm daily.* 🖼

Celebrated for its distinctive Tibetan-styled, 167-ft (51-m) white dagoba (stupa or funerary mound) designed

by a Nepalese architect, the Miaoying Temple (Miaoying Si) dates to 1271, when Beijing was under Mongol rule. In addition to its conventional Drum and Bell Towers, Hall of Heavenly Kings, and Main Halls, this Buddhist temple has a remarkable collection of small Tibetan Buddhist statues and a collection of 18 bronze *luohan* (disciples).

Beijing Zoo 28

北京动物园

137 Xizhi Men Wai Dajie, Haidian. Ⓜ *Beijing Zoo.* **Tel** *(010) 6831 5131.* ◯ *7:30am–6pm.* 🖼 **www**.beijingzoo.com

West of the Beijing Exhibition Hall, Beijing Zoo is a relic of a bygone era, with outdated concrete and glass cages. The Panda Hall is one of its better enclosures, and the bears are at their liveliest in the mornings. The real reason for visiting is the huge **Aquarium**, with coral reefs, an Amazon rainforest, and an impressive shark pool. An array of aquatic mammals, including whales and dolphins, completes the collection.

F-5 fighter planes, Military Museum of the Chinese People's Revolution

Summer Palace
颐和园

Bronze dragon

The sprawling grounds of the Summer Palace (Yihe Yuan) served the Qing dynasty as an imperial retreat from the stifling summer confines of the Forbidden City. Despite existing as an imperial park in earlier dynasties, it was not until the time of Emperor Qianlong, who reigned from 1736 to 1795, that the Summer Palace assumed its current layout. The palace is most associated, however, with the Empress Dowager Cixi who had it rebuilt twice: once following its destruction by French and English troops in 1860, and again in 1902 after it was plundered during the Boxer Rebellion.

Suzhou Street
A recreation of the shopping street originally built for the Qianlong emperor.

Temple of the Sea of Wisdom

Marble Boat
Cixi paid for this extravagant folly with funds meant for the modernization of the Imperial Navy. The super-structure of the boat is made of wood painted white to look like marble.

Boat pier

The Bronze Pavilion, weighing 207 tons (188 tonnes), is a highly-detailed metal replica of a timber-framed building.

STAR SIGHTS

★ Longevity Hill

★ Garden of Virtue and Harmony

★ Long Corridor

★ Longevity Hill
The Tower of the Fragrance of the Buddha dominates this slope covered with impressive religious buildings.

EMPRESS DOWAGER CIXI

Empress Cixi, 1835–1908

Along with the Tang dynasty, Empress Wu Zetian, Cixi, is remembered as one of China's most powerful women. Having borne the Xianfeng emperor's son as an imperial concubine, Cixi later seized power as regent to both the Tongzhi and Guangxu emperors (her son and nephew respectively). Cixi prevented Guangxu from implementing state reforms and, in her alliance with the Boxer Rebellion, paved the way for the fall of the Qing Dynasty in 1911.

VISITORS' CHECKLIST

6 miles (10 km) NW of Beijing.
Tel (010) 6288 1144. M Xizhi
Men then bus No. 32, or 808 from
zoo. ⛴ from Yuyuan Tan Park,
and Exhibition Center near zoo
(not in winter). ◻ 7am–5pm
daily. 🎫 ⊘ 🍴 🏤 ♿ 🛍️

★ **Garden of Virtue and Harmony**
This three-story building served as a theater, where the court's 348-member opera troupe entertained Cixi, who watched from the surrounding gallery.

Back Lake

The Garden of Harmonious Pleasures was Cixi's favorite fishing spot.

Hall of Happiness and Longevity

Hall of Jade Ripples

East Palace Gate (main entrance)

★ **Long Corridor**
The beams along the length of this 2,388-ft (728-m) walkway are decorated with over 14,000 scenic paintings.

Hall of Benevolence and Longevity
The principal ceremonial hall, this single-eaved building houses the throne upon which Cixi sat.

Exploring the Summer Palace

Following the conventions of Chinese gardens *(see pp28–9)* the palace grounds are arranged as a microcosm of nature, its hills *(shan)* and water *(shui)* creating a natural composition further complemented by bridges, temples, walkways, and ceremonial halls. Even after repeated restoration, the Summer Palace tastefully harmonizes the functional and fanciful, with administrative and residential quarters leading to the pastoral vistas of the grounds, as well as numerous peaceful temples and shrines. Despite the Summer Palace's popularity a little walking takes you to peaceful corners among the most idyllic in Beijing.

A pleasure cruise on Kunming Lake aboard a dragon ferry boat

🏯 Palace Complex

The grounds of the Summer Palace are extensive, but the main buildings can all be visited by those with sufficient energy and time.

The main entrance at the **East Palace Gate** (Gong Dong Men) leads to the official and residential halls of the palace complex. Just inside the main gate stands the **Hall of Benevolence and Longevity** (Renshou Dian), where the Empress Dowager Cixi and her nephew the puppet-emperor Guangxu gave audience. The bronze statues in front of this ceremonial hall, include the symbol of Confucian virtue, the mythical *qilin*, a hybrid, cloven-hoofed animal with horns and scales, sometimes incorrectly referred to as China's unicorn.

To the west, by the lake-side, the **Hall of Jade Ripples** (Yulan Tang) is where Cixi incarcerated Guangxu during her extended stays here after he supported the abortive 1898 Reform Movement

betrayed by Yuan Shikai. Cixi's former residence, the **Hall of Happiness and Longevity** (Leshou Tang), is full of Qing-era furniture and supposedly left as it was at the time of her death in 1908. To the south is the jetty from where Cixi would set sail across the lake; to the east is the **Garden of Virtue and Harmony** (Dehe Yuan) with Cixi's private theater. The theater buildings now contain an exhibition of Qing-era artifacts of daily use, from vehicles, to costumes and glassware.

🏯 Longevity Hill

From the Hall of Happiness and Longevity the **Long Corridor** (Chang Lang), decorated with painted landscapes and other scenes, zigzags along the shore of the lake, interrupted along its length by four pavilions.

At the corridor's halfway point, a series of religious and administrative buildings ascends the slopes of **Longevity Hill** (Wanshou Shan), artificially raised to improve the view in Qianlong's time. The start of the sequence is marked at the lakeside by a fabulous decorative gate *(pailou)*, beyond which stands the **Cloud Dispelling Gate**, with two bronze lions sitting alongside it.

The first main hall, the **Cloud Dispelling Hall** (Paiyun Dian), is a double-eaved structure that was the throne room when the court was at the palace. In the center of the hall is the Empress Dowager's nine-dragon throne, where she sat to receive tribute. Above the hall, rising from a great stone platform, stands the prominent, octagonal, four-eaved **Tower of the Fragrance of the Buddha** (Foxiang Ge). The stiff climb is worth the effort for views from the balcony over the yellow roofs of the halls and pavilions to the lake below.

West of the Tower of the Fragrance of the Buddha is the **Bronze Pavilion**, more properly known as the **Precious Clouds Pavilion** (Baoyun Ge), which imitates the construction of other wooden pavilions, but is built entirely in metal. Dating from

Door to the Temple of the Sea of Wisdom with glazed Buddha effigies

Seventeen-arch Bridge linking South Lake Island to the mainland

the 18th century, the building is one of a handful that, although damaged, survived the destruction wrought by English and French troops during the Second Opium War. The same is true of the magnificent **Temple of the Sea of Wisdom** (Huihai Si), which is directly behind the Tower of the Fragrance of the Buddha. It has an exterior decorated with green and yellow tiles and façades embellished with glazed Buddhist effigies, many of which have been vandalized. From here you can look down or descend to the **Back Lake** (Hou Hu) and **Suzhou Street**, a row of recently recreated historical commercial buildings. Here the Qianlong emperor, his concubines and eunuchs, would play at being part of the common herd, acting out the roles of shoppers, shopkeepers, and pickpockets. Today these buildings house snack vendors and souvenir stalls, with staff dressed in Qing-era costume.

The eastern shore's bronze ox

🛕 South Lake
The buildings at the north end of the lake are more than enough to fill a single day, however the southern end of the grounds can be blissfully

free of crowds. Boat trips to **South Lake Island** depart from the jetty near the **Marble Boat**, also known as the Boat of Purity and Ease, which is found at the very westernmost end of the Long Corridor. (North of here are the imperial boathouses.) Alternatively, if time will allow, hire a boat for a leisurely row around Kunming Lake, or in muggy summer heat, a slow but battery-powered alternative.

On South Lake Island, the **Dragon King Temple** (Longwang Miao) is dedicated

to the god of rivers, seas, and rain. Cixi would come here to pray for rain in times of drought. The island is connected to the eastern shore by the elegant **Seventeen-arch Bridge** (Shiqi Kong Qiao). A marble lion crowns each of the 544 balusters along the bridge's length, all supposedly individual. A large **bronze ox**, dating back to 1755 but looking entirely modern, reposes on the eastern shore; it was believed to pacify the waters and prevent floods.

Across on the western side of Kunming Lake, steep-sloped **Jade Belt Bridge** links the mainland to the West Causeway, which slices through the lake to its southern point.

PLAN OF GROUNDS
The grounds of the Summer Palace cover 716 acres (290 hectares), with Kunming Lake lying to the south of Longevity Hill. South Lake Island is just off the east shore and a stroll around the entire shoreline takes about two hours.

① Jade Belt Bridge
② West Causeway
③ South Lake Island
④ Bronze ox

Longevity Hill

Kunming Lake

West Lake

South Lake

KEY

☐ Area illustrated *(see pp80–81)*

| 0 meters | 800 |
| 0 yards | 800 |

Remnants of the Yuanming Yuan, once said to resemble Versailles

Yuanming Yuan
圆明园

28 Qinghua Xi Lu, Haidian.
M Yuanmen Yuan Park.
7am–5pm daily.

The Yuanming Yuan (Garden of Perfect Brightness, sometimes called the Old Summer Palace), now sits isolated from the main Summer Palace, but was a collection of princely gardens fused into the main mass by the Qing Qianlong emperor in the mid-18th century. He commissioned Jesuits at his court to design and construct a set of European-style buildings in one corner, which they likened to Versailles. Unfortunately, all the traditional Chinese halls were burned down by British and French troops during the Second Opium War in 1860. Later the European-style buildings were pulled down, and much of the remains carted away by the locals for building purposes. Chinese narrations of the devastation criticize both the marauding European troops and the ineffectual Qing rulers.

Today, Yuanming Yuan is a jumble of sad, yet graceful fragments of stone and marble strewn in the **Eternal Spring Garden** in the park's northeastern corner. A small museum displays images and models of the palace, depicting its scale and magnificence. The **Palace Maze** has been recreated in concrete to the west of the ruins. The rest of the park is a pleasant expanse of lakes, pavilions, gardens, and walks.

Great Bell Temple
大钟寺

31a Beisanhuan Xi Lu, Haidian.
300, 367. **Tel** (010) 6255 0819.
8:30am–4pm daily.

Home to a fascinating collection of bells, the 18th-century Dazhong Si follows a typical Buddhist plan, with the Heavenly Kings Hall, Main Hall, and the Guanyin Bodhisattva Hall. Its highlight is the 46.5-ton (47,246-kg) bell – one of the world's largest – that is housed in the rear tower. The bell was cast between 1403 and 1424, and brought here from Wanshou Temple in the reign of the Qianlong emperor. Buddhist *sutras* in Chinese and Sanskrit embellish its surface. During the Ming and Qing dynasties, the bell was struck 108 times to bring in the New Year, and could be heard for 25 miles (40 km). The gallery above has a display on bell casting,

Heng, Biyun Temple deity

and visitors can toss a coin into a gap at the top of the bell for luck. Hundreds of bells from the Song, Yuan, Ming, and Qing eras can be seen in a separate hall on the west side.

Xiang Shan Park
香山公园

Wofosi Lu, Xiang Shan, Haidian district. 333 from Summer Palace, 360 from Zoo. 6am–7pm. **Botanical Gardens** daily.

This wooded parkland area, also known as Fragrant Hills Park, is at its scenic best in the fall, when the maples turn a flaming red. Its main attractions are the fine views from **Incense Burner Peak**, accessible by a chairlift, and the splendid **Biyun Temple**, or Azure Cloud Temple, close to the main gate. The temple is guarded by the menacing deities Heng and Ha in the Mountain Gate Hall. A series of halls leads to the Sun Yat Sen Memorial Hall, where his coffin was stored in 1925, before being taken to Nanjing. At the temple's rear is the distinctive 112-ft (34-m) high Diamond Throne Pagoda. About a mile (2 km) east of Xiang Shan Park are the **Beijing Botanical Gardens**, with pleasant walks and some 3,000 plant species. The gardens' **Sleeping Buddha Temple** is renowned for its magnificent bronze statue of a reclining Buddha. China's last emperor, Pu Yi (*see p65*), ended his days here as a gardener.

The Great Bell Temple, or Dazhong Si

National Olympic Stadium ㉝
奥林匹克体育中心

Olympic Green. Ⓜ *Olympic Park* 🚍 **Water Park** *Tel* *(010) 8437 3011.* ⏰ *10am–4pm daily.* 📷 **www**.n-s.cn

Beijing's National Olympic Stadium was the stunning centerpiece of China's massive building program for the 2008 Olympics. It is part of the city's "Olympic Green" development, which includes a large landscaped park, an Olympic Village, and many other stadia including the National Indoor Stadium and Water Cube National Aquatics Center.

Swiss architects Herzog and de Meuron won the competition for the stadium, working in combination with Beijing-based artist and architect Ai Wei Wei, with a bird's nest-like structure of apparently random, intertwined ribbons of steel and concrete that simultaneously form both façade and structure. The gaps in the concrete lattice of the roof are filled with translucent inflated bags, making the building waterproof while allowing light to filter down to the spectators within.

In 2010, a vast water park opened at the Water Cube Center. The park features a wavepool, 13 giant slides, and other colorful, high-tech aquatic attractions.

798 Art District ㉞
七九八艺术区（大山子）

2-4 Juxian Qiao Lu, Da Shan Zi, Chaoyang. 🚍 *915 or 918 from Dong Zhi Men to Da Shan Zi, or 420 from Beijing Station.* ⏰ *10:30am–7:30pm daily.* **www**.798space.com

Although it has spilled out of its original home and into neighboring moribund industrial buildings to form the Da Shan Zi Art District, the lively arts scene here is still mostly known for the abandoned No. 798 Electronics Factory. This was the first to be converted into

Contemporary art meets obsolete industry at 798 Space in Da Shan Zi

a complex of studios, workshops, and galleries called 798 Space. Built in the Bauhaus style in the 1950s by East Germans with Soviet funding, the area was once the center of Chinese high-tech, said to have produced parts for China's first nuclear bombs and satellites. Now its industrial chic is put to more peaceful purposes with art in all media for sale both in galleries and directly from the artists themselves. Wandering among the galleries reveals a different and interesting side to the city – there are large Communist-style sculptures making ironic reflections on history and new Mao-kitsch graffiti on the walls next to the original 1950s slogans exhorting workers. Cafés and restaurants have sprung up to add to the allure of the area.

China Railway Museum ㉟
中国铁道博物馆

1 Jiuxiang Qiao Bei Lu, Chaoyang. 🚍 *Tel* *(010) 6438 1317.* ⏰ *9am–4pm Tue–Sun.* 📷

The last passenger steam services in China came to an end in 2006, but a short taxi ride northeast of the 798 Art District, the Railway Ministry Science and Technology Center has a vast modern hall displaying 53 old locomotives. The collection includes some of the vast black engines imported by the Japanese when they controlled Manchuria, as well as huge Chinese beasts from Datong, and tiny Thomas the Tank Engine-scaled machines that once worked narrow-gauge extensions to French-built lines in Yunnan Province. The most ancient model is from Beijing's first railway line, which ran to Tongzhou, east of Beijing, directly connecting the city with the northern terminus of the Grand Canal, and vital food supplies from the south. Some of the cabs can be boarded by those sufficiently agile. An exhibition on the history of China's railways is promised, but in the meantime the engines themselves are a must for small boys of all ages. It is rumored that some machines will occasionally be in steam; call ahead to enquire.

Communist-era locomotives at the China Railway Museum

FARTHER AFIELD

Beijing continues to expand ring road by ring road but – for now – there is still relief from the crowds to be found in the surprisingly lush landscapes beyond the city limits. The Great Wall meanders across hilly territory to the north, always making for the highest point, and frequently doubling back on itself. There are several official access points with coach parks and souvenir shops, and an unlimited number of unofficial ones.

To the west, ancient temples nestle on green hillsides where rural life goes on much as it has for centuries. A trip out here offers a glimpse of the realities of existence for two-thirds of China's population. This is the world of tiny two-stroke tractors

and water buffalo; of orderly patchworks of tiny wheat, corn, and sorghum fields; of bee-keeping and pig husbandry. Most temples have simple guest rooms, while at the well-preserved Ming- and Qing-era village of Cuandixia you can stay with the villagers themselves.

The countryside also harbors the vast necropolises of the Ming emperors and, more interestingly, the much less visited but more elaborate resting places of the Qing, to the east and southwest of the city. Also to the southwest is the 300-year-old stone Marco Polo Bridge and neighboring Wanping, a rare surviving example of a walled city. Both are an easy suburban bus ride from the city.

SIGHTS AT A GLANCE

**Tombs, Temples, and
Historic Buildings**
Eastern Qing Tombs ❸
Great Wall of China
pp90–92 ❷
Jietai Temple ❻
Marco Polo Bridge ❹
Ming Tombs *pp88–9* ❶
Tanzhe Temple ❺

Town and Villages
Cuandixia ❽
Shidu ❼

KEY

▢	City limits
✈	International airport

═══	National highway
▬▬▬	Major road
═══	Minor road
───	Railroad
▬▬▬	Great Wall of China
‑ ‑ ‑	Beijing Province border

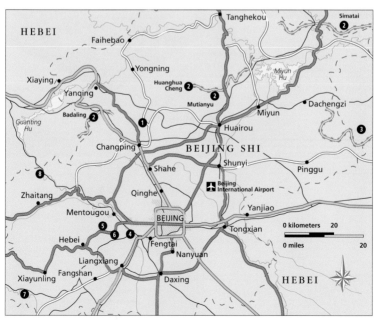

◁ **The Great Wall meandering along the ridges of mountainous terrain just north of Beijing**

Ming Tombs: Chang Ling ❶
明十三陵

Mythical *qilin* on Spirit Way

The resting place for 13 of the 16 Ming emperors, the Ming Tombs (Shisan Ling) are China's finest example of imperial tomb architecture. The site was originally selected because of its auspicious *feng shui* alignment; a ridge of mountains to the north cradles the tombs on three sides, opening to the south and protecting the dead from the evil spirits carried on the north wind. The resting place of the Yongle emperor (1360–1424), the Chang Ling is the most impressive tomb and the first to be built. It has been beautifully restored, although the burial chamber, where Yongle, his wife, and 16 concubines are thought to be buried, has never been excavated.

★ Spirit Way
Part of the 4-mile (7-km) approach to the tombs, the Spirit Way is lined with 36 stone statues of officials, soldiers, animals, and mythical beasts.

★ Hall of Eminent Favor
One of China's most impressive surviving Ming buildings, this double-eaved sacrificial hall is erected on a three-tiered terrace.

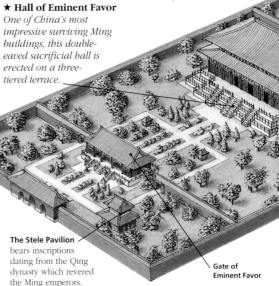

RECONSTRUCTION OF CHANG LING
This shows the Chang Ling tomb at the time of the burial of the Yongle emperor in the 15th century.

The Stele Pavilion bears inscriptions dating from the Qing dynasty which revered the Ming emperors.

Gate of Eminent Favor

THE MING TOMBS
The 13 tombs are spread over 15 square miles (40 sq km), so are best visited by taxi. Chang Ling, Ding Ling, and Zhao Ling have been restored and are very busy. Unrestored, the rest are open yet quiet.

① Chang Ling (1424)
② Yong Ling (1566)
③ De Ling (1627)
④ Jing Ling (1435)
⑤ Xian Ling (1425)
⑥ Qing Ling (1620)
⑦ Yu Ling (1449)
⑧ Mao Ling (1487)
⑨ Tai Ling (1505)
⑩ Kang Ling (1521)
⑪ Ding Ling (1620)
⑫ Zhao Ling (1572)
⑬ Concubine cemeteries
⑭ Si Ling (1644)

Spirit Way

pailou (archway)

0 kilometers 4
0 miles 4

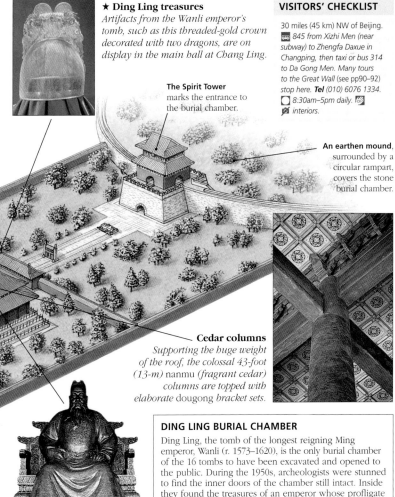

★ Ding Ling treasures
Artifacts from the Wanli emperor's tomb, such as this threaded-gold crown decorated with two dragons, are on display in the main hall at Chang Ling.

The Spirit Tower
marks the entrance to the burial chamber.

An earthen mound,
surrounded by a circular rampart, covers the stone burial chamber.

Cedar columns
Supporting the huge weight of the roof, the colossal 43-foot (13-m) nanmu *(fragrant cedar) columns are topped with elaborate* dougong *bracket sets.*

VISITORS' CHECKLIST

30 miles (45 km) NW of Beijing.
845 from Xizhi Men (near subway) to Zhengfa Daxue in Changping, then taxi or bus 314 to Da Gong Men. Many tours to the Great Wall (see pp90–92) stop here. **Tel** (010) 6076 1334.
8:30am–5pm daily.
interiors.

Statue of the Yongle Emperor
Yongle, the third Ming emperor, moved the capital from Nanjing to Beijing, where he then oversaw the construction of the Forbidden City.

STAR FEATURES

★ Hall of Eminent Favor

★ Spirit Way

★ Ding Ling treasures

DING LING BURIAL CHAMBER

Ding Ling, the tomb of the longest reigning Ming emperor, Wanli (r. 1573–1620), is the only burial chamber of the 16 tombs to have been excavated and opened to the public. During the 1950s, archeologists were stunned to find the inner doors of the chamber still intact. Inside they found the treasures of an emperor whose profligate rule began the downfall of the Ming dynasty.

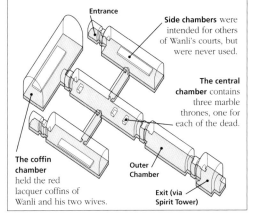

Entrance

Side chambers were intended for others of Wanli's courts, but were never used.

The central chamber contains three marble thrones, one for each of the dead.

The coffin chamber
held the red lacquer coffins of Wanli and his two wives.

Outer Chamber

Exit (via Spirit Tower)

Great Wall of China ❷
长城

A symbol of China's historic detachment and sense of vulnerability, the Great Wall snakes through the countryside over deserts, hills, and plains for several thousand miles. Originally a series of disparate earthen ramparts built by individual states, the Great Wall was created only after the unification of China under Qin Shi Huangdi (221–210 BC). Despite impressive battlements, the wall ultimately proved ineffective; it was breached in the 13th century by the Mongols and then, in the 17th century, by the Manchu. Today, only select sections of its crumbling remains have been fully restored.

Crumbling ruin
Most of the wall is still unrestored and has crumbled away leaving only the core remaining.

★ Panoramic views
Because the wall took advantage of the natural terrain for defensive purposes following the highest points and clinging to ridges, it now offers superb panoramic views.

Ramparts enabled the defending soldiers to fire down on their attackers with impunity.

Surface of stone slabs and bricks

Tamped layer of earth and rubble

Bigger rocks and stones

Kiln-fired bricks, cemented with a mortar of lime and glutinous rice

Large, locally quarried rocks

RECONSTRUCTION OF THE GREAT WALL
This shows a section of the wall as built by the most prolific wall builders, the Ming dynasty (1368–1644). The section at Badaling, built around 1505, is similar to this and was restored in the 1950s and 1980s.

STAR FEATURES

★ Panoramic views

★ Watchtowers

★ Watchtowers
A Ming addition, these served as signal towers, forts, living quarters, and storerooms for provisions.

For hotels and restaurants in this region see p182 and p202

Towers were spaced two arrow shots apart to leave no part unprotected.

Cannons
Another Ming addition, cannons were used to defend the wall and summon help.

Signal beacons were used to warn of attack by burning dried wolf dung.

The carriageway is on average 8 m (26 ft) high and 7 m (21 ft) wide.

TIPS FOR VISITORS

• The wall is exposed to the elements so be prepared for all outcomes: wear layers of clothing and a waterproof top, but also bring some suncream.
• Bring plenty of water.
• The wall can be very steep in places, so make sure you have strong footwear with a good grip such as hiking boots or tough waterproof runners.

Multi-function wall
The wall enabled speedy communications via smoke, flares, drums, and bells, as well as allowing for the rapid transport of troops across the country.

THE GREAT WALL OF CHINA (MING DYNASTY)

0 kilometers 400

0 miles 400

Inner Mongolia

Yellow River

Datong

Beijing

Taiyuan

Tianjin

Bo Hai

Qinghai Lake

Lanzhou

Yellow Sea

Most visitors travel to the wall from Beijing (*see p92*), but it is worth seeing the wall anywhere along its length. Also impressive are the restored forts at Juyong Guan, Jiayu Guan, and Shanhaiguan.

Places to visit
① Jiayu Guan
② Badaling & Juyong Guan
③ Mutianyu & Huanghua Cheng
④ Simatai
⑤ Shanhaiguan

Exploring the Great Wall of China

A trip to the wall is a must for any visitor to Beijing.
Most hotels will be able to organize this for you,
usually combined with a visit to the Ming Tombs
(see pp88–9). However, be sure to find out whether
there are any unwanted diversions planned to cloisonné
workshops, jade factories, or Chinese medicine clinics.
Small groups can have a more personalized visit, and
see the more remote parts of the wall, by hiring a taxi
for the day from Beijing and sharing the cost.

Stall selling tourist paraphernalia at the Great Wall, Badaling

🏯 Badaling

44 miles (70 km) northwest of
Beijing. *Tel (010) 6912 1890.*
🚌 1 from Qian Men. 🕐 6:40am–
6:30pm daily. 🎫 🖼 🛗 🔲
Equipped with guardrails,
cable car, pristine watchtowers,
and tourist facilities, the
restored Ming fortification at
Badaling is the most popular
section of the Great Wall.
The reward for coming to
Badaling is the breathtaking
view of the wall winding its
way over the hills. To fully
appreciate this, get away
from the crowds by walking
as far as you can along the
wall either east or west of the
entrance. The ticket includes
admission to the Great
Wall Museum. The pass at
Juyong Guan is on the way
to Badaling and is often
quieter than Badaling. With
unscalable mountains on
either side it is easy to see
why this spot was chosen for
defense. There are also some
authentic Buddhist carvings
on a stone platform, or "cloud
terrace," in the middle of the
pass that date back to the
Yuan dynasty (1279–1368).

🏯 Mutianyu

56 miles (90 km) north of Beijing,
Mutianyu Town, Huairou County. 🚌
6 from Xuanwu Men. 🕐 7:30am–
6pm daily. 🎫 🛗 & chair lifts.
The appeal of Mutianyu lies in
its dramatic hilly setting and
less intrusive tourist industry.
With a series of watchtowers
along its restored length, the
wall you can see here dates
from 1368 and was built upon
the foundations of the wall
built during the Northern Qi
dynasty (AD 550–77).

🏯 Huanghua Cheng

37 miles (60 km) north of Beijing,
Huairou County. 🕐 daily. 🎫 🛗
Situated on the same stretch of
wall as Mutianyu, Huanghua is
an exhilarating section of Ming
wall that is far less developed
than other parts of the wall.
The great barrier is split into
two here by a large reservoir;
most travelers take the right
hand route on the other side of
the reservoir, as the left-hand
section is more difficult to
reach. Devoid of guardrails, the
masonry at Huanghua Cheng
can be uneven and treacherous,
so be careful. Because of its
crumbling state, access has

Ruins at Huanghua Cheng clinging to the steep hillside

been limited by the authorities.
Due to ongoing reconstruction,
it may not always be possible
to visit Huanghua Cheng.

🏯 Simatai

68 miles (110 km) northeast of
Beijing, Miyun County. 🚌 6 from
Xuanwu Men. 🕐 6am–6pm daily.
🎫 🛗 (Apr–Nov).
The wall at Simatai has only
been partially repaired, afford-
ing a more genuine impression
of the original wall. The steep
and hazardous parts of the
wall are also a lot riskier to
navigate. Most visitors clamber
along the eastern section of
wall at Simatai, which leads to
much steeper sections of wall,
and later, impassable ruins.
Despite the tourist trappings,
the views are superb here.
There is a four-hour trek from
Simatai to Jingshanling that
provides spectacular vistas,
too. Some parts of Simatai
are being renovated until late
2013, and have been cordoned
off to visitors.

The restored section of the wall at Badaling, northwest of Beijing

Eastern Qing Tombs ❸
清东陵

77 miles (125 km) east of Beijing, Zunhua County, Hebei Province. 🚗
May–Oct: 8am–5:30pm daily; Nov–Apr: 9am–4:30pm daily. 🎫 📷 📷

The remoteness of the Eastern Qing Tombs east of Beijing and over the border in Hebei province makes them far less popular than the Ming ones *(see pp88–9)*, despite the fact that the setting is even more splendid. In fact, the Eastern Qing tombs make up the largest and most complete imperial cemetery in China, built on as grand a scale as the Forbidden City itself *(see pp62–7)*. Of the many tombs scattered throughout the area,

Spirit Way to Emperor Shunzhi's tomb at the Eastern Qing Tombs

Incense burners in front of a spirit tower at the Eastern Qing Tombs

only five are the burial places of Qing emperors: the tombs of the Shunzhi emperor (r. 1644–61), Kangxi (r. 1661–1722), Qianlong (r. 1736–95), and Xianfeng (r. 1851–61) are open, while that of the Tongzhi emperor (r. 1862–74), at a distance from the main tomb grouping, is not. A 3-mile (5-km) Spirit Way, an approach lined with guardian figures, leads to Shunzhi's tomb, Xiao Ling, at the heart of the main tomb cluster, while several of the other tombs have their own smaller Spirit Ways. Southwest of here lies Yuling, Qianlong's tomb, with its incredible chamber adorned with Buddhist carvings and Tibetan and Sanskrit scriptures (rare features at imperial and principally Confucian tombs). The devious Empress Cixi

(see p82) is buried at Ding Dong Ling to the west, in the right-hand tomb of a complex of twin tombs, the other being the resting place of Ci'an, eldest wife of the Xianfeng emperor. Although both tombs were built in 1879, Cixi had her magnificent tomb lavishly restored in 1895. The marble carriageway up to the Hall of Eminent Favor notably locates the carving of the phoenix *(feng)*, symbol of the empress, above the carving of the dragon *(long)*, symbol of the emperor. West of Ding Dong Ling, Ding Ling is partially open and approached via a set of stone animal statues. Look for the smaller tombs of imperial concubines, their roofs tiled in green (not the yellow of emperors and empresses).

EMPEROR YONGZHENG

The son of the Kangxi emperor and a maidservant, Yongzheng (r. 1723–35) chose not to be buried at the Eastern Qing Tombs, but perversely started a necropolis as far away as possible in the Western Qing Tombs (Yixian County, Hebei Province). Perhaps, racked with guilt, he could not face burial alongside his father, whose will he had thwarted. For after Kangxi's death, Yongzheng seized the throne from his brother (his father's chosen successor), and declared himself the legitimate heir, ruthlessly eliminating any other brothers and uncles who may have been a threat to his rule. Despite this shaky start, Yongzheng was an able ruler and a devout Buddhist, punishing dishonesty among his officials and seeking to improve the morals and education of his people. Another possible reason for the switch was that he just wasn't satisfied with the Eastern Tombs and chose an area with a better natural setting. Whatever the reason, those keen on Chinese tomb architecture will enjoy the peace of the Western Qing Tombs. Nearby, moved in 1995 to a commercial cemetery, are the remains of Pu Yi, the last emperor of China.

Yongzheng in robes embroidered with symbols of his power

Brick stupas at the Stupa Forest Temple, also known as Talin Si

Marco Polo Bridge ❹
芦沟桥

Wanping town, Fengtai District. 10 miles (16 km) SW of city center. 🚌 *339 from Beijing's Lianhuachi bus station; 309 from WAZI (near Beijing West Railway Station).* ⏰ *7am–7pm daily.*
🖼 **Museum of the War of Resistance against Japan** 101 Wanpingcheng Nei Jie. **Tel** *(010) 8389 2355 ext 281.* ⏰ *9am–4pm Tue–Sun.* 🖼

Straddling the Yongding River in Wanping town, the 876-ft (267-m) long marble bridge was first built during the Jin dynasty in 1189 but destroyed by a flood. The current structure dates to 1698. Known as Lugou Qiao in Chinese, the bridge acquired its English name after Marco Polo described it in his famous account of his travels. At the bridge's eastern and western ends are stelae inscribed by the Qing emperors, Kangxi and Qianlong. The poetic observation by Qianlong on a stele at the eastern end reads *"lugou xiaoyue,"* meaning "Moon at daybreak at Lugou."

Stone lion, Marco Polo Bridge

The balustrades along the length of the bridge are decorated by more than 400 carved stone lions, each one slightly different in appearance. Local legend has it that these fierce-looking statues come alive at night. Despite the widening and extensive restoration work done over the centuries, a surprising amount of the bridge is original. In addition to its antiquity, it is significant as the site of the disastrous Marco Polo Bridge Incident. This is where, on July 7, 1937, the Japanese Imperial Army and Nationalist Chinese soldiers exchanged fire – an event that led to the Japanese occupation of Beijing and a full-scale war. For those with a keen interest in this period of history, the incident is marked by some gruesome displays in Wanping's **Museum of the War of Resistance against Japan**.

Tanzhe Temple ❺
潭柘寺

Mentougou district. 28 miles (45 km) W of Beijing. Ⓜ *to Pingguo Yuan (1 hr), then bus 931 or tourist bus 7.* **Tel** *(010) 6086 2505.* ⏰ *8am–6pm daily.* 🖼

This enormous temple dates back to the 3rd century AD, when it was known as Jiafu Si. It was later renamed Tanzhe Temple, after the adjacent mountain Tanzhe Shan, which in turn got its name from the nearby Dragon Pool (Long Tan) and the surrounding cudrania *(zhe)* trees. It has a splendid mountainside setting, and its halls rise up the steep incline. The temple is especially famous for its ancient trees, among which is a huge ginkgo known as the Emperor's Tree. A slightly smaller tree close by is called The Emperor's Wife.

The most fascinating sight, however, is the **Stupa Forest Temple** (Talin Si) near the parking lot, with its marvelous collection of brick stupas hidden among the foliage. Each stupa was constructed in memory of a renowned monk. The towering edifices were built in a variety of designs, including the graceful *miyan ta* or dense-eave stupa, characterized by ascending layers of eaves. The earliest among them dates from the Jin dynasty (1115–1234).

The 11-arched Marco Polo Bridge, known locally as Lugou Qiao

The gilded Buddha atop its plinth at Jietai Temple

Jietai Temple ➏
戒台寺

Mentougou district, 20 miles (32 km) W of Beijing en route to Tanzhe Temple. **M** *to Pingguo Yuan (1 hr), then bus 931 or tourist bus 7.* ⬜ *8am–6pm daily.* 🎫

The Jietai (Ordination Terrace) Temple has been used for the ceremony of elevating monks to higher levels of the Buddhist hierarchy as far back as the Liao dynasty (907–1125), and it is well worth a visit on the way to or from the nearby Tanzhe Temple. The "terrace" referred to in the temple's name is a finely carved marble plinth used for the ordination ceremonies. Its three layers feature 113 niched statues. Topped with a gilded Buddha and chairs for three masters and seven witnesses, the plinth stands inside a magnificent and unusual square hall, surrounded by lesser courtyards dotted with pines and cypresses. The temple is located about a half-mile (one-km) walk uphill from the bus stop.

Shidu ➐
十渡

Fangshan district. 62 miles (100 km) SW of Beijing. 🚌 *bus 917 from Beijing's Tianqiao station to Shidu.* **Tel** *(010) 6134 9009.* 🎫

Shidu offers a fabulous escape from the commotion of urban Beijing and a chance to enjoy some stunning natural scenery. Before the new road and bridges were built, travelers had to cross the Juma River ten times as they journeyed through the gorge between Shidu and nearby Zhangfang village, hence the name Shidu meaning "Ten Ferries" or "Ten Crossings." Pleasant walking trails wind along the riverbank between impressive gorges and jagged limestone formations. Visitors can stop en route to paddle in the shallow river and picnic under the towering peaks. The main sights are around Qingjiang Gou and the lovely Gushan Zhai, marred somewhat by bungee jumping and other entertainment ventures.

Cuandixia ➑
川底下

Near Zhaitang town. 56 miles (90 km) NW of Beijing. **M** *to Pingguo Yuan (1 hr), then bus 929 to Zhaitang (3 hrs), then taxi.* ⬜ *daily.* 🎫

Despite the rather laborious expedition required to get here, a trip to the tiny village of Cuandixia (Under the River) is well worth the effort as the crumbling hamlet survives as a living museum of Ming and Qing dynasty village architecture. Situated on a steep mountainside, it is a picturesque outpost of courtyard houses *(siheyuan)* and rural Chinese buildings. Because of the close-knit nature of the original village all the courtyards were interconnected by small lanes. The entry ticket allows access to the entire village, all of which can be explored within a few hours. Look out for the Maoist graffiti and slogans that survive on the boundary walls; similar graffiti from the Cultural Revolution has been whitewashed in most other Chinese towns.

Cuandixia's population consists of about 70 people spread over a handful of families. Accommodations can be arranged for those wanting to explore the surrounding hills or simply experience the rural hospitality. Alive to the opportunities brought by tourism, quite a few of the old homesteads provide basic facilities at a reasonable price.

Traditional Ming and Qing dynasty houses, Cuandixia village

TWO GUIDED WALKS

Beijing is famous for its centuries-old alleys known as *hutongs*. The *siheyuan* (courtyard houses) that line them were built with their backs turned on the outside world with the main entrance set in otherwise blank walls. But these alleys and their distinctive homes have been disappearing ever more rapidly since 1949. At first they fell victim to Soviet-style edifices celebrating Communist achievements, then to multi-story apartment towers, and now to road widening and new cross-town highways. These multi-lane highways and burgeoning traffic problems do not always make Beijing the best place to explore on foot but it is worth giving it a go as you can see much more detail at walking pace. Look for the original carved wooden surrounds framing new shop fronts, and the stone "guardians" often found outside the original gates and doors.

Of course, what is charm to some visitors is merely slum living to others. The historic buildings are often almost invisible beneath improvised lean-tos, with windows knocked through external walls to create the tiny and scantily-stocked shops known as *xiaomaibu*.

A walk around Hou Hai *(see pp100–101)* takes in still standing areas of ancient *hutongs*, some of which are undeniably tatty and some of which have been well renovated. It eventually weaves its way around the Back Lakes and their willow-fringed shores, home to myriad small bars and cafés. Despite the area's popularity it is always possible to step into a small alleyway and, for the time being at least, be immediately transported back into the past. If in places things moulder as they have done for centuries, on the walk around Pudu Si *(pp98–9)* the traditional has been rebuilt from the ground up, and you could cut your finger on the sharp edges of the 20th-century "Ming" brickwork. This walk sandwiches restored *hutongs* between a handful of historical imperial temples and modern-day shopping opportunities.

Early morning exercise

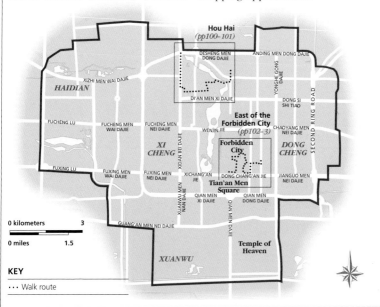

KEY

··· Walk route

A 90-Minute Walk East of the Forbidden City

This walk starts at the Imperial Ancestral Temple, a place often overlooked by visitors to the neighboring Forbidden City. Not far from these grand halls lie courtyard houses rebuilt from scratch (after leveling the originals and inserting an underground car park), which now serve as comfortable homes for officials with a taste for the traditional. The route also takes in the very much unpreserved and unreconstructed *hutong* residences of ordinary Beijingers, whose presence at the very heart of the city is surely unlikely to survive much longer. It ends on pedestrianized Wangfujing, the city's premier shopping street.

CourtYard restaurant ⑦

Tian'an Men, gateway to the Forbidden City ①

Park of the People's Culture

Make your way by subway to Tian'an Men Square. Facing the portrait of Mao that hangs on the **Tian'an Men** ①, turn right and walk east along the Imperial City wall. You soon arrive at an entrance overlooked by almost all. Go through this to the five-bay **Halberd Gate** ② and the Tai Miao, or **Imperial Ancestral Temple** ③, one of the most important in the city. A series of vast halls runs north in mimicry of the main sequence of "Harmony" halls inside the Forbidden City itself. Yet the entire site is usually deserted.

On reaching the canal at the rear of the temple, turn left to exit. This back way in to the complex was opened as a

short cut ④ for the Qianlong emperor in his old age. Cross the canal, turn right and follow the dog-leg of the **moat** ⑤ round to the north to reach the **Dong Hua Men** ⑥, or east gate of the Forbidden City (closed to the public).

As you recross the moat by bridge, immediately on the left is the famed restaurant **CourtYard** ⑦ (not open for lunch) and its basement gallery. Although this is an ancient courtyard house, the interior has completely remodeled and internationalized.

Nan Chizi Dajie

Cross over at the first junction and head south down Nan Chizi Dajie. Take the first left into narrow Pudu Si Xi Xiang and follow it round to the right and south for instant relief from traffic noise. There are left turns to explore at whim, but continuing south soon brings you to the magnificent double-eaved hall of the **Mahakala Temple** ⑧,

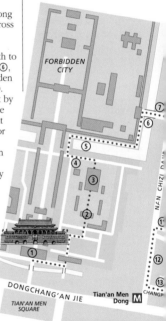

KEY

••• Walk route

Ⓜ Subway station

or Pudu Si, raised on a mound to the left. Back in the 15th century the temple was the home of a deposed Ming emperor, and later of the man who led Qing troops into Beijing in 1644. It became a lamasery in the 18th century, and housed a famous statue of Mahakala, whose cult the Qing had absorbed from the Mongols. In modern times its halls have echoed with the chanted lessons of primary

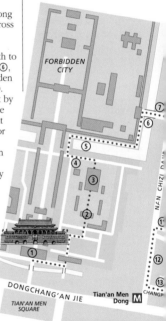

Entrance to the little visited Mahakala Temple, or Pudu Si ⑧

For hotels and restaurants in Beijing see pp178–82 and pp198–202

school children. The children are now gone, and the once sagging halls have been made shiny and new in preparation for their occupation by the land tax office.

At one time the area around the temple was filled with the ramshackle residences of ordinary people. These have now been totally rebuilt in a reproduction of antiquity and house local government officials. Security guards patrol the alleys, ready to protect the haves from the have-nots.

Continue south down the east side of the underground car park (the west side will also do) looking for **old pillar bases** ⑨ set in the new grey walls. At the end turn right

Children in the Changpu He Park ⑬

into **Duanku Hutong** ⑩, the name of which – Satin Warehouse Alley – reveals the use to which the surrounding buildings were once put. Follow the alley round to the left; the odd surviving shop sign in green and white **Arabic lettering** ⑪ reveals that many in the cloth trade were Muslims. The alley jogs right again to rejoin Nan Chizi Dajie. Resume your progress south and you will encounter the old **Imperial Archive** ⑫ a little farther down on the left. Unfortunately, the main hall, which dates back to 1536, is not open but it is still an impressive complex to wander around. Neighboring halls sell made-for-tourist art that recycles the old clichés.

Da Tian Shui Jing Hutong

Continue south down Nan Chizi and you'll soon come to an area where the ancient housing has been removed to create the narrow but pleasant **Changhe Pu Park** ⑬. This park follows the eastward course of the stream that flows in front of the Tian'an Men. Turn left along the stream bank, passing 21st-century **pastiche Qing buildings** ⑭ on the left. The park ends at a main road: cross and head north, then turn right where the bicycle route is indicated. This takes you into **Da Tian Shui Jing Hutong** ⑮ (Big Sweetwater Well Hutong) – Beijing's wells were notoriously brackish and good water would have been worth noting. For as long as it lasts, this is real *hutong* life, right in the

heart of the city. The lane is filled with tiny restaurants advertising Chongqing-style hotpot (very spicy) and noodles, all for real Beijing prices – less than ¥5 per dish. After passing a group of video parlors the alley re-engages with modernity, emerging into **Wangfujing Snack Street** ⑯, a tourist-pleasing but enjoyable food market, where you'll pay five times as much for the same dish as back in the *hutong*.

Turn left to reach the pedestrianized shopping street of **Wangfujing Dajie** ⑰ *(see p72)*, with its fashionable shops with permanent sales, and McDonald's and other imports. Those still with some walking in their legs can then enjoy some shopping.

TIPS FOR WALKERS

Length: 1.8 miles (3 km).
Getting there: Subway to Tian'an Men Dong.
Galleries at the Imperial Archive: Open 10am–noon & 1pm–6pm daily.
Stopping off points: There are Western and Chinese restaurants around the Nan Chizi crossroads near the CourtYard restaurant. In summer, stands around the Imperial Archive offer cold drinks for sale. The restaurants in Da Tian Shui Jing Hutong are grubby, but authentic and cheap. Otherwise, Wangfujing Dajie and its malls sport numerous Western and local fast food outlets and branches of coffee chains, as well as several superior Chinese and international restaurants.

0 kilometers 1
0 miles 0.5

GHUAMEN DAJIE DONG'ANMEN DAJIE
CAICHANG HUTONG
DARUANFU HUTONG ⑰
DA TIAN SHUI JING HUTONG ⑮
⑯
NANHEYAN DAJIE
HUALONG JIE
WANGFUJING DAJIE
XIAGONGFU JIE
ZHENGYI LU
Wangfujing Ⓜ

Doorway to a courtyard home in Duanku Hutong ⑩

A Two-Hour Walk around Hou Hai

Hou Hai (Back Lakes) is a cluster of three linked bodies of water just over a mile or so north of the Forbidden City. They lie at the heart of a district of labyrinthine old *hutongs* (alleys), studded with a handful of monuments of modest grandeur. This walk takes you through areas of mouldering housing to a renovated courtyard dwelling, and past abandoned mansions to one that has been largely preserved. It meanders through an area undergoing revitalization as a lively nightlife hub before winding up at a couple of ancient towers, which you can ascend to look back over the area which you have just explored.

Women exercise beside the lake shore at Hou Hai ⑩

Xinjiekou Bei Dajie
The walk starts at the Circle Line subway station of Jishuitan. Leave by exit C, turn left down Xinjiekou Bei Dajie, cross the road and continue south past **clothing and shoe shops** ①, all with prices far lower than home. The building set back from the road with a sign on top in green characters, is the **Xu Beihong Memorial Hall** ②. This is worth a look in for the lively watercolors of horses that made Xu (1885–1953) internationally famous.

Xu Beihong statue ②

means "in the depths of many flowers," a reference to a time when the *hutong* was famous for its hothouses, which had carefully ducted steam to ensure that the flowers bloomed just in time for the major festivals and temple fairs. One of the biggest such fairs used to be held at the **Protect the Nation Temple** ⑤, or Huguo Si. Take the first right into Huguo Si Xi Xiang which leads down

Continue on south past lots more small shops and cross back to the east side of the road at the traffic signals. Note the **model shop** ③ on the corner of Hangkong Hutong with large supplies of hard to obtain plastic kits at cheap prices. Walk on past electric guitar shops and jewelers to take the next left turning but one into **Bai Hua Shen Chu** ④. The name

past ramshackle housing to the temple's sole surviving hall. This was formerly the home of a Yuan dynasty prince, banished for treason in 1355; it was turned into a temple a decade later. The institution was funded by imperial eunuchs and doubled as a retirement home for them. These haunting remains represent the sad state of historic conservation in Beijing: abandonment leading to eventual ruin.

Huguo Si Jie
At the bottom end of Huguo Si Xi Xiang turn left onto the busier main road of Huguo Si Jie. You pass take-away snack shops, vegetable and meat vendors, and an art shop, before coming to the **Mei Lanfang Memorial Hall** ⑥. This is a traditional *siheyuan* (courtyard house) in a fine state of preservation, which shows what can be done with old Beijing when tourism income is anticipated. This was the home of Beijing Opera's greatest performer (1894–1961), *see pp30–31*. The rear rooms have been left with their traditional furniture,

Street entrance to the Mei Lanfang Memorial Hall ⑥

For hotels and restaurants in Beijing see pp178–82 and pp198–202

exactly as they were when Mei died. Other rooms contain hagiographic accounts of his life, diagrams of the stylized movements required by the form, and a video of Mei, already 61, but still playing the young girl roles for which he was famous.

Crossing the next junction, which is with busy Desheng Men Nei Dajie, look in the next gate on the left for a glimpse of part of the former **Mansion of Prince Qing** ⑦, which has not fared as well as Mei Lanfang's residence. Continue east, cross Songshu Jie, and turn left along the

The Silver Ingot Bridge between Hou Hai and Qian Hai ⑪

Shrine with offerings at the Mansion of Prince Gong ⑧

KEY

••• Walk route

Ⓜ Subway station

outer wall of the **Mansion of Prince Gong** ⑧ *(see p68)*. It is worth making time for a look around this extensive former royal residence with its beautiful gardens. The sad fact is that this is the last intact house of its kind in an area that once held several similarly grand mansions.

The Back Lakes
On exiting Prince Gong's mansion turn right and follow the compound wall around to the right and into **Da Xiang Feng Hutong** ⑨, looking for drum stones, carved panels, and door guardians adorning the fronts of the old houses. Just before the end of the *hutong* you'll catch a glimpse of the waters of **Hou Hai** ⑩ down a narrow left turn: head this way. You now hit tourist territory. The shores of the lake are hugely popular with both foreign visitors and locals and are lined with Chinese karaoke and faux-Western bars and restaurants. The hub of all activity is the bottleneck of the **Silver Ingot Bridge** ⑪, which arches over the narrow channel between the Hou Hai and Qian Hai, and gives modestly pretty views in two directions.

Once over the bridge go straight ahead and jink left then right into **Yandai Xiejie** ⑫, a terrifically vibrant small street with corner street-food sellers and an odd mix of gift shops and bars mixed in with the practical, such as a bicycle repair shop. Look up for glimpses of finely carved wood here and there that belongs to ancient façades to which modern shop fronts have been attached. There is a former bathhouse here that's now a boutique and a temple that's now a café.

Turn left at the end onto main Di'an Men Wai Dajie, to see the **Drum Tower** ⑬ rearing up ahead; the **Bell Tower** ⑭ is just behind. The balconies of both give views back across the labyrinth you've just navigated.

TIPS FOR WALKERS

Length: 2.5 miles (4 km).
Getting there: Subway to Jishuitan.
Xu Beihong Memorial Hall: Open 9am–4pm Tue–Sun.
Mei Lanfang Memorial Hall: Open 9am–4pm Tue–Sun, but closed for a month in Jan–Feb.
Mansion of Prince Gong: Open 8:30am–4:30pm daily.
Bell Tower and Drum Tower: Open 9am–5pm daily.
Stopping off points: After turning left onto Huguo Si Jie, turn right at the next crossroads down Hucang Hutong, to find Jing Wei Lou on the right at the corner with the major avenue, Ping'an Da Dao. This is a bustling restaurant with a picture menu of dishes. Just before the entrance to Prince Gong's Mansion is Sichuan Fandian, one of Beijing's oldest restaurants, serving excellent fiery Sichuan food. Some bars along the lake shore offer dishes that faintly resemble the Western foods for which they are named.

SHOPPING IN BEIJING

From some of the world's biggest and glitziest shopping malls selling global brands, to thriving street markets where everything from counterfeit designer goods to reproduction antiques can be found, there is almost nothing you can't buy in Beijing. A new Ferrari? There has been a dealership in Beijing since 1994. Tiffany, the New York jeweler, opened its first branch in the city in 2001. But, as with the likes of Japanese electronics and Swiss watches, severe import duties ensure these foreign products all cost substantially more here

Chairman Mao lighter

than they would at home. Beijing should certainly not be mistaken for the duty-free haven of Hong Kong.

Traditionally, Wangfujing Dajie and its side turnings are the heart of Beijing's shopping, along with The Village mall and plaza in Sanlitun, which was opened for the 2008 Olympics. But Beijing's historic symmetry means there's a similar concentration west of the Forbidden City at Xi Dan. There are also department stores and markets scattered throughout the city's residential quarters, many with far better prices than the central locations.

SHOPPING ETIQUETTE

The frantic sanitization of Beijing has removed many of the traditional small side-street markets, and has driven all the better-known larger markets under the cover of purpose-built sites. If you do come across any surviving street markets on your travels – you may still encounter them in residential areas – then they are always worth browsing for cheap prices.

Always bargain hard, not just at markets, but also at supposedly fixed price shops too, just as the Chinese do. Or try to buy from stalls where you can see people making and selling craft items, as this will benefit the local residents.

Wherever you go, shop with caution. If you are told that something is supposedly old, rare, or intrinsically

Caged birds for sale at a traditional Beijing street market

Stallholder selling silks and fabrics at Hong Qiao Market

expensive, it is most likely a fake. China is not the place to shop for valuable antiques, gems, or jewelry (including jade and pearls) unless you really are an expert. Nothing with an internationally traded value can be bought cheaply in either Beijing or Shanghai. Famous brand-name goods, from Louis Vuitton bags and Calvin Klein apparel to Apple iPods, are all commonly faked. At the very least with high-value locally-made items like carpets, considerable time should first be spent visiting carpet dealers and learning about quality, manufacturing methods, and prices.

At the end of the day if you like the item and it seems a reasonable deal to you, go ahead and buy it, but don't assume you have got a real bargain or something of great value cheaply.

ANTIQUES, CRAFTS, AND CURIOS

Genuine antiques are almost impossible to find, and all purchases should be made on the assumption that what is being bought is fake. Objects dating between 1939 and 1795 cannot officially be taken out of the country without a certificate, something any honest dealer with a genuinely ancient item would help you to acquire. Anything older may not be exported at all. The most interesting market for so-called antiques and curios is **Panjiayuan Market** in the southeast of town but even vendors admit that 80 percent of what is on sale is fake. However, there is nowhere better to do all your gift shopping in one go, although you may find yourself hoarse by the end of the day from bargaining for items such as Russian optical equipment, gramophones, stuffed deer heads, framed calligraphy, and bamboo-and-bone *mah jong* sets. Even for anybody who doesn't like shopping, Panjiayuan is worth visiting as a sight in its own right. Neighboring **Beijing Curio City** also has a vast array of ceramics, furniture, jewelry, and Tibetan art on several floors, although authenticity is equally suspect.

The large **Hong Qiao Market** near the Temple of Heaven has an odd range of clothing, souvenirs, and low quality (or fake) pearls up on the third and fourth floors.

Spend a few hours browsing through the pleasant little shops of **Liulichang** (see p61), which specialize in lacquerware, ceramics, paintings, and assorted crafts. China has a long tradition of making excellent furniture and **Huayi Classical Furniture** sells classical antique, restored, and reproduction furniture, some of which, at least, is clearly marked as being what it is. The trendy store **Sattva**, near the Lama Temple, sells hand-dyed rugs and furniture sourced personally by the owner from Tibet and Qinghai. Assorted extras include drums, art, and jewelry. Another hip store is **Lost & Found**, which sells good-quality furniture, porcelain, clothing, and home accessories.

Perhaps the most unusual curios are those connected

Curios and reproduction antique furniture at Panjiayuan Market

with Beijing's four traditional pastimes of flowers, birds, fish, and insects *(hua, niao, yu, chong)*. While the animals can not be exported to your home country, some of the associated paraphernalia – ornate bird cages, tiny feeding dishes, gourd homes for insects, and perhaps even tapes for teaching your mynah Mandarin – will certainly make excellent conversation pieces and are genuine souvenirs of Beijing. Even for those who don't do shopping, the **Huasheng Tian Qiao Market** offers a compelling aural and visual feast, as the chirrups and clicks of the insects compete with the wider ranging whistles of the birds.

ART AND CALLIGRAPHY

Paintings done in traditional styles and of traditional subjects can be found at all curio markets and souvenir shops, and hundreds if not thousands of copies will be painted of anything foreigners find appealing. Modern painting in Western styles also tends to choose tourist-pleasing subject matter, attaching prices that show an understanding of Western art markets – although such pieces could rarely be sold on for

Hanging scroll painted with elegant script

anything like the same price outside of China. There is tourist kitsch aplenty at the galleries in the **Imperial Archive** (see p99); for more serious efforts, but still often conscious of Western preferences and beliefs about China, try the **Red Gate Gallery** (see p73) and the **CourtYard Gallery**, attached to the restaurant of the same name. Serious art shoppers should consider visiting the dozens of artists' studios and galleries that make up the **798 Art District** (see p85). Prices will be prohibitive to all but the most committed and deep-pocketed of collectors, but there is no charge for looking. The Caochangdi Art Village is also a great place for art enthusiasts. Chinese artist Ai Weiwei has a studio here and top galleries such as **Pekin Fine Arts** and **Platform China** are located in the area. A good place for affordable Chinese contemporary art is **Affordable Art Beijing**, which sells both online and from its office near the Confucius Temple.

BOOKS

Take your own reading material when traveling to China, as the choice of imported and English-language fiction in Beijing is limited. The best selection is on the top floor at the **Foreign Languages Bookshop** on Wangfujing. However, English books on cultural and travel topics and coffee-table photography books on Chinese themes are plentiful (although often marked-up in price for the foreign market). **The Bookworm**, in Chaoyang, offers a range of such English-language books, as does Beijing's largest bookshop, **Tushu Dasha**. Specialist art bookshops can be found in and around the **National Art Museum of China** (see p72).

Traditional-style painting on parchment – a popular souvenir

Detail from a traditional embroidered men's robe

CARPETS, TEXTILES, AND CLOTHING

Beijing's markets sell a variety of carpets from Tibet, Gansu, and Xinjiang. Try the **Qian Men Carpet Company**, which has antique, imitation antique, and new carpets for sale. It also arranges shipping. The **Beijing Silk Store** is the best starting point for silk and related fabrics at local prices. Tour groups are often taken to the popular **Yuanlong Silk Corporation**, which has fabrics and a large selection of ready-made silk garments. What is known as the **Xiushui Silk Market**, is in fact almost entirely free of silk – its four floors of vendors mostly stock counterfeit designer goods at prices that indicate they know the ignorance of foreign shoppers. None of this stops it from reportedly being one of the city's biggest tourist attractions after the Forbidden City and Great Wall. Sanlitun's **Yaxiu Market** (sometimes written Yashow) also has four floors of clothes, fabric, and curios, plus a tailoring services for those who want a figure-hugging *qipao* (*cheongsam*).

For unique textile designs and jewelry by local designers, try **Torana House**, located in the Europlaza Mall. This flagship store specializes in hand-woven Tibetan carpets and Chinese rugs.

Modern decorative beaded purse

DEPARTMENT STORES AND SHOPPING MALLS

In the west of the city, the **Season's Place** mall is big, glitzy, and modern, with brands like Lane Crawford and Louis Vuitton, plus an excellent basement supermarket and several restaurants. **The Village** at Sanlitun is the city's busiest mall, with a broad open plaza and plenty of brands including an Apple Store, Nike, Adidas, Agnès B, and Diesel, as well as several cafes, restaurants, and bars. Another large and popular mall is **The Place** on Guanghua Lu, which has a lot of brand shopping and an extraordinary multimedia canopy roof showing videos and interactive art. The **Oriental Plaza** on Dong Chang'an Jie boasts a glittering array of international names, from Paul Smith and Armani to an Apple computer store. The basement level has a large Watson's pharmacy, a supermarket, and an excellent Southeast Asian-style food court. **Sun Dong'an Plaza**, on Wangfujing, holds international fashion stores mixed in with branches of retailers originating from Hong Kong.

ELECTRONICS

Despite what you might think, China is not a good source of cheap electronics. If the equipment is imported then it is going to be more expensive than in the West; if it is locally made then it usually comes with a Chinese operating system, pirated software, and a guarantee that is no use outside China. However, China is excellent value for accessories such as cables and converters, and media such as blank CDs, Mini-Discs, and DVDs. Zhongguang Cun in the northwest district of Haidian is the main place for all such things, but it is a long way to travel. A better option is the **Bai Nao Hui** computer market, which is more central. **Apple Store** is at The Village in Sanlitun as well as at the Oriental Plaza.

Anywhere tourists go to shop or play, vendors will be found with fake DVDs of Hollywood movies. Setting aside legal issues, copies may be of foreign language versions with no English option, subtitles may be for a different film altogether, the disc may stop playing partway through, and copies of recent titles will have been made by placing a camera at the back of a cinema auditorium. The authorities

Wangfujing Dajie, Beijing's modern, mall-lined main shopping street

in China are cracking down on this piracy, and occasionally there are arrests and fines. But it is such a big industry and there is such a gap between the cost of legitimate goods and the average wage in China that the trade will be impossible to stamp out completely. At around as little as US$1 per disk, pirated DVDs are understandably still very popular.

TEA

Malian Dao Lu has all the teas in China, available from endless rows of tiny shops on either side of the street, and from the four stories of the **Malian Dao Cha Cheng** with

Chinese children's kite

dozens of stalls. Rare and expensive teas should be avoided unless you're an expert, but few foreigners come here, and most stalls

have thimble-sized cups to give you a taste. Packaging is often very attractive, and bricks of the cheapest tea, pounded into a mould with an assortment of patterns, make attractive if slightly heavy souvenirs.

TOYS

You can find everything from the Chinese edition of Monopoly to Gameboys, jigsaw puzzles, and radio-controlled cars, all at bargain prices under one roof at the **Hong Qiao Toy City**. **Jack's Toys** is also good, and more toys can be found at China's first flagship **Lego** store, which stocks the whole lego series and limited edition collections.

DIRECTORY

ENTERTAINMENT IN BEIJING

Literary and cultured, but still too much under the thumb of a highly conservative government to be truly progressive, Beijing nevertheless offers entertainment that includes the tourist-pleasing, the traditional, and the reasonably recherché. This is, of course, the home of the world-famous Beijing Opera, which continues to be performed at venues across the city on a nightly basis, although the majority of these shows cater for foreign visitors. The

Lurid Beijing cocktails

same is true of the various acrobatic performances that take place. The rock and pop scene, on the other hand, is vibrant and wholly targeted at a young, local audience. Performing arts in general have received a shot in the arm thanks to the National Center for the Performing Arts. This vast, mercury bubble of a building, controversially designed by French architect Paul Andreu, is worth a visit for the spectacle of the structure itself.

PRACTICAL INFORMATION

For details of performances – from large-scale stadium rock concerts to dance troupes appearing on handkerchief-sized stages – see the listings in the expat-produced listings magazines such as *Agenda*, *The Beijinger*, *City Weekend*, and *Time Out Beijing*. These are available free in hotel lobbies and at many restaurants and bars. Only these bi-weekly and monthly publications can hope to keep up with frantic schedules, rapid changes in fashion, and the may-fly existence of some venues that close almost as soon as they've opened.

Tickets are generally bought at the venue box offices and paid for in cash. At small music clubs, pay on the door. Most hotel concierges can usually help in securing seats.

Seating area of Atmosphere in the China World Summit Tower

Bar at the Apothecary, Sanlitun Road

BARS AND CLUBS

Sanlitun is the one district that all Beijing expats know intimately. Sanlitun Road (once known as Sanlitun Bar Street) was redeveloped in time for the 2008 Olympics and includes The Village and Nali Patio, home to some of the city's best bars. Chic cocktail lounges **D Lounge** and **Apothecary** can be found here, while **The Tree**, a long-standing favorite, marries draught beer with wood-fired pizza and remains a popular spot. On Sanlitun North Road **Enoterra** sees Shanghai's favorite French-owned wine bar trying its hand in the capital with similar success. Its well-priced wine menu, specials board, and light French cuisine is the same as in the Shanghai branch, as is the eager embrace from Beijing wine lovers. **The Hutong** and **Riverbank Café** are two hip café-bars that double as mini cultural centers, showing movies and hosting dance and theater performances. New bars and cafés are springing up all the time along the eastern shore of Hou Hai, where the pick of the bunch is the understated and wholly original **No Name Bar**. The first bar to open in the area, it benefits from a wonderful waterside site just south of the Silver Ingot Bridge.

Across the lake on the western shore is Lotus Lane, which is a developer's attempt to recreate Sanlitun, but the bars and clubs here are a little tawdry and suffer from a lack of inspiration. Instead, head north and east into the *hutongs*. Nearby, Bei Luogu Xiang is an up-and-coming area with boutiques, cafés, and bars, including **Mai**, a popular cocktail lounge and jazz venue.

Farther north, a couple of alleys up past the Bell Tower, **Bed Bar** is a multi-courtyarded venue whose labyrinth of rooms is filled with Chinese-style four-posters and other beds. It is a wonderful fusion of the hip and the traditional, and delivers a truly Beijing-style bar experience. Also worth a look is **Stone Boat**, a small pub that "floats" in a corner of the Ri Tan Park lake.

Beer in a local bar can cost as little as ¥5, but in foreigner-frequented venues it will more commonly be anything from ¥15–¥30. You also pay inflated prices for imported pleasures such as cocktails, particularly if you take them in foreign-run places where they are done best, such as **Centro** at the Kerry Center Hotel (whose deep-pocketed customers consume more Moët et Chandon between them than those of any other mainland venue). Also pricey is the fashionable **Atmosphere**, a Beijing hotspot located on the 80th floor of the China World Summit Tower. This is the capital's highest bar and a place to "see and be seen" but the views are exceptional. For another great view, the cocktail terrace at **Capital M** overlooks Tian'an Men Square. This upscale restaurant and lounge bar is the sibling of M on the Bund in Shanghai.

For late-night high jinks, **Yugong Yishan** remains Beijing's most eclectic and down-to-earth club, offering live music and alternative DJs most nights of the week.

BEIJING OPERA

For most non-Chinese, Beijing Opera *(see pp30–31)* is a taste not easily acquired. Incomprehensible plots, unfamiliar sounds, and performances lasting up to three hours can make for uncomfortable viewing. However, there's no denying the acrobatic ability and dramatic splendor of the event, so everyone should try it once. Performances are best seen in the splendid Ming-dynasty **Zhengyici Theater** or Qing-dynasty **Huguang Guildhall**. During the warmer months, there are evening shows at the **Mansion of Prince Gong** *(see p68)* at 7:30pm. Given the choice, you would opt for any of these over the **Liyuan Theater** in the Qian Men Hotel, which is where tour groups are taken.

Beijing Opera star

CINEMA

Government-imposed restrictions mean that cinemas show a very limited number of imported English-language films. **Culture Yard**, an independent movie club, shows mostly Chinese movies, while **Riverbank Café** screens classic movies from around the world. **The Hutong** culture center also shows international films.

Beijing Opera – difficult to follow, but the color is dazzling

For the latest international movies on huge screens head for **Wanda International Cinema Complex**. There is also a games arcade and a few cafés here. During the summer months keep a look out for movies screened outdoors in various park locations.

CLASSICAL CONCERTS

Take the chance to see and hear a Chinese orchestra, if at all possible. Sections of unfamiliar plucked string, bowed string, woodwind, and percussion instruments compete for attention in swirling arrangements.

The **National Center for the Performing Arts**, just one block west of Tian'an Men Square, is a spectacular multi-purpose venue that puts on classical concerts, ballet, and opera, as well as providing space for art exhibitions. Its central location and impressive architecture alone certainly merit a visit.

National Center for the Performing Arts – or, as it is more commonly known, "the Egg"

Popstars performing an outdoor concert in Beijing

ROCK AND POP

The question of which city has the best tunes provokes regular shouting matches between the youth of Beijing and Shanghai, but there is no argument really: Beijing wins.

Beijing-based Cui Jian, the Bob Dylan-like old man of Chinese rock, became the first famous indigenous name in rock with his protest songs, including "Nothing to My Name," with its references to the events in Tian'an Men Square of June 1989. As a result he was forbidden to play large venues until 2006.

But the once lone voice of rock is now drowned out by the innumerable punk bands for which Beijing is famous, and Chinese versions of every kind of popular music. Most of the new generation think Cui Jian should retire, although he played small venues across North America in 2005, and was the support act for the Rolling Stones when they played Shanghai for the first time in 2006.

Many Chinese rock and pop musicians take Western music genres as a starting point, on to which they then overlay Chinese characteristics. Singing in Mandarin isn't enough: they will also perhaps add an electrified *erhu (see p31)* to the line-up, or use vocal styles from Chinese opera. The results range from appalling to appealing, but there's no lack of talent and enthusiasm.

Sanlitun's **Workers' Stadium** is the usual venue for large-scale rock, filled regularly by Taiwanese and Hong Kong stars, but also by a few mainland pan-Asia mega-stars

such as the infinitely talented Wang Fei (Faye Wong to her Cantonese-speaking fans). Tickets are always hard to get, and there is always a thriving trade for them on the black market.

Among the many smaller venues for live music, all with rosters of rock, blues, jazz, punk, and anything else that seems likely to bring in the masses, the **Yugong Yishan** bar is the current favorite for its cheap drinks and eclectic programing policy. Also popular is the rocking student venue, **Mao Livehouse**, which attracts both local and international live acts from across the underground music spectrum (it is part-owned by a Japanese record label).

TEAHOUSES

China's long history of growing and drinking tea has led to considerable refinement in its production, preparation, and serving. A very elaborate tea ceremony may include the use of a sniffing cup into

which a small amount of tea is poured and then emptied before the residual aroma is savored. In fact, most ceremonies involve a lot of filling and spilling, or tipping away – the aim is to provide a good number of exquisitely small cups of perfect tea, all at the same strength, from one pot of tea leaves. Teahouses such as the **Purple Vine** near the west gate of the Forbidden City, offer calm interiors with antique furnishings, and a respite from the city's bedlam. The **Xi Hua Yuan Teahouse**, which is across the street from Purple Vine, adds a Chinese-speaking mynah bird to the attractions. The **Ji Gu Ge Teahouse** offers a wide selection of traditional teas and also boasts a small gallery and shop.

At such establishments the prices of various teas are clearly given on a menu, and a demonstration of the traditional preparation of tea is included in the cost of the more expensive ones.

Watch out for English-speaking Chinese who strike up conversations at tourist sites. Sometimes the visitor is asked whether they have ever seen a Chinese tea ceremony? A short walk to a tucked-away teahouse, and a few samples of tea later, a bill that is the equivalent of well over a hundred US dollars or more is presented. Your new Chinese friends will profess to be horrified, as they had no idea it would be so expensive, but of course they are party to the con.

The elaborate art of tea drinking

PUPPET THEATER AND ACROBATICS

When it comes to theater, language truly is a barrier. However, there is always traditional Chinese puppet theater. Plays with wooden puppets *(mu'ouxi)* involve elaborate and colorfully dressed marionettes. The fun is as much in admiring the craftsmanship and dexterity as attempting to work out the plot; see what's on at the **China Puppet Art Theater**.

Enterprising entrepreneurs have also put together performances of "teahouse art," which may include acrobatics, story-telling, singers, jugglers, and short

Chinese acrobatic troupe performing with bicycles

extracts from Beijing Opera. These bite-sized cultural morsels are usually served in recreated period atmosphere

with tea and a meal. Try the **Lao She Teahouse** (which has shows at 7:50pm daily), just south of Tian'an Men Square, and the **Tian Qiao Happy Teahouse**.

China has a worldwide reputation for its gymnasts who perform breathtaking routines that showcase their unnerving flexibility. Displays of balance often involve props such as chairs and plates, with one of the most popular tricks being to pile 20 or so acrobats on a bicycle. Venues include the **Chaoyang Theater** and **Tiandi Theater**, both with nightly shows, and occasionally the **Poly Theater**. All of these theaters are in the eastern district of Sanlitun.

DIRECTORY

BARS & CLUBS

Apothecary
D302, 3/F, Nali Patio, 81 Sanlitun Road, Chaoyang. **Map** 3 F3.
Tel (010) 5208 6040.

Atmosphere
80/F, China World Summit Tower, 1 Jianguo Men Wai Dajie. **Map** 3 F5. **Tel** (010) 6505 2299 ext. 6433.

Bed Bar
17 Zhangwang Hutong, off Jiu Gulou Dajie. **Map** 2 A2. **Tel** (010) 8400 1554.

Capital M
3/F, Qianmen Dajie, Chongwen. **Map** 4 C2. **Tel** (010) 6702 2727.

Centro
Kerry Center Hotel, 1 Guanghua Lu. **Map** 3 F5. **Tel** (010) 6561 8833 ext. 42.

D Lounge
Courtyard 4, Gongti Bei Lu, Chaoyang. **Map** 3 F3. **Tel** (010) 6593 7710.

Enoterra
D405, 81 Sanlitun North Road. **Map** 3 F3. **Tel** (010) 5208 6076.

The Hutong
1 Jiu Dao Wan Zhong Xiang. **Map** 2 C2. **Tel** (159) 0104 6127.

Mai
40 Bei Luogu Xiang. **Map** 2 B2. **Tel** (0138) 1125 2641.

No Name Bar
Qianhai Dong Yan, S. of Silver Ingot Bridge. **Map** 2 A2. **Tel** (010) 6401 8541.

Riverbank Café
Ground Floor, FX Hotel, 39 Maizidianxi Jie. **Tel** (010) 6506 8277.

Stone Boat
Southwest corner of Ri Tan Park. **Map** 3 E5. **Tel** (010) 6501 9986.

The Tree
43 Sanlitun Bei Lu. **Map** 3 F3. **Tel** (010) 6415 1954.

Yugong Yishan
3–2 Zhangzizhong Lu, Gulou. **Map** 2 B3. **Tel** (010) 6404 2711.

BEIJING OPERA

Huguang Guildhall
3 Hufang Lu. **Map** 4 B3. **Tel** (010) 6351 8284.

Liyuan Theater
Qian Men Hotel, 175 Yong an Road, Xuan Wu. **Map** 4 B3. **Tel** (010) 6301 6688.

Mansion of Prince Gong
14 Liuyin Jie, off Hou Hai Nan Yan. **Map** 2 A2. **Tel** (010) 6616 8149.

Zhengyici Theater
220 Xiheyan Dajie. **Map** 4 B2. **Tel** (010) 8315 1649.

CINEMA

Culture Yard
10 Shique Hutong. **Map** 2 C2. **Tel** (010) 8404 4166.

Wanda International Cinema Complex
3/F, Building 8, Wanda Plaza, 93 Jianguo Lu, Chaoyang. **Map** 3 F5. **Tel** (010) 5960 3399.

MUSIC

Mao Livehouse
111 Gulou Dong Dajie, Dongcheng. **Map** 2 B2. **Tel** (010) 4402 5080.

National Center for the Performing Arts
Xi Chang'an Jie, W. of Great Hall of the People. **Map** 4 C1. **Tel** (010) 6655 0000.

Workers' Stadium
Gongren Tiyuchang Bei Lu. **Map** 3 E3. **Tel** (010) 6501 6655.

TEAHOUSES

Ji Gu Ge Teahouse
132-6 Liulichang Dong Jie. **Map** 4 B2. **Tel** (010) 6301 7849.

Purple Vine
2 Nan Chang Jie. **Map** 2 A5. **Tel** (010) 6606 6614.

Xi Hua Yuan Teahouse
Bei Chang Jie, across from west gate of Forbidden City. **Map** 2 A5. **Tel** (010) 6603 8534.

PUPPET THEATER AND ACROBATICS

Chaoyang Theater
36 Dongsanhuan Bei Lu. **Map** 3 F4. **Tel** (010) 6526 8228.

China Puppet Art Theater
A1 Anhua Xi Li. **Tel** (010) 6424 3698.

Lao She Teahouse
3 Qian Men Xi Dajie. **Map** 4 C2. **Tel** (010) 6301 7454.

Poly Theater
Poly Plaza, 14 Dong Zhi Men Nan Dajie. **Map** 3 D3. **Tel** (010) 6500 1188.

Tiandi Theater
10 Dong Zhi Men Nan Dajie. **Map** 3 D3. **Tel** (010) 6502 3984.

Tian Qiao Happy Teahouse
1 Bei Wei Lu. **Map** 4 C3. **Tel** (010) 6304 0617.

BEIJING STREET FINDER

The map references given with all sights, hotels, restaurants, shops, and entertainment venues described in this chapter refer to the following maps only. The first figure of the map reference indicates which map to turn to, and the letter and number that follow are the grid reference. The key map below shows which parts of Beijing's city center are covered in this Street Finder. A complete index of street names follows the maps. Note that there are different ways of presenting Chinese names, so, for example, the main street Jianguo Men Nai Dajie might appear on signs in Beijing as Jianguomennai Dajie. For more on street names see page 168. Modern Beijing has extended a long way beyond the main city center zone depicted below and outlying areas are shown on the Beijing Farther Afield map on page 87.

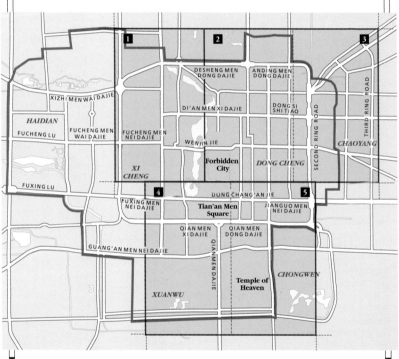

KEY TO STREET FINDER

- ▪ Major sight
- ▪ Place of interest
- ▫ Other important building
- ▣ Train station
- ▣ Long-distance bus station
- Ⓜ Subway station
- ▭ City bus station
- ℹ Tourist information
- ✚ Hospital
- ⊠ Post office
- ⛩ Temple
- ✝ Church
- ☪ Mosque

SCALE OF MAP ABOVE

0 kilometers   2

0 miles   2

SCALE OF MAPS 1–5

0 meters   500

0 yards   500

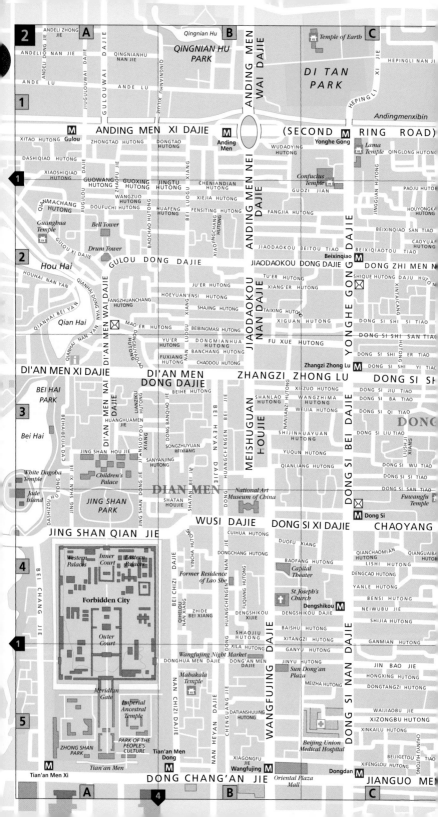

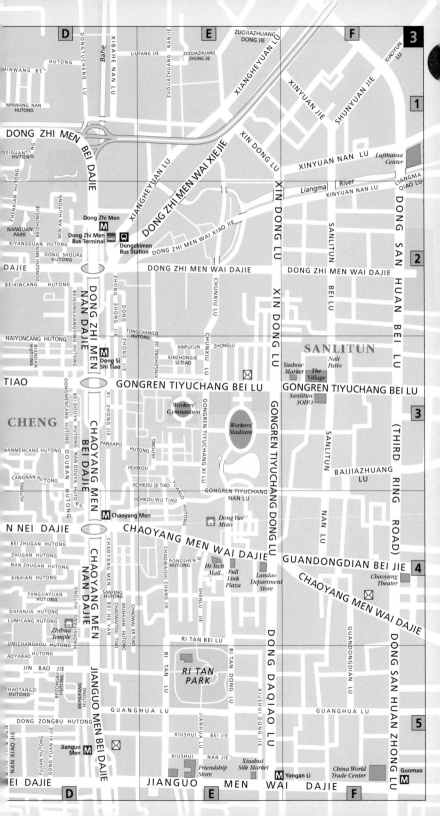

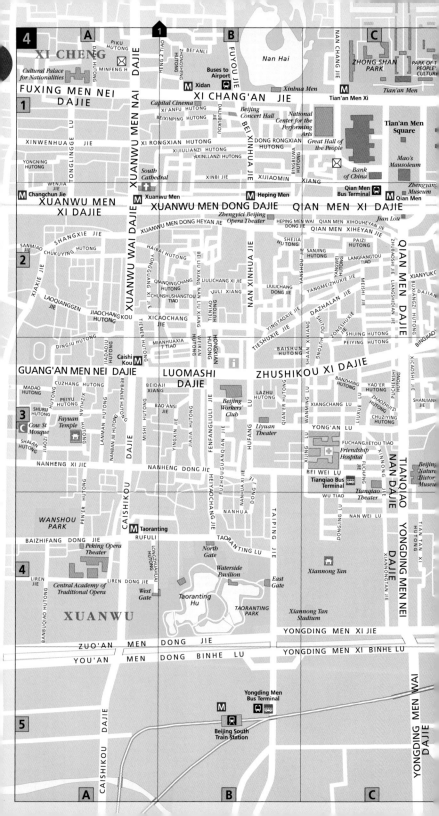

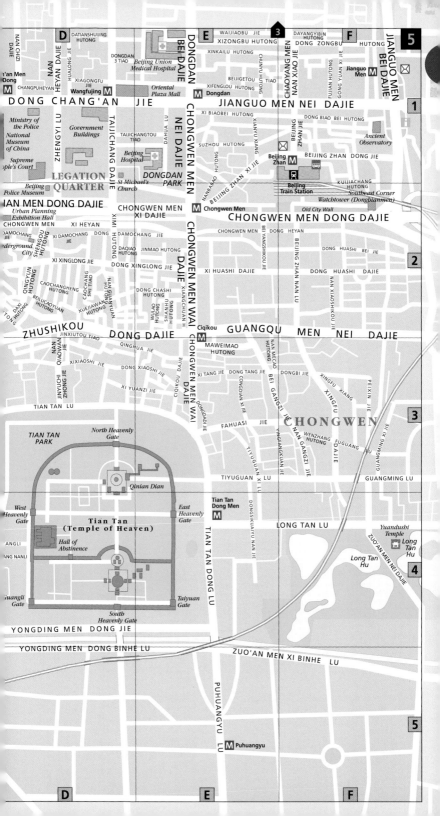

Beijing Street Finder Index

SHANGHAI

Exploring Shanghai

Shanghai has three main areas of interest to the visitor. The Old City is typically Chinese, with alleys, markets, and temples. It is also home to the very lovely Yu Gardens. The former concession areas, once under the direct rule of the French, British, and Americans, boast the Bund, the riverside avenue lined with grand colonial buildings, as well as the city's two main shopping streets, Nanjing Road and Huaihai Road. Pudong, Shanghai's newest district, on the Huangpu's east bank, is an immense business and residential zone, with a clutch of museums and some of the highest buildings in the world.

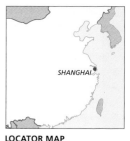

SHANGHAI

LOCATOR MAP

SEE ALSO

- ***Where to Stay*** pp182–7
- ***Where to Eat*** pp202–7

SIGHTS AT A GLANCE

Historic Buildings, Sites, and Neighborhoods

The Bund pp122–3 1
Bund Sightseeing Tunnel 12
French Concession 8
Jinmao Tower 16
IFC Tower 15
Longhua Cemetery of Martyrs 22
Nanjing Road 2
Oriental Pearl TV Tower 13
Shanghai Exhibition Center 9
Shanghai World Financial Center 17
Site of the First National Congress of the Chinese Communist Party 6
Soong Qingling's Former Residence 20
World Expo Site (2010) 23

Temples and Churches

Jade Buddha Temple 11
Jing'an Temple 10
Xujiahui Catholic Cathedral 21

Parks and Gardens

Century Park 18
Fuxing Park 7
Hongkou Park 19

People's Park & Square 3
Yu Gardens & Bazaar pp130–31 5

Museums

Shanghai Museum pp126–9 4
Shanghai Ocean Aquarium 14

Towns and Areas of Natural Beauty

She Shan 24

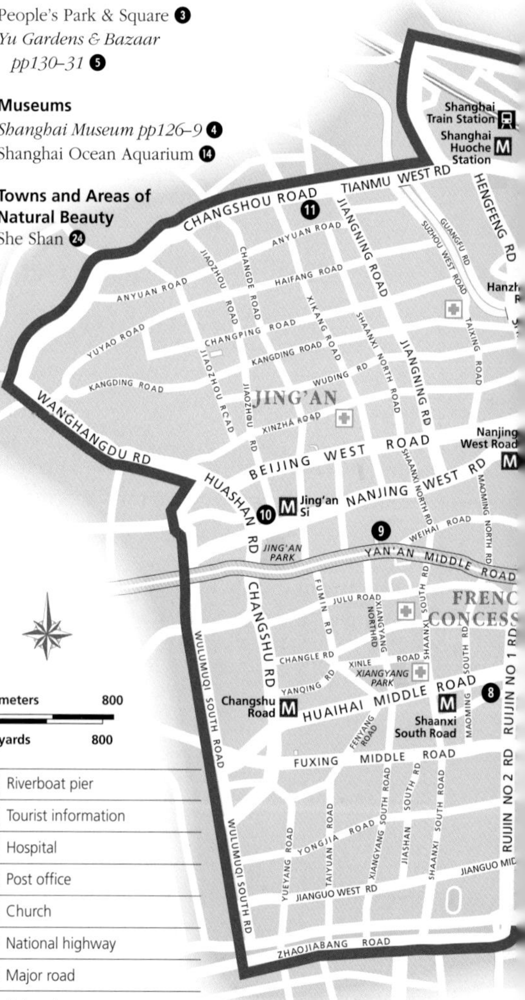
Shanghai Train Station
Shanghai Huoche Station
TIANMU WEST RD
HENGFENG RD
CHANGSHOU ROAD
JIANGNING ROAD
ANYUAN ROAD
HAIFANG ROAD
SUZHOU WEST ROAD
GUANGFU RD
JIAOZHOU ROAD
CHANGDE ROAD
XIKANG ROAD
YUYAO ROAD
CHANGPING ROAD
KANGDING ROAD
SHAANXI NORTH ROAD
TAIXING ROAD
WUDING RD
JING'AN
XINZHA ROAD
WANGHANGDU RD
BEIJING WEST ROAD
Nanjing West Road
HUASHAN RD
Jing'an Si
NANJING WEST RD
MAOMING NORTH RD
WEIHAI ROAD
JING'AN PARK
YAN'AN MIDDLE ROAD
CHANGSHU RD
FUMIN RD
JULU ROAD
XIANGYANG NORTH RD
FRENCH CONCESSION
WULUMUQI SOUTH ROAD
CHANGLE RD
XINLE ROAD
XIANGYANG PARK
YANQING RD
Changshu Road
HUAIHAI MIDDLE ROAD
Shaanxi South Road
RUIJIN NO 1 RD
FENYANG ROAD
FUXING MIDDLE ROAD
RUIJIN NO 2 RD
YONGJIA ROAD
TAIYUAN ROAD
YUEYANG ROAD
JIASHAN ROAD
SHAANXI SOUTH ROAD
JIANGUO WEST RD
ZHAOJIABANG ROAD
0 meters 800
0 yards 800

KEY

- Street-by-Street area: *see pp130–31*
- Domestic airport
- International airport
- Train station
- Subway station
- Bus terminus
- Ferry terminal
- Riverboat pier
- Tourist information
- Hospital
- Post office
- Church
- National highway
- Major road
- Railroad

◁ **Futuristic architecture along the banks of the Huangpu River, Pudong, Shanghai**

GETTING AROUND

The subway is the best way to get around Shanghai. At the time of writing there are twelve lines and the network is still expanding (see p226). Taxis are also convenient, cheap, and plentiful. Buses tend to be extremely crowded and slow due to traffic congestion, especially during the morning and evening rush hours. Road tunnels link the east and west banks of the Huangpu River but it's more fun to take a ferry.

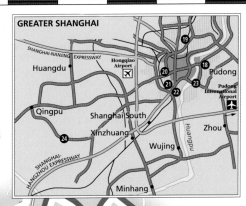

GREATER SHANGHAI

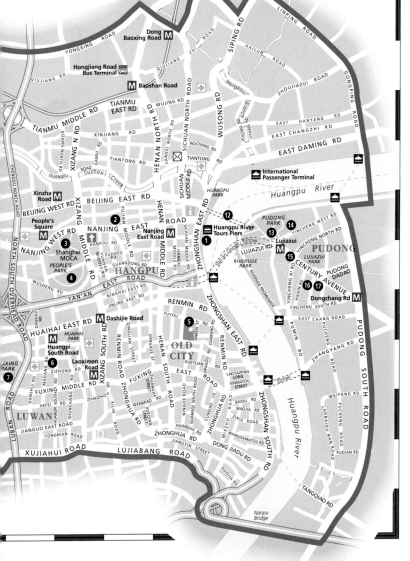

The Bund ❶
外滩

Lion, symbol of colonial power

Some places are forever associated with a single landmark and in the case of Shanghai it is surely the Bund. Also known as Zhongshan East No.1 Road, the Bund was at the heart of colonial Shanghai, flanked on one side by the Huangpu River and on the other by the hotels, banks, offices, and clubs that were the grandiose symbols of western commercial power. Most of the old buildings are still in place and a walk along here can easily absorb a couple of pleasant hours. The Bund was extensively relandscaped for the World Expo 2010.

The Bund, at its peak the third biggest financial center in world

★ Shanghai Pudong Development Bank
Built in 1921 when it was vaunted to be the most beautiful building in Asia, it boasts delightful murals.

Customs House ★
The entrance hall is decorated with some handsome marine mosaics.

The bronze lions' paws and head are rubbed for good luck.

Russo-Asiatic Bank Building

Former Bank of Communications

★ River promenade
On the river side of the Bund is a wide pavement, a wonderful place to stroll and watch locals practising tai ji quan (tai chi). It is also a great spot for photographing the Pudong skyline.

STAR SIGHTS

★ River promenade

★ Shanghai Pudong Development Bank

★ Customs House

★ View of Pudong

★ View of Pudong
In the evening the Bund throngs with people enjoying the river breeze and the spectacular lights of Pudong's modern skyline.

Former Palace Hotel
The Palace Hotel was built in 1906 and was for a long time one of the best hotels in Shanghai. It is now the Swatch Art Peace Hotel.

Bank of China
Blending 1920s American and traditional Chinese styles, this impressive block was built by a rival of Sassoon, H.H. Kung.

Chartered Bank Building of India, Australia, and China.

Former Bank of Taiwan

North China Daily News Building

Fairmont Peace Hotel
Originally the Cathay Hotel, built in 1930 by Sir Victor Sassoon, this is now a lavish hotel with impressive views of the Huangpu River. The jazz bar is still at the heart of its events.

Chen Yi's statue
The bronze statue looking down the Bund is not Chairman Mao but Chen Yi, revolutionary commander and first mayor of Shanghai after 1949.

Nanjing Road ❷
南京路

Map 1 D3/E3/F2 & 2 A2/B2/C2.
Ⓜ *Nanjing East Road (for pedestrian shopping street), Nanjing West Road (for People's Square).*

Nanjing Road has traditionally been Shanghai's foremost shopping street, although since the 1990s it has faced increasing competition from Huaihai Road in the French Concession. The street is divided into two distinct halves: Nanjing East Road stretches between the Bund and People's Park; Nanjing West Road runs from People's Park out past Jing'an Temple. Together the two parts total close to six miles (10 km).

The "shopper's paradise" has always been **Nanjing East Road**. Before 1949, all the major stores were located here. One of them, the Sun Department Store, is now the **Shanghai No. 1 Department Store**, which continues to attract thousands of customers every day with its exotic window displays. Many of the other department stores have been replaced with modern malls, but it is worth a walk down the street by night because, when the sun goes down,

Statues on Nanjing Dong Lu

Birds for sale at the Fish & Flower Market on Jiangyin Road

Nanjing East Road resembles a Chinese Las Vegas with its shop fronts illuminated by a multitude of garish neon signs.
Nanjing West Road once went by the charming name of Bubbling Well Road, after the well near Jing'an Temple (*see p134*). A grand relic of those times survives in the **Park Hotel**, across from People's Square, which when built in 1934 was the tallest building in Shanghai – a record it held until 1988 – not to mention, one of the most fashionable addresses. Beside the Park, **Huanghe Road** is a great place for street food. **Wujiang Road**, which loops off Nanjing Road west of People's Square now has an impressive and popular shopping plaza.
Beyond the point at which it is rejoined by Wujiang Road, Nanjing West Road is lined by a series of exclusive shopping and commercial centers such as the Westgate Mall, CITIC Square, and Plaza 66 (*see p162*), all filled with multiple levels of designer shops, including names such as Armani, Louis Vuitton, and Cartier, with prices even higher than at home. A little farther along is the **Shanghai Center**, one of the earliest such developments, with several good restaurants, a popular bar, and airline offices clustered around the Portman Ritz-Carlton Hotel.

The Park Hotel, formerly one of the most fashionable addresses in town

People's Park & Square ❸
人民广场

Nanjing West Road. **Map** 2 A2 & A3.
Ⓜ *People's Square.*

What used to be a racecourse (*see p125*) is now occupied by the pleasantly landscaped People's Park (Renmin Gong Yuan) in the northern half, and People's Square and the **Shanghai Museum** (*see pp126–9*) in the southern section. Locals visit the park to walk, gossip, exercise, or fly kites but, in addition to the museum, there are several other sights and cultural monuments to attract the visitor. Quite literally over-shadowed by the gleaming glass and steel skyscrapers that surround it, **Mu'en Tang**, the Merciful Baptist Church, lies on the eastern side of the square. It was built in 1929 as the American Baptist Church. An inter-denominational survivor of China's many revolutions, it is open to all, although the services are in Chinese only.
On the northeast side of the square, the building with four inverted tents for a roof is the **Urban Planning Exhibition Hall**. The Yangzi River delta is the world's fastest-growing urban area and that is reflected here with the world's largest model. The model, which can be viewed from a gallery above, sprawls across 100 square meters, and depicts the Shanghai of the not-too-distant future. This,

unsurprisingly, takes the form of a forest of skyscrapers, all lovingly detailed at a scale of 1:2000. Other floors have maps of more construction to come, and exhibitions on the city's signature *shikumen* housing and colonial-era Shanghai. The top floor houses a quiet café.

The elegant glass box of **MOCA Shanghai**, the Museum of Contemporary Art, opened in 2005. Its two floors house regularly changing exhibitions of cutting-edge art and design, which have included work by Alexander Calder, David Hockney, Jenny Holzer, and Matazo Koyama, and the 80th-anniversary showcase of the Salvatore Ferragamo couture house.

At the northwest corner of the park is the Former Shanghai Jockey Club, an elegant old racecourse clubhouse. The lavish marbled interiors of this 1930s Neo-Classical building are particularly impressive. This beautiful building was once the home of the eclectic Shanghai Art Museum, which has now moved to the World Expo Site (2010) *(see p139)*. On the top floor is the bar-restaurant, **Kathleen's 5**, which boasts marvelous views over the park from its roof terrace. On your way up the stairs, keep an eye out for the horses' heads

THE OLD RACECOURSE

The old racecourse was the center of Shanghai social life in the early 20th century, and its Race Club was one of the most profitable corporations in China. It also boasted a swimming pool and a cricket pitch. After the Communists came to power in 1949, the course became a symbol of Western decadence, and was turned into a park and an adjacent square that was used for political rallies. It was later landscaped to accommodate the Shanghai Museum. When the grandstand became the Shanghai Art Museum, all that remained of the racecourse was its old grandstand clock on the park's west side.

A view of Shanghai's racecourse prior to 1949

worked into the decoration of the banisters.

Behind the Former Shanghai Jockey Club is the striking **Shanghai Grand Theater** made almost entirely of glass and topped by a spectacular convex roof. It is definitely worth a visit, for a meal with a view or just to look around; official tours are also available.

🔼 **Mu'en Tang**
315 Xizang Middle Road. ◯ *five daily services, see entrance for times.*

🏛 **MOCA Shanghai**
People's Park, 231 Nanjing West Road. ◯ *10am–9:30pm daily.* **www**.mocashanghai.org

🎦 **Shanghai Grand Theater**
People's Square. ◯ *10:30am– 5:30pm daily.*

🏛 **Urban Planning Exhibition Hall**
100 People's Avenue.
◯ *9am–4pm Mon–Thu, 9am–5pm Fri–Sun.* **www**.supec.org
¥30.

Ornamental flower display in the beautifully maintained People's Park, at the heart of Shanghai

Shanghai Museum ❹
上海博物馆

Bronze coin (AD 927–51)

With a collection of over 120,000 pieces, the Shanghai Museum displays some of the best cultural relics from China's neolithic period to the Qing dynasty, a span of over 5,000 years. While the highlights are the bronze ware, ceramics, calligraphy, and painting, it also has excellent displays of jade, furniture, coins, and Chinese seals or "chops." The museum was established in 1952, and the current building opened in 1995 with a design that recalls some of the exhibits and symbolizes "a round heaven and a square earth."

Shanghai Museum, reminiscent of a Shang-dynasty bronze *ding* pot

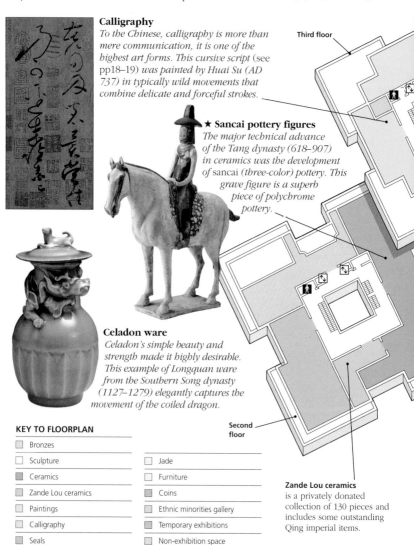

Calligraphy
To the Chinese, calligraphy is more than mere communication, it is one of the highest art forms. This cursive script (see pp18–19) was painted by Huai Su (AD 737) in typically wild movements that combine delicate and forceful strokes.

Third floor

★ Sancai pottery figures
The major technical advance of the Tang dynasty (618–907) in ceramics was the development of sancai (three-color) pottery. This grave figure is a superb piece of polychrome pottery.

Celadon ware
Celadon's simple beauty and strength made it highly desirable. This example of Longquan ware from the Southern Song dynasty (1127–1279) elegantly captures the movement of the coiled dragon.

Second floor

KEY TO FLOORPLAN

- Bronzes
- Sculpture
- Ceramics
- Zande Lou ceramics
- Paintings
- Calligraphy
- Seals
- Jade
- Furniture
- Coins
- Ethnic minorities gallery
- Temporary exhibitions
- Non-exhibition space

Zande Lou ceramics is a privately donated collection of 130 pieces and includes some outstanding Qing imperial items.

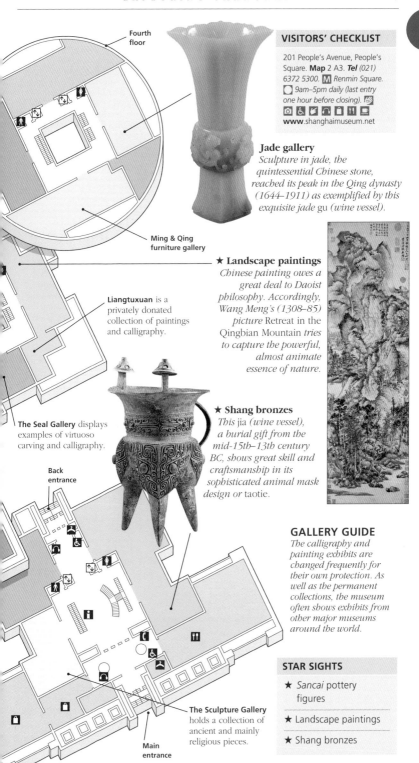

Fourth floor

Ming & Qing furniture gallery

Liangtuxuan is a privately donated collection of paintings and calligraphy.

The Seal Gallery displays examples of virtuoso carving and calligraphy.

Back entrance

Main entrance

VISITORS' CHECKLIST

201 People's Avenue, People's Square. **Map** 2 A3. **Tel** (021) 6372 5300. M Renmin Square. 9am–5pm daily (last entry one hour before closing). www.shanghaimuseum.net

Jade gallery
Sculpture in jade, the quintessential Chinese stone, reached its peak in the Qing dynasty (1644–1911) as exemplified by this exquisite jade gu (wine vessel).

★ Landscape paintings
Chinese painting owes a great deal to Daoist philosophy. Accordingly, Wang Meng's (1308–85) picture Retreat in the Qingbian Mountain *tries to capture the powerful, almost animate essence of nature.*

★ Shang bronzes
This jia (wine vessel), a burial gift from the mid-15th–13th century BC, shows great skill and craftsmanship in its sophisticated animal mask design or taotie.

GALLERY GUIDE
The calligraphy and painting exhibits are changed frequently for their own protection. As well as the permanent collections, the museum often shows exhibits from other major museums around the world.

STAR SIGHTS

★ *Sancai* pottery figures

★ Landscape paintings

★ Shang bronzes

The Sculpture Gallery holds a collection of ancient and mainly religious pieces.

Exploring the Shanghai Museum

Eleven galleries display a selection of the museum's permanent collection and three others are used to show temporary exhibitions from around the world. The scope and quality of the exhibits mean that one visit may not be enough for the interested visitor. The displays and interpretation are probably the best in China and, as such, should be savored. There's also an excellent shop within the museum with one of the best selections of books on China that you are likely to find anywhere.

pieces date back as far as the Tang dynasty (618–907). Despite the concrete and bedlam of modern Shanghai just outside, here's a reminder of the Chinese delight in nature and wildlife that goes back centuries. Waterfalls plunge down mountains topped with gnarled pines and inhabited by pheasants and other wild birds. Notable treasures include the only surviving original painting by Sun Wei of the Tang dynasty, showing seven hermits disporting themselves in a bamboo forest.

Bronze *ding* (food vessel), mid Western Zhou (10th century BC)

BRONZES

China's Bronze Age (18th to 3rd century BC) is represented by an extraordinary collection of wine vessels, three-legged *ding* (cooking vessels), and bells, all cast in bronze using ceramic moulds. Particularly attractive are the *zun* wine vessels, such as one in the shape of a sturdy ox, 2,500 years old, complete with horns and nose-ring and covered in incised decoration. The intricacy of the metalwork – quite impractical for everyday items – is evidence that these beautiful works of art were used for ritual offerings of food and wine, and that the society that created them was possessed of a sophisticated level of technology. It would also have taken powerful rulers, great organization, and vast amounts of manpower to mine, transport, and refine such large amounts of metal ore and then create these wonderful pieces, setting a precedent for Chinese societies to come.

SCULPTURE

Buddhism's arrival in China and its gradual absorption into the mainstream is reflected in over 120 pieces of bronze, wood, stone, and pottery dating from around 475 BC to AD 1644, the end of the Ming dynasty. Gradually, the high-cheekboned slender figures of a North Indian and Central Asian aesthetic take on the plumper, moon-faced shapes of the Chinese. There are also legions of tomb figurines from different dynasties, and fine examples of the polychrome equestrian figures that characterize sculpture during the Tang dynasty period.

Gilt bronze Buddha

PAINTING

A lighting system in each display cabinet that only comes on as visitors approach helps to protect the 120 delicate exhibits on display in the museum's third-floor painting gallery. Some of the

CALLIGRAPHY

Calligraphy in China is said to have already atttained maturity by the time of the Eastern Zhou dynasty (770–221 BC). However, the art's greatest exponent is often said to be Wang Xizhi (c. AD 303–361), who is known as the "Sage of Calligraphy". Few Chinese these days can understand much of the classical script of these scrolls, and perhaps the foreign visitor's appreciation of their beauty is enhanced because it is undistracted by any flashes of meaning, allowing concentration on the shapes alone. Stylistic differences can be identified even by the non-specialist, such as the difference between the running style and the more flamboyant cursive style, while the characters adorning the seals seem from another language altogether.

Hermits, a hand scroll by Sun Wei, Tang dynasty (AD 618–907)

Polychrome glazed pottery, Tang dynasty (AD 618–907)

CERAMICS

The museum is particularly proud of its display of 500 pieces from all over China, which together illustrate 8,000 years of ceramic production. Some are incredibly rare and were deemed too delicate for public presentation until the current modern facility was built. It is visibly a long journey from the clumsy solidity of some of the early pots displayed here to the *famille verte* of the Qing Kangxi emperor's era, delicately painted with traditional scenes, and the *famille rose* of his successors with their flowery over-decoration and rococo elements designed to pander to the Orientalism of European markets. Better than either is the fine, white-glaze porcelain of the Jin dynasty. Also notable are the delicate celadon hues of Song dynasty wares and the charm of the underglaze paintings of fish and flowers in blue or red of the Ming dynasty. This one gallery alone makes a visit to Shanghai worthwhile.

Porcelain vase of Jingdezhen origin

JADE

The precious substance most closely linked with China, at least by foreigners, is jade, a word the Chinese use to describe a variety of different stones of various hues, but principally the bluish green nephrite and jadeite. Never particularly abundant in China, stocks are now largely exhausted. Some of the jade objects here are described as dating back to the 51st century BC. These early examples were symbols of status, as the dense stone requires a great deal of effort to shape. In the late Zhou period, around 2,500 years ago, jade's symbolic value was augmented by an appreciation of its beauty. The stone began to be used for ornaments such as wine cups and brooches. The museum's collection includes examples carved into dragons, turtles, and tigers of marvellous delicacy.

FURNITURE

Up on the topmost floor of the museum is the furniture gallery, where Ming-dynasty constructions of elegant simplicity sit alongside over-elaborately decorated later Qing pieces. Should any of these items take your fancy, most can be found copied in "antique" furniture stores in both Shanghai and Beijing. Two beautiful brick-floored rooms contain recreations of the layouts of studies of both eras. Perhaps best of all are the miniature wooden furniture sets, together with a procession of wooden figurines, retrieved from Ming tombs.

SEALS

Seals, or chops, as they are also known, remain essential when important documents are signed, even in modern China. They are easily purchased, coming in straightforward plastic and rubber forms. But those in the museum's collection of more than 500 include miniature works of art in ivory, jade, and soapstone. Some are in the shapes of animals or mythical creatures, and some are carved with tiny landscapes. This is rightly regarded as the best such collection in China, although anyone visiting Hangzhou may also want to visit the Museum of the Seal Engravers Society (see p153).

OTHER DISPLAYS

Other displays include pottery, costume, embroidery, and lacquerware from a few of the 55 or so ethnic minorities that make up the peoples of China. Also as one of the first countries to systematically use coins and then notes there's an extensive collection of these items from throughout China's history.

Sandalwood Qing-dynasty throne chair with carved cloud and dragon design

Yu Gardens and Bazaar ❺
豫园

**Chinese
lion statue**

The old-style buildings of the Yu Gardens bazaar are not really old, but the fanciful roofs are nevertheless very appealing. The shops here peddle everything from tourist souvenirs to traditional medicines and, despite inflated prices, the area is incredibly popular. It is best to arrive early and go straight to the beautiful and relatively peaceful Ming-dynasty Yu Gardens (Yu Yuan). A dumpling lunch, before the restaurants get too busy, will set you up for a hectic afternoon of shopping and haggling, followed by a cup of tea in the quaint Huxinting teahouse.

Yu Gardens Bazaar, modern shops in old-fashioned buildings

Restaurants surround the lake – you can see the dumplings being made in the morning.

Yu Gardens Bazaar
Despite being a bit of a tourist trap, there is plenty of fun to be had wandering among the stalls and haggling over prices.

Street performers
Every now and then a colorful troupe of performers appears bearing young children on top of poles to entertain the thronging crowds.

**Shanghai Old Street
(Fangbang Road) and an
entrance to the Bazaar**

★ City God Temple
Dating back to the Ming era, the temple once housed the patron god of Shanghai and encompassed an area as large as the bazaar. Now this small restored temple is very popular with tourists.

STAR SIGHTS

★ City God Temple

★ Huxinting Teahouse

★ Huge rockery,
Yu Gardens

For hotels and restaurants in Shanghai see pp182–7 and pp202–7

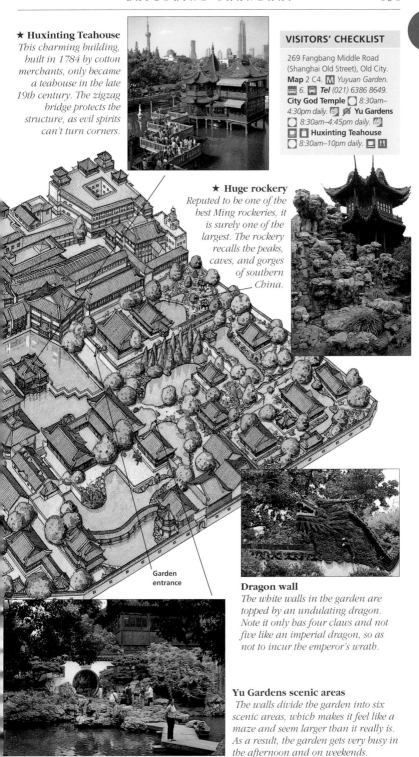

★ **Huxinting Teahouse**
This charming building, built in 1784 by cotton merchants, only became a teahouse in the late 19th century. The zigzag bridge protects the structure, as evil spirits can't turn corners.

VISITORS' CHECKLIST

269 Fangbang Middle Road (Shanghai Old Street), Old City. **Map** 2 C4. Ⓜ *Yuyuan Garden.* 🚍 6. 🚗 *Tel* (021) 6386 8649. **City God Temple** ☐ 8:30am– 4:30pm daily. 📷 📷 **Yu Gardens** ☐ 8:30am–4:45pm daily. 📷 🅿 🚻 **Huxinting Teahouse** ☐ 8:30am–10pm daily. 🖥 🍴

★ **Huge rockery**
Reputed to be one of the best Ming rockeries, it is surely one of the largest. The rockery recalls the peaks, caves, and gorges of southern China.

Garden
entrance

Dragon wall
The white walls in the garden are topped by an undulating dragon. Note it only has four claws and not five like an imperial dragon, so as not to incur the emperor's wrath.

Yu Gardens scenic areas
The walls divide the garden into six scenic areas, which makes it feel like a maze and seem larger than it really is. As a result, the garden gets very busy in the afternoon and on weekends.

Entrance, First National Congress of the Chinese Community Party

Site of the First National Congress of the Chinese Communist Party ❻
中共一大会址纪念馆

374 Huangpi South Road. **Map** 2 A4. Ⓜ *Huangpi South Road.* ⭕ *9am–4pm.* 🏛

This house in the French Concession was the venue for a historic meeting, where representatives of China's communist cells met to form a national party on July 23, 1921. Officially, there were 12 participants including Mao Zedong, but it is believed that many others also attended. The police discovered the meeting and the delegates were forced to escape to a boat on Lake Nan, in Zhejiang. The house has a reconstruction of the meeting, with the original chairs and teacups used by the delegates. The exhibition hall tells the history of the Chinese Communist Party.

Fuxing Park ❼
复兴公园

Fuxing Middle Road. **Map** 1 F4. Ⓜ *Xintiandi.* **Sun Yat Sen Memorial Residence** 7 Xingshan Road. *Tel (021) 6372 6083.* ⭕ *6am–6pm daily.* 🏛 **Zhou Enlai's Former Residence** 73 Sinan Road. ⭕ *9am–4pm daily.* 🏛

The French bought this private garden, located in the French Concession, in 1908. It was

known then as the "French Park," and has elements of a formal Parisian *jardin*, with meandering paths flanked by cherry trees. It was renamed Fuxing, meaning "revival," in 1949.

Close by on Xiangshan Road is the **Sun Yat Sen Memorial Residence**, a typical Shanghai villa where the leader and his wife, Soong Qingling, lived between 1918 and 1924. The interior is just as it was in Sun's time, with many of his personal items such as his gramophone and books. South of the park, 73 Rue Massenet (now Sinan Road) was the **Former Residence of Zhou Enlai**, who lived here when he was head of the city's Communist Party in the 1940s. It is another excellent example of a European-style Shanghai villa.

Statue of Sun Yat Sen, Sun Yat Sen Memorial

French Concession ❽
法国花园

Ⓜ *Shaanxi South Road.* **Map** 1 E4.

The former French Concession, stretching from the western edge of the Old City to Avenue Haig (Huashan Road), comprises boulevards, shops, and cafés, and its residents

were mainly White Russians and Chinese. It had its own electrical system, judiciary, and police force, whose highest ranking officer "Pockmarked Huang," was the leader of the infamous Green Gang which controlled the opium trade.

Today, the Concession is centered on **Huaihai Road** – a vibrant street lined with boutiques, candy stores, hair salons, and bars – and the charming **Jinjiang Hotel** on Maoming Road. The hotel's compound includes the Grosvenor Residence, pre-war Shanghai's most exclusive property. The VIP Club, in the hotel's old wing, retains its 1920s architecture. The adjacent street, Maoming Road, is currently under redevelopment. Another interesting building is the **Ruijin Guesthouse** at the corner of Fuxing Middle Road and Shaanxi South Road. This Tudor-style manor is now an inn set in a quiet compound. **The Children's Palace** at the western end of Yan'an Road was part of an early 1920s estate, and is now a children's arts center. The tourist office arranges tours to watch its singing and dancing shows.

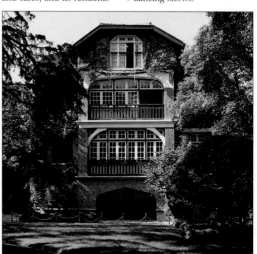

The European-style villa that was Zhou Enlai's former residence

The Huangpu River

The Huangpu River is a mere 68 miles (110 km) in length from its source, Dianshan Lake, to its junction with the Yangzi River, 17 miles (28 km) downstream from Shanghai. As a spectacle, however, it is fascinating and there is much for the eye to take in, from the majestic but elderly waterfront at the Bund, and burgeoning modern metropolis on Pudong,

Cargo ships, Huangpu River

to the bustling docks that line the Huangpu all the way to the mouth of the Yangzi. The boat departs from the wharves on the Bund between Nanjing Road and Yan'an Road (see pp120–21). The one-hour trip takes visitors as far as the Yangpu Bridge, but there is also the longer three-and-a-half hour trip, all the way to the Yangzi River.

The Yangzi River ⑦
The color of the water changes markedly here, as the oily Huangpu meets the muddy and turbulent Yangzi. A lighthouse marks the confluence of the two.

Shanghai Docks ④
The Shanghainese proudly claim that nearly a third of all China's international trade enters via the perennially busy Huangpu river.

Wusong Fort ⑥
The site of a decisive battle against the British in 1842, it consisted of a crescent-shaped fort with ten imported cannons.

Yangpu Bridge ③
Built in 1993, this is one of the world's longest cable-stay bridges – cables are anchored to each tower.

Gongqing Forest Park ⑤
This large and pleasantly landscaped park was reclaimed from marshland and is popular with the Shanghainese on weekends.

Huangpu Park ②
At the northern tip of the Bund, this park is home to the Monument to the People's Heroes.

Huangpu River

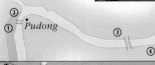

0 km		6
0 miles		3

Pudong

TIPS BOX

Length: 37 miles (60 km).
One-hour trip: 10 miles (16 km).
Boat trips: The boats vary in size and facilities, so make sure you know what you are getting. The more expensive ones do food and even entertainment of sorts.
Times: 9am, 2pm, 7pm Mon–Fri, 11am, 3:30pm, 8pm Sat & Sun. The one-hour trips leave more frequently (times can vary).

The Bund ①
The best way to enjoy the Bund's grandiose skyline is from a boat, which also gives the visitor a view of the city that would have greeted all expatriates on their arrival here before 1949.

Façade of the Soviet-style Shanghai Exhibition Center

Shanghai Exhibition Center ❾
上海展览中心

1000 Yan'an Middle Road. **Map** 1 E3. **Tel** (021) 2216 2216. Ⓜ Jing'an Temple. ◯ 8am–5pm daily.

The enormous Shanghai Exhibition Center is one of the few reminders of the influence the Soviet Union once had in Shanghai. Built in 1954, it was known as the Palace of Sino-Soviet Friendship, and was designed as a place for exhibiting China's technological and agricultural advances since the founding of the People's Republic in 1949. Ironically, the building stands on the site of the estate of millionaire Silas Hardoon – Shanghai's biggest capitalist in the 1920s. The Center is worth seeing for its grimly florid Soviet-style architecture. It has an impressively ornate entrance, with columns decorated with red stars, and a gilded spire. Today, it is a gigantic mall, filled with shops selling furniture and souvenirs.

Nearby on Xinle Road, in the former French Concession, is the old **Russian Orthodox Church** with its distinctive onion-shaped domes. It served thousands of refugees from the Russian Revolution in 1917. The area around Julu Road and Changle Road,

nearby, has a number of interesting Art Deco and early 20th-century villas and mansions constructed by Shanghai's wealthy residents.

Jing'an Temple ❿
静安寺

1686 Nanjing West Road (near Huashan Road). **Map** 1 D3. Ⓜ Jing'an Temple. ◯ 7:30am–5pm daily.

Located opposite the attractive Jing'an Park, which contains the old Bubbling Well Cemetery, Jing'an Temple (Temple of Tranquility) is one of the city's most revered places for ancestor worship. Originally founded in the Three Kingdoms Period, the current structure dates to 2007 when the temple was completely rebuilt. In the 1930s, it was Shanghai's wealthiest Buddhist temple, headed by the influencial abbot Khi Vehdu, who was also a gangster with a harem of concubines and White Russian bodyguards. It is said **Wall detail, Jade** that his bodyguards **Buddha Temple** went with him everywhere, carrying bulletproof briefcases as shields in the event of an attack. The temple was closed during the Cultural Revolution, but has reopened to become one of the best examples of an active Buddhist shrine in the city. It is a popular place to offer coins and pray for financial success.

Jade Buddha Temple ⓫
玉佛寺

170 Anyuan Road. **Map** 1 D1. **Tel** (021) 6266 3668. Ⓜ Hanzhong Road then taxi. ◯ 8am–4:30pm daily.

The most famous of Shanghai's temples, Yufo Si lies in the northwest part of the city. It was built in 1882 to enshrine two beautiful jade Buddha statues that were brought from Burma by the abbot Wei Ken. The temple was originally located elsewhere, but shifted here in 1918, after a fire damaged the earlier structure. After being closed for almost 30 years, it reopened in 1980, and today has some 100 monks. Built in the southern Song-dynasty style, it has sharply curved eaves and figurines on the roof. Its three main halls are connected by two courts. The first hall is the **Heavenly King Hall**, where the four Heavenly Kings line the walls. The **Grand Hall of Magnificence** houses three incarnations of the Buddha, while the **Jade Buddha Chamber** contains the first jade statue – that of a large reclining Buddha. The finer of the two statues, however, lies upstairs. Carved from a single piece of jade, this jewel-encrusted seated Buddha is exquisite. Visitors should note that photography is forbidden here.

Golden Buddhas in the Jade Buddha Temple

Old Shanghai

Until 1842 Shanghai was a minor Chinese river port, worthy of a protective rampart but otherwise undistinguished. In that year the Chinese government capitulated to western demands for trade concessions resulting in a number of ports along China's eastern seaboard, including Shanghai, becoming essentially European outposts. Their key feature was that of extra-territoriality – foreign residents were answerable only to the laws of their own country. Thus the

Calendar girls, 1930s

Americans, British, and French had their own "concessions" – exclusive areas within the city with their own police forces and judiciary – a situation that attracted not only entrepreneurs, but refugees, criminals, and revolutionaries. This mix was a potent one and Shanghai's reputation for glamor and excess derives from the politically combustible period between the two world wars. It all came to an end in the 1940s when foreigners gave up their rights in the face of growing Chinese opposition.

The Bund, *also known as Zhongshan East No. 1 Road, was the wide thoroughfare running along Huangpu River. This was where all the major players in Shanghai commerce built their offices and created the distinctively grandiose skyline that still greets the river-going traveler today.*

The Great World *was a quintessential Shanghai creation, a mixture of freakishness, fashion, sex, and theater under one roof, owned by the gangster Pockmarked Huang.*

The Race Course, *located in the area of today's People's Park, was an indispensable part of expatriate life, where, just as in the numerous clubs and institutions for non-Chinese, expats were able to socialize as if they were at home.*

Opium, trafficked commercially *with claims for free-trade by British companies like Jardine Matheson, was the foundation of Shanghai's prosperity and dens dotted the city. When the mercantile veneer was jettisoned, opium became the currency of Shanghai's gangster underworld.*

Nanking Road, *as it was then known, was, and still is, Shanghai's retail hub. Divided in two parts (the western end then known as Bubbling Well Road), it was home to China's first department stores, where Chinese and expatriates mixed on an equal footing.*

Shanghai Ocean Aquarium

Bund Sightseeing Tunnel ⑫
外滩观光隧道

The Bund at Beijing East Road, and near the foot of the Oriental Pearl TV Tower in Pudong. **Map** 3 D2. **Tel** (021) 5888 6000. Ⓜ *Nanjing West Road (Bund) or Lujiazui (Pudong).* ◯ *8am–10:30pm daily (8am–10pm winter).* 📷

Part high-tech, computer-controlled subway ride, part low-tech, fairground haunted house, and wholly ridiculous, the oddly named Sightseeing Tunnel offers a brief but surreal 2,132-ft (650-m) jaunt beneath the Huangpu river. Passenger cars zip down a tunnel assailed en route by a neon and laser light show,

The psychedelic experience that is the Bund Sightseeing Tunnel

with inflatable figures and an accompanying soundtrack. Official government promotional materials imaginatively describe the experience as *pavonine* (peacock-like). You may just consider it kitsch. However, it is a very Shanghai experience and something that should be done at least once. For the return journey, consider taking the ferry: at ¥2 it costs a fifteenth of the fare on the Sightseeing Tunnel and it delivers rather better sightseeing opportunities.

Oriental Pearl TV Tower ⑬
东方明珠广播电视塔

1 Century Avenue. **Map** 3 D2. **Tel** (021) 5879 1888. Ⓜ *Lujiazui.* 🚌🚇 ◯ *Tower and Shanghai History Museum 8am–9pm daily.* 📷🍴🖥

One of the first modern towers to rise above the rubble of the peasant homes that once fringed the river on the Pudong side. When it was completed in 1994 the 1,500-ft (457-m) Oriental Pearl instantly became China's most recognizable modern icon. Despite all the high-rises that have gone up since, it is still one of the most striking buildings in Shanghai. It houses an assortment of entertainments, including

viewing platforms at various heights, rotating restaurants, and, in the basement, the **Shanghai History Museum**. This museum uses ingenious technology to conjure up recreations of long-vanished city life. Models of early Shanghai street scenes ring with the traditional cries of vendors, and projected figures re-enact episodes of Shanghai domestic life. The museum also displays the original bronze lions made to guard the Shanghai Pudong Development Bank *(see p122)* – the pair on the Bund are replicas.

Shanghai Ocean Aquarium ⑭
上海海洋水族馆

1388 Lujiazui Ring Road, east of the Oriental Pearl TV Tower. **Map** 3 E2. **Tel** (021) 5877 9988. Ⓜ *Lujiazui.* 🚌 ◯ *9am–6pm daily.* 📷🍴🖥📷 **www**.sh-aquarium.com

Rated by enthusiasts as one of the best in the world, this vast, US$55 million aquarium features more than 10,000 temperate and tropical fish representing more than 300 species, as well as turtles and other sea creatures. It boasts 480 feet (150 m) or so of underwater, clear viewing tunnels that even include a submarine escalator to bring visitors up close to the marine life. There are also careful recreations of different aquatic environments from around the world including Antarctica, Africa, and the Amazon, as well as displays highlighting the endangered aquatic species native to China. Feeding times take place mid-morning and mid-afternoon.

IFC Tower ⑮
上海国金中心

8 Century Avenue. **Map** 3 E3. **Tel** (021) 2020 7000. Ⓜ *Lujiazui.* **www**.shanghaiifc.com.cn

The glassy, 58-story Shanghai IFC Tower – the sibling of the two IFC towers in central Hong Kong – makes an impressive mark on the Pudong skyline. Opened in 2010, the lower floors comprise a glitzy mall featuring 180 leading name retailers, including several luxury flagship stores, an Apple store, and a vast basement supermarket. There are also several restaurants and a six-screen cinema. The mall connects directly to subway lines 2 and 14. On the upper floors of the tower is the luxury 285-room Ritz-Carlton Shanghai, Pudong hotel. On the hotel's 58th floor is Flair, an al fresco bar and restaurant with a terrace offering dramatic views.

Jinmao Tower ⑯
金茂大厦

88 Century Avenue. **Map** 3 E3. **Tel** (021) 5047 6688. Ⓜ *Lujiazui.* 🚇 🚌 ◯ *8:30am–9pm daily (observation deck).* 🈂 🍴 www.jinmao88.com

American architects Skidmore, Owings & Merrill get credit for one of the finest towers in Pudong, the US$540 million, 88-story, 1,379-ft (421-m) Jinmao Tower. For a time it was the tallest building in China. It has a basement food court, 42 floors of offices, and the luxurious Grand Hyatt hotel between the 53rd and 87th floors. This is topped by an 88th-floor enclosed viewing gallery.

The tower is known as the "Golden Prosperity Building" and has a silvery exterior, wrapped with rails, which narrows in steps, pagoda-like, to a sharp point. According to the architects, the building is

The skyscraping, silvery, pagoda-like form of the Jinmao Tower

---

THE MAGLEV TRAIN

This is, for the moment at least, the fastest you'll ever travel without flying. The German-built "magnetically levitated" train travels the roughly 18.6 miles (30 km) from Long Yang Road metro station in Shanghai's eastern suburbs to Pudong Airport in under eight minutes, briefly reaching a speed in

A super-fast Maglev train slows as it approaches the terminus

excess of 267 mph (430 kph) with considerable smoothness and limited noise. A counter in each carriage tells you how fast you are actually going. However, lower than expected passenger numbers due to high ticket prices, the rather limited service, and the inconvenient location of the Shanghai terminus (you still need a taxi to get into the city) mean that the trains travel half-empty most of the time.

---

a pen, the curved roof of the attached exhibition hall a book, and the Huangpu itself the ink. Express elevators to the viewing gallery or the Sky Lounge, a more comfortable alternative to the observation deck, are reached via the basement, but equally breathtaking is the view up the 33-story interior atrium from the Grand Hyatt's 56th-floor reception.

Shanghai World Financial Center ⑰
上海环球金融中心

100 Century Avenue. **Map** 3 E3. **Tel** (4001) 100 555. Ⓜ *Lujiazui or Dongchang Road.* 🚇 🚌 ◯ *Observatory 8am–11pm daily.* 🈂 🍴 🖥 www.swfc-observatory.com

Built by Japan's Mori Corporation and opened in 2008, the 101-story, 1,614-ft (492-m) Shanghai World Financial Center was designed by architects Kohn Pederson Fox, and is China's tallest building. The signature feature of the tower for most visitors – which some say resembles a standing bottle-opener owing to the aperture at its peak – is the Skywalk 100, an 180-ft (55-m) long glass corridor observatory which soars 1,555 ft (474 m) above the ground, providing breathtaking views of the Huang Pu River and downtown Shanghai below.

There is another observatory platform on the 97th floor, which features a retractable roof. It is also home to the world's highest hotel, Park Hyatt Shanghai.

Century Park ⑱
世纪广场

Century Avenue and Yanggao Middle Road intersection. **Tel** (021) 6892 2000. Ⓜ *Shanghai Science and Technology Museum.* 🚌 **Science and Technology Museum** ◯ *9am–5pm Tue–Sun (last ticket sold at 4:30pm).* 🈂

Shanghai's largest square is dominated by a giant sculpture called "Oriental Light" that features an arrow piercing a disk that looks a bit like a sundial; it is meant to signify time. The square is graced by flower beds spelling out the characters of its name – Shiji Guangchang, in Chinese – as well as assorted sculpture and water features. It is flanked by local government buildings, the striking **Oriental Arts Center**, designed in the form of a blooming magnolia (the city flower of Shanghai), and the **Science and Technology Museum**. The latter is well-intentioned but the lack of clear interpretation or a coherent purpose to the museum renders most exhibits baffling. The museum also has two IMAX cinemas and an IWERKS 4-D theater.

Brightly colored boats alongside the lake pier at Hongkou Park (Lu Xun Park)

Hongkou Park ⑲
虹口公园

146 East Jiangwan Road.
Ⓜ *Hongkou.* ⬜ *daily.* 🅿

To the north of Suzhou Creek and Waibaidu Bridge lies the Japanese section of the former International Settlement, which once had a Zen temple, a Japanese school, and specialist Japanese shops. The area's most interesting spot is Hongkou Park, which is a pleasant place to pass the time and watch the Chinese taking boat rides on the lake, playing chess, practising *tai ji quan* or simply relaxing. It is also known as Lu Xun Park due to its strong associations with the great Chinese novelist Lu Xun (1881–1936), who lived nearby. His most famous work is *The True Story of Ah Q*, which lampooned the Chinese national character. Lu Xun was also an early proponent of the *baihua* or plain speech movement, which championed the simplification of the Chinese script and the use of spoken Chinese in literature. **Lu Xun's Tomb**, where his ashes were interred in 1956 to mark the 20th anniversary of his death, is also in the park. To the right of the park's main entrance lies a **Memorial Hall** dedicated to the novelist, where visitors can view early editions of his work and his correspondence with various intellectuals including George Bernard Shaw. Just south of

Statue, Lu Xun's Tomb

Hongkou Park is **Lu Xun's Former Residence**, where the novelist spent the last three years of his life at a house on Shanyin Road. It is an interesting example of a typical 1930s Japanese-style residence, but is perhaps even more sparsely furnished than other houses of the time. Lu Xun's rattan chairs and writing desk are also on display.

🏛 Lu Xun's Former Residence
9 Dalu Xincun, Shanyin Rd.
⬜ 9am–4pm daily. 🅿

Soong Qingling's Former Residence ⑳
宋庆龄故居

1843 Huaihai Middle Road.
Ⓜ *Hengshan Road.* **Tel** *(021) 6474 7183.* ⬜ *9am–4:30pm daily.* 🅿

At the southwestern edge of the city is the fine villa that was the residence of Soong Qingling, wife of the

revolutionary leader Dr. Sun Yat Sen. All the Song siblings – three sisters and a brother – came to wield a lot of influence in China. Of the three sisters, Song Meiling married Chiang Kai Shek, the head of the Nationalist Republic of China from 1928 to 1949; Ailing married H.H. Kung, the director of the Bank of China, and Soong Qingling married Sun Yat Sen. Her brother, known as T.V. Song, became Chiang Kai Shek's finance minister. Soong Qingling stayed in China once the Communists took over and became an honorary Communist heroine. She lived in Shanghai after her husband's death, initially in the house they had shared in the former French Concession *(see p132)*, before moving to this villa. She died in Beijing in 1981.

The house is a charming example of a mid-20th-century Shanghai villa. It has some wonderful wood paneling and lacquerwork. Her limousines are still parked in the garage, and some of her personal items are also displayed.

Soong Qingling's Former Residence – a charming early 20th-century villa

Xujiahui Catholic Cathedral ㉑
徐家汇堂

158 Puxi Road. *Tel* (021) 6438 2595.
Ⓜ *Xujiahui.* ◯ *1pm–4pm Sat, Sun.*

The red-brick Gothic Cathedral of St. Ignatius that stands at a southwestern corner of Shanghai has long been associated with foreign nationals. The land originally belonged to a member of the Xu clan, Xu Guangqi (1562–1633), who was converted to Catholicism by Matteo Ricci. Upon his death, Xu left land to the Jesuits for the building of a church, seminary, and observatory. The cathedral, with its 164-ft (50-m) twin towers, was built in 1906. It was partly destroyed during the Cultural Revolution, but was rebuilt, and now holds Sunday services. The interior is an interesting mix of traditional Catholic decoration and Chinese embellishment. Xu Guangqi is buried nearby in Nandan Park.

Longhua Cemetery of Martyrs ㉒
龙华烈士陵园

2887 Longhua Road. Ⓜ *Shanghai Stadium then taxi. Tel* (021) 6468 5995. 🚌 *No. 41.* ◯ *6am–4:30pm daily.* 🎟 **Longhua Temple** 2853 Longhua Road. ◯ *7am–4:30pm daily.* 🎟

This site honors those who died for the communist cause before the People's Republic was established in 1949. At the center is a Memorial Hall, while many commemorative sculptures dot the park. The cemetery is situated on the site of the Nationalist Party's execution ground, where hundreds of Communists were put to death by Chiang Kai Shek.
Nearby is **Longhua Temple** and an octagonal pagoda. A temple has existed on this site since AD 687, and a pagoda since AD 238–251. The foundations of the current pagoda, with its upturned eaves, date to AD 977, while the temple buildings were built during the late Qing era. The temple has several halls and

Commemorative statue at the Longhua Cemetery of Martyrs

is very active. The surrounding area is pretty in spring, when the peach trees are in bloom.

World Expo Site (2010) ㉓
中国2010年上海世博会官方网站

Pudong. Ⓜ *Shibo Ave & Lupu Bridge.*

Spanning the banks of the Haungpu River on each side of the Lupu Bridge, the 2010 World Expo site hosted over 200 nations with spectacular pavilions showcasing culture, technology, gastronomy, and art. The site reopened as the Shanghai Convention Center in 2011 but a handful of the original venues remain, including the China Pavillion and the Expo Performance Center, rebranded as the Mercedes Benz Arena.
In addition, the Shanghai Art Museum, renamed the China Art Museum, has relocated here. The former Urban Future Pavilion has been converted to the state-owned Shanghai Museum of Contemporary Art.

She Shan ㉔
佘山

22 miles (35 km) SW of Shanghai. Ⓜ *She Shan.* 🚌 *from Wenhua Guangchang bus stop or Xi Qu bus station in Shanghai.*

She Hill or She Shan is a mere 328 ft (100 m) high, and is surmounted by a grand, red-brick Catholic church, **Our Lady of China**. In the 1850s, European missionaries built a chapel here. Later, a bishop took refuge in the area and vowed to build a

church. The basilica was built between 1925 and 1935. Services, often in Latin, take place on Christian holidays and particularly in May, when pilgrims stream here. The route to the top represents the Via Dolorosa (The Way of Suffering), the road that Christ took to his crucifixion. It is a pleasant walk past bamboo groves, but there is a cable car that goes to the summit. The hill also has an ancient observatory that houses an earthquake-monitoring device of a jar with dragon heads around the outside and a pendulum inside. Each dragon has a steel ball in its mouth. When an earthquake occurred, the pendulum would swing, knock a dragon, causing its mouth to open and a ball to drop out and thereby point out the quake's direction.

Exterior of the grand She Shan church, Our Lady of China

FARTHER AFIELD

Despite Shanghai's vast sprawl, it is not too difficult to escape to greener and more pleasant spots. The spongy landscape of the surrounding region is laced with canals and dotted with picturesque towns and villages, each claiming to be the "Venice of China." The best known and largest of these canal towns is Suzhou, which is a 30-minute "bullet" train ride from Shanghai. Once a favored abode of retired scholars and officials, it combines the attractions of boat rides and ornamental gardens with centuries of history. Suzhou was also once a center for the production of one of China's most famous exports – silk. The trio of nearby, smaller canal towns of Tongli, Wuxi, and Zhouzhuang all boast pleasant waterways as well. The towns are fast developing but still continue to retain their charm.

Hangzhou, the delight of poets for centuries, perhaps now lacks the peace they once associated with it, and even boasts a sprinkling of noteworthy modern buildings, not to mention showrooms for the likes of Ferrari sports cars. But the real joy of the poets was around the West Lake, where narrow causeways still provide today's visitor with tranquility. And there is always the option of escape onto the water – with a few sweeps of the oars of a hired boatman, the roar of traffic becomes no more than a gentle murmur.

SIGHTS AT A GLANCE

Towns and Cities
Hangzhou pp150–51 ❻
Suzhou pp144–5 ❺
Tongli ❶
Wuxi ❸
Zhouzhang ❷

Lakes and Areas of Natural Beauty
Tai Hu ❹

KEY

	City limits
	International airport
☒	Domestic airport
═	National highway
▬	Major road
═	Minor road
—	Railroad
- -	Shanghai Province border

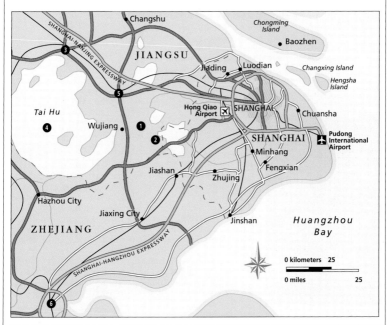

◁ **Waterside pavilion in the Humble Administrator's Garden, Suzhou**

Houses fronting canals in Zhouzhuang's old town

Tongli ❶
同里

16 miles (25 km) SE of Suzhou.
🚶 45,000. 🚌

A pretty little water town
typical of the region, Tongli
gives visitors a good idea of
what Suzhou must have been
like in its heyday. All its
houses open out on to a
network of canals that are
spanned by dozens of stone
bridges and are busy with
transportation and trading
boats. Some of its buildings
are open to the public, such
as **Jiayin Hall**, the former
home of Liu Yazi, an early
20th-century actor renowned
for his rather bizarre
collection of gauze caps. The
other interesting sight is **Tuisi
Yuan**, a classical garden dating
from the late Qing period.

♣ **Tuisi Yuan**
🕐 7:45am–5:30pm daily. 🈺

Sightseeing boats on one of Tongli's
numerous canals

Zhouzhuang ❷
周庄

12 miles (20 km) W of Shanghai.
🚶 32,000. 🚌 Shanghai, Suzhou.
🚤 to Tongli. **Old Town** tickets from
Quangong Road.

A small town on the Jinghang
Canal, which links Suzhou
and Shanghai, Zhouzhuang
was once a flourishing port,
specializing in silk, pottery,
and grain. It attracted scholars
and officials who built fine
bridges and houses between
the Yuan and Qing eras. The
charming **Old Town** can be
explored on foot or via a boat
tour on the canals. Among the
sights are the Ming-era Hall
of Zhang Residence with 70
rooms, and the Hall of Shen's
Residence, with 100 rooms
connected to the main hall.
The Chengxu Temple, located
near the museum, is a Song-
dynasty Daoist shrine.

Wuxi ❸
无锡

25 miles (40 km) NW of Suzhou.
🚶 4,320,000. 🚌 🚇 🚤 services
to Hangzhou & Suzhou. 🛈 88
Chezhan Road. **Tel** (0510) 401 6081.

The highlights of a trip to
Wuxi are the scenic Tai Hu
(Lake Tai) and the Grand
Canal. According to legend,
the town was established
3,500 years ago as the capital
of the Wu Kingdom and was
a center for the production of
tin. When the mines ran dry
(Wuxi means "without tin"),
the capital moved west, but
Wuxi remained significant

due to its location on the
Grand Canal. **Xihui Park** in the
west of town was established
in 1958, and houses the
Jichang Yuan garden. At the
park's entrance, a path leads
to the Dragon Light Pagoda
on top of Xi Shan. A cable car
connects Xi Shan to nearby
Hui Shan. The **Wuxi Museum**
has exhibits dating back 6,000
years, and includes some
Qing-dynasty cannons.

♣ **Xihui Park**
Huihe Road. 🕐 6am–6pm daily. 🈺

🏛 **Wuxi Museum**
71 Huihe Road. 🕐 9am–4pm daily. 🈺

The scenic cable car ride, Xihui
Park, Wuxi

Tai Hu ❹
太湖

3 miles (5 km) SW of Wuxi.

One of China's largest lakes,
Tai Hu is famous for its rocks,
an indispensable feature of a
traditional garden (see pp28–
9). The lake's northern shores
are fringed with scenic spots
including **Mei Yuan** (Plum
Garden), spectacular in spring
when its 4,000 fruit trees
blossom. **Yuantou Zhu** (Turtle
Head Promontory) is a
favorite with the Chinese,
with tea houses and pretty
lake views. Nearby, **Sanshan
Island** is a former bandit's
haunt with temples and tall
Buddha statues. However,
none is as tall as the 289-ft
(88-m) Lingshan Buddha on
Ma Shan peninsula, a short
bus ride from the other sights.
The area also has a handful
of lakeside theme parks.

♣ **Mei Yuan & Yuantou Zhu**
🕐 7am–5pm daily. 🈺

The Grand Canal

Boat for canal cruises

The Grand Canal, started in 486 BC, was built in sections over the next one thousand years, with the aim of linking the Yangzi with the Yellow River, and one capital with another. It remains the world's largest man-made waterway. The earliest northern section was built for military reasons but large-scale construction began in the 7th century under the Sui Wendi emperor, involving over 5 million conscripted males aged between 15 and 55, supervised by a vast and brutal police force. Linking the comparatively populous north with the southern rice-producing region, it reached Beijing only in the 13th century. In the early 20th century, a combination of the altered course of the fickle Yellow River and the rise of the railways saw its gradual demise.

This map *shows the route of the 1,112-mile (1,900-km) canal from Beijing to Hangzhou. Crossing the traditional battlefields between north and south, the canal supplied food throughout the empire. The hilly terrain led to the first recorded use of double locks in AD 984.*

KEY

━ Grand Canal

The Sui Yang Di emperor *is said to have celebrated the completion of his work by touring the canal with a flotilla of dragon boats hauled by the empire's most beautiful women.*

Tourist boats *are now the only way to enjoy a journey on the canal as road and rail transport is favored by the locals. Regular tourist boats operate overnight services between Hangzhou and Suzhou or Wuxi, whilst boats can also be chartered for day-trips between the major tourist stops.*

Barges splutter *their way along the canal laden with agricultural produce and factory supplies. The busiest sections are in the south and north of the Yangzi to the border with Shandong.*

The canal banks *are lively with people performing domestic tasks. Families, even if they have houses, may live on board the boats when they are working.*

Suzhou ⑤
苏州

Milefo Buddha at the base of Beisi Ta

A network of canals, bridges, and canal-side housing characterizes the city of Suzhou. Its history dates back to the 6th century BC, when the first canals were built to control the area's low water table. The construction of the Grand Canal *(see p143)*, 1,000 years later, brought prosperity as silk, the city's prized commodity, could be exported to the north. During the Ming dynasty, Suzhou flourished as a place of refinement, attracting an influx of scholars and merchants, who built themselves numerous elegant gardens. The city has plenty of sights, and is dissected by broad, busy roads laid out in a grid.

🅱 Beisi Ta
1918 Renmin Road. **Tel** (0512) 6753 1197. ⬜ 8am–6pm daily. 🖼
The northern end of Renmin Road is dominated by the Beisi Ta (North Pagoda), a remnant of an earlier temple complex, which has been rebuilt. The pagoda's main structure dates from the Song dynasty, but its foundations supposedly date to the Three Kingdoms era (AD 220–265). Towering 249 ft (76 m) high, it is octagonal in shape, and has sharply upturned eaves. Visitors can climb right to the top, from where there are good views of the city, including Xuanmiao Guan and the Ruiguang Pagoda.

The octagonal Beisi Ta

🏛 Suzhou Silk Museum
2001 Renmin Road. **Tel** (0512) 6753 6505. ⬜ 9am–5pm daily. 🖼
The Suzhou Silk Museum is a pleasure to visit, mainly because its exhibits are well-documented with English captions. It traces the history of silk production and its use from its beginnings in about 4000 BC to the present day. Exhibits include old looms with demonstrations of their workings, samples of ancient silk patterns, and a section explaining the art of sericulture. The museum's most interesting exhibit is its room full of live silk worms, eating mulberry leaves and spinning cocoons.

🏛 Suzhou Museum
204 Dongbei Street. **Tel** (0512) 6757 5666. ⬜ 9am–4pm Tue–Sun. 🖼
The municipal museum is housed in a lavish modernist reinvention of a Suzhou villa and garden designed by Chinese-American architect I. M. Pei, who spent his childhood summers in Suzhou. The stunning fusion of traditional and modern Chinese architecture more than makes up for a rather dry collection that concentrates on Suzhou's association with canal construction and silk production. Some of the exhibits, especially the early maps, are of interest.

🌸 Humble Administrator's Garden
See pp146–7

🌸 Shizi Lin
23 Yuanlin Road. ⬜ daily. 🖼
The Lion Grove Garden is considered by many the finest in Suzhou. However, visitors unfamiliar with the subtleties of Chinese garden design may find it rather bleak, as rocks are its main feature. Ornamental rocks were a crucial element of classical gardens, and symbolized either the earth or China's sacred mountains. Dating to 1342, the garden was originally built as part of a temple. The large pool is spanned by a zigzag bridge and buildings with unusually fine latticework, while part of the rockery forms a labyrinth.

🌸 Ou Yuan
Cang Street. ⬜ 8am–5pm daily. 🖼
The Ou Yuan (Double Garden) is not as busy as many of the city's other classical gardens, and is a pleasure to visit. It takes its name from its two garden areas, separated by buildings and corridors. A relaxing place, Ou Yuan has rockeries, a pool, and a fine, open pavilion at its center, which is surrounded by several tea-houses. It is situated in a charming locality filled with some of the most attractive houses, canals, and bridges in the city.

The charming Ou Yuan Garden

Mural in the Hall of Literary Gods, Xuanmiao Guan

🏛 Museum of Opera & Theater

14 Zhongzhangjia Xiang. **Tel** *(0512) 6727 3334.* ⬭ *9am–4pm daily.* 🎟

Housed in a beautiful Ming-dynasty theater of latticed wood, the Museum of Opera and Theater (Xiqu Bowuguan) is a fascinating and highly visual museum. Its display halls are filled with examples of old musical instruments, delicate hand-copied books of scores and lyrics, masks, and costumes. It also exhibits other paraphernalia including a life-size orchestra and vivid photographs of dramatists and actors. Traditional Suzhou Opera, known as *kun ju*, is renowned as the oldest form of Chinese opera, with a history of about 5,000 years. The museum is the venue for occasional performances, while the adjacent teahouse stages daily shows of *kun*-style opera and music.

VISITORS' CHECKLIST

32 miles (50 km) NW of Shanghai. 🏠 *5,750,000.* 🚆 *Suzhou Train Station.* 🚌 *Bei Men Station, Nan Men Station, Wu Xianshi Station.* 🚢 *ferries to Hangzhou.* 🚢 *tours of the Grand Canal.* ℹ *195 Shiquan Street (0512) 6520 3131.*

🏛 Xuanmiao Guan

Guanqian Street. **Tel** *(0512) 6777 5479.* ⬭ *8:30am–4:30pm daily.* 🎟

The Daoist Temple of Mystery was founded during the Jin dynasty but like many Chinese temples, has been rebuilt many times. The Hall of the Three Pure Worshipers dates to the Song dynasty, and is the largest ancient Daoist hall in China. The intricate structure of the roof in particular is worth scrutiny. Located in Suzhou's commercial center, the temple was associated with popular street entertainment, and although the musicians and jugglers have gone, it retains a casual atmosphere.

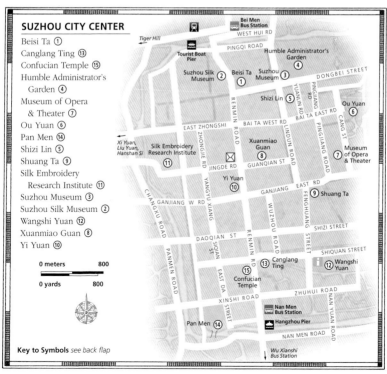

SUZHOU CITY CENTER

| 0 meters | 800 |
| 0 yards | 800 |

Key to Symbols *see back flap*

Humble Administrator's Garden

拙政园

Tai Hu rock display

Suzhou's largest garden, Zhuozheng Yuan, the Humble Administrator's Garden is also considered the city's finest. It was established in the 16th century by a retired magistrate, Wang Xianchen, and developed over the years as subsequent owners made changes according to the fashion of the day. A 16th-century painting shows that originally the garden was less decorative than it is now. The garden is separated into three principal parts, east, central, and west. The eastern section has colorful flowers but is of less interest than the other two. There is also a museum that explains the history and philosophy of Chinese gardens.

Covered walkway – a way to enjoy the garden even in the hot sun

Western section of the garden

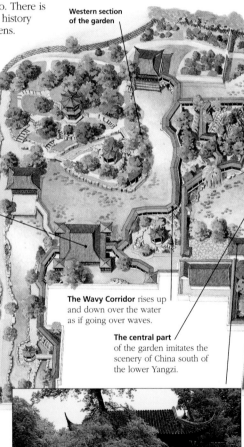

★ Mandarin Duck Hall
Split into two equal rooms, this arrangement allowed visitors to enjoy the cooler north-facing chamber in summer, and the warmer south-facing one in winter.

The Wavy Corridor rises up and down over the water as if going over waves.

The central part of the garden imitates the scenery of China south of the lower Yangzi.

STAR SIGHTS

★ Fragrant Isle

★ Mandarin Duck Hall

★ Hall of Distant Fragrance

★ Fragrant Isle
This pavilion and terrace is supposed to resemble the deck and cabin of a boat. As it projects out over the water, it gives excellent views of the garden from all sides.

THE HUMBLE ADMINISTRATOR'S GARDEN

Area illustrated below

① Entrance
② Eastern Garden
③ Garden Museum
④ Penjing Nursery *(see p29)*

0 meters 100
0 feet 300

VISITORS' CHECKLIST

178 Dongbei Street, Suzhou.
Tel (0512) 6751 0286.
8am–5:30pm daily (last
admission 5pm). includes
the Garden Museum.
www.szzzy.cn

Orange Pavilion
*Artificial mountains
were an important
element in Chinese
gardens and were ideal
for contemplation.*

Little Flying
Rainbow
Bridge

Entrance to the
central section

**Secluded Pavilion of Firmiana
Simplex and Bamboo**
*The most famous view of the
garden, the "borrowed view"
(see p29) of Beisi Ta, the
Northern Pagoda reflected in
the water, is visible from here.*

★ Hall of Distant Fragrance
*The main hall of the garden,
is named after the perfume of
the large lotus pond nearby
that delicately wafts in.*

The octagonal Song dynasty twin pagodas, Shuang Ta

🔳 Shuang Ta

Dinghui Si Xiang. ⬭ *daily.* 🖼

Once part of a temple, these 98-ft (30-m) high twin pagodas date to the early Song era. According to an inscription, they were first built in AD 982 by the students Wang Wenhan and his brother in honor of their teacher, who helped them pass the imperial civil service exams. Twin pagodas are commonly found in India but are a rarer feature of Chinese temples, as pagodas were largely built as single edifices.

🍀 Garden of Happiness

343 Renmin Road.

⬭ *7:30am–4:30pm daily.* 🖼

The Garden of Happiness is one of Suzhou's newer gardens, dating from the late Qing dynasty. It was built by a government official, who utilized rocks and landscape designs from other abandoned gardens. The garden appears to have originally covered a larger area; today its central feature is a pool encircled by rockeries and spanned by a zigzag bridge. The best

viewpoint is from the Fragrant Lotus Pavilion, while another pavilion that juts into the pool is known for catching cooling breezes. Look out for the calligraphy by famous scholars and poets.

🏛 Silk Embroidery Research Institute

280 Jingde Road. ⬭ *daily.* 🖼

Housed in the Huan Xiu Shan Zhuang (Surrounded by Majestic Mountains) Garden, this institute creates exquisitely fine silk embroidery, work that is mainly done by women. In order to produce the painting-like effect of their designs, the women sometimes work with silk strands that are so fine, they are almost invisible. They specialize in double-sided embroidery – for example, a cat with green eyes on one side and blue on the other.

🍀 Master of the Nets Garden

11 Kuojiatou Xiang. **Tel** *(0512) 6529 3190.* ⬭ *7:30am–5pm daily.* 🖼

It is said that the Master of the Nets Garden was named after one of its owners – a retired official who wished to become an accomplished

fisherman. Dating to 1140, it was completely remodeled in 1770 and for many people, is the finest of all Suzhou's gardens. Although small, it succeeds, with great subtlety, in introducing every element considered crucial to the classical garden *(see pp28–9)*. It includes a central lake, discreet connecting corridors, pavilions with miniature courtyards, screens, delicate latticework, and above all, points which "frame a view", as if looking at a perfectly balanced photograph. The best known building is the Pavilion for Watching the Moon, from where the moon can be viewed in a mirror, in the water, and in the sky. Regular evening performances of Chinese opera, including local *kun ju*, take place here.

🍀 Dark Blue Wave Pavilion Garden

3 Canglang Ting Street, Renmin Road. **Tel** *(0512) 6529 3109.* ⬭ *daily.* 🖼

The Dark Blue Wave Pavilion Garden – whose name is suggestive of a relaxed and pragmatic approach to life – is perhaps Suzhou's oldest garden, first laid out in 1044 by a scholar, Su Zimei, on the site of an earlier villa. His successor, a general in the imperial army, enlarged it in the 12th century, and it was rebuilt in the 17th century. It is known for its technique of "borrowing a view", allowing the scenery beyond the garden's confines to play a role in its design. Here, it is

The Pavilion for Watching the Moon, Master of the Nets Garden

Gateway to the Confucian Temple

achieved by lowering walls on the north side of some of the pavilions, allowing views across water; elsewhere the southwest hills can be seen. The central feature is a mound that is meant to resemble a wooded hill. Gardens were ideal places for contemplation and writing poetry, a fact demonstrated by the engravings of verses dotting the area.

🍀 Pan Men Scenic Area
2 Dong Da Road. ◯ 8am–5pm daily. 🖼 🔲 📷 🎧

This area has been extensively restored but it still contains some of the city's most interesting historical sights. Pan Men is a unique fortified gate that controlled access to the city by both land and water nearly 700 years ago, although most of the present construction is more recent. Other highlights include the graceful Wu Men Bridge and the views of the city from the 140-ft (43-m) high Ruigang Pagoda. The bridge and pagoda both date back to the Song dynasty, although each has been rebuilt since.

🏛 Confucian Temple
45 Renmin Road. ◯ daily. 🖼

The original Song-dynasty temple was rebuilt in 1864 after it was destroyed during the Taiping Rebellion. Its main hall, dating from the Ming dynasty, has several stone carvings including China's oldest surviving city map, depicting Suzhou, or Pingjiang as it was known in 1229. Also on display is a star chart dating from 1247 that

maps the positions of stars and celestial bodies in the heavens. It is one of the earliest surviving maps of its kind.

🍀 Tiger Hill
Huqiu Road. **Tel** (0512) 6532 3488. ◯ 7:30am–5pm daily. 🖼

In the city's northwest is the popular Tiger Hill (Huqiu Shan), the burial place of He Lu, the King of Wu and founder of Suzhou. His spirit is said to be guarded by a white tiger, which appeared three days after his death and refused to leave.

The main attraction is the Song-dynasty leaning pagoda (Yunyan Ta or Cloud Rock Pagoda), built in brick, which leans more than 7 ft (2 m) from the perpendicular at its highest point. Some 10th-century Buddhist *sutras* and a record of the year that it was constructed (959–961) were

Ceremonial urn, Tiger Hill

discovered during one of the attempts to prevent it from falling. The park is quite large, with pools and flowerbeds filled with blooms in spring and early summer. One of the many boulders is split in two, allegedly the result of He Lu's swordsmanship. He is supposedly buried nearby along with 3,000 swords.

🏛 Hanshan Temple
24 Hanshansi Long. **Tel** (0512) 6533 6634. ◯ 8am–5pm daily. 🖼

First constructed in the Liang dynasty, the Cold Mountain Temple was named after a Tang-dynasty poet-monk. A stone rendition of him and his fellow monk, Shi De, is to be seen here. The temple was rebuilt in the 19th century, after it was destroyed during the Taiping Rebellion. Located close to the Grand Canal, it was immortalized by the Tang-dynasty poet Zhang Ji, who arrived here by boat and anchored nearby. His poem "Anchored at Night by the Maple Bridge" is inscribed on a stone stele, and contains the lines that made Hanshan Temple famous: "Beyond Suzhou lies Hanshan Temple; at midnight the clang of the bell reaches the traveler's boat." The bell alluded to here was subsequently lost, and the temple's current bell was presented by Japan in 1905. Nearby, a beautiful arched bridge offers views along the Grand Canal.

Incense burners in the grounds of Hanshan Temple

Hangzhou
杭州

Renowned in medieval China as an earthly paradise, Hangzhou became the splendid capital of the Southern Song dynasty between 1138 and 1279. Later, when the conquering Mongols chose what is now Beijing as their new capital, Hangzhou continued to be a thriving commercial city. Its glories were extolled by Marco Polo *(see p153)*, who allegedly visited Hangzhou at the height of its prosperity and described it as "the City of Heaven, the most magnificent in all the world." Although most of the old buildings were destroyed in the Taiping Rebellion, the attractive West Lake and its surrounding area are still worth visiting.

Statue of Yue Fei

Entrance archway to Yue Fei Mu (Tomb of Yue Fei)

⛩ Yue Fei Mu
Bei Shan Road. **Tel** (0571) 8796 9670. ⏲ 7:30am–5.30pm daily. 📷
Just north of the West Lake lies the tomb of the Song general, Yue Fei, a popular Chinese hero revered for his patriotism. His campaigns against the invading Jin were so successful that his Song overlords began to worry that he might turn against them. He was falsely charged with sedition and executed, only to become a martyr whose exploits were widely celebrated in painting.

The Yue Fei Temple is a late 19th-century construction, and the tomb lies beside it. Leading to the tomb is a small avenue of stone animals. The central tumulus belongs to Yue Fei, while the smaller one is his son's, who was also executed. The kneeling figures in iron represent his tormentors – the prime minister, his wife, a jealous general, and the prison governor. It was customary to spit on them, but this is no longer encouraged.

🌺 Huanglong Dong Park & Qixia Shan
North of West Lake (Xi Hu).
This hilly area, crisscrossed with paths, has several sights of interest. Huanglong Dong Park, nestling in the hills, is very attractive with its teahouses, ponds, and flowers, and a pavilion where musicians perform traditional music in summer. To the east is **Baoshu Ta**, a 20th-century rebuild of a Song-era pagoda. Looming close by is **Qixia Shan** (Lingering Clouds Mountain), with the **Baopu Daoist Temple** located halfway up its slopes. This active temple has services on most days. It makes an interesting stopover, where visitors can watch pilgrims, priests, and perhaps even one of the frequent ancestral worship ceremonies.

🏛 Hu Qingyu Tang Museum of Chinese Medicine
95 Dajing Xiang. **Tel** (0571) 8702 7507. ⏲ 8:30am–5pm daily. 📷
This interesting museum is housed in a beautiful old apothecary's shop. It was established by the merchant Hu Xueyan during the Qing dynasty and traces the history of traditional Chinese medicine, which goes back thousands of years. It is still an active dispensary and pharmacy.

🌺 West Lake
See pp152–3.

🏛 China National Tea Museum
88 Longjing Road. **Tel** (0571) 8796 4221. ⏲ 8:30am–5:30pm daily. 📷
Tracing the history of tea production, the China National Tea Museum, located on a working tea plantation, has lots of interesting information regarding the different varieties of tea, its cultivation, and the development of tea-making and tea-drinking vessels. Fortunately, many of the captions are in English.

Wood panel carving at Baopu Daoist Temple

🏯 Longjing Village
SW of Tea Museum. 📷
The village of Longjing (Dragon Well) produces one of China's most famous varieties of green tea. Visitors can wander around the tea terraces, catching glimpses of the different stages of production, such as cutting, sorting, and drying, and also buy the tea, which varies in price according to its grade.

Inside the main hall of the Hu Qingyu Tang Museum of Chinese Medicine

Lingyin Si

1 Fayun Long, Lingyin Road. *Tel (0571) 8796 8665.* ◯ *6am–6pm daily.*

The hill area known as Feilai Feng (The Peak that Flew Here) is home to some of the city's main sights, including Lingyin Si. Founded in AD 326, this temple once housed 3,000 monks who worshiped in more than 70 halls. Though now much reduced in size, it is still one of China's largest temples. It was damaged in the 19th-century Taiping Rebellion, and then again by fire in the 20th century. It is said to owe its survival to Zhou Enlai, who prevented its destruction during the Cultural Revolution. Still, some parts of the temple are ancient, such as the stone pagodas on either side of the entrance hall, which date from AD 969. Behind this hall is the **Great Buddha Hall**, with an impressive 66-ft (20-m) statue of the Buddha carved in 1956 from camphor wood.

The **Ligong Pagoda** at the entrance was built in honor of the Indian monk, Hui Li, who gave the mountain its eccentric

Buddha sculptures at Feilai Feng

name. Hui Li thought it was the spitting image of a hill in India and asked whether it had flown here. Feilai Feng is known for the dozens of Buddhist sculptures carved into the rock, many dating from the 10th century.

Six Harmonies Pagoda

16 Zhijiang Road. *Tel (0571) 8659 1401.* ◯ *5:30am–6:30pm daily.*

Standing beside the railway bridge on the northern shore of the Qiantang River, Liuhe Ta is all that is left of an octagonal temple first built in AD 970 to placate the tidal bore, a massive wall of water that rushes upstream during high tide. Over 197-ft (60-m) high, it served as a lighthouse up until the Ming dynasty.

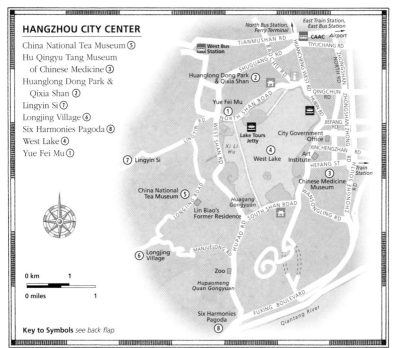

HANGZHOU CITY CENTER

China National Tea Museum ⑤
Hu Qingyu Tang Museum of Chinese Medicine ③
Huanglong Dong Park & Qixia Shan ②
Lingyin Si ⑦
Longjing Village ⑥
Six Harmonies Pagoda ⑧
West Lake ④
Yue Fei Mu ①

Key to Symbols see back flap

West Lake
西湖

**Metal work,
Xiaoying Island**

Long considered one of the scenic wonders of China, covering over three square miles (8 sq km), West Lake (Xi Hu) is situated at the heart of Hangzhou. Surrounded by gentle green hills, the lake's willow-shaded causeways and fragrant cover of lotus blossoms have long been an inspiration for artists. Originally the lake was an inlet off the estuary of the Qiantang River, becoming a lake when the river began to silt up in the 4th century. The lake had a tendency to flood, so several dykes were built, including the Bai and Su Causeways. Hiring a private boat from the eastern shore for an afternoon on the water is highly recommended, as is a leisurely stroll along the shady causeways.

★ Three Pools Reflecting the Moon
Three small stone pagodas rise from the waters near Xiaoying Island. At full moon candles are placed within and their openings are covered in paper to create reflections resembling the moon.

XI LI HU

Huagang Garden
This garden is intended as a place for viewing fish. Designed by a Song-dynasty eunuch, its pools are filled with shimmering goldfish in a restful setting of grasses and trees.

STAR FEATURES

★ Xiaoying Island

★ Three Pools Reflecting the Moon

★ Su Causeway

★ Xiaoying Island
Often called San Tan Yin Yue Island, referring to the three moon-reflecting pagodas off its shores, Xiaoying Island consists of four enclosed pools fringed by pavilions first built in 1611. The zig-zagging Nine Bend Bridge was built in 1727.

For hotels and restaurants in this region see p187 and p207

VISITORS' CHECKLIST

Hangzhou. 🚌🚢 *daily from eastern shore near Hubin Road. Boats for hire on Gu Shan Island.* **Zhejiang Provincial Museum** 25 Gushan Road. **Tel** *(0571) 8798 0281.* ◻ *1–4pm Mon, 9am–4pm Tue–Sun.* 🖼 *www.*zhejiangmuseum.com

★ Su Causeway

The longer of the two causeways takes its name from the Song-dynasty poet, Su Dongpo, who also served as governor. Linked by six stone bridges, the causeway is a peaceful thoroughfare running along the lake's western edge.

Bridge to Quyuan Garden

This bridge leads to a stunning garden surrounded by lotus flowers. It is considered one of the ten prospects from where the lake can be seen to best advantage.

The Seal Engravers Society is open in the summer months.

GU SHAN

Zhejiang Provincial Museum

XI HU

BEI LI HU

MARCO POLO

Whether Marco Polo ever visited China is much disputed. However, according to the book he dictated to a ghost writer who embroidered it substantially, Polo became governor of nearby Yangzhou for three years during the Yuan dynasty. He describes Hangzhou as paradise and the finest city in the world, with fascinating markets, pleasure boats, and prostitutes. Hangzhou was indeed a cosmopolitan city, ever since the Southern Song dynasty made it their capital. *The Travels of Marco Polo*, however, may be based on earlier journeys by his father and uncle, and stories from other merchants.

Engraving of Marco Polo, 1254–1324

Bai Causeway

Named after the 9th-century poet-governor Bai Juyi, this dyke leads to Gu Shan, an island first landscaped during the Tang dynasty, and now containing a tea house and the provincial museum.

TWO GUIDED WALKS

After the grandiose sweep of the Bund, the best walking in Shanghai is through the areas where the *shikumen*, or stone-gate houses, of ordinary people stand next to the vast European-styled villas and mansions erected in the early years of the 20th century for foreign business magnates.

Although the city is best known for its foreign influences, something even Shanghainese highlight first when talking about their home town, the Chinese side of Shanghai should not be forgotten. After the Opium Wars of the 1840s and 1850s, the original modest walled city became surrounded by swathes of foreigner-controlled territory. But it is in what survives of the Old City that the remnants of more traditional Chinese culture can still be found.

The first walk begins at the heart of this district, taking in temples, street vendors, and bustling markets of all kinds. It ends with a look at a successful modern attempt to recycle the city's traditional buildings with the shopping, dining, and entertainment

Art Deco detailing

district of Xin Tiandi ("New Heaven and Earth"), which recreates the buildings of Old Shanghai for more modern purposes.

West of Xin Tiandi, the French Concession offers some of the best of the surviving colonial-era villas and mansion blocks. Some are now hotels, or restaurants and bars, and some have been preserved through the accident of having at some point been occupied by those the ruling Communist Party promotes as "Great Men."

The second walk visits some of the more notable examples of Concession architecture. It traces a century's worth of history written in brick and stone, from the party town that was Shanghai in its 1930s heyday, through the rather more dour Party decades post 1949, to the rebirth of the city, as most visibly exemplified by the high-end international retailers now crowding fashionable Huaihai Road. The walk also includes the Maoming Road Bar Street. Once a run-down area, it is being redeveloped to include a luxury hotel complex and shopping plaza.

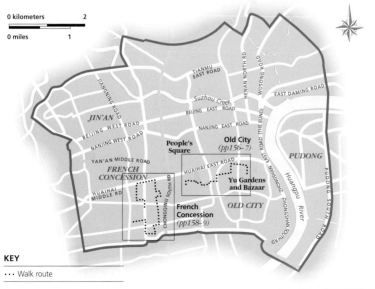

KEY

··· Walk route

◁ **Kommune Cafe near Taikang Road, Shanghai**

A 90-Minute Walk through the Old City

Although the city walls of the original Chinese settlement were pulled down early last century, their former path is still clearly visible on maps, marked by a perfect circle of road. Within this ring you'll find everything from bustling produce markets full of pajama-clad vendors and shoppers, to some delightful old timber and brick architecture. The Old City is also home to the famous Yu Gardens, and to places of worship of every shape, size, and religious persuasion. After time spent observing back-street reminders of Shanghai's history, the walk ends with the ultra-fashionable, rebuilt oldness of Xin Tiandi.

Dajing Road food market ⑦

Fangbang Middle Road ②

Fangbang Middle Road

The walk begins on Fangbang Middle Road at the southern entrance to the Yu Gardens and Bazaar complex. Just inside is the **City Temple** ①. Once much larger, the temple is now squeezed by tall mock-traditional department stores, but it remains a popular place of worship and is fascinating to visit. After seeing the temple, return to **Fangbang Middle Road** ② and walk west past dealers in "antiques," along with sellers of tea, furniture, peasant art, and traditional blue-and-white batik-style cloth. The shops are worth browsing, but they are also prone to over-charging anyone who does not know better.

Where the bazaar comes to an end turn right and head north towards the large **decorative gate** ③, or *pailou*. However, before reaching it turn left and then take the first right; this will take you

by the long, mustard-colored wall of the **Chengxiang Ge Buddhist Temple** ④. Turn left at the top of the alley and dodge the enthusiastic pearl vendors whose shops cluster near the temple entrance. The three large halls that make up

the complex remain home to a sizeable community of nuns.

Continue west a short distance to the **Fuyou Road Mosque** ⑤, Shanghai's oldest place of Islamic worship (1868) – a green sign indicates its location down a tiny alley.

Dajing Road

At Henan South Road turn left and pass beneath another gaudy **reconstructed arch** ⑥.

The courtyard of the Chengxiang Ge Buddhist Temple ④

KEY

••• Walk route

Ⓜ Subway station

A lively street café in popular Xin Tiandi ⑬

Dajing Tower museum ⑧

Continue south for a little while before turning right into Dajing Road, which soon becomes a bustling **food market** ⑦.

Depending on the time of day, you'll see groups of wizened ladies sorting through leafy piles of greens, chefs tossing blackened woks full of noodles and traditional Shanghai dumplings, and fishmongers scaling the catch of the day. Stay on this road until you reach the junction with Renmin Road, which is where you'll find the **Dajing Tower** ⑧. Originally part of the city's defences and then an active temple, the tower now houses an interesting small museum with a model of the old city walls and an exhibition of black-and-white photos. Sadly, there is virtually nothing left of the

original city walls. This whole area, especially the fringes where any remaining bits of wall once were, are fast being redeveloped.

Dongtai Road

Busy **Renmin Road** ⑨ follows the line of the walls that formerly encircled the Old City. Despite Shanghai's growing number of cars it still resembles a cycle track in rush hour. Leave it to turn right into Kuaiji Road, cross main Xizang South Road, and continue along Liuhekou Road, where there's an indoor **bird and flower market** ⑩, full of cricket enthusiasts (the insect, not the game), who gather with their jars of twitching creatures. A little further on is **Dongtai Road Market** ⑪, optimistically called an "antiques market," but in view of the unlikelihood of finding any authentic treasures, it is more accurately described as a flea market.

Dongtai Road Antiques Market ⑪

Xin Tiandi

Head north up Dongtai Road and turn left on Chongde Road, following the street until it turns right into Taicang Road. This borders **Huahai Park** ⑫ for a bit, and then a few hundred yards farther west is **Xin Tiandi** ⑬, an area of *shikumen* (stone tenements) redeveloped into a smart shopping, dining, and hotel complex. This district has been completely redesigned and transformed into a lively area by day and night. It is now said to be the most popular tourist sight in Shanghai for out-of-town Chinese, and a model for downtown redevelopments across China.

TIPS FOR WALKERS

Length: 2 miles (3.2 km).
Getting there: Take a taxi to the Yu Gardens Bazaar.
Yu Gardens: Open 8:30am–5:30pm daily.
Chengxiang Ge: Open 7am–4pm daily.
Dajing Tower: Open 9am–4pm daily.
Bird and Flower Market: Open 8am–6pm daily.
Dongtai Lu Antiques Market: Open 9am–5pm daily.
Stopping off points: Huxinting Teahouse in the Yu Gardens is the most famous spot for tea and snacks, and the Nanxiang Steamed Bun Restaurant has Shanghai's most famous dumplings, but both may have long queues. At Xin Tiandi, try Crystal Jade for a dim sum lunch, the KABB for beers, wines, and cocktails, Element Fresh for cakes and salads, or T8 for a reasonably priced set lunch.

A 90-Minute Walk around the French Concession

In 1843, the British negotiated a deal with the Chinese that led to the creation of the International Concession, a zone of self-rule for foreign powers in Shanghai. The French, however, declined to join. They made a separate deal to found their own concession, beginning with a narrow finger of land between the old Chinese city and what is now Yan'an Lu, and later spreading to cover a large area to the west. Redevelopment is constantly removing the old villas and apartment buildings that formerly made this area of Shanghai resemble a typical French provincial town, but there remains much to see and this is a very walkable part of town.

labyrinth of lanes lined by cafés, craft shops, boutiques, and galleries. Side turnings are lined with fine examples of *shikumen*, the houses with

Taikang Road ⑥

Ruijin No. 2 Road and Taikang Road

Start by taking a taxi to 27 Shaoxing Road for morning coffee or Chinese tea at the **Old China Hand Reading Room** ①. This is a quiet café with elegant period furnishings that also sells books on the old architecture of Shanghai and elsewhere produced by the team of American-born but long-time Shanghai resident Tess Johnston and local photographer Deke Erh.

From the café head off east along Shaoxing Road, a lovely street with a number of small galleries. Turn right down **Ruijin No. 2 Road** ② and look above the modern shop fronts for hints of the city's Art Deco past, and other oddities such as the particularly **Germanic mansion** ③ at No. 152. Cross the junction with Jianguo Middle Road and take the next left into **Taikang Road** ④, which is lined with art shops with foreigner-pleasing watercolors, and tailors happy to make traditional *qipao* dresses. At Zui Zhu Zhai (No. 322) framed calligraphy by a living master is available from about ¥600 – much cheaper than in Xin Tiandi or elsewhere.

Cross over the road for a fascinating **wet market** ⑤, full of live fish, frogs, eels, and snakes, then pass under an arch leading into **Taikang Road** ⑥. This is a

stone-framed entrances that are this city's counterpart to Beijing's *siheyuan* dwellings.

Sinan Road

At the top of the alley turn right along Jianguo Middle Road, then left into Sinan Road, past mansions with hints not only of France, but Spain and Germany too. These were spacious enough to attract

Café-cum-bookshop-cum-library: Old China Hand Reading Room ①

senior figures from both the rival Nationalist and Communist parties in their day. On the right you come to the **Former Residence of Zhou Enlai** ⑦ *(see p132)*, Premier and Foreign Minister under the People's Republic. The spartan interior of the residence is left furnished much as it was in Zhou's time. Just on the corner of

Cafés and bicycles on Maoming North Road ⑭

Sinan Road and Fuxing Middle Road is the **Sinan Mansions** ⑧, a cluster of 1930s mansions that have been redeveloped as bars, cafés, and restaurants. Sample the Fat Olive for mezze and wine, or Chicha for modern Peruvian cuisine. Hotel Massenet, a boutique hotel housed in a series of restored mansions, is also located here. The hotel gets its name from the street's French Concession-era name, Rue Massenet. Farther along is the **Sun Yat Sen Memorial Residence** ⑨ *(see p132)*. Many of Sun's personal items are on display here.

Huaihai Middle Road
Immediately east of the Sun Yat Sen residence is the French-created **Fuxing Park** ⑩ *(see p132)*, which is worth a detour, before returning to Sinan Road via Gaolan Road and a visit to the onion-domed former **Russian Orthodox Church of St. Nicholas** ⑪, built in 1933 and dedicated to the last Tsar.
Continuing north brings you to **Huaihai Middle Road** ⑫. Once the French Concession's principal boulevard, this is one of the city's premier shopping streets, mixing international big brand names with an array of smaller boutiques. Walking west, after a short time you'll see the spire-topped Art Deco exterior of the **Cathay Theater** ⑬ over on the north side of the road. Built in the 1930s it is still in use as a cinema. It also hosts the Shanghai

Sun Yat Sen, founder of the Nationalist Party ⑨

0 meters   500
0 yards   500

KEY

••• Walk route

Ⓜ Subway station

Former Residence of Zhou Enlai ⑦

International Film Festival in June *(see p35)*.
Turn right into **Maoming North Road** ⑭. A short way along this road there are two heritage buildings, facing each other. On the left is the **Okura Garden Hotel** ⑮, formerly the Cercle Sportif Français (French Sports Club). Built in 1926, the original colonnaded building remains a spectacular sight. Opposite is the **Jinjiang Hotel** ⑯ which houses the Art Deco Grosvenor Mansions apartment block. The Shanghai Communiqué was signed by Mao Zedong and the then US President Richard Nixon in the hotel's Grand Hall in 1972.

SHOPPING IN SHANGHAI

Intricate paper cut, found in craft stores

Where Beijing boasts a thousand-plus years of imperial history and asssociated monuments, Shanghai reigns supreme when it comes to the modern passions of eating and shopping. With the latter, the enticements begin with the likes of Chinese cotton slippers, sold two pairs for a dollar at the street market, and run all the way up to high-fashion labels such as Louis Vuitton, Gucci, and Prada at the Plaza 66 luxury brands mall. The former main shopping street of Nanjing East Road is being redeveloped, but its flagship the No. 1 Department Store remains, where you can buy Mao-label tea and cigarettes in a packet emblazoned with a golden Oriental Pearl TV Tower. Shanghai shoppers also throng Huaihai Road, which is lined with high-gloss malls at its eastern end, with boutique shopping farther west. One block south, the Xin Tiandi mall is housed in recon-structed *shikumen* stone tenements. Markets are thinner on the ground than in Beijing but, even so, only the most morose opponent of consumerism could fail to find fun shopping in Shanghai.

PRACTICAL INFORMATION

Most shops are open seven days a week from around 10am through until 9pm or even later. Markets will start and finish earlier. Credit cards are not as widely accepted as you might expect; some places only take local cards and many don't take any form of plastic at all. You need to carry cash. If you run short, ATMs are not hard to find.

SHOPPING ETIQUETTE

When bargaining at any market that sees plenty of foreign shoppers – Fangbang Road or Dongtai Road, for example – don't listen to advice that says half or one third of the first offer made by the vendor is reasonable. This first-named price may easily be five, ten or even fifteen times what

A Western fashion house advertises in the windows of a Shanghai mall

any local would consider a reasonable sum. A counter-offer of only half the vendor's price marks you down as easy prey. Offer far less – maybe as little as 10 percent of the price you were quoted. Your first counter-offer says, "I'm not as stupid as you think. And maybe I'm not that interested anyway." It's hard to make an offer that's too low, and you also have nothing to lose. Either the vendor will dramatically lower his or her price, or he or she will let you walk away, in which case you can improve your offer. Your second offer should be no more than a fraction higher than your first.

It is worth remembering that since there is nothing original or truly antique in Shanghai's markets, there is little that is unique either. You should always try your

Modern twists on classic Chinese fashion at Shanghai Tang

luck with a number of vendors before settling on any purchase.

Always do everything in a friendly way and with a smile.

Refunds are impossible, so be certain that you have what you want before you pay.

ANTIQUES

There aren't any true antiques on sale in Shanghai and if there were you'd need special permission to export them anyway. What there is, how-ever, is lots of Mao-era memorabilia. The place for this is **Dongtai Road**, which is just east of the Xin Tiandi complex. Referred to as an antiques market, the stalls that line this fairly short street are in fact filled with an assortment of Communist Party kitsch and other miscellaneous junk, much of which is grossly overpriced. Still, it is fun to browse, and you never know when a foot-high, pewter Mao figurine is going to come in handy. There are similar pickings on **Fuyou Road** (open Sunday only) and **Fangbang Road**. Fangbang Road's **Hubao Building Basement Market**, which is part of the busy Yu Gardens Bazaar complex, is the city's largest indoor antiques market.

Over in the French Concession, **Madam Mao's Dowry** is a curiosity store of odd bits and pieces of recent heritage collected by its magpie owners, from vintage clothing to Socialist-Realist posters. Everything here is the genuine article – no repros.

Other stores worth a visit include the state-run **Shanghai Antique & Curio Shop**, just off the Bund, which is something of an antique itself, having been around for over a hundred years, while over in the Hongkou district **Duolun Road** has a row of shops selling antiques and curios.

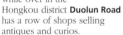

Antique radio for sale at a street market

ART

The Shanghai equivalent of Beijing's 798 Art District is the M50 art hub on Mogan Shan Road. This is a street north of Jing'an, not far from the train station on the west bank of Suzhou Creek. Here, an area

of light industrial buildings has been taken over by artists' ateliers and workshops, as well as a number of commercial galleries. These include the well-respected **ShanghART**, as well as **Art Scene China**, which represents over 20 of China's leading contemporary artists.

In the former French Concession, **Art Labor** has cutting-edge contemporary works of art by Chinese and international artists. Jewelry, home accessories, and other creations by Chinese contemporary designers can be bought at the **Shanghai Museum of Contemporary Art (MOCA) Shop**, in the heart of People's Square.

For something less polished, **Taikang Road** is an attempt to foster a district of arts, crafts, boutiques, and cafés based around a former candy factory and several lanes of old *shikumen* houses. There are a handful of art galleries, plus some handicraft workshops and interesting jewelry and ethnic clothing boutiques. The area is visited as part of one of the Shanghai Guided Walks (see p158).

BOOKS

Shanghai beats Beijing hands down for English-language books. Like its counterpart in the capital, the state-run

Mao's "Little Red Book" – still widely available in Shanghai

Foreign Languages Bookstore has a reasonable selection of English-language novels, as well as plenty of souvenir picture books. **Garden Books**, at the heart of the French Concession, combines bookselling with a pleasant café and ice-cream counter, while the **Shanghai Museum Shop** is as good as it gets when it comes to books about not just Shanghai, but China as a whole.

The **Confucius Temple** in the Old City has a book market every Sunday that makes for fun browsing. There are also bookstores in shopping malls such as the top floor of **CITIC Square** mall on Nanjing Road and Xujiahu's **Grand Gateway Plaza**, where Xinhua sells a small selection of English-language books.

CHINESE PHARMACIES

If you know your Chinese medicine, speak Chinese, or are just plain curious to see dried seahorses and the like, **Tong Han Chun** is a venerable example of a traditional Chinese medicine store – one reputedly established in 1783. Claiming even older roots, **Lei Yun Shang Pharmacy** first opened in Suzhou in 1662 but is a relative newcomer to Shanghai, having arrived only in 1860. It still maintains its old-fashioned wooden interior. For modern pharmacies, the Hong Kong pharmacy retailer Mannings now has several outlets across downtown Shanghai.

Browsing for antiques and trinkets on Dongtai Road

Boutique clothes store on Huaihai Middle Road, French Concession

CLOTHES & TEXTILES

Most major clothing brand names from Europe, the US, and Japan are represented in Shanghai. Although there are some bargain clothes items, with factories originating in China, some shops still have prices in line with Europe and the US. The main shopping streets are **Huaihai Road** in the French Concession and **Nanjing Road** west of People's Square, where you will find modern, high-end malls such as **CITIC Square** and **Plaza 66**.

For something a bit different, tree-lined **Changle Road**, particularly between Shaanxi South Road and Fumin Road, has some stylish boutiques, as does Anfu Road. Styles are Western, although sizes are Eastern (small). Many of these places specialize in factory seconds of items by well-known designers.

Maoming Road and Xin Tiandi both have a branch of **Shanghai Tang**, the glamorous retro-Asian, Hong Kong high-fashion store which can also be found in Pudong. Shaanxi North Road and Xinle Road also have several boutiques representing Chinese designers.

The city has revived its tradition of fine tailoring. Maoming Road, just north of Huaihai Road, is famous for its strip of tailors selling custom-made *qipao* dresses, which were high fashion in the 1920s, and still worn by elegant, high-society women.

W.W. Chan & Sons Tailor Ltd. is noted for high quality at fair prices. Fabrics by the meter or the bolt are sold at the **Shanghai Nan Waitan (South Bund) Textile Market**. Filling four floors, it resembles a provincial shopping mall, but it sells only fabric. Most stalls also have a resident tailor ready to whip up made-to-measure cashmere coats, cotton shirts, or silk dresses. They can follow any pattern provided, or even make copies from fashion pictures clipped from a magazine. It typically takes a week for garments to be made but rush jobs can be done for a little more. A shirt will cost the equivalent of around $10, trousers $20.

CRAFTS

It is never good practice to shop near sites with a high volume of tourist traffic, and as you might imagine there is a lot of trash for sale around the **Yu Gardens Bazaar** *(see pp130–31)*. But even Shanghainese visit the quieter corners of the complex for items such as tea, teapots, and tea sets. For porcelain in general, some of the best buys are the fine reproductions of classic designs available at the **Shanghai Museum Shop** *(see pp126–9)*. The shop also has lots of other beautiful items, from calligraphy to carved jade, jewelry, and silk slippers. Although expensive, the work sold here is of better

Silk embroidered coasters

quality than almost anything else on the market. Handicrafts made by some of China's myriad ethnic minorities, as well as by people of neighboring countries, including Nepal, are available at shops dotted along Nanjing Road.

DEPARTMENT STORES & MALLS

The Shanghainese have caught the mall craze and multi-story retail plazas have sprung up everywhere. Nanjing West Road has three in a row: six-story **CITIC Square**, the plush **Plaza 66**, and the more egalitarian **Westgate Mall**. Other excellent malls include the **IFC Shanghai Mall** and the **Superbrand Mall**, both near the Lujiazui metro station in Pudong. **Hong Kong Plaza** on Huaihai Road is another trendy mall. All these places are full of luxury-brand Western goods (at significantly higher than Western prices). Now that the municipality has shut down the fake market, and the old fabric market has moved under cover, Shanghai is severely lacking in open-air commerce. Another upscale shopping district in Shanghai is **Xin Tiandi Shopping Mall**, housed in rebuilt 19th-century *shikumen* buildings. Visitors can browse brand-name shops, eat in world-class restaurants, or simply take in the scenery.

Plaza 66, one of three adjacent modern malls on Nanjing West Road

ELECTRONICS

There are no bargains to be had on computers or other electronic items. Almost everything is imported and so costs as much, if not more than, in the US or Europe. There are a few exceptions such as Sony shortwave radios, made in China for export, which may be bargained down to decent prices. Cheap Chinese MP3 players or DVD players are often multi-lingual and multi-voltage, but there's no warranty except with a very few global Chinese brands. Accessories and media such

Nanjing East Road, once Shanghai's main shopping street

as disks, tapes, leads, and convertors, all made in China, are cheaper than the identical item packaged up for sale

at home. The IFC Shanghai Mall in Pudong houses the stylish **Apple Store**. The cylindrical entrance to the store is an impressive sight.

PEARLS & JEWELRY

Jewelry shops abound all over the city, particularly in the Old City around the Yu Gardens Bazaar and along pedestrianized Nanjing East Road. Pearls are a specialty, both fresh- and saltwater. One of the best shops is **Shanghai Pearl City**. Prices are competitive, but you do need to know what you are looking at.

Directory

ANTIQUES

Dongtai Road Antiques Market
Dongtai Road, off Chongde Road, near Xin Tiandi.
Map 2 B4.

Fuyou Road Market
Cangbao Road, Fangbang Middle Road 457, Old City. **Map** 2 C4.

Hubao Building Basement Market
Fangbang Road, Old City. **Map** 2 C4.

Madam Mao's Dowry
207 Fumin Road, French Concession.
Tel *(021) 5403 3551.*

Shanghai Antique & Curio Shop
218–226 Guangdong Road, by Jiangxi Middle Road, Huangpu District.
Map 2 C3.
Tel *(021) 6321 4697.*

ART

Art Labor
Building 4, 570 Yongjia Road. **Map** 1 E5.
Tel *(021) 3460 5331.*
www.artlaborgallery.com

Art Scene China
2/F, Building 4, 50 Mogan Shan Road, Putuo District.
Tel *(021) 6277 4940.*
www.artscenechina.com

Shanghai Museum of Contemporary Art (MOCA) Shop
231 Nanjing West Road.
Map 2 A3.
Tel *(021) 6327 9900.*
www.mocashanghai.com

ShanghART
Building 16, 50 Mogan Shan Road, Putuo District.
Tel *(021) 6359 3923.*
www.shanghart.com

BOOKS

Confucius Temple Book Market
215 Wenmiao Road, Old City. **Map** 2 B5.

Garden Books
325 Changle Road, French Concession.
Map 1 E4.
Tel *(021) 5404 8728.*

Foreign Languages Bookstore
390 Fuzhou Road, Huangpu District. **Map** 2 B3. **Tel** *(021) 6322 3200.*

Shanghai Museum Shop
201 People's Avenue, People's Square. **Map** 2 A3. **Tel** *(021) 6372 3500.*

CHINESE PHARMACIES

Lei Yun Shang
2 Huashan Road, Jing'an District. **Map** 1 D3.
Tel *(021) 6217 3501.*

Tong Han Chun
20 Yuyuan Xin Road, by Jiuxiao Road, Old City.
Map 2 C4.
Tel *(021) 6355 0308.*

CLOTHES AND TEXTILES

Shanghai Nan Waitan (South Bund) Textile Market
399 Lujiabang Road, Huangpu District.

Shanghai Tang
Lane 333 Huangpi South Road, Xintiandi North Block. **Map** 2 A4.
Tel *(021) 6377 3333.*

W.W. Chan & Sons Tailor Ltd.
129 Maoming South Road, by Huaihai Middle Road, French Concession.
Map 1 E4.
Tel *(021) 5404 1469.*

CRAFTS

Yu Gardens Bazaar
Fuyou Road, Old City.
Map 2 C4.

DEPARTMENT STORES & MALLS

CITIC Square
1168 Nanjing West Road, Jing'an District. **Map** 1 E3.

Grand Gateway
11 Hongqiao Road, Xujiahu. **Map** 2 A5.
Tel *(021) 6404 0111.*

Hong Kong Plaza
Corner of Huaihai Middle Road and Songshan Road. **Map** 2 B4.
Tel *(021) 2327 8888.*

IFC Shanghai Mall
8 Century Avenue, Pudong. **Map** 3 E3.
Tel *(021) 6311 5588.*

Plaza 66
1266 Nanjing West Road, Jing'an District.
Map 1 E3.

Superbrand Mall
168 Lujiazui West Road, Pudong.
Map 3 E3.
Tel *(021) 688 7788.*

Westgate Mall
1038 Nanjing West Road, Jing'an District
Map 1 E3.

Xin Tiandi Shopping Mall
Huangpi South Road, Old City.
Map 2 A4.
Tel *(021) 6311 2288.*

ELECTRONICS

Apple Store
LG2–27 IFC Shanghai Mall, 8 Century Avenue. **Map** 3 E3.
Tel *(021) 2033 5300.*

PEARLS & JEWELRY

Shanghai Pearl City
3721 Hongmei Road, Hongqiao.

ENTERTAINMENT IN SHANGHAI

It is frequently said that Beijing produces the art and culture, and Shanghai sells it. There is some truth in this. Beijing has the happening music scene; its film academy has produced almost every director of note of recent times; and it is the home of traditional art forms such as Beijing Opera. But in the last decade Shanghai has pulled ahead in building arts and entertainments venues, including theaters, concert halls, and galleries. The city prides itself on being cosmopolitan and, as a result, venues

Sax player on bar balcony

tend to host Western shows such as *Cats*. However, this is changing and centers now showcase Chinese and Asian musicians and orchestras.

Shanghai's modern nightlife once existed in the shadow of the reputation of the famously wild 1920s and 1930s. Many of the hotel bars and seedier expat hang-outs played on this reputation, with female wait staff dressed in the figure-hugging *qipao* (dresses) of old, live jazz, and cocktails. Today, the city's nightlife is thriving, diverse, and improving all the time.

Shanghai Grand Theater, the city's premier venue for performing arts

PRACTICAL INFORMATION

For details of what's on in town pick up one of the English-language listings magazines, such as *Shanghai Talk*, *City Weekend*, and *That's Shanghai*. These publications are available free in hotel lobbies and at restaurants and bars.

Tickets are generally bought at the venue box offices and paid for in cash. At small music clubs, pay on the door. Most hotel concierges can usually help with securing seats at the theaters.

CLASSICAL MUSIC AND THE PERFORMING ARTS

The major theaters – which include the **Shanghai Grand Theater**, **Lyceum Theater**, **Majestic Theater**, **Oriental Art**

Center, and the **Shanghai Center** – put on large-scale concerts of Chinese and foreign music and Western musicals, as well as some home-grown dance and musical spectaculars. Other theaters put on more traditional Chinese Opera performances, notably the **Yifu Theater**. The 2010 World Expo Site's handful of permanent attractions includes the oyster shell-shaped **Mercedes-Benz Arena**, which hosts concerts, theater, and large stage shows.

Shanghai is most famous for its acrobatic shows. Although most performances are now constructed with tourists in mind, complete with theatrical lighting and sequined costumes, this makes them no less valid or spectacular. Lissom adults and children who seem more fluid than solid make towers

out of themselves and assortments of tables, chairs, and umbrellas, and disappear into the objects the same size as carry-on luggage.

BARS AND PUBS

Shanghai's image in the West links it inextricably to the cocktail, and certainly there are now many suitably luxurious locations in which to drink one. Hotel bars offer the most dramatic settings and include the Park Hyatt's dizzying 91st-floor **100 Century Avenue** bar, the Hyatt on the Bund's **Vue** skydeck bar, with views of the Bund, Huangpu River, and the Pudong skyline, the expensive 14th-floor outdoor terrace of **Sir Elly's** at the Peninsula Hotel on the Bund, and **The Long Bar** at Waldorf-Astoria Shanghai on the Bund, which recreates a 1930s bar of the same name. These bars all offer views that may quickly induce the slightly colonial feeling of being master of all you survey.

International sophistication spreads well beyond the big hotels. **Bar Rouge**, with snooty patrons awash in Veuve Cliquot, is one of the few places in China where a dress code is enforced. If you're anything less than "smart casual" look elsewhere, although it's a shame to miss the terrace overlooking the Huangpu. **Barbarossa** offers a North African theme with sequined pillows and a

Cotton's, one of the city's many watering holes

terracotta-tiled rooftop terrace overlooking a small lake in central People's Park. Most chic of all perhaps is **Glamour Bar**, the cocktail venue attached to restaurant M on the Bund. It boasts regular live acts, which range from the eccentric to the internationally renowned; it is a place for a pre-dinner martini, a post-dinner liqueur, or simply to spend the whole evening wallowing in glam.

The Fuxing Road area of the French Concession has become something of an after-dark hotspot with cool cocktail lounges like **The Apartment** and **El Coctel**, plus the city's best microbrewery pub **Boxing Cat Brewery**. Another popular bar is the Yunnan-themed **Mask**, which forms the first floor of Lost Heaven restaurant.

As an alternative to the cocktail scene, there is no shortage of down-to-earth pubs. **O'Malley's** is possibly the best – by a leprechaun's nose – of the city's many Irish pubs. It has the usual Celtic clutter on the walls, international sport on large screens, and Guinness at prices that reflect how far it has traveled. In the French Concession district, **Sasha's** bar and grill is set in a historic mansion with a beautiful patio garden. This stalwart of Shanghai was one of the city's first real international standard bars. It is particularly popular for its weekend brunch and it also makes good wood-fired pizzas. In the same grounds, **Zapata's** is a Mexican bar, restaurant, and club that targets a younger, more clubby crowd than Sasha's.

The **Paulaner Brauhaus** brews its own, expensive ale, with schnitzels and wurst to help it down, and views of the lights coming on along the Bund in the early evening. **Cotton's** is a big old house with rooms galore, each furnished with a grand fireplace.

Just north of Nanjing West Road, Tongren Road has the American-style bar, **Malone's**, the **Spot Bar**, with TV sports, large bar-food menu, and both tap and bottled beers, and the Canadian-owned **Big Bamboo Sports Bar**, the city's best venue for watching international soccer and other sports matches. Another popular sports bar, especially for Australian sports, is **The Camel** on Yueyang Road. Upscale Xin Tiandi has a good selection of pubs including **Kabb**, a trendy bar and grill, great for sophisticated cocktails, or try classy wine bar **Dr Wine**, perfect for lunch or a night out.

CLUBS

You're unlikely to travel to China just to go clubbing, but Shanghai regularly attracts big-name foreign DJs and hiphop acts. Again, see the local English-language press for details. If you have ever wondered what Shanghainese rap sounds like, then you can join the crowds as Hong Kong and Taiwanese DJs appear at long-standing favorite **Guan Di** in Fuxing Park, playing trance, house, and hip hop at high volumes, while VIPs recline on the fringes drinking Chivas and green tea (and that's in the same glass). Another glimpse at nouveau riche Chinese partying is on offer at **Bar 88**, a cavernous, lavishly designed mix of a club, karaoke house, and late night bar. It's loud and decadent but great fun.

FILM

Cinemas in Shanghai suffer the same handicaps as movie houses in Beijing, namely heavy censorship, a strict limiting of the number of foreign movies that can be screened, and the fact that you can get any new release on DVD for less than a dollar long before it reaches the big screen. For all these reasons, Shanghai possesses far fewer cinemas that you would expect. The most modern and high-tech venue is the **Paradise Warner Cinema City**, a multiplex in the Xujiahui district. However, probably more convenient for

A superb hotel bar, some 80 floors above street level

The foyer of the Cathay Theater, one of Shanghai's 1930s cinemas

Shanghai is trying its best to catch up with the capital. There are still relatively few live music bars in the city, in part due to a heavy crack down in the lead up to, and during, the 2010 World Expo. Many venues have closed indefinitely since that time but the scene is starting to pick up again. A popular choice among locals is the hip underground bar and club **The Shelter**, which features regular live music and DJs.

Xin Tiandi, the Hong Kong-financed rebuild of *shikumen* housing into a playground for the well-heeled, is where you will find many clubs and bars with cover bands and live music. This upscale area of bars, restaurants, and shops is a popular place for wealthy locals and visitors to the city to hang out.

most visitors is the **UME International Cineplex** in Xin Tiandi. For a taste of cinema-going of old, visit the 1930s Art Deco **Cathay Theater** in the French Concession. It often screens international movies with Chinese subtitles.

Shanghai is also the venue for an international film festival, held every June *(see p35)*. Films screenings are open to the public and the movies shown are not subject to the usual censorship.

JAZZ

The last living relic of the "Whore of the Orient" era, the nonagenarian band at the **Fairmont Peace Hotel Jazz Bar**, is more novelty act than any kind of serious musical proposition, although concierges and guide books will usually direct you to them. The bar has been revamped as part of a three-year overhaul of the Fairmont hotel. Serious blues lovers head for the **Cotton Club**, which has been around long enough to garner a good reputation and is typically packed at weekends. Try also **Club JZ**, a regular venue for visiting overseas jazzers and sessions of improvization. It is also where you may see famous local singer Coco.

The **House of Blues and Jazz**, located on Fuzhou Road, two blocks back from the Bund, is bluesier, and also features many touring bands from overseas, many of whom have played in top clubs in cities like New York. Drink prices at all these venues tend to be high. Foreign jazz acts also appear at **Brown Sugar** in Xin Tiandi, and at some other cocktail venues, including the **Glamour Bar** on the Bund,

ROCK AND POP

Beijing claims the crown when it comes to live contemporary music, but

TEA HOUSES

Normally the traditional Chinese tea house offers a respite from the crowds of the city, but Shanghai's most famous, the **Huxinting** or "mid-lake pavilion," is set amid the bedlam of the Yu Gardens and its attendant shopping, and is anything but calm. However, its 200-year-old willow pattern looks, with access only via a ghost-thwarting zig-zag bridge (ghosts can only travel in straight lines) makes it the most popular place to experience a Chinese tea ceremony. Past visitors have included the likes of Queen Elizabeth II, Bill Clinton, and other heads of state.

Fangbang Middle Road, the street that runs to the south of the Yu Gardens complex, has several similar operations of greater modernity, most selling tea as well as providing a place to drink it.

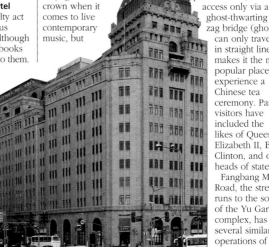

The Fairmont Peace Hotel, home of Shanghai's oldest jazz band

DIRECTORY

CLASSICAL MUSIC AND THE PERFORMING ARTS

Lyceum Theater
57 Maoming
South Road, French
Concession.
Map 1 E4.
Tel (021) 6217 8530.

Majestic Theater
66 Jiang Ning Road,
Jing'an District.
Map 1 E2.
Tel (021) 6217 3311.

Mercedes-Benz Arena
1200 Expo Avenue,
Pudong.
Map 3 E5.
Tel (086) 400 181 6688.

Oriental Art Center
425 Dingxiang Road.
Tel (021) 6854 1234.

Shanghai Center
1376 Nanjing West Road,
Jing'an District.
Map 1 E3.
Tel (021) 6279 8600.

Shanghai Grand Theater
300 Renmin Avenue,
Renmin Square.
Map 2 A3.
Tel (021) 6386 8686.

Yifu Theater
701 Fuzhou Road,
Huangpu District.
Map 2 B3.
Tel (021) 6351 4668.

BARS, PUBS, AND CLUBS

100 Century Avenue
91/F Park Hyatt Shanghai,
Century Boulevard,
Pudong. **Map** 3 F4.
Tel (021) 6888 1234.

Bar 88
2/F, 291 Fumin Road,
French Concession.
Map 1 D4.
Tel (021) 6136 0288.

Bar Rouge
7th Floor, Bund 18,
18 Zhong Shan Dong
Yi Lu, The Bund.
Map 2 C2.
Tel (021) 6339 1199.

Barbarossa
Nanjing West Road 231,
inside People's Park.
Map 2 A3.
Tel (021) 6318 0220.

Big Bamboo Sports Bar
132 Nanyang Road,
Jing'an District.
Map 1 D3.
Tel (021) 6256 2265.

Boxing Cat Brewery
82 Fuxing Road, French
Concession.
Tel (021) 6431 2091.

Brown Sugar
Building 15,
Xintiandi North
Block, Lane 181
Taicang Road.
Map 2 A4.
Tel (021) 5382 8998.

Club JZ
46 Fuxing West
Road, French Concession.
Tel (021) 6431 0269.

Cotton Club
1428 Huaihai
Middle Road, French
Concession.
Map 1 E4.
Tel (021) 6437 7110.

Cotton's
132 Anting Road,
Xuhui District.
Tel (021) 6433 7995.

Dr Wine
177 Fumin Road.
Map 1 D4.
Tel (021) 5403 5717.

El Coctel
2/F 47 Yongfu
Road, French Concession.
Tel (021) 6433 6511.

Fairmont Peace Hotel Jazz Bar
20 Nanjing East Road,
The Bund.
Map 2 C2.
Tel (021) 6138 6883.

Glamour Bar
M on the Bund,
6th Floor, 20
Guangdong Road,
The Bund.
Map 2 C3.
Tel (021) 6350 9988.

Guan Di
2 Gaolan Road,
inside Fuxing Park,
French Concession.
Map 1 F4.
Tel (021) 5383 6020.

House of Blues and Jazz
60 Fuzhou Road,
French Concession
(Nanjing East Road
metro).
Tel (021) 6321 1214.

Kabb
181 Taicang Road,
Xin Tiandi.
Map 2 A4.
Tel (021) 3307 0798.

Malone's
255 Tongren Road,
Jing'an District.
Map 1 D3.
Tel (021) 6247 2400.

Mask
38 Gaoyou Road, French
Concession.
Tel (021) 6433 5126.

O'Malleys
42 Taojiang Road,
Jing'an.
Map 1 D5.
Tel (021) 6474 6166.

Paulaner Brauhaus
Binjiang Avenue,
by Pudong
Shangri-La.
Map 3 D3.
Tel (021) 6888 3935.

Sasha's
11 Dong Ping Road &
Hengshan Road,
French Concession.
Tel (021) 6474 6628.

Sir Elly's
13/F, The Peninsula
Shanghai Hotel, 32
The Bund.
Map 3 D2.
Tel (021) 2327 2888.

Spot Bar
331 Tongren Road,
Jing'an.
Map 1 D3.
Tel (021) 6247 3579.

The Apartment
3/F 47 Yongfu Road,
French Concession.
Tel (021) 6437 9478.

The Camel
1 Yueyang Road,
French Concession.
Map 1 D5.
Tel (021) 6437 9446.

The Long Bar
Waldorf-Astoria
Shanghai on the Bund,
2 The Bund.
Map 3 C3.
Tel (021) 6322 9988.

The Shelter
5 Yongfu Road,
near Fuxing West
Road.
Tel (021) 6437 0400.

Vue
32–33/F, Hyatt on
the Bund Hotel, 199
Huangpu Road, near
The Bund (north).
Tel (021) 6393 1234.

Zapata's
5 Hengshang Road,
French Concession.
Tel (021) 6433 4104.

FILM

Cathay Theater
Huaihai Middle Road
870, French Concession.
Map 1 E4.
Tel (021) 5404 2095.

Paradise Warner Cinema City
6th Floor, Grand
Gateway, 1 Hong Qiao
Road, Xuhui District.
Tel (021) 6407 6622.

UME International Cineplex
2nd Floor, Lane 123,
Xingye Road,
Xin Tiandi.
Map 2 A4.
Tel (021) 6373 3333.

TEA HOUSES

Huxinting
257 Yu Yuan Road,
Old City.
Map 2 C4.
Tel (021) 6355 8270.

SHANGHAI STREET FINDER

The map references given with all sights, hotels, restaurants, shops, and entertainment venues described in this chapter refer to the following maps only. The first figure of the map reference indicates which map to turn to, and the letter and number that follow are the grid reference. The key map below shows which parts of Shanghai's city center are covered in this Street Finder and the symbols used in the Street Finder are listed below. A complete index of street names follows the maps. In contrast to Beijing street names, which still use Pinyin, Shanghai street names now use the English term for their suffixes and directionals: "lu" is now road, "dong" is east, "bei" is north, "nan" is south, "zhong" is middle, "jie" is street, and "dadao" is avenue.

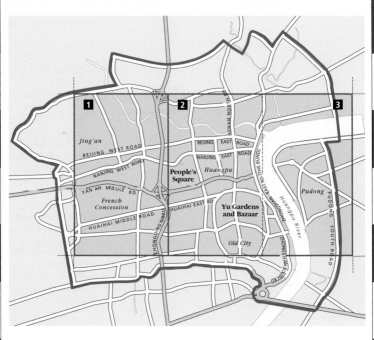

KEY TO STREET FINDER

Major sight		Tourist information	
Place of interest		Hospital	
Other important building		Post office	
M Subway station		Church	

SCALE OF MAP ABOVE

0 kilometers   2

0 miles   1

SCALE OF MAPS 1–3

0 meters   500

0 yards   500

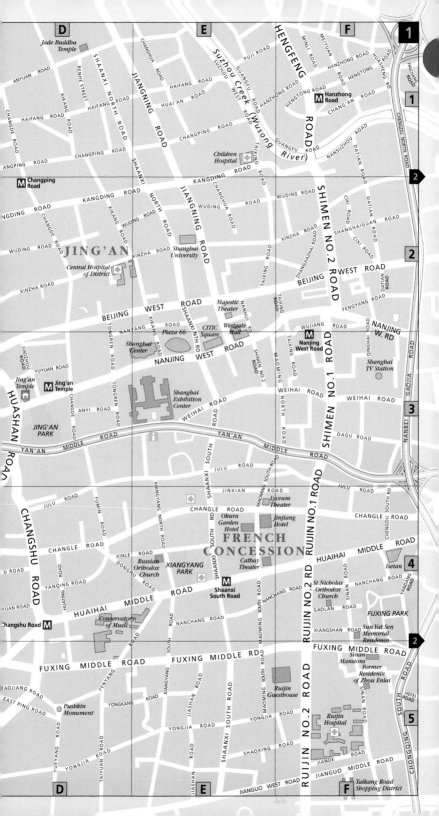

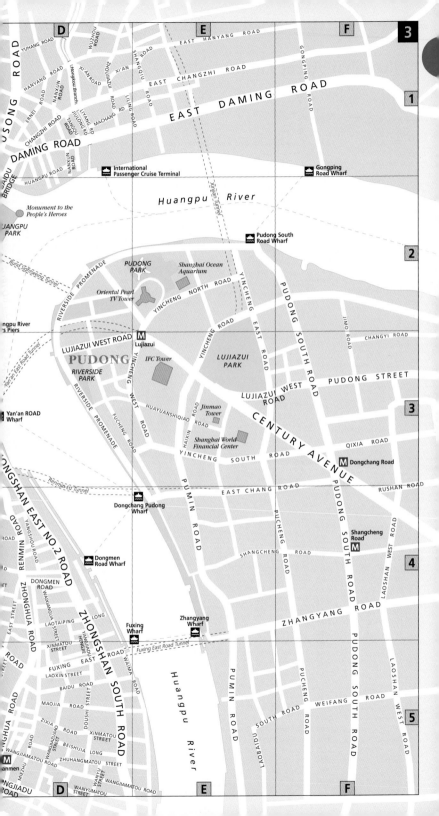

Shanghai Street Finder Index

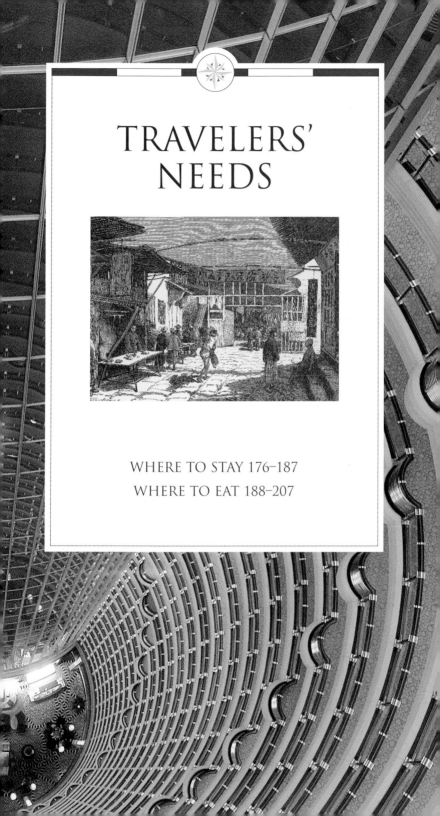

TRAVELERS'
NEEDS

WHERE TO STAY

Traditional red
lantern

Beijing and Shanghai together offer the most glamorous hotels in mainland China, and some of the most historic too. Four- and five-star hotels, many belonging to foreign chains, are plentiful. Boutique hotels are now opening in both cities, though standards vary. Beijing also has a num-ber of "courtyard" hotels, which are conversions of traditional old Chinese homes, and Shanghai has some old lane houses con-verted into boutique hotels and bed and breakfasts. There are plenty of other comfortable mid-range choices, and for budget travelers dirt-cheap need not mean dirty.

The courtyard of Beijing's Lu Song
Yuan Binguan Hotel

INTERNATIONAL AND CHINESE-RUN HOTELS

Visitors in search of interna-tional standards of comfort and service should stick either to five-star hotels managed by familiar Western chains, or the Singapore- and Hong Kong-based luxury companies.

Chinese-run hotels do their best to emulate Western operations and hospitality standards were greatly improved across the board during the lead up to the Olympics in Beijing and the World Expo in Shanghai. However, the level of service still does not match their Western counterparts.

The Chinese star system of grading hotels can be confusing as it does not follow international norms, and some hotel grades can be overstated. Rather than be involved in the star-rating system, some international hotels choose to go starless, but can be far superior to neigh-boring Chinese-run, five-stars. As a general rule for Chinese-run hotels, the newer the hotel, the better the facilities.

BUDGET HOTELS & OTHER TYPES OF ACCOMMODATIONS

Beijing has ample budget accommodations, including a new breed of sparkling hostels. In Shanghai things are more difficult, although dormitory beds can still be had for ¥70 or less.

Neither city has any sort of official camping grounds, and camping at random may lead to arrest.

BOOKING A HOTEL

In China, the real price of a hotel room is what the customer is willing to pay. Locals will always ask for a discount and you should too.

For most foreign-run hotels and newer Chinese hotels, the best available price will be on the hotel's own website. Prices can drop nearer to the planned day of stay, but it can be risky to wait too long as demand at international hotels is often high, particularly in Shanghai.

Be wary of websites adver-tising Chinese hotels, some of which quote a wildly inflated rack rate. Specialist websites often claim to offer huge discounts, so it is best to stick to reputable sites such as elong.net and ctrip.com.cn.

Most non-budget hotels will accept international credit cards but many charge a transaction fee. Foreign exchange facilities in hotels are becoming less reliable, and holders of travelers' checks, in particular, may be sent to the nearest large branch of the Bank of China. Particularly in more modest Chinese hotels, always be prepared to pay in local currency. Wherever you stay, you will always be asked for a credit card or cash deposit to cover hotel extras.

HIDDEN COSTS

The prices quoted by major international hotels do not include their service charges. Many Chinese-run, upper-end hotels have begun to levy service charges of between 5 and 15 percent, plus 3 percent VAT (Value Added Tax). Most Chinese customers refuse to pay the charges, and

Luxurious bedroom at the Portman Ritz-Carlton, Shanghai

◁ Grand Hyatt Shanghai, looking down multi-story atrium to patio below hotels rarely insist, but ask before you check in. Note that minibar contents are as overpriced in China as they are elsewhere in the world. However, only a modest service charge is added on top of the cost of international phone calls made from your hotel room.

SEASONAL DEMAND

The busiest travel periods are during the week-long national holiday around October 1, and during the Spring Festival or Chinese New Year (see p34). But most of the travel is away from the big cities, and so demand for hotel rooms in Beijing and Shanghai isn't usually any higher than at most other times of the year. Exhibitions and conferences pose more of a problem – and dates are mostly unpredictable – but these tend to affect upper-end accommodations only, although the April dates of Shanghai's Formula One Grand Prix should be avoided. During the Chinese New Year and October holidays, accommodations in Suzhou, Nanjing, and Hangzhou may be very hard to find.

Reception at the courtyard Bamboo Garden Hotel, Beijing

GENERAL OBSERVATIONS & PRECAUTIONS

It is common for Chinese-run hotels to request payment for the room in advance. Check-out is usually noon (some hotels may charge for late check out), but you can pay half the nightly rate to keep the room until 6pm.

Many hotels in China advertise facilities such as night clubs and karaoke bars, but these are often fronts for prostitution. Be wary of unexpected telephone calls to your room offering massage. It is nearly always a mistake to arrange transportation

through your hotel, as it often costs four times as much as it would if you found a taxi on your own. Taxis hovering near the doors of upmarket hotels should also be approached with caution.

FACILITIES FOR CHILDREN & THE DISABLED

Most hotels allow under-12s to stay with their parents free of charge. Most will also add an extra bed for an older child for a nominal (and negotiable) fee.

In general, China is not a suitable destination for the disabled, although facilities are becoming more widespread. Only the newest and best international hotels make any serious effort to provide wheelchair access, or fully adapted rooms.

TIPPING

Traditionally there is no tipping in China, but because of the increasing number of visitors that do tip regardless, this is starting to change. This is most particularly true in hotels in heavily touristed areas and in more upmarket establishments.

DIRECTORY

HOTEL CHAINS

Crowne Plaza
Tel 1-800 801 881 (US).
0800 8222 8222 (UK).
www.ichotelsgroup.com

Fairmont
Tel 1-800 257 7544 (US).
0800 0441 1414 (UK).
www.fairmont.com

Four Seasons
Tel 1-800 819 5053 (US).
0800 6488 6488 (UK).
www.fourseasons.com

Grand Hyatt
Tel 1-866 233 1234 (US).
0845 888 1234 (UK).
1-800 481 034 (Ireland).
www.hyatt.com

Hilton
Tel 1-800 774 1500 (US).
0800 4488 22073 (UK).
www.hilton.com

Holiday Inn
Tel 1-800 465 4329 (US).
0800 405 060 (UK).
www.ichotelsgroup.com

Howard Johnson
Tel (021) 6886 8840.
www.hojochina.com

Hyatt Regency
Tel 1-866 233 1234 (US).
0845 888 1234 (UK).
www.hyatt.com

InterContinental
Tel 1-800 424 6835 (US).
0800 405 060 (UK).
www.ichotelsgroup.com

Marco Polo
www.marcopolohotels.
com

Marriott
Tel 1-888 236 2427 (US).
0800 1927 1927 (UK).
www.marriott.com

Novotel
Tel 1-800 666 0835 (US).
www.novotel.com

Park Hyatt
Tel 1-866 233 1234 (US).
0845 888 1234 (UK).
1-800 481 034 (Ireland).
www.hyatt.com

Peninsula
Tel 1-866 382 8388 (US).
0800 2828 3888 (UK).
www.peninsula.com

Radisson
Tel 1-800 805 164 (US).
0800 374 411 (UK).
1-800 557 474 (Ireland).
www.radisson.com

Ritz-Carlton
Tel 1-800 542 8680 (US).
0800 234 000 (UK).
1-800 145 004 (Aus).
www.ritzcarlton.com

St. Regis
Tel 1-800 325 3589 (US).
0800 3257 8734 (UK).
www.starwood.com

Shangri-La
Tel 1-866 565 5050 (US).
0800 028 3337 (UK).
www.shangri-la.com

Sheraton
Tel 1-888 625 5144 (US).
0800 3253 5353 (UK).
www.starwood.com

Sofitel
Tel 1-800 763 4835 (US).
0871 663 0625 (UK).
1300 884 400 (Aus).
008 133 388 (China).
www.sofitel.com

Westin
Tel 1-888 625 5144 (US).
0800 3259 5959 (UK).
www.starwood.com

Choosing a Hotel

The hotels in this guide have been selected across a wide range of price categories for the excellence of their facilities, location, or character. The chart below lists the hotels in price categories within the chapters of the book. Many hotels have business facilities, gyms, and swimming pools, but only the best have been listed.

PRICE CATEGORIES
The following price ranges are for a standard double room (or single dorm bed) and taxes per night during the high season. Breakfast is not included.
Ⓨ under ¥200
ⓎⓎ ¥200–¥400
ⓎⓎⓎ ¥400–¥800
ⓎⓎⓎⓎ ¥800–¥1400
ⓎⓎⓎⓎⓎ Over ¥1400

BEIJING

Downtown Backpackers (Dongtang Qingnian Lüshe)   Ⓨ
85 Nan Luogu Xiang **Tel** *(010) 8400 2429* **Rooms** *20*   **Map** *2 B2*

Good value in the heart of Nanluo Guxiang *hutong* district, minutes from the imperial lakes, Drum and Bell Towers, and myriad restaurants and bars. Offers clean single rooms, doubles with attached bath, and 6–8 bed dorms, plus bike hire and laundry facilities. **www.backpackingchina.com**

Red Lantern House   Ⓨ
5 Zhengjue Hutong, Xinjiekou Nandajie **Tel** *(010) 8328 5771* **Rooms** *12*   **Map** *1 E2*

This family-run hotel occupies a traditional *siheyuan* and is excellent value for money. The rooms are set around an inner courtyard and are simple and clean, while the friendly owners go out of their way to offer guests advice and help with onward bookings. A good option for budget travelers. **www.redlanternhouse.com**

Saga Hostel (Shizhu Qingnian Lüshe)   Ⓨ
9 Shijia Hutong **Tel** *(010) 6527 2773* **Fax** *(010) 6524 9098* **Rooms** *24*   **Map** *2 C4*

Tranquil if slightly inconvenient *hutong* location south-west of Chaoyang Men subway. Featuring spotless doubles, triples, and dorm rooms, a communal kitchen and café, and a rooftop patio. Helpful English-speaking management organize bike hire, ticket bookings, and tours. **www.sagayouthhostelbeijing.cn**

Sweet Garden Hostel (Tianyuan Qingnian Lüguan)   Ⓨ
19 Dong Si Qi Tiao **Tel** *(010) 6405 1538* **Rooms** *13*   **Map** *2 C3*

Peaceful, family-run hostel in a converted courtyard residence close to Dong Si Shi Tiao subway offers simple single, double, and 4–6 bed dorm rooms. Management speak little English but arrange bike hire, booking services, and even airport pick-up. Rates include Chinese breakfast.

Beijing City Youth Hostel (Beijing Chengshi Guoji Qingnian Lüshe)   ⓎⓎ
1–5 Beijing Zhan Qian Jie **Tel** *(010) 8511 5050* **Fax** *(010) 6525 9066* **Rooms** *200*   **Map** *5 F1*

Good value budget accommodations and extremely convenient for those with early morning trains from Beijing Station. Reasonably priced twin rooms and dorms are modern and clean, and there are also cooking facilities and a 24-hour shop on site. **www.centralhostel.com**

Beijing Citycourt Hotel   ⓎⓎ
14 Liulisi Hutong, Dongcheng **Tel** *(010) 6712 5588* **Fax** *(010) 6718 6069* **Rooms** *24*   **Map** *2 B2*

Located in a renovated Qing-dynasty *hutong* courtyard in a quiet but central location, this small hotel has plenty of character, with Chinese lanterns and an interior courtyard patio with painted beams and pillars. There is also a Chinese restaurant and bar as well as a café. **www.citycourthotelbeijing.cn**

Far East International Youth Hostel (Yuan Dong Qingnian Lüshe)   ⓎⓎ
90 Tieshuxie Jie **Tel** *(010) 5195 8811* **Fax** *(010) 6318 0324* **Rooms** *24*   **Map** *4 B3*

The city's most charming YHA hostel, with dorms (110 beds in total) and private rooms available both in a pleasantly decorated conventional hotel building and a courtyard house across the street. The surrounding area was an Imperial-era red-light district and maintains its lively atmosphere. **www.fareastyh.com**

Feiying Binguan   ⓎⓎ
10 Xuanwu Men Xi Dajie **Tel** *(010) 6317 1116* **Fax** *(010) 6315 1165* **Rooms** *46*   **Map** *4 A2*

Among the cheapest of the Youth Hostelling International hotels in Beijing, and the most convenient for transportation. Private twins and dorm rooms are pristine, and management are fairly helpful. Facilities on offer include a bar and restaurant. **www.hihostels.com**

Red Hotel (Ruixiu Binguan)   ⓎⓎ
10 Chunxiu Lu **Tel** *(010) 6417 1066* **Fax** *(010) 6416 7600* **Rooms** *40*   **Map** *3 E2*

Dorms, hotel rooms, and apartments with kitchen and laundry facilities for short- or long-term rent. Rooms feature dark wooden floors, faux-antique furnishings, and multi-jet capsule showers. There's a popular football bar on the ground floor, and it's just a few minutes' walk to the entertainment district of Sanlitun. **www.red-hotel.com**

Key to Symbols *see back cover flap*

Xindadu Youth Hostel (Xindadu Guoji Qingnian Lüshe)

21 Chegongzhuang Dajie **Tel** *(010) 6831 9988 ext. 180* **Fax** *(010) 8837 3701* **Rooms** *38*

YHA hostels are beginning to take over Beijing's budget accommodations. Dorm beds (there are 200 in total here) are the only option, but the rooms are pristine and Xindadu's rates are some of the lowest in the city. Convenient access to Beijing West Railway Station.

Zhaolong International Youth Hostel (Zhaolong Qingnian Lüshe)

8 An Ping Xiang, Zhao Deng Yu Lu **Tel** *(010) 6597 2299 ext. 6111* **Fax** *(010) 6597 2288* **Rooms** *24*   **Map** *1 E3*

A quiet option despite the proximity to Sanlitun bar district. Dorms are decently tidy and guests have access to a self-catering dining room, games room, reading room, and bike rentals. Staff keep strict order, locking doors at 1am even on weekends.

4 Banqiao

4 Banqiao Hutong, Beixinqiao **Tel** *(010) 8403 0968* **Rooms** *18*   **Map** *2 C2*

In a great location in the heart of Beijing's historical *hutong* area, this inexpensive courtyard hotel is very popular. Rooms are furnished to a higher standard than you would expect for the price – there are antiques and nice touches such as handmade bed spreads. Book well in advance and expect good discounts off season. **www.4banqiao.com**

Aloft

Tower 2, 25 Yuanda Lu, Haidian District **Tel** *(010) 8889 8000* **Fax** *(010) 8889 8666* **Rooms** *186*

A good-value option, Aloft is located in the university disctrict, close to the Summer Palace. It has hip, contemporary decor and excellent facilities for both leisure and business visitors. The open-plan lounge features computers and a pool table. There is a special program of activities for kids under 12 years. **www.alofthotels.com/beijing**

Bamboo Garden Hotel (Zhuyuan Binguan)

24 Xiao Shi Qiao Hutong, Jiugulou Lu **Tel** *(010) 5852 0088* **Fax** *(010) 5852 0066* **Rooms** *40*   **Map** *2 A1*

Close to the lakes, this is the oldest of Beijing's traditional hotels, with the largest and most elaborate courtyards, although rooms are mostly located in two buildings that lack the intimacy and charm of other smaller competitors. Rockeries and covered pathways make for pleasant lounging surrounds. **www.bbgh.com.cn**

Comfort Inn & Suites

6 Gongren Tiyuchang Bei Lu **Tel** *(010) 8523 5522* **Fax** *(010) 8523 5577* **Rooms** *96*   **Map** *3 D3*

Rooms are tastefully decorated, with large desks, comfortable sofas, and plush duvets. Catering more for business people on lengthy stays, service can be found wanting. The location nevertheless provides access to Sanlitun's many bars, restaurants, and shops. **www.comfortinn.com**

Courtyard 7

7 Qiangulouyuan Hutong, Nanluoguxiang **Tel** *(010) 6406 0777* **Rooms** *19*   **Map** *2 B2*

This small, tastefully converted 300-year-old courtyard hotel is set back off one of Beijing's most interesting *hutongs* and makes for a peaceful refuge. The small rooms and bathrooms have been sympathetically modernized and the charming courtyard is the perfect place to while away some time. **www.courtyard7.com**

Cuimingzhuang Binguan

1 Nan Heyan Dajie **Tel** *(010) 6513 6622* **Fax** *(010) 6526 1516* **Rooms** *134*   **Map** *2 B5*

This hotel is conveniently located and affordable. Rooms are simple but clean, and are surprisingly large compared to other hotels in the area. The service staff are more pleasant than normally found in a Chinese hotel: quiet, unobtrusive, and unusually fastidious.

Emperor Hotel

33 Qihelou Jie **Tel** *(010) 6526 5566* **Fax** *(010) 6523 8786* **Rooms** *55*   **Map** *2 B4*

Injecting some coolness into the Forbidden City area, this boutique hotel has very modern, colorful rooms – each one named after a different Emperor – and hip modular furniture. There is an in-house restaurant and a rooftop bar boasting stellar views over the Forbidden City. **www.theemperorbejing.cn**

Fraser Residence Beijing

Block B, Ocean International Centre 58, Dong Si Huan Zhonglu **Tel** *(010) 5870 9188* **Fax** *(010) 5870 9199* **Rooms** *228*

Superbly appointed and stylishly designed serviced apartments of varying sizes. Each apartment has living, dining, kitchen, and bedroom areas and facilities include high-speed Internet connection, cable TV, and air-conditioning. Service is fast and responsive. **beijing-east.frasershospitality.com**

Lu Song Yuan Binguan

22 Banchang Hutong **Tel** *(010) 6404 0436* **Fax** *(010) 6403 0418* **Rooms** *50*   **Map** *2 B3*

The details are similar to those in other courtyard hotels, but here they somehow add up to a more comfortable atmosphere. A good variety of accommodations from cheap youth hostel-style facilities right up to suites as well as a charming teahouse and well-stocked bookshelves. **www.lusongyuanhotel.com**

Scitech Hotel

Jianguo Men Wai Dajie 22 **Tel** *(010) 6512 3388* **Fax** *(010) 6512 3545* **Rooms** *294*   **Map** *3 F5*

A good-value option for shoppers and hedonists, four-star Scitech abuts a large department store and popular nightclub Banana. Standard rooms decorated in earthy tones are small, but are otherwise comfortable and well-appointed. **www.scitechhotel.com**

3 + 1 Bedrooms

17 Zhangwang Hutong, Jiu Gulou Dajie **Tel** *(010) 6404 7030* **Rooms** *4*   **Map** *2 A1*

A world away from traditional Beijing, this tiny boutique injects some minimalist chic into the courtyard hotel scene. Run by a stylish Singaporean, there are just three bedrooms and a suite. The stark whiteness of the rooms contrast nicely with the colorful local street life visible from the rooftop terrace. **3plus1bedrooms.com**

Crowne Plaza

48 Wangfujing Dajie **Tel** *(010) 5911 9999* **Fax** *(010) 5911 9998* **Rooms** *360*   **Map** *2 B4*

The Crowne Plaza has comfortable rooms with tasteful decoration. Facilities include a health club with spa and swimming pool. Reasonable value, and within walking distance of Wangfujing subway and the Forbidden City. **www.crowneplaza.beijing.ichotelsgroup.com**

Fairmont Hotel Beijing

8 Yong An Dong Li, Jianguomen Wai Dajie **Tel** *(010) 8511 7777* **Fax** *(010) 8507 3999* **Rooms** *222*   **Map** *3 E5*

The Fairmont is one of Beijing's five-star hotels and its golden colored decor is glamorous without being gaudy. North facing rooms have good views over the city and come with plenty of added extras including Bose music systems, Nespresso coffee machines, and TVs in the bathrooms. **www.fairmont.com/beijing**

Grace Beijing

Jiuxianqiao Lu, 2 Hao Yuan, 798 Art District **Tel** *(010) 6436 1818* **Fax** *(010) 6438 1810* **Rooms** *30*

Located in the 798 Art District, this boutique hotel offers smart, European-style rooms with spacious bathrooms, satellite TV, and free Internet. There is a charming patio terrace and a highly acclaimed bistro restaurant, Yi House, which is very popular for Sunday brunch. Art exhibitions are shown in the lobby, restaurant, and bar. **www.gracebeijing.com**

Hilton Beijing Wangfujing

8 Wangfujing Dong Daji **Tel** *(010) 5812 8888* **Fax** *(010) 5812 8886* **Rooms** *255*   **Map** *2 B5*

The latest Hilton in Beijing attracts praise for its central location – it is walking distance from Tian'an Men Square and the Forbidden City – its spacious, open-plan rooms, and its warm service. The large pool and luxurious spa area provide a wonderful refuge after a day of sightseeing. **www.hilton.com**

Hotel G

A7 Gongti Xi Lu **Tel** *(010) 6552 3600* **Fax** *(010) 6552 3606* **Rooms** *110*   **Map** *3 E3*

Beside the Workers' Stadium and a 15-minute walk from Sanlitun, this glamorous boutique hotel is an excellent choice. Well-priced rooms come with seductive velvet drapes, darkly colored 1960s retro furniture, iPod docks, and Nintendo Wiis. Scarlet, the in-house bar and restaurant, is very popular. **www.hotel-g.com**

Howard Johnson Paragon

18A Jianguo Men Nei Dajie **Tel** *(010) 6526 6688* **Fax** *(010) 6527 4020* **Rooms** *288*   **Map** *5 F1*

Comfortable and close to both Beijing Station and its subway stop, and just a short taxi ride to Wangfujing and Tian'an Men Square. Rooms, although not large, are comfortable, and international standards ensure a quality of service not found in most other nearby hotels. **www.hojochina.com**

InterContinental Financial Street Beijing

11 Jinrong Jie (Fucheng Men Nan Dajie) **Tel** *(010) 5852 5888* **Fax** *(010) 5852 5999* **Rooms** *332*   **Map** *1 D5*

This luxury boutique hotel located in "Financial Street," Beijing's rapidly growing western business district, features tasteful, modern decor throughout. Although far from tourist sights, spacious rooms are good value with large plasma TVs and impressive bathrooms. **www.ichotelsgroup.com**

Novotel Xin Qiao

1 Chong Wen Men Xi Dajie **Tel** *(010) 6513 3366* **Fax** *(010) 6512 5126* **Rooms** *700*   **Map** *5 E2*

Big discounts and a central location near Tian'an Men Square, Chongwen Men subway station, and shopping centers compensate for bland rooms and poor service. Still, rooms are cable Internet-equipped and restaurants are varied and reasonably priced. **www.novotel.com**

Park Plaza Hotel

97 Jin Bao Jie **Tel** *(010) 8522 1999* **Fax** *(010) 8522 1919* **Rooms** *216*   **Map** *2 C5*

Set back from the street, the stylish Park Plaza is a peaceful oasis in a fast-developing precinct. Rooms are modish in decoration, with bathrooms featuring designer touches including mosaic tiles. Convenient for the Forbidden City and a short walk from Wangfujing. **www.parkplaza.com/beijingcn**

Sofitel Wanda Beijing

93 Jianguo Lu, Tower C, Wanda Plaza **Tel** *(010) 8599 6666* **Fax** *(010) 8599 6686* **Rooms** *407*

The Beijing outpost of this French chain has sober, stylish rooms where everything is controlled with the push of a button. The Sofitel has a good location next to the Central Business District and is 10 minutes' walk from the nearest subway stop. Le Pre Lenotre, the hotel's fine-dining French restaurant, is one Beijing's best. **www.sofitel.com**

The Orchid

65 Baochao Hutong, Dongcheng District **Tel** *(010) 8404 4818* **Fax** *(010) 8418 1987* **Rooms** *10*   **Map** *2 A1*

A stylish boutique hotel, The Orchid is housed in a renovated courtyard building located in the increasingly hip Baochao Hutong. The comfortable guestrooms feature contemporary decor and modern amenities. The rooftop bar and lounge affords fine views over the *hutongs* towards the Drum and Bell Towers. **www.theorchidbeijing.com**

Key to Price Guide *see p178* **Key to Symbols** *see back cover flap*

Traders Hotel Beijing

1 Jianguo Men Wai Dajie **Tel** *(010) 6505 2277* **Fax** *(010) 6505 0838* **Rooms** *570*   **Map** *3 F5*

In the heart of the business district, thoroughly wired, and offering every possible business facility, but also comforts such as a very popular Southeast Asian buffet that spills onto a terrace in summer. Next to the China World Shopping Mall, Convention Center, and the subway. **www.shangri-la.com**

Aman at Summer Palace

1 Gongmenqian Jie **Tel** *(010) 5987 9999* **Fax** *(010) 5987 9900* **Rooms** *51*

Fit for an emperor, this stunning hotel, part of the luxurious Amanresorts group, consists of converted Summer Palace courtyards, linked up by covered walkways in stunning grounds. Guests enjoy private access to the Summer Palace *(see pp80–3)* as well as a cinema, spa, and subterranean swimming pool. **www.amanresorts.com**

Duge Courtyard Hotel

26 Qianyuanensi Hutong, Nanluoguxiang **Tel** *(010) 6406 0686* **Fax** *(010) 6406 0628* **Rooms** *10*   **Map** *2 B2*

Tucked down an alley, this tiny, exclusive hotel was part designed by jeweler Jehanne de Biolley and is flamboyant and colorful. The hotel provides a luxurious hideaway with each of its ten rooms uniquely decorated; the Imperial suite, with burnished gold decor, will make guests feel like royalty. **www.dugecourtyard.com**

Grand Hyatt Beijing

1 Dong Chang'an Jie **Tel** *(010) 8518 1234* **Fax** *(010) 8518 0000* **Rooms** *825*   **Map** *2 B5*

In the glittering Oriental Plaza shopping complex on Wangfujing, no other Beijing luxury hotel is better located, and few are as well equipped. Cantonese, Beijing, and Japanese restaurants here are among the city's finest, and fitness and spa facilities are among the best. **www.beijing.grand.hyatt.com**

JW Marriott Hotel Beijing

83 Jianguo Lu **Tel** *(010) 5908 6688* **Fax** *(010) 5908 6699* **Rooms** *588*

With a great selection of food and beverage outlets, including Loong Bar with its dazzling dragons, the JW is very popular with locals. It is also a good choice for business travelers as it is near the Central Business District. Next to the hotel is the ritzy Shin Kong Place shopping center and a subway stop. **www.marriott.com**

Kempinski Hotel

50 Liangma Qiao Lu **Tel** *(010) 6465 3388* **Fax** *(010) 6410 4080* **Rooms** *366*   **Map** *3 F1*

Near the embassy district, the Kempinski offers excellent service. The real selling point is its access to Western conveniences in the attached Lufthansa Center, including airline offices, medical facilities, restaurants and bars, and high-end shopping. **www.kempinski.com**

Kerry Center Hotel

1 Guanghua Lu **Tel** *(010) 6561 8833* **Fax** *(010) 6561 2626* **Rooms** *487*   **Map** *3 F5*

The youngest of Shangri-La's Beijing stable combines the group's high service standards with bright, modern room design. Part luxury shopping complex, the Kerry is also home to one of Beijing's best Cantonese restaurants, the city's hottest cocktail bar (Centro), and extensive health facilities. **www.shangri-la.com.cn**

Park Hyatt Beijing

2 Jianguomenwai Dajie **Tel** *(010) 8567 1234* **Fax** *(010) 8567 1000* **Rooms** *237*   **Map** *3 F5*

Soaring above the heart of Beijing's Central Business District, this luxury hotel is located in one of the city's tallest skyscrapers. The contemporary accommodation is understated and chic, and filled with high-tech amenities, while the hotel's bars and restaurants are popular with discerning Beijingers. **beijing.park.hyatt.com**

Peninsula Beijing Hotel

8 Jinyu Hutong **Tel** *(010) 8516 2888* **Fax** *(010) 6510 6311* **Rooms** *530*   **Map** *2 C5*

Luxurious rooms each with large plasma TVs, marble bathrooms with another small screen TV, and all amenities. Several outstanding restaurants, a luxury mall with names like Prada and Gucci, excellent service, and a central Wangfujing location, make this one of the city's best choices. **www.peninsula.com**

Ritz-Carlton Financial Street

57 Jin Cheng Fang East Street, Financial District **Tel** *(010) 6601 6666* **Fax** *(010) 6601 6029* **Rooms** *253* **Map** *4 B1*

Bright, chic, and functional interiors represent a departure from the Ritz-Carlton's classical style, but the elegance and superb facilities are still much in evidence here in the Financial district, west of Tian'an Men Square. A good range of fine-dining options completes the picture. **www.ritzcarlton.com**

Shangri-La Beijing

29 Zizhuyuan Lu **Tel** *(010) 6841 2211* **Fax** *(010) 6481 8002/3* **Rooms** *528*

The Shangri-La is peacefully located in gardens to the west of the city, not far from the Summer Palace. Decorated to a high standard, with the addition of a tower and excellent restaurants and bars, not to mention the hotel's usual five-star service. **www.shangri-la.com**

Shangri-La China World Summit Wing

1 Jianguo Men Wai Dajie **Tel** *(010) 6505 2299* **Fax** *(010) 6505 8811* **Rooms** *716*   **Map** *3 F5*

One of the most comprehensively luxurious hotels in Beijing is housed in the city's tallest tower, with magnificent views over the capital. Located in the heart of the main business district, with connections to the subway and a swish shopping mall, it houses some of the best restaurants in town, including Grill 79. **www.shangri-la.com**

St. Regis Beijing

21 Jianguo Men Wai Dajie **Tel** *(010) 6460 6688* **Fax** *(010) 6460 3299* **Rooms** *273* — **Map** *3 F5*

Close to the main embassy area and business district, the St. Regis has had an extensive revamp. It has small, but beautifully decorated rooms with free access to an on-call butler. There are excellent Italian and steak restaurants, as well as an exclusive health club and outdoor putting green. **www.starwoodhotels.com**

The Opposite House

The Village, Building 1, 11 Sanlitun Lu, Chaoyang **Tel** *(021) 6417 6688* **Fax** *(010) 6417 7799* **Rooms** *99* — **Map** *3 F3*

This upscale boutique hotel was designed by Japanese architect Kengo Kuman with a theme of "nature indoors" so unpolished wood and stone predominate. The super-swish ambiance continues in the open-plan rooms, all with excellent amenities and large bathrooms. **www.theoppositehouse.com**

The Westin Beijing Chaoyang

7 North Dongsanhuan **Tel** *(010) 5922 8888* **Fax** *(010) 5922 8999* **Rooms** *550* — **Map** *3 F1*

Luxurious comfort and outstanding service from well-trained staff are complemented by the Westin's stylish property, the brand's second location in the city. While being set on a ring road is not ideal, sights and shopping areas are only a short taxi ride away. **www.starwoodhotels.com**

BEIJING FARTHER AFIELD

SHUIGUAN Commune at the Great Wall

Badaling Express Way Exit 53 Shuiguan Section **Tel** *(010) 8118 1888* **Fax** *(010) 8118 1866* **Rooms** *212*

A popular retreat for Beijing-based expats, the major attraction here is private access to a part of The Great Wall. Originally a collection of architect-designed houses, the hotel has majorly expanded its number of rooms. The Kid's Club gets high praise from grateful parents, as does the fancy Antanara Spa. **www.commune.com.cn**

XIAGUANDI Red Capital Ranch

No. 28 Xiaguandi Village, Yanxi Township **Tel** *(010) 8401 6152* **Fax** *(010) 6402 7153* **Rooms** *10*

Guests looking for a rustic and romantic stay will find it at one of Red Capital's 10 stone cottages, filled with interesting artifacts from around the country. A quiet stretch of the Great Wall is walking distance away. Closed December to February. **www.redcapitalclub.com.cn**

YINGBEIGOU Brickyard Inn

Yingbeigou Village **Tel** *(010) 6162 6506* **Rooms** *16*

This small bed and breakfast occupies an old glazed-tile factory and offers 16 rooms, all with private terraces. There is free Wi-Fi throughout and the Mutianyu section of the Great Wall is nearby. The owners are careful to employ local people as part of their belief in sustainability. Closed December to February. **www.brickyardatmutianyu.com**

SHANGHAI

Captain Hostel

37 Fuzhou Road **Tel** *(086) 400 001 9990* **Fax** *(021) 6321 9940* **Rooms** *21* — **Map** *2 C3*

The best cheap option in Shanghai. A stone's throw from the Bund, with river views from the rooftop bar. Dorm beds (132 in total) and rooms are clean and comfortable. All typical hostel extras (day trips, Internet, bicycle hire) are available. The Captain has a sister hostel in Pudong. **www.captainhostel.com.cn/en**

Astor House Hotel (Pujiang Fandian)

15 Huangpu Road **Tel** *(021) 6324 6388* **Fax** *(021) 6324 3179* **Rooms** *130* — **Map** *3 D2*

This historic building was, a century ago, Shanghai's most luxurious hotel. The decor suggests it aspires to former glories, yet the Astor remains primarily a budget option. Still, spacious rooms with wood-paneled floors are available, some with fantastic Bund views. **www.pujianghotel.com**

Ling Long Hotel

939 Yan'an West Road **Tel** *(021) 6225 0360* **Rooms** *15*

An excellent choice for budget travelers, this small hotel was once a private residence and still retains its intimate atmosphere. The slightly old-fashioned decor adds to the charm, but light sleepers should be aware that the hotel is on a busy street. While staff do not speak fluent English, they will do their best to help guests.

Motel 168

1119 Yan'an West Road **Tel** *(021) 5117 7777* **Rooms** *510*

Leading the charge of budget hotels across China's main cities, Motel 168 offers no-frills accommodations with clean, compact rooms, and features walls in bright colors. The Yan'an Road branch, near Jing'an Temple, has the best location of the ten in Shanghai. **www.motel168.com**

Key to Price Guide *see p178* **Key to Symbols** *see back cover flap*

Broadway Mansions

20 Suzhou North Road **Tel** *(021) 6324 6260* **Fax** *(021) 6306 5147* **Rooms** *234*   **Map** *2 C1*

Replete with 20th-century history, this distinctive brick building was constructed in 1934 on Suzhou Creek. Located just minutes north of the Bund, the Broadway offers eight room types with wildly varying prices and views. Staff here are friendly and helpful. **www.broadwaymansions.com**

Bund Garden Hotel

200 Hankou Road **Tel** *(021) 6329 8800* **Rooms** *9*   **Map** *2 C2*

Located right next to the Bund, this small hotel is spread across several 1930s-era houses. The leafy garden is a delight, as are the charming, 1930s-style rooms. Breakfast is Chinese style and served in your room. Not all staff speak English, but there is usually someone who will be able to help guests.

City Hotel

5–7 Shanxi South Road **Tel** *(021) 6255 1133* **Fax** *(021) 6255 0211* **Rooms** *270*   **Map** *1 E3*

On the northern fringe of the French Concession, this is a decent, central four-star option with a business bent. The basic, good-value rooms won't win design awards, but do have broadband and satellite TV. Skip the Shanghainese restaurant for the excellent eateries nearby. **www.cityhotelshanghai.com**

Green Garden Hotel

328 Weifang Road **Tel** *(021) 5081 2222* **Fax** *(021) 5058 0117* **Rooms** *151*   **Map** *3 F5*

Environmentally friendly four-star hotel aimed at business travelers, particularly Japanese, offering *tatami* suites, Inax bidets, and a Japanese restaurant. Well located in the Lujiazui Financial District but less convenient for Shanghai's main tourist spots. **www.greengardenhotel.com/en**

Hengshan Moller Villa

30 Shanxi South Road **Tel** *(021) 6247 8881* **Fax** *(021) 6289 1020* **Rooms** *45*   **Map** *1 E3*

Built by a 1930s shipping magnate with a castle fetish, this bizarrely bricked and turreted edifice is less impressive inside than out, with unexceptional, frumpy rooms and a particularly dreary modern annexe. A novelty, but not a bargain. **www.mollervilla.com**

Hengshan Picardie Hotel

534 Hengshan Road **Tel** *(021) 6437 7050* **Fax** *(021) 6433 5732* **Rooms** *233*

Well located on one of the city's prettiest streets, and opposite Xujiahui Park, the Hengshan Picardie Hotel is a perfect starting point for French Concession walks. Choose a room with care, however, as rooms vary in size and quality, from smart and spacious to smoky and poky. **www.hengshanhotel.com/en**

Metropole Hotel

180 Jiangxi Middle Road **Tel** *(021) 6321 3030* **Fax** *(021) 6321 7365* **Rooms** *141*   **Map** *2 C3*

The fabulous Art Deco exterior and a location close to the Bund recall 1930s Shanghai. Unfortunately so does the hotel's lighting: entertainment areas and rooms are gloomy, and the restaurant lacks charm. Staff are approachable and, for the most part, affable. **www.metropolehotel-shanghai.com**

Okura Garden Hotel Shanghai

58 Maoming South Road **Tel** *(021) 6415 1111 or (021) 6415 8866* **Fax** *(021) 6415 8866* **Rooms** *492*   **Map** *1 E4*

This Japanese-managed luxury hotel has an almost unsurpassed location, close to the subway, the French Concession, and vibrant Maoming Road. Lush gardens, potable tap water in the marble bathrooms, and staff members with excellent language ability complete the plush picture. **www.gardenhotelshanghai.com**

Old House Inn (Lao Shiguang)

No.16, Lane 351, Huashan Road **Tel** *(021) 6248 6118* **Fax** *(021) 6249 6869* **Rooms** *12*

Perhaps the best of Shanghai's handful of boutique hotels, the Old House Inn is central yet peaceful: the creaking of wooden floors is all you'll hear. Delightful old furniture highlights the dozen unique rooms; shuttered windows open onto a courtyard. There's an innovative Western restaurant downstairs. **www.oldhouse.cn**

Pacific Hotel

108 Nanjing West Road **Tel** *(021) 6327 6226* **Fax** *(021) 6375 0350* **Rooms** *180*   **Map** *2 A2*

Wedged between Shanghai's famous Art Deco Park Hotel and a Radisson, the Pacific Hotel still exudes grandness, thanks to its Bund-matching façade and elegant clock tower, sadly unmatched by some tired interior areas. Rooms facing People's Park are easily the best. **www.pacifichotelshanghai.cn**

Quintet

808 Changle Road **Tel** *(021) 6249 9088* **Fax** *(021) 6249 2198* **Rooms** *5*   **Map** *1 E4*

Tasteful and charming, Quintet is highly recommended by travelers looking for intimate bed and breakfast accommodation. The five rooms have comfortable, king-size beds with luxurious white linens, and bathrooms have oversized bathtubs. Breakfast can be served on the rooftop area, weather permitting. **www.quintet-shanghai.com**

Tai Yuan Villa

160 Taiyuan Road, near Yongjia Road **Tel** *(021) 6471 6688* **Fax** *(021) 6471 2618* **Rooms** *19*   **Map** *1 D5*

Perfect for history buffs, this 1920s mansion has housed Ho Chi Minh and Kim Il Sung, and was home to Jiang Qing (Mao's last wife). Inside, polished wood and curios abound; outside is a delightful garden. Business-minded gym junkies might prefer the Grand Hyatt. **www.ruijinhotels.com**

The Seagull on the Bund

60 Huangpu Road **Tel** *(021) 6325 1500* **Fax** *(021) 6324 1263* **Rooms** *128*

Map 3 D2

With its hard-to-beat waterfront location where Suzhou Creek meets the Huangpu River, the Seagull's refurbished rooms are only adequate but there's the compensation of views of the Bund and Lujiazui. Enjoyable rooftop dining under the glow of the neon Epson advertisement which crowns the hotel. **www.seagull-hotel.com**

Donghu Hotel

70 Donghu Road **Tel** *(021) 6415 8158* **Fax** *(021) 6415 7142* **Rooms** *271*

Map 1 E4

A stone's throw from bustling Huaihai Road, this lush garden hotel is encircled with high walls that make it a haven and help emphasize its long history. The newer buildings lack character so aim for Building 1, with its traditional Chinese furniture. **www.donghuhotel.com**

Howard Johnson Huaihai Hotel

1 Fenyang Road **Tel** *(021) 5461 9898* **Fax** *(021) 6415 1551* **Rooms** *167*

Map 1 E4

Centrally located on the corner of Huaihai Road and Fenyang Road, this smart, contemporary hotel offers easy access to the stores, museums, restaurants, and nightlife in downtown Shanghai, as well as the fine architecture of the former French Concession.

Jia Shanghai

931 West Nanjing Road **Tel** *(021) 6217 9000* **Fax** *(021) 6287 9001* **Rooms** *55*

Map 1 E4

This super-chic boutique hotel is in the heart of downtown Shanghai. The rooms are relatively small but exquisitely styled and have excellent facilities. The Issimo restaurant by Japan-based restaurateur Salvatore Cuomo is one of Shanghai's finest Italian eateries. **www.jiashanghai.com**

Jinjiang Hotel

59 Maoming South Road **Tel** *(021) 3218 9888* **Fax** *(021) 6253 0929* **Rooms** *434*

Map 1 E4

Once known as the Cathay Mansions and the scene of some important political events, this famous garden hotel in the French Concession has restyled itself for the 21st century. Rooms are elegant, facilities numerous, and the surrounding area houses a number of superb restaurants. **www.jinjianghotels.com**

Park Hotel

170 Nanjing West Road **Tel** *(021) 6327 5225* **Fax** *(021) 6327 6958* **Rooms** *252*

Map 2 A2

The tallest building in Asia when it was completed in 1934, the 22-story Park Hotel is now dwarfed by nearby offices. Still, the Art Deco feel and convenient Nanjing Road and People's Square location make for a quirky stay. Service is inconsistent. **www.parkhotel.com.cn**

Park Hyatt Shanghai

Shanghai World Financial Center, 100 Century Av **Tel** *(021) 6888 1234* **Fax** *(021) 6888 3400* **Rooms** *174* **Map** *3 E3*

The world's tallest hotel was also the Park Hyatt's debut property in mainland China. Located on floors 79–93, all rooms have magnificent views as well as excellent, hi-tech facilities. The Water's Edge Spa is on the 88th floor and a three-level atrium-style bar and restaurant sits on the top floors. **www.shanghai.park.hyatt.com**

Pudong Shangri-La Shanghai

33 Fucheng Road **Tel** *(021) 6882 8888* **Fax** *(021) 6882 6688* **Rooms** *957*

Map 3 D3

A stately tower with an elegant lobby and a modern counterpart with superbly designed rooms place this among the largest hotels in Shanghai. Shangri-La is justly famed for its service standards, and many rooms have fine views across the river to the the Bund. **www.shangri-la.com**

Purple Mountain Hotel

778 Dongfang Road **Tel** *(021) 6886 8888* **Fax** *(021) 6886 8866* **Rooms** *400*

An excellent business choice and close to Shanghai's exposition and convention facilities, this spotless five-star offers sizeable, stylish rooms, great views of Pudong, and a delightful outdoor pool popular for weekend parties in summer. It's a half-hour taxi ride to the French Concession though. **www.pmhotel.com.cn**

Radisson Blu Plaza Xing Guo Hotel

78 Xingguo Road **Tel** *(021) 6212 9998* **Fax** *(021) 6212 9996* **Rooms** *190*

A historic hotel with perhaps the best gardens of any accommodations in Shanghai – Chairman Mao was once a frequent guest. With serene, spacious rooms, the Radisson's only drawback is its distance from the Bund, although the attractions of the French Concession are just a short walk away. **www.radisson.com**

Regal International East Asia Hotel

516 Hengshan Road **Tel** *(021) 6415 5588* **Fax** *(021) 6445 8899* **Rooms** *330*

Located on tree-lined Hengshan Road in a consular district of the French Concession, the Regal has bright rooms with plenty of space and pleasant views. Sports buffs will enjoy the squash court, bowling alley, and Shanghai International Tennis Center. **www.regalhotel.com**

Ruijin Guesthouse

118 Ruijin No. 2 Road **Tel** *(021) 6472 5222* **Fax** *(021) 6473 2277* **Rooms** *62*

Map 1 F5

The 1917 mock-Tudor home of a British industrialist, now with a slightly shabby elegance but with large, modern bathrooms, is now the central building of a collection of villas standing in 17 acres (7 hectares) of gardens, recalling Shanghai's heyday. **www.ruijinhotelsh.com**

Key to Price Guide *see p178* **Key to Symbols** *see back cover flap*

Sofitel Shanghai Hyland

505 Nanjing East Road **Tel** *(021) 6351 5888* **Fax** *(021) 6351 4088* **Rooms** *389*   **Map** *2 B2*

Excellent downtown location – the check-in counter is only a few yards from Shanghai's most bustling streets – with great views from higher floors of the 30-story tower. The rooms are adequate, though slightly poky. A German restaurant contributes to the hotel's European feel. **www.sofitel.com**

Urbn Hotel

183 Jiaozhou Road, near Xinhua Road **Tel** *(021) 5153 4600* **Fax** *(021) 5153 4610* **Rooms** *26*   **Map** *1 D3*

China's first carbon-neutral hotel combines eco-friendliness with style. The hotel occupies a former factory and recycled materials, such as bricks from demolished factories, line the corridors. In-room sunken baths are a feature and the low Asian-style beds are perfect for lounging on. The restaurant is very popular with locals. **www.urbnhotels.com**

Waterhouse at South Bund

1–3 Maojiayuan Road, off Zhongshan South Road **Tel** *(021) 6080 2988* **Fax** *(021) 6080 2999* **Rooms** *19* **Map** *3 E5*

This boutique hotel, in a renovated 1930s warehouse beside the Huangpu River, is popular with visiting celebrities. Rooms feature ultra-modern furnishings. The casual hotel restaurant, Table No. 1, serves modern European cuisine, while the rooftop cocktail garden offers spectacular views of the city skyline. **www.waterhouseshanghai.com**

88 Xin Tiandi

380 Huangpi South Road **Tel** *(021) 5383 8833* **Fax** *(021) 5383 8877* **Rooms** *53*   **Map** *2 A4*

Impressive boutique hotel set within the Xin Tiandi entertainment district, comprising chic apartment-style rooms with comprehensive business facilities and kitchenettes (including microwave and refrigerator). Yet with Xin Tiandi's legion of restaurants at the doorstep, you'll hardly need to cook. **www.88xintiandi.com**

Fairmont Peace Hotel

20 Nanjing East Road **Tel** *(021) 6321 6888* **Fax** *(021) 6329 1888* **Rooms** *380*   **Map** *2 C2*

Dating from the late 1920s, this copper-towered building at the junction of the Bund and Nanjing Road has been fully restored and returned to its former glory. The restyled rooms are historically themed but feature all modern comforts. There are several fine-dining restaurants plus the legendary Jazz Bar *(see p123)*. **www.fairmont.com/peacehotel**

Four Seasons Hotel Shanghai

500 Weihai Road **Tel** *(021) 6256 8888* **Fax** *(021) 6256 5678* **Rooms** *421*   **Map** *1 F3*

One of the more up-market establishments on the Puxi side, the Four Seasons is held in high regard by regular visitors to Shanghai for its butler service, large marble bathrooms, and luxurious health club. The location is not great but it's a short walk to People's Square and the French Concession. **www.fourseasons.com/shanghai**

Grand Hyatt Shanghai

Jinmao Tower, 88 Century Avenue **Tel** *(021) 5049 1234* **Fax** *(021) 5049 1111* **Rooms** *555*   **Map** *3 E3*

This spectacular hotel begins at the 53rd of 88 stories in Shanghai's Jinmao Tower. Large, ultra-modern rooms with spacious bathrooms and separate shower cubicles have bird's-eye views over the Bund and Pudong, as do an assortment of excellent restaurants. **shanghai.grand.hyatt.com**

Hilton Shanghai

250 Huashan Road **Tel** *(021) 6248 0000* **Fax** *(021) 6248 3868* **Rooms** *772*

A favorite with business travelers since it opened in 1987, the Hilton's status seems to be under threat as newer hotels emerge. Still, service is first rate, the spa is superb, and the top-floor bar commands enviable views of the French Concession. **www.hilton.com**

Holiday Inn Pudong Shanghai

899 Dong Fang Road **Tel** *(021) 5830 6666* **Fax** *(021) 5830 5555* **Rooms** *362*

Dull rooms and tiny bathrooms, but the Holiday Inn boasts full supporting facilities including an Irish pub, and at lower prices than the other familiar brand names on the Pudong side of the river. A business rather than a leisure choice, perhaps. **www.ichotelsgroup.com**

Hong Qiao State Guest House

1591 Hong Qiao Road **Tel** *(021) 6219 8855* **Fax** *(021) 6219 5036* **Rooms** *216*

Travelers who've tired of international high-rise hotels will enjoy the Hongqiao State Guest House whose vast, grassy grounds are dotted with villas. Rooms are clean and airy. Aside from a nearby street of shops in Gubei district, you'll need taxis to reach the sights. **www.hqstateguesthotel.com**

Howard Johnson Plaza

595 Jiujiang Road **Tel** *(021) 3313 4888* **Fax** *(021) 3313 4880* **Rooms** *364*   **Map** *2 B2*

Nanjing Road's pedestrian mall looks shabbier every day, yet fresh luxury hotels continue to rise in its vicinity. The only-just-five-star Howard Johnson Plaza has comfortable rooms, a trendy wine bar, and responsive staff, all making for an agreeable stay. **www.howardjohnsonplazahotel.com**

Hyatt on the Bund

199 Huangpu Road **Tel** *(021) 6393 1234* **Fax** *(021) 6393 1313* **Rooms** *631*   **Map** *3 C2*

An elegant luxury hotel spread across two towers perched on the bend of the Huangpu River. Rooms have magnificent views and the service is excellent. One of the restaurants, Xindalu, has a specially imported brick oven for roasting the finest Peking Duck in Shanghai. **www.shanghai.bund.hyatt.com**

JW Marriott Hotel Tomorrow Square

399 Nanjing West Road **Tel** *(021) 5359 4969* **Fax** *(021) 6375 5988* **Rooms** *342*   **Map** *2 A3*

Wood-paneled doors, exceptional service and remarkable 360-degree views of People's Square and central Shanghai are just some of the attractions. Checking in on the 38th floor with its floor-to-wall windows is an exhilarating experience in itself. Among Shanghai's best hotels. **www.marriott.com**

Le Royal Meridien

789 Nanjing East Road **Tel** *(021) 3318 9999* **Fax** *(021) 6361 3388* **Rooms** *761*   **Map** *2 B2*

Just off the busy pedestrianized section of Nanjing Road, the huge Royal Meridien overlooks People's Square and is a pleasant, brightly lit hotel with open-plan bedrooms and bathrooms. The in-house Chinese restaurant is popular for dim sum and the Sunday brunch is a local institution. **www.starwoodhotels.com**

Les Suites Orient

1 Jinling East Road **Tel** *(021) 6320 0088* **Fax** *(021) 6320 3399* **Rooms** *168*   **Map** *3 C3*

The rooms at this classy hotel next to the Bund are sleekly styled with modern amenities. Breakfast is included in the room rate, as is a cell phone for making local calls, which is installed with city information and maps. Rooms on the upper levels have excellent views over the Huangpu River and the Pudong district. **www.hotelsuitesorient.com**

Mansion Hotel

82 Xinle Road **Tel** *(021) 5403 9888* **Fax** *(021) 5403 7077* **Rooms** *32*   **Map** *1 E4*

The former residence of a Shanghai gangster, this small boutique hotel, with its walled courtyard garden, captures the essence of old Shanghai. The reception area is filled with a stunning collection of 1930s Shanghai memorabilia, while the stylish rooms have fine stone balconies. Roof terrace with great views. **www.chinamansionhotel.com**

Portman Ritz-Carlton

1376 Nanjing West Road **Tel** *(021) 6279 8888* **Fax** *(021) 6279 8800* **Rooms** *610*   **Map** *1 E3*

The most thoughtful and attentive service in China: omnipresent when needed, invisible when not. The tower has its feet in an array of top-notch shopping, banking, ticket agencies, and more. Smart rooms have every facility and expansive views across Puxi. **www.ritzcarlton.com**

Renaissance Shanghai Pudong Hotel

100 Changliu Road **Tel** *(021) 3871 4888* **Fax** *(021) 6854 5928* **Rooms** *369*

Conveniently located for conference delegates or business travelers, this stylish Pudong hotel has an attention to aesthetic detail often lacking in five-star properties. Rooms and public areas follow an East-meets-West theme, with antique cabinets, mosaics, and calligraphy-etched glass. Staff also impress. **www.marriott.com**

Shanghai Marriott Hotel Hongqiao

2270 Hong Qiao Road **Tel** *(021) 6237 6000* **Fax** *(021) 6237 6222* **Rooms** *313*

The five-star Marriott boasts spacious, well-appointed rooms, impeccable service, and advanced business facilities, with wireless broadband available throughout the hotel. There are excellent steaks at the Manhattan Steak House. Close to the domestic airport and zoo. **www.marriott.com**

Sheraton Shanghai Hongqiao

5 Zunyi South Road **Tel** *(021) 6275 8888* **Fax** *(021) 6275 5420* **Rooms** *496*

The Sheraton has ornate rooms and a stunning lobby featuring imported Italian marble. It is conveniently close to the domestic airport, though hardly central. The Bauernstube farmhouse-style delicatessen has some of the best imported meats and cheeses in China. **www.sheratongrand-shanghai.com**

The Langham Xintiandi

99 Madang Road, Xintiandi **Tel** *(021) 2330 2288* **Fax** *(021) 2330 2233* **Rooms** *357*   **Map** *2 A4*

Located in the heart of downtown Xintiandi, this luxury hotel offers elegant rooms with a mix of traditional and modern decor. Amenities include a 24-hour health club and gym. Guests can unwind in the XTD open-air bar and restaurant. There are also plenty of facilities for business travelers. **www.xintiandi.langhamhotels.com**

The Peninsula Shanghai

32, Zhongshan East No. 1 Road **Tel** *(021) 2327 2888* **Fax** *(021) 2327 2000* **Rooms** *235*   **Map** *2 C2*

Located at the northern end of the Bund, the Shanghai outpost of the Peninsula group is just as sophisticated as its sister hotels. Guestrooms feature top-notch electronics and bathrooms with spa tubs, music, and mood lighting. Get picked up in their vintage Rolls for the ultimate airport collection. **www.peninsula.com**

The Puli Hotel and Spa

1 Changde Road **Tel** *(021) 3203 9999* **Fax** *(021) 3251 8989* **Rooms** *229*   **Map** *1 D1*

Billing itself as an urban retreat, this independent member of the Design Hotels collection has an interesting location overlooking Jing'an Park. As befits a hotel which emphasizes relaxation, the Anantara Spa is excellent, as are the spacious, Southeast Asian-themed rooms with Chinese furniture. **www.thepuli.com**

The Ritz-Carlton Shanghai, Pudong

Shanghai IFC, 8 Century Avenue **Tel** *(021) 2020 1888* **Fax** *(021) 2020 1889* **Rooms** *285*   **Map** *3 E3*

Conveniently located in Pudong's Lujiazui financial and shopping district, this plush hotel occupies the upper floors of the 58-story IFC Tower. The rooms are decorated in an Art Deco style and feature the latest hi-tech gadgetry. Flair, an alfresco bar and restaurant, offers some of the best views of Shanghai. **www.ritzcarlton.com**

Key to Price Guide *see p178* **Key to Symbols** *see back cover flap*

Waldorf-Astoria Shanghai on the Bund

2 The Bund **Tel** *(021) 6322 9988* **Fax** *(021) 6321 9888* **Rooms** *260*   **Map** *2 C3*

Housed in a heritage building, this luxurious hotel boasts a Neo-Classical facade dating back to 1911. Period-themed decor evokes Shanghai's decadent 1930s era. The Parisian-style Salon de Ville is great for high tea, while the exquisite Long Bar offers an extensive drinks menu. **www.waldorfastoriashanghai.com**

SHANGHAI FARTHER AFIELD

HANGZHOU Amanfayun

22 Fayun Nong, Xihuijiedao **Tel** *(0571) 8732 9999* **Fax** *(0571) 8732 9900* **Rooms** *63*

A 20-minute drive from Hangzhou, this Amanresorts outpost is as stylish and exclusive as you would expect from the brand. Tucked away in an ancient village in a picturesque valley, Amanfayun is surrounded by tea fields, quaint villages, and Buddhist temples. The beautiful rooms are set in restored cottages. **www.amanresorts.com**

HANGZHOU Four Seasons Hangzhou at West Lake

5 Lingyin Road **Tel** *(0571) 8829 8888* **Fax** *(0571) 8829 2298* **Rooms** *73*

Located in a small complex of traditional Chinese buildings, ponds, and courtyards beside Hangzhou's West Lake, the Four Seasons is reminiscent of a Qing Dynasty palace. Rooms boast stunning views of temples and tea plantations. The Jin Sha restaurant serves Hangzhou cuisine in 11 different private pavilions. **www.fourseasons.com/hangzhou**

HANGZHOU Fuchun Resort

339 Jiangbin Dongdadao, Dongzhou Jiedao **Tel** *(0571) 6341 9500* **Fax** *(0571) 6346 1222* **Rooms** *86*

One of the Yangzi Delta's best resorts. With traditional architecture and advanced facilities, the hotel is impressive enough, although Fuchun's five fully serviced villas are its crowning glory, each with a dramatic indoor swimming pavilion and sweeping views of tea-laden terraces. **www.fuchunresort.com**

HANGZHOU Hyatt Regency Hangzhou

28 Hu Bin Road **Tel** *(0571) 8779 1234* **Fax** *(0571) 8779 1818* **Rooms** *390*

Hyatt's China property is a smarter-than-average horseshoe-shaped mansion, with a vast lobby incorporating indoor/outdoor café and extensive shopping. Many rooms have lake views, and others have private terraces with miniature gardens. **hangzhou.regency.hyatt.com**

HANGZHOU Sofitel Westlake Hangzhou

333 Xi Hu Avenue **Tel** *(0571) 8707 5858* **Fax** *(0571) 8702 8466* **Rooms** *200*

Smart, colorful interior decor, sharp service, and relatively small scale make this hotel a deservedly popular choice, along with its central, lake-side position, handy for the burgeoning Xi Hu Tiandi bar and restaurant area. Rooftop bar with splendid lake views. **www.sofitel.com**

KUNSHAN Fairmont Yangcheng Lake

3668 West Ma'anshan Road **Tel** *(0512) 5780 0888* **Fax** *(0512) 5780 7255* **Rooms** *200*

Located on the shores of Yangcheng Lake – home to the famous Hairy Crab winter delicacy – this excellent, upscale hotel is popular with both business and weekend leisure travelers. The well-appointed rooms come with all expected contemporary amenities and the hotel's Cantonese restaurant is highly regarded. **www.fairmont.com/yangchenglake**

SUZHOU Hotel Soul Suzhou

27–33 Qiaosikong Xiang, Ping Jiang District **Tel** *(0512) 6777 0777* **Fax** *(0512) 6777 0088* **Rooms** *225*

This courtyard-style boutique hotel, located in the heart of the old city, is regarded as one of Suzhou's most stylish, . blending traditional Suzhou architecture and contemporary design. Amenities include a rooftop garden, a juice bar, a French brasserie, a gym, and a spa. **www.hotelsoul.com.cn**

SUZHOU New World Aster Hotel

488 Sanxiang Road **Tel** *(0512) 6829 1888* **Fax** *(0512) 6829 1838* **Rooms** *366*

This hotel is ten minutes west of the city center, at the junction of the old town and the burgeoning economic district. Views from the sightseeing elevators and top-floor restaurant are superb. Rooms are well furnished and recreational facilities abound. **www.aster.com.cn**

SUZHOU Pan Pacific

259 Xinshi Road **Tel** *(0512) 6510 3388* **Fax** *(0512) 6510 0888* **Rooms** *407*

The architecture of this impeccable hotel reflects the heritage of old Suzhou, with a central building modeled on the city's famous Panmen Gate. Canals wind through the quiet, elegant gardens, and the luxurious rooms feature spacious marble bathrooms. **www.panpacific.com/suzhou**

SUZHOU Suzhou Garden Hotel

99 Dai Cheng Qiao Road **Tel** *(0512) 6778 6778* **Fax** *(0512) 6778 6888* **Rooms** *236*

Set across leafy gardens in the heart of old Suzhou, this hotel comprises several restored, low-rise houses and cottages. Rooms are large and comfortable with excellent facilities. The Thai-themed spa, fitness club, and pool are among the city's best. Breakfast is included in the room rate. Note that only Chinese credit cards are accepted. **www.gardenhotelsz.com**

WHERE TO EAT

Bamboo steamer of dim sum

Once you dine in Beijing or Shanghai, you may start to question your prior conceptions of Chinese food. The local restaurants in these two cities serve up cuisines of such variety and delight that it will quickly dissolve memories of the pale imitations of Chinese food experienced back home. Beijing's slender wheat noodles, *jiaozi* dumplings, and roast duck are vastly different from Shanghai's rope-like noodles, *shengjian* fried buns, and braised crabs. But both cities also offer the best of China's regional cuisines, from fiery Sichuanese and Hunanese, and subtle Cantonese (quite different from that served at home), to the lesser-known sweet and fruity tastes of sub-tropical Yunnan in the southwest, the vinegary noodles of Shanxi, and the hard-to-define but always excellent dishes of the Hakka (Kejia) minority of the southeast. Chinese consider the opportunity to sample different foods one of the main reasons to travel, and so should you.

Elegant interiors of Crystal Jade *(see p203)*, a popular Cantonese restaurant

TYPES OF RESTAURANT

Whether you are looking to eat in the splendor of an imperial pavilion in Beijing or a chic Shanghai emporium, you will find a restaurant boom taking place in China. Entrepreneurs are thinking up tempting new ways to indulge in the country's favorite pastime. You never have to walk far to find restaurants in China and when you do, do not let first appearances put you off – many gourmet restaurants boast simple decor and harsh lighting. Look instead for happy crowds of diners and a different concept of "atmosphere:" in Chinese eyes, the more lively and noisy *(renao)* a restaurant is, the better.

OPEN ALL HOURS

You can breakfast on the street by 6am, but all hotels should serve breakfast until 10am. Lunch is typically from 11am until 1pm, after which some restaurants shut until the evening shift starts around 5pm. In the evening closing times can be very late, while some places never shut. At one time, booking was rare, except for the most popular and high-end establishments, but these days it's always wise to book in advance, particularly in Shanghai.

HOTEL FOOD

If you are tired and hungry, and staying at one of China's more expensive hotels, then room service can provide the usual international fare, and unchallenging made-for-foreigners Cantonese one-dish meals.

In Beijing and Shanghai many of the best restaurants, both Chinese and foreign, are located in hotels. The English menus are convenient, but prices can be inflated. The more intrepid diner who makes a few forays outside the comfort of four- or five-star hotels will reap handsome dividends. Some of the best restaurants are now stand-alone, with hotels no longer dominating the scene.

STREET FOOD

Street-food vendors have smartened up, due to the 2010 World Expo. These vendors' portable stalls form a vital part of the everyday life of China, selling cheap and popular foods such as breakfasts of dough sticks *(youtiao)* and beancurd *(doujiang)*, or snacks like scallion pancakes *(jian bing)*, sweet potatoes *(shanyu)* roasted in old oil drums, deep-fried beancurd cubes *(zha doufu)*, and local fruits. A reliable way to locate delicious street food is to stroll through a night market *(ye shi)*, a culinary and visual

Scorpion kabobs (kebabs) – cooking renders the sting ineffective

Steaming food on the street – simple, fast, and efficient

feast where clouds of vapour escape from bamboo steamers, and the sky glows red from the flames of oil-drum stoves. The sizzle of cooking and clamor of vendors shouting for business should stir your appetite, and if deep-fried scorpions or cicadas on skewers prove too exotic, be assured that plenty of other foods will take your fancy. If the food is hot and freshly cooked, hygiene problems are rare. The market off Wangfujing Street (see p72) in Beijing is the most famous of the night markets.

LITTLE EATS

Cheap and nourishing snacks such as those found at night markets are known collectively as *xiao chi*, or "little eats." Restaurants that specialize in them are called *xiao chi dian*; they sell different types of noodles or dumplings, stuffed buns, or pancakes. Open early for breakfast, they may serve simple stir-fried dishes too, and shut only when the last guest leaves. The setting is usually basic, but the food is hearty, tasty, and very reasonably priced.

The very visible success of Western fast-food restaurants (McDonald's and KFC are everywhere) has led to local restaurant chains adopting the same style to serve native Chinese fast-food dishes and snacks. These are generally far tastier and healthier than their Western counterparts.

THE OTHER CHINA

Beijing and Shanghai showcase not only regional cuisine from all over Han China, but also a whole range of ethnic specialties belonging to the 55 minority nationalities, from the Korean border to the Tibetan plateau. Minorities' restaurants are an "exotic" attraction for Chinese as well as foreign tourists. In some Dai restaurants, offering the Thai-like cuisine of southern Yunnan, guests are greeted with scented water, given a lucky charm, and may later be invited to join in the singing and dancing. In more upmarket Uighur restaurants, serving lamb-heavy dishes from the Muslim northwest,

Rice and chopsticks

belly dancing is sometimes included as part of the entertainment.

VEGETARIAN SURPRISE

The Chinese understanding of a good life is inextricably associated with meat. They find it hard to understand why someone who could afford to eat meat would choose not to. Nevertheless, you will find an increasing number of vegetarian restaurants in Beijing and Shanghai. Some use soya protein to imitate meat with extraordinary authenticity. Others simply use Chinese cooking methods to bring out the best in pulses and vegetables. Ordinary restaurants can lay on good vegetarian meals too, as long as you can repeat, "Wo shi chi su de. Wo bu chi rou," ("I'm vegetarian. I don't eat meat"), and don't mind the odd bit of meat or chicken stock.

INTERNATIONAL FOOD

Almost all kinds of foreign food, from Brazilian to Indian can be found in Beijing and Shanghai. Italian is probably the most popular of Western cuisines, ravioli and spaghetti being easy concepts for the dumpling- and noodle-loving Chinese to appreciate. Some have justifiably earned wide acclaim, such as Maison Boulud in Beijing, and M on the Bund in Shanghai. Other Asian cuisines, namely Korean, Japanese, Indian, and Thai, are also well represented, and more readily accepted by the chopstick-wielding Chinese.

Eating together, an important aspect of Chinese social life

Dining Etiquette

The Chinese are quite informal at meal times. Confucius may have been renowned for his silence while eating, but these days a busy Chinese restaurant can be a deafening place as waiters crash plates about and diners shout orders at the waiters. It may seem daunting but just join in and expect praise for your chopstick skills – even if you struggle, your willingness to try will be appreciated.

Dinner in a private room, a popular Chinese way of doing business

EARNING SOME FACE

The Chinese do not expect visitors to be fully versed in proper banquet etiquette, but awareness of a few essentials can earn "face" both for yourself and your host, whatever the occasion. The other guests will appreciate that you have some respect for Chinese culture and traditions.

When attending, or hosting, a formal meal, note that the guest of honor is usually placed on the seat in the middle, facing the door. The host, traditionally positioned opposite the guest, now more often sits to his or her left.

If you come as a guest, be punctual and do not sit down until you are given your seat – seating arrangements can be very formal and based on rank. Once seated, do not start on the food or drink before your host gives the signal. Some of the delicacies on offer may test your courage but it is an insult if the food is untouched. Leave some food on the plates: empty bowls imply that the host is too poor or mean to lay on a good spread.

In addition to the above, there are further rules that should be kept in mind. If you are applauded as you come into the room, don't feel shy about applauding back Reply to any welcome toast with your own (short) speech and toast. In your speech and any subsequent conversation avoid broaching sensitive subjects, in particular Chinese politics.

Show respect to your elders and superiors by ensuring that the rim of your glass is lower than theirs when clinking glasses, and drain your drink in one swift movement.

THE ART OF ORDERING

If you are someone's guest, you may be asked to order something, or state some sort of preference – if you do not do so, a ten-course banquet could soon appear. Feel free to name your favorite dish, or point at the object of your desire, possibly something swimming in a fish tank at the entrance to the restaurant. Freshness is all-important in Chinese cuisine.

A meal might begin with cold starters such as pickled vegetables, 1,000-year old eggs, seasoned jellyfish, or cold roasted meats. Main courses should be selected for harmony and balance. A typical order would be a variety of different meats and vegetables, cooked in different and complementary ways. The last dish, or *cai*, is usually soup. Then comes *fan*, a grain staple such as rice, noodles, or bread (*mantou*), without which a Chinese diner may feel they have not eaten. At informal meals you can have rice at the start of the meal – although you may want to remind the waiting staff of this – but not at a banquet, or your host will assume his dishes are inadequate.

English-language menus are becoming more common. An increasing number of restaurants actively encourage visitors to get out of their chairs and choose ingredients from tanks, cages, and supermarket-type shelves. Your Chinese friends (and waiters and onlookers) will likely be

A variety of dim sum dishes – no need to finish them all

delighted by any interest you show in the whole experience. In the end, when language or phrase book fail, simply look around and point at whatever appeals on other tables, or even head into the kitchen to find what you want.

INVITED TO DINNER

A formal meal often takes place in a private room and usually begins with a toast. The host serves his guest with the choicest morsels, and then everyone is permitted to help themselves. Simply watch others for guidelines on when to use serving utensils, and when, more informally, your own chopsticks will do.

Only in restaurants regularly frequented by lots of foreigners, or which also have Western dishes on the menu will knives and forks be available.

Seafood – abundant in Beijing and Shanghai

The host almost always orders more dishes than is necessary. While it is, as stated earlier, polite to try everything, it is far from necessary to finish it all.

DOS AND DON'TS

The Chinese are fairly relaxed about table manners. Slurping shows appreciation, enables better appreciation of flavor, and sucks in air to prevent burning the mouth. Holding your bowl up to your mouth, to shovel rice in, is another practical solution. You may happily reach across your neighbors, but do not spear food with your chopsticks, and do not stand them upright in a bowl of rice either, as it looks like an offering to the dead. If you have finished with the chopsticks lay them flat on the table or on a rest. You shouldn't suck greasy fingers, or use them to pick bones out of your mouth – spit bones or shell onto the table, into the saucer that was under your bowl, or more delicately into

---

HOW TO HOLD CHOPSTICKS

1) Place the first chopstick in the crook of your thumb and forefinger. Support it with the little and ring fingers, and keep it there with the knuckle of the thumb.

Third finger acting as a rest for the lower stick

Thumb and first finger controlling the top stick

2) Hold the second chopstick like a pencil, between middle and index fingers, anchored by the pad of your thumb.
3) When picking up food, keep the lower stick stationary and the tips even. As the index finger moves up and down, only the upper stick should move, using the thumb as an axis.

---

a napkin. Toothpicks are ubiquitous, but do cover the action with your free hand.

And generally don't be shy about shouting for attention as enthusiasm for food is much appreciated. Eating alone is alien to the Chinese way of thinking. They believe that eating in a group – sharing both the dishes and the experience – significantly increases the enjoyment.

THE END OF THE MEAL

A platter of fresh fruit and steaming hot towels signal the end of the meal is coming. In more formal meals, just as you should await the start of a meal, do not stand up before your host, who will rise and indicate that the dinner has ended and ask if you've had enough. The correct answer is "yes." The person who invited you

Dining outdoors in Shanghai, possible for much of the year

usually shoulders the full weight of the bill, so accept graciously. Offering to pay is fine, even polite; insisting too hard suggests that you doubt the host's ability to pay.

Prices are fixed and written down in most restaurants, and on bills. Tipping is not necessary and the only places that include a service charge are the upmarket restaurants within hotels. These are also the only places likely to take international credit cards.

PARTY FOOD

In a culture obsessed with both symbolism and eating, many foods that have earned special meaning and must be consumed on set occasions. Round mooncakes, dotted with moon-like duck egg yolks, are a must at Mid-Autumn Festival. At Spring Festival, the whole family cooks *tangyuan*, round sweet dumplings made of glutinous rice flour, because *yuan* can also mean "reunion." Fish is auspicious, because the character for fish (*yu*) sounds like the one for "abundance" and offers the hope of good fortune in the year ahead. Meat dumplings (*jiaozi*) are another New Year favorite as their shape is said to resemble the symbol for prosperity. Birthdays are often celebrated with noodles, a symbol of longevity, while red beans are a metaphor of longing and love. To celebrate new arrivals, parents hand out eggs painted red for luck – an even number for a boy, an odd number for a girl.

What to Eat in Beijing

Communities developed beside the Yellow River before 6000 BC, but it is not until about 1500 BC, when written records started, that a picture of the dietary habits of the ancient Chinese becomes clear. They kept pigs and grew millet, wheat, barley, and rice and even fermented their grain to make alcoholic beverages. Later (around 1100 BC), soybeans were added to the Chinese diet, then by-products such as soy sauce and beancurd (tofu). Late-founded Beijing had no distinctive cuisine of its own, but as the center of a mighty empire it imported elements and influences from a variety of sources.

Chinese leaf, also known as Tianjin cabbage

Candied apples, a common Beijing street food

ingredients – shark's fin, bird's nest soup, and abalone, all imported from the south – feature as well as artistic presentation and poetic names. Beijing cuisine can be summed up as the distillation of the creations of generations of Imperial Palace chefs over almost a millennium.

THE PALACE KITCHEN

Kublai Khan made Beijing the capital in 1271 and brought simple Mongolian influences to the imperial kitchens – lamb, roasting, and the hotpot. These were foods that didn't require a lot of equipment, ideal for pastoral nomads and armies on the move. Elaborate preparation and expensive

MONGOLIAN AND MUSLIM CUISINE

One highly successful alien invader is the Mongolian hotpot, a simple one-pot dish. Although Buddhists, the Mongol minority within China are not vegetarians – their traditional nomadic lifestyle made vegetable

Marinated, roast duck

Steamed pancakes

Scallions

Sliced cucumber

Special duck sauce

A whole Peking duck with traditional accompaniments

REGIONAL DISHES AND SPECIALTIES

Peking duck – an Imperial meal – must be the best known dish in north Chinese cuisine. The duck, a local Beijing variety, is carefully dried, and then brushed with a sweet marinade before being roasted over fragrant wood chips. When ready it is carved by the chef and eaten wrapped in pancakes with a special duck sauce, and slivered scallions and cucumbers. To accompany the duck, diners might also be served duck liver pâté, and duck soup to finish. Beijing is also known for a wide variety of cold dishes that start a meal, for stuffed breads and pastries, and for *jiaozi* (dumplings). Look out for *zha jiang mian* (Clanging Dish Noodles), in which ingredients are added at the table to a central bowl of noodles, the bowls loudly clanged together as each ingredient goes in.

Duck pears – like a duck's head

Mu xu pork: *stir-fried tiger lily buds, scrambled egg, black fungus, and shredded pork – eaten with pancakes.*

growing impractical, and the hotpot is served with a choice of finely shaved lamb or beef, or sometimes more exotic meats. Modern Beijing has a great many dedicated hotpot restaurants, and it is one of the cheapest ways of group eating.

Chinese Muslims are treated as a separate ethnic minority in China, known as the Hui, with enclaves in every major city. Beijing also has small pockets of Turkic Uighur people from the Xinjiang region of the Northwest, also Muslim, so none eat pork. Xinjiang men, originally from the far northwest of China, can often be found hunched over troughs of coals at the

The art of pouring tea, exhibited in a Beijing restaurant

streetside, selling *kao rou chuan*, or lamb kabobs dusted with cumin. Another Uighur specialty are thick *lao mian* or "pulled noodles" made by endlessly doubling, twisting, and stretching a rope of dough, and widely available in Beijing.

Some of the wide variety of foods on display at a night food market

SHANDONG

Shandong is the birthplace of Confucius, and its cuisine is generally regarded as the oldest and best in China. Shandong has produced the largest number of famous master chefs, and it is said that the iron wok originated here. Most of the Chinese influences in Beijing cooking come from this province. As one of the most important agricultural areas of China, Shandong supplies Beijing with most of its ingredients – its main crops are wheat, barley, sorghum, millet, and corn. Additionally, fisheries are widely developed along the Yellow River and the north China coast, particularly the Shandong peninsula where the specialties are all kinds of fish, shrimp, shellfish, abalones, sea slugs, and sea urchins.

ON THE MENU

Drunken empress chicken Supposedly named after Yang Guifei, an imperial concubine overly fond of her alcohol.

Stir-fried kidney-flowers These are actually pork kidneys criss-cross cut into "flowers" and stir-fried with bamboo shoots, water chestnuts, and black fungus.

Fish slices with wine sauce Deep-fried fish fillet braised in a wine sauce.

Phoenix-tail prawns King prawn tails coated in batter and bread crumbs, then deep fried.

Lamb in sweet bean sauce Tender fillet of lamb sliced and cooked in sweet bean paste with vinegar to give it that classic sweet and sour taste.

Hot candied apples A popular Chinese dessert.

Lamb and scallions: *sliced lamb rapidly stir-fried with garlic, leeks or scallions, and sweet bean paste.*

Mongolian hotpot: *thinly sliced lamb, vegetables, and noodles dipped in boiling water and an array of sauces.*

Sweet and sour carp: *the quintessential Shandong dish traditionally made with Yellow River carp.*

What to Eat in Shanghai

Shanghai draws its population from neighboring provinces, and these people have brought with them their regional tastes and preferences. The surrounding provinces are traditionally referred to as the "Lands of Fish and Rice," and indeed the Yangtze River Delta is one of the country's leading agricultural regions with some of the most fertile land. Both wheat and rice are grown here as well as barley, corn, sweet potatoes, peanuts, and soybeans. Freshwater fisheries abound in the network of lakes and rivers, while deep-sea fishing has long been established on the coast.

Garlic chives and bok choi

Market stall displaying the wide variety of dried goods available

SHANGHAI

The characteristics of Shanghai cuisine are summarized as "exquisite in appearance, rich in flavor, and sweet in taste." A favorite ingredient is the hairy crab from the Yangzi estuary (although overfishing means they actually come from elsewhere nowadays) and the eel. The sweetness and oiliness of many Shanghai dishes is balanced by lighter elements from neighboring older schools of cuisine – Huaiyang and Suzhe. Among the dishes Shanghai is famous for are its thick fried noodles, its *shengjian mantou*, which are bread dough balls stuffed with meat and "steamed in oil," and *xiao long bao*, little pasta sacks filled with pork, crab meat, and scalding soup. Calling both of these *mantou* rather than *bao* as elsewhere in China marks you out as a local. The distinctive pungent smell of *chou doufu*, or "stinky" tofu, invented not far away in Shaoxing is also found gusting around Shanghai streets.

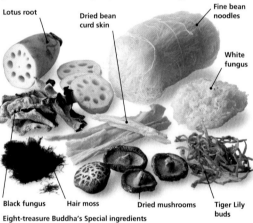

Lotus root

Dried bean curd skin

Fine bean noodles

White fungus

Black fungus   **Hair moss**   **Dried mushrooms**   **Tiger Lily buds**

Eight-treasure Buddha's Special ingredients

REGIONAL DISHES AND SPECIALTIES

Fermented bean curd

Two of the area's great cities, Nanjing and Hangzhou, were at different times dynastic Chinese capitals. Whenever there was a change of capital, the vast imperial kitchens changed location bringing the staff with them resulting in a cross-fertilization of recipes and methods from one region to another. One favorite imperial dish despite its lowly name is Beggar's Chicken – a whole chicken is stuffed with vegetables and herbs, wrapped in lotus leaves, and encased in clay before being baked. The clay container is then broken at the table releasing the beautifully concentrated aromas. (For hygiene reasons, top hotels find clayless solutions to the same delicious result.) Another specialty is *Dongpo rou*, a soya pork dish named for the Song poet exiled to Hangzhou. Freshwater crabs are best during the months of October and November.

Lions' heads: *pork meatballs braised with Chinese leaf – meant to look like lions' heads and manes.*

HUAIYANG AND SUZHE

Based specifically around the deltas of the Huai and Yangzi Rivers, Huaiyang cuisine is most famous for its excellent fish and shellfish – the freshwater crabs from the waters of Tai Hu are superb. Suzhe cuisine, however, covers a wider area – the provinces of Jiangsu and Zhejiang – and includes culinary centers such as Nanjing and Hangzhou that both served as capital cities. Along with stews flavored with a light stock, the region is famous for its "red cooking" – food braised in soy sauce, sugar, ginger, and rice wine. "Chinkiang Vinegar" is black rice vinegar from Zhenjiang, Jiangsu, and is acknowledged to be the best rice vinegar in China. The province of Zhejiang, of course, produces China's best rice wines from Shaoxing and top quality hams from Jinhua. It is also worth trying the Long Jing (Dragon Well) green tea grown around West Lake in Hangzhou.

Park cafés – popular places to snack on some filled dumplings

ANHUI

Shanghai is also influenced by the little known Anhui cuisine, from farther inland.

Despite being landlocked, Anhui still enjoys a lot of fish thanks to its extensive network of lakes and rivers. The province is also another of the key agricultural regions in China, and it produces a great number and variety of crops and vegetables. One of Anhui's most famed ingredients are its tender white bamboo shoots. These crisp shoots feature large in the vegetarian cuisine prepared in the Buddhist mountain retreats and are often combined with a variety of exotic woodland mushrooms. Finally the world-famous Keemun red tea comes from the hills of Yimeng in south Anhui.

Hairy crabs, a Shanghai delicacy

ON THE MENU

Beggars chicken A whole chicken stuffed with flavorings and cooked in a clay pot.

Fried prawns in shells Prawns still in their shells are rapidly fried and then braised in a soy and tomato sauce.

Three-layer shreds Steamed shredded ham, chicken, and pork with bamboo shoots and black mushroom – should be called five-layer shreds.

Freshwater crabs Simply steamed with scallions, ginger, soy, sugar, and vinegar.

Steamed belly pork with ground rice Also known as Double-braised Pork, this long-cooked dish literally melts in your mouth.

Eight-treasure Buddha's Special A generic name for a delicious vegetarian dish which can actually contain any number of different ingredients.

Tofu casserole: *tofu with sea cucumbers, ham, prawns, mushrooms, bamboo shoots, and bok choi in a stew pot.*

Squirrel fish: *a bream is filleted, coated with batter, deep-fried, and served with a sweet-and-sour sauce.*

Sweet and sour spare ribs: *deep-fried, bite-size pork spare ribs braised in soy, sugar, and vinegar.*

What to Drink

Tea of course is the most popular drink in China. There are countless arguments for drinking the infusion of the bush *Camellia sinensis,* and just as many legends about its origin. But if tea is the most popular drink, there is a wide range of others for the visitor. Beer is popular with meals and wine is available in many upscale restaurants. Chinese spirits can range from the extremely pleasant to the almost dangerous. Likewise approach the "health tonics," like snake wine, with caution – as if the reptilian "sediment" in the bottle isn't enough, they can be fiercely alcoholic.

Fresh tea leaves

Tea may be served both during and after a meal

TYPES OF TEA

Green is the most common tea, baked immediately after picking. Flower tea is a mixture of green tea with flower petals. Black tea colors during the fermentation process and the reddish brew that results explains its Chinese name – red tea. The most highly prized is oolong, a lightly fermented tea, and Longjing tea from Hangzhou. Brick tea is black or green, pressed into blocks. Eight Treasure tea *babaocha* has many ingredients including dates, dried longan, and wolfberry, and Tibetans enjoy yak butter tea.

Gaiwan or three-piece tea cup

Lid keeps leaves in the cup, not the mouth

Saucer to prevent fingers burning

Black: hongcha, *actually called "red tea" in Chinese.*

Green: lucha, *uses leaves dried without fermentation.*

Pu'er: *from Yunnan, is compressed into "bricks."*

Flower: huacha *a mix of petals – jasmine, rose, and chrysanthemum.*

The famous "Hairy Peak" green tea

Coffee: *as café culture enters China, coffee drinking is fashionable among the middle classes. Starbucks may have an outlet inside the Forbidden City, but freshly-ground coffee is rare outside major hotels.*

Tea and coffee drink: *those who want a fashionable coffee drink, but cannot do without their daily shot of tea, can try this blend of tea and coffee.*

SOFT DRINKS

Even as a cold drink, tea is dominant. Iced tea is very popular, especially with the young. Besides the usual array of fruit juices, there is hawthorn juice in Beijing, pomegranate juice from Xinjiang, and lychee and sugar cane juice from down south. As well as the global drink brands, local challengers include Tianfu Cola, and the energy drink Jianlibao, made with honey. As China overcomes its dairy aversion, milk and yoghurt drinks multiply, as well as soya-bean *(doujiang)* and coconut milk.

Bamboo cane juice

Iced green tea

Coconut milk drink

BEER

The Germans first introduced beer to China in the early 20th century, giving the Tsingtao beer the reputation it has today; in the 21st century, China has taken over as the world's biggest brewer. Both Beijing and Shanghai have their own local breweries.

Tsingtao beer   **Yanjing beer**

Great Wall   **Dragon Seal**

WINE

Although grape seeds traveled the Silk Roads, China has historically preferred grain alcohol. The quality is rapidly improving, but red wine is still a safer order than white – considered good for the heart, and a lucky color too.

SPIRITS

For millennia the Chinese have been distilling grains into *baijiu* or "white spirits" ranging from strong to deadly. Classified into three types: the *qingxiang*, or light bouquet, group includes Fenjiu from Shaanxi; Guizhou's famous Maotai is a classic *jiangxiang*, soy bouquet; *nongxiang*, strong bouquet, is championed by Sichuan giant Wuliangye.

Maotai *"eight times fermented and seven times distilled" is favored for toasts at banquets. At the other end of the scale* erguotou *is cheap and effective – the people's drink.*

Maotai   **Erguotou**

RICE WINE

Despite being called "wine," some care is required as this can vary in strength from a mild 15–16% alcohol, to the double- or triple-fermented wines at up to 38% ABV. Good rice wine is best drunk warm and goes well with cold starters.

Shaoxing rice wine

Shaoxing: *This is among the best of the* huangjiu *(yellow spirits), noted for its moderate alcohol content (about 16%) and mellow fragrance.*

Strong rice wine

DRINKING CULTURE

Teahouses are enjoying something of a revival in China, as appreciation of traditional tea culture recovers after years of proletarian austerity. While *cha* (tea) stimulates quiet contemplation, *jiu* (alcohol) lubricates noisy celebrations. Despite reveling in the drunkenness of their poets such as Li Bai *(see p20)*, the Chinese have not been as badly affected by alcoholism as many other societies. Public drunkenness is frowned upon – except maybe in the ever more popular karaoke (known as KTV) bars. Traditionally only soup was drunk with meals, but this is changing, especially when eating with foreigners. "Gan bei!" or "dry the cup" is the repeated clarion call to toasting bouts and drinking games. Beware the legendary drinking capacity of the northeast Chinese, and don't drink alone or on an empty stomach.

Chinese youth drinking in a local modern teahouse

Choosing a Restaurant

Chosen for their excellent food, good value, and convenient or interesting location, the restaurants in this guide cover a wide price range. They are listed by town or city in the same order as the chapters appear in this book. Where a restaurant has both an English and a Chinese name, the English name is given first.

PRICE CATEGORIES
The following price ranges are the equivalent of a meal for two made up of a range of dishes, served with tea, and including any service charges.

¥ under ¥100
¥¥ ¥100–¥250
¥¥¥ ¥250–¥500
¥¥¥¥ over ¥500

BEIJING

Baoyuan Jiaozi Wu   Ⓥ   ¥
6 Maizidian Jie **Tel** *(010) 6586 4967*

Cheap and cheerful, head here for Beijing's best dumplings. The dumplings are dyed different colors using vegetables such as spinach, carrot, and beetroot. One order (a *liang*) comprises six dumplings and they are so inexpensive you can order with abandon. Try the purple dumplings filled with crispy rice, carrot, and pork. English menu.

Beijing Roast Duck Restaurant (Beijing Dadong Kaoyadian)   ¥
Building 3, Tuanjiehu Beikou, Dong San Huan Bei Lu **Tel** *(010) 5169 0329*   **Map** *3 F4*

There's no finer Beijing duck than that served here – full-flavored and with just the right balance between tender meat and crispy skin. Far less famous than the Quanjude establishments that dot Beijing, it nevertheless surpasses its rival on every level, including price.

Crescent Moon   ¥
16 Dongsiliutiao (just off Dongsi Bei Dajie) **Tel** *(010) 6400 5281*   **Map** *2 C3*

Juicy kebabs, rich stews, and lots of naan bread are on the menu at this basic but authentic Xinjiang restaurant located down an atmospheric *hutong*. The food from China's far west is very different in style to the rest of the country, and the food at Crescent Moon is some of the best in Beijing. English menu.

Ding Ding Xiang   ¥
2/F, Yuanjia International Apartments (opposite East Gate Plaza), Dongzhongjie **Tel** *(010) 6417 9289*   **Map** *3 D3*

Hot pot is very popular in Beijing, especially during the freezing winter months, and this local favorite is a good place to sample it. Parties share a huge vat of steaming broth into which you dunk thin slices of meat and vegetables before dipping them in a thick, tangy sauce. Lots of fun and an English menu.

Lao Beijing Zhajiang Mian Da Wang   🗐   ¥
29 Chongwen Men Wai Dajie **Tel** *(010) 6705 6705*   **Map** *5 E3*

This bustling institution near the Temple of Heaven is decorated with Ming-style ornaments and serves traditional Beijing snacks like *mifen rou* (steamed pork belly with rice powder) and *zhajiang mian* (bean sauce noodles). Kitsch and a bit touristy, but cheap and very tasty fare.

Noodle Loft   🗐   ¥
20 Xidawang Lu, 33 Guangshunjie **Tel** *(010) 6774 9950*

A surprisingly sleek, modern restaurant dishing up regional Shanxi dishes with tidy presentation and a modern twist. Excellent snacks and cold starters such as the salty mashed pumpkin and fungus and caraway salad complement fresh noodle dishes and main courses. Excellent value.

Private Kitchen 44   Ⓥ   ¥
44 Xiguan Hutong **Tel** *(010) 6400 1280*   **Map** *2 C2*

This lovely restaurant down an atmospheric alley serves food from Guizhou province in the southwest. The restaurant boasts stylish bohemian surrounds and diners sit in tiny rooms off a central courtyard. The English menu helps you navigate your way around what may be unfamiliar cuisine, but you can't go wrong with specialties like sour fish soup.

Yuxiang Renjia   ¥
20 Chaoyang Men Wai Dajie, 5/F, Union Plaza **Tel** *(010) 6588 3841*   **Map** *3 D4*

One of a chain of swish but economical Sichuan restaurants scattered all over the city, Yuxiang Renjia is at least as good, and far cheaper, than its many more famous competitors. This is real Sichuanese: oily, intensely spicy, and totally addictive.

Alameda   🍴●🖪   ¥¥
Nali Market, 81 Sanlitun Lu **Tel** *(010) 6417 8084*   **Map** *3 F3*

Trendy, intimate restaurant serving Brazilian-inspired contemporary cuisine. Succinct but well-balanced menu includes a handful of excellent value set meals that change weekly with the availability of fresh ingredients, with consistently good steaks. The small wine list is carefully chosen but expensive. Service is attentive.

Key to Symbols *see back cover flap*

Bei

The Opposite House hotel, 11 Sanlitun Lu, Chaoyang **Tel** *(010) 6410 5230*

Map *3 F2*

Frequently voted one of Beijing's top restaurants, this elegant diner serves up-and-coming chef Max Levy's acclaimed takes on North Asian dishes. Japanese, northern Chinese, and Korean cuisine all feature, with an emphasis on inventive seafood dishes. Everything here is skilfully prepared and exquisitely presented. Closed Sun.

Bellagio (Lu Gang dia Zhen)

Xiaoyun Lu 35 (opposite Renaissance Hotel) **Tel** *(010) 8451 9888*

Map *3 E3*

Packed around the clock with hip, young Beijingers, this Taiwanese chain serves quality Hakka dishes from China's south such as "three cup chicken," as well as fruit smoothies and red-bean ice desserts in a bustling, modern dining room with floor-to-ceiling windows. There are several other branches around the city.

Cafe Sambal

43 Doufuchi Hutong **Tel** *(010) 6400 4875*

Map *2 A2*

A stylish Malaysian restaurant that's a big favorite with expatriates in want of an alternative to Chinese fare. The exquisite dishes are prepared by a genuine Malay chef. The attractive courtyard setting makes for a great place to relax over a drink or meal in summer.

Da Zhai Men

20 Shouti Nan Lu **Tel** *(010) 8835 6687*

Specializing in palace cuisine but also serving Cantonese, Sichuan, and Beijing snacks, this cavernous restaurant is dressed up like an imperial court. Locals praise the food's authenticity; foreigners enjoy the floorshow, which includes acrobats, magicians, kung fu, and clowns.

Dali Courtyard

16 Xiaojingchang Hutong, Gulou Dong Dajie **Tel** *(010) 8404 1430*

Map *2 B2*

Beautifully lit by candles at night, this atmospheric courtyard venue wins top marks for its ambience and excellent set menus. The cuisine is made up of classic dishes from the Yunnan province in the southwest. If you are vegetarian, inform staff on arrival and they will tailor the menu for you. English menu.

Element Fresh

58–31, The Village, 19 Sanlitun Lu **Tel** *(010) 6417 1318*

Map *3 F3*

Perennially popular with locals and tourists alike, this bright and airy Western café is staffed with young enthusiastic servers. Fare includes huge dishes of creative salads and pasta, as well as sandwiches and a few Asian favorites. Plenty of freshly squeezed juices too and an English menu.

Hatsune

3/F, The Village, 19 Sanlitun Lu **Tel** *(010) 6415 3939*

Map *3 F3*

Charmingly creative rolls at surprisingly affordable prices make this one of the city's best modern Japanese options. Stylish surroundings, attentive service, and fresh fish flown in regularly from Japan suggest a much more expensive experience. A place to indulge yourself.

Kong Yiji

Desheng Men Nei Dajie, on the Hou Hai shore **Tel** *(010) 6618 4915*

Map *1 C2*

Perpetually packed with local epicures, this is simply among the best two or three Chinese restaurants of any style in the city. There's an enormous range of delicate dishes from the Yangzi River delta and the atmosphere is pure Chinese-style culinary joy.

Liqun Kaoyadian

11 Beixiangfeng Hutong (enter from Zhengyi Lu, off Qian Men Dong Dajie) **Tel** *(010) 6705 5578*

Map *5 D2*

Peking duck at this chaotic, little courtyard restaurant tucked away in a *hutong* east of Qian Men, can be sublime or disappointing. Generally worth trying your luck, though, if only for the rough-and-ready ambience. Very popular, so book ahead.

Lotus in Moonlight

Gate 4, Gongti Dong Men **Tel** *(010) 6268 1318*

Map *3 E1*

With its bright, pastel interior, Lotus practically glows with health and is popular for its range of vegetarian options, including traditional "fake meat" dishes and innovative modern vegetable combinations, as well as an extensive tea selection. Like meat, alcohol is prohibited here.

Makye Ame

2/F, A11 Xiushui Nan Jie, Jianguo Men Wai Dajie **Tel** *(010) 6506 9616*

Map *3 F5*

This branch of a popular Lhasa restaurant is pricey but it does offer a fantastic ethnic atmosphere and live folk entertainment that more than justifes the expense. Dishes use Tibetan ingredients but are slightly more fanciful than authentic Tibetan fare.

Mosto

3/F, Nali Patio, 81 Sanlitun Lu **Tel** *(010) 5208 6030*

Map *3 3F*

International classics with a contemporary twist, served in a buzzy central Sanlitun location. This European-style bistro has plenty of fans thanks to its relaxing ambience and immaculate service. The superb wine list is another draw. English menu and a good-value set menu available at lunchtime.

Salt

1/F, Trio Building, Jiangtai Xi Lu **Tel** *(010) 6437 8457*

Something of a local legend, this restaurant attracts plenty of diners for its innovative European menu and great service. Both lunchtimes and evenings offer a reasonable, fixed-price menu that changes daily. Well worth the 15-minute drive out of town. English menu.

Serve the People

Feijiacun Yuan, 8 Laiguangying Dong Lu, Chaoyang **Tel** *(010) 8470 4792*   **Map 3 F2**

This long-standing backstreet restaurant near Sanlitun serves up spicy dishes from Thailand and Vietnam. Prices are reasonable and the vibe is casual and lively most evenings. Weekend lunch and dinner slots are popular so reservations are recommended. There is a nice outdoor terrace where ice-cold beers are served to offset the often peppery cuisine.

South Silk Road

3/F, Soho Tower, 88 Jianguo Lu **Tel** *(010) 8580 4286*   **Map 1 F3**

Serves authentic but stylish Yunnanese food. Diners can sample all manner of flowers, insects, and mysterious animal parts, as well as more conventional dishes such as bacon and herb rolls. Classy private rooms upstairs with gorgeous lake views.

Southern Barbarian

107 Baochao Hutong **Tel** *(010) 6401 3372*   **Map 2 A2**

An offshoot of the popular Shanghai original, this delightful restaurant is located in the up-and-coming Baochao Hutong. It serves authentic Yunnan cuisine, along with a wide variety of bottled beers from Asia and Europe, in a smart interior. Service is excellent and the friendly owner is a real character.

Susu

10 Xi Xiang, Qianliang Hutong **Tel** *(010) 8400 2699*   **Map 2 B3**

Tucked away in a quiet *hutong* courtyard in the heart of old Beijing is this authentic Vietnamese restaurant. Simple, yet tasty dishes such as spring rolls and chicken pho are prepared by two chefs from Saigon, and there is a good selection of vegetarian options. The rooftop terrace is excellent for a romantic evening.

The Tree

42 Bei Sanlitun, opposite Sanlitun Hospital. **Tel** *(010) 6415 1954*   **Map 3 F2**

An amiable, expat-frequented pub hidden in a Sanlitun *hutong* serving good wood-fired pizzas with Belgian beers on tap. Enjoy soothing acoustic tunes from Filipino cover bands and gaze at abstract nude portraits on the walls. Regulars swear by the wood-fired pizzas.

The Veggie Table

19 Wudaoying Hutong **Tel** *(010) 6446 2073*   **Map 2 C1**

This charming American-owned restaurant serves generous portions of both Asian- and Western-style vegan and vegetarian meals. Specialties include vegetarian burgers and salads, and there is a wide selection of healthy juices and teas. Wine and beer are also available.

Three Guizhou Men

3 Guanghua Xilu **Tel** *(010) 6502 1733*   **Map 3 F5**

This popular restaurant in stylish surroundings reflects Guizhou province's culinary links with Southeast Asia. Expect excellent spicy food – huge plates of braised ribs with chili and garlic, and cold noodle salads in piquant sauces. If you are not a fan of too much spice, ask the staff to tone it down a little. English menu.

Capital M

3/F, 2 Qianmen Pedestrian Street **Tel** *(010) 6702 2727*   **Map 4 C2**

Boasting a prestigious address and enjoying a stellar view over Tian'an Men Square, this excellent contemporary restaurant is the sibling of Shanghai's legendary M on the Bund. The glamorous interior alone is worth a visit but for something even more memorable, dine on the terrace. Afternoon tea and Sunday brunch are also served. English menu.

Cuisine Cuisine

2/F, West Tower, WFC, 1 Dongsanhuan Zhong Lu **Tel** *(010) 5891 7626*

This outstanding restaurant boasts lavish and ornate interiors with an emphasis on gold and scarlet decor. The menu offers a modern take on classic Cantonese dishes. The attentive staff and the refined, elegant atmosphere together make for a memorable dining experience. Not recommended for vegetarians.

Din Tai Fung (Ding Tai Feng)

24 Xinyuan Xili Zhong Jie **Tel** *(010) 6462 4502*   **Map 3 E2**

Internationally acclaimed Taiwanese chain restaurant serving pricey Shanghainese cuisine and specializing in delicious *xiao long bao* (soup-filled dumplings). Slick decor across two stories, numerous private rooms, and an open kitchen/steamer room to entertain diners. Service is as attentive as the price warrants.

Duck de Chine

1949 The Hidden City, Gongti Bei Lu, Chaoyang **Tel** *(010) 6501 8881*   **Map 3 F3**

Located in an old factory complex dating from 1949, Duck de Chine has a sparsely designed dining room with heavy wooden beams, floorboards, and Chinese lanterns. The restaurant's signature Peking Duck is prepared with French-influenced ingredients and roasted in traditional Beijing duck ovens.

Key to Price Guide *see p198* **Key to Symbols** *see back cover flap*

Fat Duck 🍽️📖 ¥¥¥
Renaissance Beijing Capital Hotel, 61 Dongsanhuan Zhong Lu, Chaoyang **Tel** *(010) 5863 8888*

Set around an open, show kitchen, this elegant restaurant is a place to see and be seen. The slick, colorful decor is complemented by an equally eclectic menu consisting of contemporary adaptations of traditional pan-Chinese dishes, especially Sichuan and Cantonese. If you want Peking Duck in fine-dining style, this is where you will find it.

Huang Ting ¥¥¥
8 Jinyu Hutong (inside the Peninsula Beijing Hotel) **Tel** *(010) 6510 6707*   **Map** *2 C5*

Old Beijing recreated with thousands of bricks from demolished *hutong*s, along with wooden screens, carved stone friezes, and door guardian stones. Dishes such as deep-fried shrimps with wasabi-mayonnaise show a Hong Kong influence, but you can also get classic Beijing roast duck.

Lost Heaven 📖 V ¥¥¥
23 Chienmen, Qianmen Dong Lu **Tel** *(010) 8516 2698*   **Map** *5 D1*

This popular restaurant offers modern, creative cuisine inspired by the traditional cooking of the Dai, Miao, and Bai ethnic minorities from the mountainous Yunnan province. The ambience is stylish, in keeping with the affluent clientele. In summer, the second-floor terrace is a pleasant spot for dinner and drinks.

Made in China 📖 ¥¥¥
1 Dong Chang'an Jie (inside Grand Hyatt Hotel) **Tel** *(010) 8518 1234 ext. 6024*   **Map** *2 B5*

Brick walls hung with cooking implements give the impression of eating with the family. The kitchen is open allowing diners to view ducks roasting and nimble fingers speedily making disks of dough and spooning in fragrant fillings to make the little parcels known as *jiaozi*, a Beijing specialty. Superb.

Maison Boulud à Pékin 🍽️🍴📖 V ¥¥¥
Chi'en Men 23, 23 Qianmen Dong dajie **Tel** *(010) 6559 9200*   **Map** *5 D1*

Sophisticated and stylish, Maison Boulud is celebrity chef Daniel Boulud's only outpost in China. The restaurant occupies a former American Legation building and serves flawless French haute cuisine with an Asian twist. Prices are high but the set lunch menu is very reasonable and equally an occasion. Dress smartly and book ahead. English menu.

My Humble House 🍴📖 ¥¥¥
W3-1/F, Oriental Plaza West Tower, 1 Dong Chang'an Jie **Tel** *(010) 8518 8811*   **Map** *2 B5*

This smart branch of the Singapore chain serves intriguing fusion cuisine in a chic, modern setting. Beautiful presentation throughout from the decorative pond in the light-filled atrium to the lines of poetry woven into the descriptions of dishes.

Noble Court ¥¥¥
1 Dong Chang'an Jie (inside Grand Hyatt Hotel) **Tel** *(010) 8518 1234 ext. 6024*   **Map** *2 B5*

Among Beijing's finest Cantonese restaurants, elegantly decorated and beautifully run, Noble Court also serves a nice range of finely crafted dim sum and Beijing-style snacks, plus excellent seafood, and customary excesses such as shark's fin and bird's nest.

Transit 📖 V ¥¥¥
N4-36, 3/F, The Village North, Sanlitun Lu **Tel** *(010) 6417 9090*   **Map** *3 F3*

Located above the Village North's boutiques, this beautifully styled, ultra-modern restaurant is a great spot for a relaxed dinner with friends. The menu offers excellent Sichuan fare, immaculately presented. Classic dishes, such as the spicy Sichuan chicken cold cut, are perfectly executed.

CourtYard 🍴📖 ¥¥¥¥
95 Donghua Men Dajie **Tel** *(010) 6526 8883*   **Map** *2 B5*

Beijing's most famous fusion restaurant isn't quite the revelation it's made out to be, but is nevertheless excellent. The menu emphasizes execution over innovation, and the wine list is unrivaled. But the biggest draw is definitely the view across the moat to the Forbidden City.

Green T. House 📖 ¥¥¥¥
6 Gongti Tiyuchang Xi Lu **Tel** *(010) 6552-8310/8311*   **Map** *3 E3*

It takes an inventive menu to distract from Beijing's most jaw-dropping, China-meets-Alice-in-Wonderland design, but from nuggets of roasted lamb nestling among woolong tea and fennel, to green tea wasabi shrimp, everything is inventive, all is superb, and all contains tea.

Jing 🍴📖 ¥¥¥¥
8 Jinyu Hutong, Wangfujing (in the Peninsula Beijing Hotel) **Tel** *(010) 6510 6714*   **Map** *2 C5*

Few restaurants in China can even dream of being as stylish as Jing, with its gleaming open kitchens, video art, and Asian-influenced fusion menu with everything from seared goose liver with caramelized apples to tandoori lamb with cumined lentils, and large wine list. Nearly perfect.

Sureño 🍴📖 ¥¥¥¥
Inside Opposite House Hotel, The Village, 11 Sanlitun Lu, Chaoyang **Tel** *(010) 6410 5240*   **Map** *3 F3*

This contemporary Mediterranean restaurant is designed in a sophisticated minimal style, with leather chairs, silk cushions, and metallic and wooden paneling. The open kitchen, featuring a wood-fired oven, serves some of the finest modern Italian-Spanish fusion cuisine in Beijing.

Temple Restaurant Beijing ⦿⧫⊡ ⓎⓎⓎⓎ

23 Songzhusi, Shatan Bei Dajie **Tel** *(010) 8400 2232*   **Map** *2 B3*

Housed in a renovated 600-year-old temple complex, this upscale establishment is one of Beijing's most acclaimed international restaurants. Specialties include pot-roasted lobster with smoked aubergine caviar, and goose liver on toast. Book in advance, especially for the very popular Sunday brunch.

Tiandi ⊡ ⓎⓎⓎⓎ

140 Nan Chizi Dajie **Tel** *(010) 8511 5556*   **Map** *2 B5*

Upscale restaurant serving expensive imperial food in a light-filled courtyard residence. Decorations artistically blend Eastern symbols with Western irony. Dishes such as *lapi* (mung bean noodles) and crispy beef, can be exquisite or unforgivably bland, but ambience and service will not disappoint.

BEIJING FARTHER AFIELD

HEGEZHUANG The Orchard ▣⧫⊡Ⓥ ⓎⓎ

Hegezhuang Village **Tel** *(010) 6433 6270*

It may be out of town, but The Orchard is very popular with expats, particularly at weekends when a buffet brunch is served. Other offerings include freshly made organic salads, platters of roast meats, and fish from their own lake – try the trout if it's available. Lovely rustic venue surrounded by apple trees. Closed Mondays.

YINGBEIGOU Xiaolumian Ⓥ Ⓨ

Yingbeigou Village **Tel** *(010) 6162 6506*

Meaning "Little Hut Noodles", this rustic eatery is set in a renovated farmhouse and has a limited menu of delicious, homemade noodles and dumplings. Guests choose their preferred noodles and pick a topping such as *zhajiang* (bean paste with pork and garlic). Tea is complimentary. Open April to October, 11am–3pm at weekends and holidays only.

SHANGHAI

Baker and Spice ▣⧫Ⓥ Ⓨ

1/F, 195 Anfu Road **Tel** *(021) 5404 2733*   **Map** *1 D4*

Part of the popular Wagas café chain, Baker and Spice bakes fresh bread and all manner of delectable pastries daily on the premises. There is a surprising amount of space given the small shopfront – a large open kitchen bustles with bakers and there are plenty of tables. It does get busy so be prepared to wait for a table.

Haya's Mediterranean Cuisine ▣⧫ Ⓨ

415 Dagu Road **Tel** *(021) 6295 9511*

Formerly in Hong Qiao, this delightful café serves authentic Mediterranean fare featuring hummus, kabobs, and crisp salads. For taste and value, the falafel wrap in laffa bread is among the city's best options for a non-Chinese lunch. Try baklava and Turkish coffee for dessert.

Ming Ming Noodles Ⓨ

269 Beihai Road **Tel** *(021) 6352 5967*   **Map** *2 B3*

Despite looking like an ordinary dining pitstop that are ten a penny in Shanghai, a large crowd heads to Ming Ming for homemade noodles, made fresh every day. Diners order at the counter (no English is spoken) and then hand the receipt to the waitress before taking a seat. Try the *la rou mian* (spicy pork noodles) for a filling meal.

Nan Xiang Steamed Bun Restaurant ▣ Ⓨ

85 Yu Yuan Road **Tel** *(021) 6355 4206*   **Map** *2 C4*

One of those rare long-standing institutions (originally founded 1900) which actually lives up to its reputation, and where the pork and crab dumplings are well worth waiting for. Walk up the stairs to a higher, more pricey dining room with a much shorter wait.

Old Station ▣ Ⓨ

201 Caoxi North Road **Tel** *(021) 6427 2233*

Well-executed Shanghai classics at budget prices in a choice of highly unusual settings: the high-ceilinged halls of a former French monastery, or two connected luxury railway carriages, one formerly used by the Dowager Empress Cixi, and the other by Song Qingling, wife of Sun Yat Sen.

Wagas ▣⧫⊡Ⓥ Ⓨ

169 Wujiang Road, Room 201 **Tel** *(021) 5292 5228*   **Map** *1 F2*

This breakfast, lunch, and dinner spot is part of the city-wide chain that serves fresh salads and other light meals, as well as coffee and desserts. Good sized portions and consistent quality food make it a popular choice, as do the free Wi-Fi and casual buzz. Friendly, well-trained staff who speak good English.

Key to Price Guide *see p198* **Key to Symbols** *see back cover flap*

Yang's Fry-dumplings ✿

2/F, 269 Wujiang Road **Tel** *(021) 6136 1391* **Map** *1 F2*

Fried *shengjian* soup dumplings filled with pork and sprinkled with sesame seeds are popular snacks in Shanghai, and this institution churns them out 24 hours a day. Join the queue, order a serving for a few *renminbi*, and eat them carefully. The trick is to puncture the dumplings first to let the steam out before sucking up the delicious soup.

Yershari Xinjiang Food ✿

106 Nandan East Road **Tel** *(021) 6468 6079*

You may have to queue here at times but this is one of the most popular Xinjiang restaurants in the city and well worth the wait. Fare includes large plates of hearty chicken and potato stew *(da pan ji),* flavorsome naan breads, and succulent lamb kebabs. The Xinjiang dancers here are very entertaining. English menu.

1221 🍴 ✿✿

1221 Yan'an West Road **Tel** *(010) 6213 2441*

1221 serves a Canton-influenced and less oily version of Shanghainese dishes, including a refreshing pork and papaya soup, garlicky string beans, and spicy boiled beef with warm sesame loaf. Away from the center of town but worth the short taxi ride.

1931 🍴 ✿✿

112 Maoming South Road **Tel** *(021) 6472 5264* **Map** *1 E4*

Eating at this cozy little restaurant is like being in a 1930s private house, the walls hung with advertising and photographs from the period. Few of the dishes are obviously Shanghainese, although all are light and pleasant, and excellent value for money.

Anadolu 🍴🍴 ✿✿

4–7 Hengshan Road **Tel** *(021) 5465 0977*

Perfectly located on beery Hengshan Road, this is Shanghai's best late-night kabob house. Forget the functional dining room at the back: order a tender lamb döner wrapped in fluffy bread and smothered in sauce and eat it at the counter too.

Azul 🍴🍴 ✿✿

8/F, 378 Wukang Road **Tel** *(021) 5405 2252* **Map** *1 D5*

Shanghainese like tapas, and most agree that Azul is among the best places to sample these snack-size Spanish delights. The friendly Peruvian-born restaurateur oversees a blue-tiled bar and alcoves full of sequined pillows, and also serves heartier mains, such as an osso buco with saffron risotto.

Bali Laguna 🍴🍴 ✿✿

1469 Nanjing West Road **Tel** *(021) 6248 6970* **Map** *2 A3*

A slice of the tropics in Shanghai, this is a wooden villa with Balinese decor, perched on the side of a lotus-filled lake in a leafy park across from Jing'an Temple. An all-Indonesian menu includes common satays and *nasi goreng* but executed with a fine touch.

Bao Luo 🍴🍴 ✿✿

271 Fumin Road **Tel** *(021) 5403 7239* **Map** *1 D4*

Blink and you'll miss the entrance – but once inside it opens out into a cavernous space with lots more rooms upstairs. A favorite of local gourmets (plus renowned chef Jean-Georges Vongerichten), Bao Luo is justifiably acclaimed for cheap and classic Shanghainese dishes, like divinely sweet stir-fried eggplant in pancakes.

Crystal Jade 🍴 ✿✿

2/F, No. 6–7 South Block Xin Tiandi, Lane 123, Xingye Road **Tel** *(021) 6385 8752* **Map** *2 A4*

Exceptional Cantonese, Shanghainese, and other Chinese favorites in the upscale Xin Tiandi complex. Highlights include the spicy, nutty *dan dan mian* (made from one long, fresh noodle), superb *xiaolongbao* (Shanghainese dumplings), and many varieties of steamed buns. Bookings are essential at weekends.

Dong Bei Ren 🍴🍴 ✿✿

46 Panyu Road **Tel** *(021) 5230 2230*

Colorfully decorated cheap-eats hall serving wholesome northeast dishes, including simply prepared *jiaozi* and surprisingly flavorful tofu. Bottles of *baijiu* are a popular accompaniment, so tables can get rowdy. Oh, and no need to sing for your food as warbling waiters will take care of that.

Element Fresh 🍴🍴 ✿✿

Shanghai Center, 1376 Nanjing West Road **Tel** *(021) 6279 8682* **Map** *1 E3*

When oodles of street noodles have lost their shine, Element Fresh provides the perfect tonic of salads and sandwiches: try a gigantic, crunchy Niçoise washed down with freshly squeezed carrot-and-apple juice. Now in three stylish locations around town.

Enoterra 🍴🍴🍴 ✿✿

53–57 Anfu Road, near Changshu Road **Tel** *(021) 5404 0050* **Map** *1 D4*

This chic, romantic wine bar offers a wide selection of new- and old-world wines and knowledgeable staff who can advise on the best wine to suit your menu choices. Food is everything from small, tapas-style dishes to intricate French cuisine for full evening meals. There is a store attached.

Gu Yi

87 Fumin Road **Tel** (021) 6249 5628

Map 1 D3

The unassuming corner of Julu and Fumin Road now boasts exceptional eateries galore, among them Gu Yi. Bland palates beware! Everything in this outstanding Hunanese restaurant comes with chili, from pork ribs to cold-pressed chicken, even a side dish of cucumbers.

Haiku by Hatsune

28B Taojiang Road **Tel** (021) 6445 0021

Map 1 D5

This Shanghai outpost of a Beijing institution is just as trendy and lively as its northern sibling. Its popularity is well deserved thanks to the uniformly excellent Californian-style Japanese food. Any of the innovative hand rolls will be good, but the 119 spicy tuna rolls, as well as the excellent Motorola rolls, are famous. Book ahead. English menu.

Lotus Eatery

85 Yangzhai Road **Tel** (021) 6282 7756

Food from Yunnan province is very trendy in Shanghai, and Lotus Eatery is one of the city's most authentic Yunnan restaurants. Specialties include spicy fish soup and the eatery's many mushroom and spicy salad dishes. There are also good value set menus and a BYO policy. English menu.

Lynn

99–1 Xikang Road **Tel** (021) 6247 0101

Map 1 E3

This sophisticated, stylishly designed restaurant serves modern Shanghainese cuisine, plus some Cantonese and other pan-Chinese dishes. The consistently well-executed and well-priced food draws locals, expats, and visitors alike; Saturday and Sunday lunchtimes are popular for dim sum.

People 7

805 Julu Road **Tel** (021) 5404 0707

Map 1 D4

People 7 is minimalist and clever, from the "trick" bathrooms to the asymmetrical glassware and chunky stone bowls that the modern Chinese food arrives in. Even the breadsticks are cutting edge. These embellishments don't overshadow the cuisine, which is generally first-rate.

Quanjude

3/F, Purple Mountain Hotel, 778 Dongfang Road, Pudong **Tel** (021) 6886 8966

There's no need to travel to Beijing to find top quality Beijing duck. This immense hall, four floors above bustling Huaihai Lu, is stuffed with eager eaters watching white-gloved waiters transform whole birds into soups and slices of tender meat for rolling up with pancakes.

Sichuan Citizen

30 Donghu Road **Tel** (021) 5404 1235

Map 1 E4

A casual, yet slightly upmarket Sichuan restaurant that combines all the spice and fire of traditional Sichuan cuisine with excellent cocktails and wines. Many of the dishes are meat based but the kitchen will adapt them for vegetarians. Very popular with 20- to 30-something Shanghainese and expats.

Simply Thai

5C Dong Ping Road **Tel** (021) 400 880 7729

1 D5

This extremely popular Thai restaurant is efficient, relaxed, and inexpensive. The soups and salads benefit from the freshness of the ingredients and all the curries are well-spiced and hearty. If the weather's right, take a table on the deck outside. There's also a branch in Xin Tiandi.

SOAHC Restaurant and Tea Garden

Xingye Road, South Block, Xin Tiandi **Tel** (021) 6385 7777

Map 2 A4

Clunky name aside ("chaos" spelt backwards), this is one of the more visually appealing restaurants in Shanghai, with ponds, polished wood, and innovative lighting. The classically presented Yangzhou cuisine, from pumpkin croquettes with sesame to eel fillet with peppercorns, is similarly impressive.

Vegetarian Lifestyle

258 Fengxian Road **Tel** (021) 6215 7566

Map 1 B2

Zao Zi Shu boasts no eggs, meat, fish, fowl, or MSG. Fake meat dishes are prominent, most of them are created with tofu, and many of the patrons are monks in flowing robes. After eating, you can browse the restaurant's new-age bookstore.

Yin

Jinjiang Hotel Gourmet Street, 2/F, 4 Hengshan Road **Tel** (021) 5466 5070

Map 1 E4

Chef Dan presides over an inventive and satisfying menu that includes his signature Guizhou-style fish in zesty sauce and sliced lamb with ten spices, along with sushi and other Shanghai staples. Stylish decor in this 1929 hotel includes antique furniture and elegant table settings, complemented by mellow yet effective service.

Yuan Yuan

1/F & 2/F, K. Wah Center, 108 Xiangyang North Road **Tel** (021) 5108 3377

Map 1 E4

Recommended by several high-profile Shanghai chefs, Yuan Yuan is an expanding chain of no-frills Shanghainese restaurants specializing in seafood, prepared in the sticky, sweet, and boozy sauces that are so cherished by locals. Sautéed yellow croaker is a favorite.

Key to Price Guide see p198 **Key to Symbols** see back cover flap

Casanova

Building 3–4, 913 Julu Road **Tel** *(021) 5403 4528*   **Map** *1 D4*

Italian expatriates flock to this quaint old house, and with good reason. Despite an unremarkable decor and a dowdy downstairs bar, Casanova comes up trumps with soft-shell crab linguine and other perfect pastas, plus complimentary biscotti and limoncello to finish.

Cucina

56/F, Jinmao Tower, 88 Shiji Avenue (inside Grand Hyatt) **Tel** *(021) 5049 1234 ext. 8908*   **Map** *3 E3*

One of a collection of restaurants ringing the 56th floor of the Grand Hyatt, this trattoria's busy show kitchen has to work hard to distract from the spectacular views (on clear days, at least), but the home-made pizzas and pastas, and excellent seafood will do it.

El Willy

South Bund 22, 22 Zhongshan South Road **Tel** *(021) 5404 5757*   **Map** *3 D3*

Named after the owner, charismatic Spanish chef Guillermo "Willy" Trullas Moreno, El Willy is one of Shanghai's busiest international restaurants. The large menu combines inventive modern tapas with more conventional Spanish fare. Latino soundtrack and buzzy ambience. Advance reservations are recommended in the evening.

Flair

58/F, The Ritz-Carlton Shanghai, Pudong, IFC Tower, 8 Century Avenue, Pudong **Tel** *(021) 2020 1888*   **Map** *3 E3*

From the 58th floor of the IFC Tower, this sky-high venue with an outdoor terrace offers one of the most spectacular views of Shanghai. The menu specializes in Asian tapas dishes, such as miso-glazed black cod, and there is also a seafood bar. The premier location makes Flair a popular choice for dinner and cocktails, so reservations are essential.

Ginger

2 Lane 299, Fuxing West Road (near Gaoyou Road) **Tel** *(021) 6433 9437*   **Map** *1 D3*

Delightfully cozy café and restaurant, with both an indoor area and a small garden patio. It serves a range of Asian dishes plus special dinner items like Japanese sushi and mixed Asian tapas. Very good service and great food make this a popular place at lunchtimes and for weekend brunch.

Issimo

Jia Shanghai hotel, Nanjing West Road **Tel** *(021) 3302 4997*   **Map** *2 C2*

Large portions of classic Italian pasta, pizza, and risotto are designed for sharing at this sumptuous bar and restaurant, which opened as part of the Jia Shanghai boutique hotel. The contemporary-style dining room has become a regular home for the city's movers and shakers.

Lost Heaven

38 Gaoyou Road **Tel** *(021) 6433 5126*   **Map** *1 D5*

Housed in a French Concession villa, just off Fuxing Road, this beautifully styled exotic restaurant is popular with celebrities and local VIPs. Dishes are a fusion of Southwestern Yunnan cuisine with the spicy flavors of Burma and Thailand. The first-floor Mask Bar is great for pre- and post-dinner drinks.

Mercato

6/F, Three on the Bund **Tel** *(021) 6321 9922*   **Map** *2 C3*

Housed in the historic Three on the Bund heritage building, Mercato is an upscale Italian eatery with a separate pizza lounge. The menu, created by Michelin-starred celebrity chef Jean-Georges Vongerichten, offers refined and inventive takes on traditional Italian dishes. Specials include crispy beef rib with a chili-chianti glaze.

Mr and Mrs Bund

6/F, Bund 18, 18 Zhongshan East No. 1 Road **Tel** *(021) 6323 9898*   **Map** *2 C3*

Considered one of Shanghai's best Western restaurants, this classy French eatery is chic yet unstuffy. With a great position on the Bund, diners come here for the views as well as the food. Famous dishes include a mouth-watering *foie gras* crumble. Booking is essential. English menu.

New Heights

7/F, Three on the Bund, 3 Zhongshan East No. 1 Road **Tel** *(021) 6321 0909*   **Map** *2 C3*

This restaurant occupies the top floor of the Three on the Bund complex and entices diners with a globe-trotting menu that ranges from a souped-up croque monsieur to Vietnamese duck and fish and chips, all at very reasonable prices. A great lunch option, especially on the outdoor terrace at weekends.

Shintori Null II

803 Julu Road **Tel** *(021) 5404 5252*   **Map** *1 D4*

Rustic paths wind through bamboo to a sliding metal door. Inside is a chic industrial space and possibly Shanghai's best Japanese food. Enjoy the beefsteak in Pu-leaf – a winning variation on Beijing duck – but leave room for the green tea tiramisu.

Sir Elly's

13/F & 14/F, The Peninsula Shanghai, 32 The Bund **Tel** *(021) 2327 6756*   **Map** *2 C2*

Named after Sir Elly Kadoorie, founder of Peninsula hotels, this restaurant serves inventive modern European and Mediterranean cuisine in an exquisite dining room. In spring and summer, guests can enjoy dinner and drinks on the hotel's 14th-floor stone terrace, which affords stunning views of the Pudong skyline.

South Beauty 881

881 Yan'an Middle Road **Tel** *(021) 6247 5878*   **Map** *1 E3*

South Beauty's setting, an ornately decorated mansion with roof terrace and vast gardens, threatens to overwhelm the Sichuan/Cantonese menu and so-so service. On the other hand, some of the hot and spicy items, particularly seafood, are innovative in presentation with remarkable flavors.

T8

181 Taicang Road, No. 8 North Block, Xin Tiandi **Tel** *(021) 6355 8999*   **Map** *2 A4*

An army of chefs work their magic in an open kitchen on intelligent combinations of Chinese and Mediterranean ideas, such as Chinese duck pizza, seared salmon with char siu pork, and mushroom soup with truffle oil, in the theatrically lit and ultra-modern interior of a reimagined traditional house.

Table No. 1

The Waterhouse at South Bund Hotel, 1–3 Maojiayuan Road, off Zhongshan Road **Tel** *(021) 6080 2918* **Map** *3 E5*

On the ground floor of The Waterhouse at South Bund boutique hotel is the chic but casual Table No. 1. The restaurant is known for its modern, seasonal European cuisine and fresh flavors created by acclaimed British chef Jason Atherton. The emphasis is on large dishes for sharing.

Yi Long Court

The Peninsula Shanghai, 32 Zhongshan East No. 1 Road **Tel** *(021) 2327 6742*   **Map** *2 C2*

Helmed by a Michelin-starred Cantonese chef, this classy establishment is perhaps Shanghai's best upscale Chinese restaurant. The Cantonese dim sum and traditional dishes are perfectly executed, the service is sublime, and the beautifully designed dining room boasts antique Chinese and Parisian furnishings.

8½ Otto e Mezzo Bombana

6–7/F, Mission Building, 169 Yuanmingyuan Road **Tel** *(021) 6087 2890*   **Map** *2 C2*

The Shanghai outpost of Hong Kong's Michelin-starred restaurant, 8½ Otto e Mezzo Bombana offers highly stylized Italian cuisine by famous chef Umberto Bombana. A-la-carte and tasting menus are available. Options include homemade artisanal pastas or chargrilled pigeon. The elegantly styled, contemporary interiors ooze luxury.

Downstairs by David Laris

183 URBN Hotel, Jiaozhou Road **Tel** *(021) 5172 1300*   **Map** *1 D2*

This stylish contemporary restaurant on the ground floor of the URBN boutique hotel is managed by ubiquitous celebrity chef David Laris. The open kitchen serves up a fusion of modern Asian, Australian, and Mediterranean cuisines. There is also a wide selection of innovative cocktails and a good wine list.

Fook Lam Moon

2/F, 33 Fucheng Road (inside Pudong Shangri-La Hotel) **Tel** *(021) 5877 3786*   **Map** *3 D3*

The latest and most luxurious branch of this legendary Hong Kong restaurant. Cold Shanghai-style appetizers keep the local clientele happy, but shark's fin and crabmeat soup, roasted suckling pig, and a wide range of southern Chinese favorites justify the unequalled reputation.

Jade on 36

33 Fucheng Road (inside Pudong Shangri-La Hotel) **Tel** *(021) 6882 3636*   **Map** *3 C3*

High on the Shangri-La's tower, Jade on 36 offers a stimulating menu of classic French cuisine that has been given a contemporary twist. Dining is in a sumptuously designed restaurant that offers jaw-dropping views from the 36th floor over the city.

Jean Georges

4/F, Three on the Bund, 3 Zhongshan No. 1 Road **Tel** *(021) 6321 7733*   **Map** *2 C3*

The Shanghai branch of Jean-Georges Vongerichten's garlanded New York restaurant offers French with hints of Asia (lemon grass, coconut), each dish small but perfect in every way. Try the seasonal set menu which makes the best of available ingredients, and something from the 5000-bottle wine cellar.

M on The Bund

7/F, 20 Guangdong Road **Tel** *(021) 6350 9988*   **Map** *2 C3*

Atop a 1920s bank building overlooking the river, the pioneer of posh Bund dining continues to excel with a menu of celebrity restaurateuse Michelle Garnaut's favorites, including signature soft-as-butter salted lamb and light-as-air Pavlova. An essential Shanghai experience.

Morton's

Unit 15–16, 4/F, IFC Shanghai Mall, 8 Century Avenue, Pudong **Tel** *(021) 6075 8888*   **Map** *3 E3*

This popular American steakhouse, born in Chicago in 1978, has opened branches all over the world. The Shanghai restaurant is the largest and boasts sleek, stylish interiors as well as an alfresco terrace and a cigar and wine lounge. Morton's specializes in hearty American cuisine, such as its prized grain-fed aged beef steaks and giant desserts.

Nadaman

33 Fucheng Road (inside Pudong Shangri-La Hotel) **Tel** *(021) 5888 3768*   **Map** *3 D3*

Five varieties of the Japanese aristocratic *kaiseki ryori* multi-course set meals, with an endless stream of small but exquisite dishes. The Nadaman is the Shanghai branch of a restaurant with 175 years of tradition, but not shy of modern invention, and a favorite with Japanese visitors.

Key to Price Guide *see p198* **Key to Symbols** *see back cover flap*

Palladio
1376 Nanjing West Road (inside Portman Ritz-Carlton) Tel (021) 6279 7188 **Map** 1 E3

Sumptuous menu of extravagant Italian dishes with hints of Napoli, suggesting meals should be taken at a gentle pace over an extended period of time, although briskly served business set lunches are excellent value for money, too. Highly recommended.

The Yongfoo Elite
200 Yongfu Road Tel (021) 5466 2727

The abalone-heavy Shanghai and Cantonese menu is a little pricey, but served in an ancient former British Consulate building, the Yongfoo Elite reputedly took two years to furnish. The results are extraordinary, from the verandah shaded by an ancient magnolia to the ornate candelabra.

SHANGHAI FARTHER AFIELD

HANGZHOU Crystal Garden
12 Dongpo Road Tel (0571) 8706 7777

Smart, brightly lit three-story interior atrium with traditional square tables and wooden stools serving Hangzhou, Shanghai, and Huaiyang cuisine. A picture menu with English makes ordering steamed mince pork and roe balls and chicken in rice wine very easy.

HANGZHOU Hangzhou House
Amanfayun, 22 Fayun Nong Tel (0571) 8732 9999

Part of the luxurious Amanfayun resort, this is a more casual, authentic eatery providing traditional fare in a simple, picturesque setting. On the menu are well-known local dishes such as Beggar's Chicken, where a whole chicken is covered in a layer of clay and baked underground before being cracked open at your table. English menu.

HANGZHOU Provence
1 Baishaquan, Shuguang Road Tel (0571) 8797 6115

This small, two-floored restaurant is owned by a team of French chefs, Maître d's, and wine connoisseurs. The cozy atmosphere and simple, well-executed Provençal cuisine is matched by an excellent wine list that includes French and European wines. Very popular at weekends and during holiday periods.

HANGZHOU Va Bene
Building No. 8, 147 Nan Shan Road, Xi Hu Tiandi Tel (0571) 8702 6333

An Italian is in charge of the large open kitchen of this latest incarnation of the Hong-Kong-based Italian chain, set among lake-edge groves of maple and bamboo in Hangzhou's answer to Shanghai's trendy Xin Tiandi area. Try beef *carpaccio* or salmon with horseradish, or reasonably priced pizzas or a set menu.

SUZHOU Chuanfulou Dajiudian
10 Gong Lane Tel (0512) 6762 5377

Sichuan and Suzhou dishes presented in a variety of stone pots and porcelain plates in a spotless yet charming setting. Highlights of the comprehensive menu include Chuan Fu roast beef (sizzling and invigorating) and stir-fried local mushrooms (simple yet stunning).

SUZHOU Deyue Lou
8 and 43 Guanqian Street Taijian Long Tel (0512) 6523 8940

This renowned 400-year-old restaurant has twice appeared on Chinese cinema screens. It's probably the best place to sample squirrel-shaped mandarin fish and other Suzhou specialties. Presentation is outstanding – particularly the dumplings, some of which come shaped like hedgehogs or geese.

SUZHOU Pingjiang Lodge
33 Niujia Lane, Pingjiang District Tel (0512) 6523 3318

A neat blend of whitewashed Suzhou architecture and modern interior design with large glass windows overlooking the picturesque Pingjiang canal district. The restaurant serves Suzhou cuisine as well as some Chinese fusion dishes; locally caught fish features heavily and comes steamed, baked, broiled, or wok fried.

SUZHOU The Bookworm
77 Gunxiufang, Shiquan Street Tel (0512) 6526 4720

An offshoot of the Beijing original, this multi-purpose café, bar, library, bookstore, Wi-Fi hangout, and cultural center serves fresh-brew coffee and an eclectic assortment of tasty dishes for breakfast, lunch, and dinner. It's a great place for a quick snack or to while away an hour or two.

SUZHOU Hai Tien Lo
259 Xinshi Road (inside Pan Pacific Suzhou Hotel) Tel (0512) 6510 3388 ext. 8500

This beautifully styled Cantonese dining room is located in the impeccable Pan Pacific Hotel (formerly the Sheraton). The restaurant serves authentic dim sum, plus a large menu of Suzhou specialties and some inventive takes on traditional southern Chinese food.

SURVIVAL
GUIDE

PRACTICAL INFORMATION

China has been through an explosion in both international and domestic tourism, so most accessible sights get very crowded, especially during the summer season. Due to the absence of any non-profit network of tourist information centers, visitors often have to rely on hotels for guidance, which can be far from reliable. China International Travel Service branches, listed on page 211, exist to sell over-priced services, not to provide impartial advice, and local

Symbol of the China Tourist Board

competitors may be better. A thorough reading of this and other books before departure is recommended. In Beijing and Shanghai the tourist infrastructure, including transportation, hotels, and restaurants, is mostly on a par with international standards. However, communication still poses some difficulties, as English is not spoken everywhere, though standards have improved since the Olympic Games in Beijing and the World Expo in Shanghai.

WHEN TO GO

Although there are great climatic disparities within China, spring and fall are generally the best months to travel, and the time when the Chinese also take to the road in far vaster numbers than those of foreign visitors. The peak foreign tourist season, however, is during summer (June to September), best avoided if you don't like the heat – it is baking hot in Beijing, and steamy in Shanghai. Winter is fiercely cold in Beijing, and rather dank and penetrating in Shanghai. Climate and rainfall charts are found on *pages 35–7*. Although planning your trip to coincide with one of the major holiday and festival periods *(see pp34–7)* can lead to a fun and colorful trip, national holidays are probably best avoided as tickets for air,

train, and bus transportation can be very difficult to acquire. Tourist sights will also be swamped with local sightseers, and most hotels and guesthouses will have raised their rates.

VISAS AND PASSPORTS

A passport, valid for at least six months, and a visa are necessary to enter the People's Republic of China. However, most foreign nationals do not require a visa for entering Hong Kong and Macau where mainland visas can be purchased more easily than anywhere else. Chinese embassies and consulates around the world issue a standard single-entry, 30-day visa, although multiple-entry 60-day visas, and 90-day visas can sometimes be obtained. Long-duration multiple-entry visas are no

A symbol of former European influence in Shanghai

longer easily obtainable in Hong Kong. When completing the visa application form, you must specify what parts of China you plan to visit. Avoid mentioning Tibet or Xinjiang, even if you plan to visit these regions, as you may be questioned about your occupation and intent of visit. Any list you provide is not binding. The vast majority of China is open to visitors and you do not need any special permits for Beijing and Shanghai. Always carry your passport, as it is an essential document for checking into hotels, and the Public Security Bureau (PSB) *(see p216)* may insist on seeing it. Photocopying the visa page and the personal information page will speed up replacement if your passport is lost or stolen. When in China, you can normally get two 30-day

Snow-covered bicycles in Beijing during winter

◁ **Beijing, Hou Hai, caged birds in the blossom-covered branches of a small tree**

Communist mementos on sale in a Shanghai market

extensions to your visa from the PSB, though the bureaucracy can be daunting and you currently need to prove you have US$3,000 in a Chinese bank account. Note that heavy fines are levied if you over-stay your visa.

CUSTOMS INFORMATION

When entering China, visitors are entitled to a duty-free allowance of 70 fluid ounces (2 liters) of wine or spirits, 400 cigarettes, and a certain amount of gold and silver. Foreign currency exceeding US$5,000, or its equivalent, must be declared. Items that are prohibited include fresh fruit, all animals (except cats and dogs as pets) and plants, and arms and ammunition. Chinese law specifies limits on the export of certain items, such as particular herbal medicines. Also, objects predating 1795 cannot be taken out of China, while antiques made after that date will need to have an official seal affixed. Although foreign visitors are largely left alone, it is not advisable to take in politically controversial literature, especially if it is written in Chinese.

EMBASSIES AND CONSULATES

Most countries have an embassy in Beijing and many also have a consulate in Shanghai. Consular offices can re-issue passports and assist in case of emergencies, such as imprisonment, hospitalization, and if you become a victim of a crime.

Your hotel can put you in touch with your nearest embassy or consulate.

TOURIST INFORMATION

China has yet to recognize the value of professional tourist information centers, either at home or abroad. Those that exist in Beijing and Shanghai are, in general, useless. The state-approved **China International Travel Service** (CITS), originally set up to cater to the needs of foreign visitors, today functions as any other local operator, offering nothing more than tours, tickets, and rented cars. There are a few government-run travel agencies abroad but they fail to offer professional and unbiased advice, instead steer customers toward group tours and standard hotels. The best advice tends to come from youth hostels, hotels and private companies, such as **Bespoke Beijing**, that are geared to the needs of tourists.

Hotel receptions – a useful source of tourist information

ADMISSION PRICES

Most temples, parks, palaces, and museums have an entrance fee. Temples charge anything from ¥5 to ¥50. Star sights, such as Beijing's Forbidden City, can charge up to ¥60 in summer, plus an assortment of extra charges for access to certain areas and special exhibitions. Shanghai's Oriental Pearl Television Tower costs ¥150 if all its various platforms and exhibitions are visited. Some sights offer a *men piao* which merely allows access to the grounds, and a *tong piao*, which includes access to buildings in the price. The sale of tickets can cease up to an hour before closing time. Guides swarm around entrances to major sights but their knowledge often amounts to no more than the Party-approved information on signs.

DIRECTORY

EMBASSIES AND CONSULATES

Australia
21 Dongzhi Men Wai Dajie, Beijing. **Tel** *(010) 5140 4111*. 22/F, CITIC Square, 1168 Nanjing West Road, Shanghai. **Tel** *(021) 2215 5200*.

Canada
19 Dongzhi Men Wai Dajie, Beijing. **Tel** *(010) 5139 4000*. 8/F, 1788 Nanjing West Road, Shanghai. **Tel** *(021) 3279 2800*.

United Kingdom
11 Guanghua Lu, Beijing. **Tel** *(010) 5192 4000*. Room 301, Shanghai Center, 1376 Nanjing West Road, Shanghai. **Tel** *(021) 3279 2000*.

USA
55 Anjia Lu, Beijing. **Tel** *(010) 8531 3000*. 1469 Huai Hai Middle Road, Shanghai. **Tel** *(021) 3217 4650*.

TOURIST INFORMATION

Bespoke Beijing
www.bespokebeijing.com **Tel** *(010) 6400 0133*.

China International Travel Service (CITS)
Beijing 1 Dongdan Bei Dajie. **Tel** *(010) 8522 8888/8522 8445*. **Shanghai** 1277 Beijing Xi Lu. **Tel** *(021) 6289 4510*. **www**.cits.net

HOLIDAYS AND OPENING HOURS

The main holiday periods are Chinese New Year (Spring Festival) and October 1 (National Day). People get around a week's holiday over both periods with the actual dates announced by the government a week in advance. There are also a number of one-day holidays throughout the year as well as the longer May holiday. Accommodation prices rise as domestic tourism peaks. Restaurants, tourist sights, and shops, mostly remain open except for a short period around Chinese New Year. The majority open every day and hours are roughly from 10am until 8pm.

LANGUAGE

The official language of China is Putonghua (literally "common speech"), known outside China as Mandarin. Putonghua is the native language of the north, but it is used across the country for communication between speakers of several other Chinese dialects, and can be used throughout China. More and more people speak English in hotels, shops, and restaurants though you should not assume you will be able to find an English speaker. The tonal nature of Putonghua makes it a difficult language to learn without a little serious study with a teacher. Pinyin, which is a written romanization system, helps in the recognition of sounds, but the diacritical marks to indicate tone are all too often omitted, and without tone there is no meaning. A few basic phrases in Putonghua are listed on *pages 238–40*.

Chinese children enjoying time in a Shanghai park

Road sign in both Pinyin and Chinese characters

PUBLIC CONVENIENCES

Away from hotels and more expensive restaurants, public bathrooms are traditionally of the squat variety. In Beijing and Shanghai they vary between being very well looked after and quite clean to horrifying. There is little privacy and toilet paper is a rarity, so carry your own. You usually have to pay around ¥0.30 to use public bathrooms. If you are unused to squat toilets, take full advantage of hotel, fast-food restaurant, and shopping mall facilities.

TRAVELERS WITH SPECIAL NEEDS

If you are a wheelchair user, China will be hard going, though the situation has improved since the Olympics and the World Expo. Beijing's new subway lines have wheelchair access and there are a few disabled access taxis, though they must be booked in advance. In Beijing and Shanghai, crowded pavements can be a challenge, as can public transport, but many hotels and restaurants are wheelchair accessible. The re-landscaped Bund area features concrete ramps enabling wheelchair access to the elevated riverside boardwalk. However, public buildings and places of interest are rarely fitted with ramps or rails. The best advice for disabled visitors is to hire a driver and stay in a foreign-run branded hotel which will have adapted rooms. Elevators are common in most hotels over three storeys high.

TRAVELING WITH CHILDREN

The Chinese love children, and they are usually welcome everywhere. Both you and your child might have to grin and bear the hair-ruffling and general enthusiastic contact that you will likely encounter on a daily basis. If it starts to get tiresome, saying that your child is very shy *(ta shi hen haixiu)* might result in people being more hands-off. Baby-changing rooms are extremely rare, and very few restaurants have child seats, but people will generally go out of their way to accommodate you. Supermarkets are well supplied with diapers, baby wipes, creams, medicine, baby food, and clothing. However, you are advised to buy foreign infant milk formula as Chinese brands have twice been found to be contaminated. Bring a set of plastic cutlery for your child, as most restaurants only have chopsticks. Bear in mind that a lot of taxis do not have seatbelts in the back with which to attach child seats.

GAY AND LESBIAN TRAVELERS

The gay and lesbian scene is growing, and Beijing and Shanghai are considered relatively open. However, the country is still a highly conventional society, and homosexuality is not considered a standard lifestyle. Both Beijing and Shanghai have several gay bars and clubs, with Destination (7 Gongti Xi Lu, (010) 6551-5138) in

Beijing being a long-term favorite and Red Station (4/F, 200 Taikang Road, (021) 6415 -8695) in Shanghai is the place to party. Bear in mind that bars are occasionally raided by the police as homosexuality is still a sensitive subject.

TRAVELING ON A BUDGET

As China goes up in the world and the value of its currency rises, so do its prices for travelers, but in general, the country is a good place to be on a budget with plenty of well-run hostels that operate tours and offer advice. However, Beijing and Shanghai are the most expensive cities to visit and accommodation isn't as cheap as you might hope; dorm beds never cost less than ¥50, a fortune compared to rural parts of the country. On the bright side, public transportation is very cheap, with buses in both cities costing ¥1 or ¥2, and food can be amazing value too, with a big bowl of noodles costing around ¥3 in local cafés. Unfortunately, international student cards or cards for the retired do not entitle you to any discounts in China.

WHAT TO TAKE

In Beijing from November until March, you will require a good, warm jacket, gloves, sweater, warm socks, thermal leggings, sturdy footwear, and lip balm. During the same period in Shanghai, you still need a raincoat, a sweater, warm clothes, and an umbrella. In summer, you only need loose-fitting shirts or T-shirts, and thin trousers. Shorts will also do. If you do not want to do any shopping for essentials, bring a first-aid kit, raincoat, sun hat, sunglasses, and a plug adapter. Make sure you have a phrase book and all the books you require for your trip.

Midday in Shanghai – so midday in Beijing too

TIME AND CALENDAR

Despite its vast size, China occupies only one time zone, and there is no daylight saving time. So, China is 7 or 8 hours ahead of Green-wich Mean Time (GMT), 2 or 3 hours behind Australian Eastern Standard Time, 15 or 16 hours ahead of US Pacific Standard Time, and 12 or 13 hours ahead of US Eastern Standard Time. The Western Gregorian calendar is used for all official work; the dates for traditional festivals follow a lunar calendar.

ELECTRICITY

The electrical current in China is 220 volts. The most common plug arrangement is two flat prongs, as in North America. Sockets will not take plugs with a third earthing pin, or those with one flat blade larger than the other. Most are also designed to take European-style two round pins, while the British three square-pin arrangement is rare outside smart hotels. Bring an adapter suitable for China to avoid problems. It is best to stay clear of cheap Chinese batteries, as they are very short-lived and may leak, but be aware that the Western-brand batteries on sale are often fakes.

Plugs with two and three prongs

RESPONSIBLE TOURISM

It is no secret that China has terrible environmental problems. People in Beijing and Shanghai still litter with abandon, but attitudes are changing, especially amongst the younger generation. Tourists can play their part by not wasting water (Beijing has almost constant drought) and being conscious of their impact on the local environment. New hotels often play lip service to being sustainable, but there is only one hotel in Shanghai that lives up to its eco-credentials – the Urbn *(see p185)* – which keeps its carbon usage to an absolute minimum. Tourists can support communities by staying in locally-owned hotels and taking small, low-impact tours. There are also food markets where you can buy locally-grown produce. China has banned the use of free plastic bags, so bring your own. In Beijing, the Sanyuanli Market (Shun Yuan Jie) near Sanlitun is excellent for locally-grown fruit and vegetables, and in Shanghai, try the Wuzhong Wet Market (328 Wulumuqi Middle Road, near to Fuxing West Road).

CONVERSION CHART

The metric system is used in all parts of China.

Imperial to metric
1 inch = 2.5 centimeters
1 foot = 30 centimeters
1 mile = 1.6 kilometers
1 ounce = 28 grams
1 pound = 454 grams
1 pint (US) = 0.473 liters
1 gallon (US) = 3.785 liters

Metric to imperial
1 centimeter = 0.4 inches
1 meter = 3 feet 3 inches
1 kilometer = 0.6 miles
100 gram = 3.53 ounces
1 kilogram = 2.2 pounds
1 liter = 2.11 pints (US)

Chinese measurements
When buying fruit and vegetables, use the following measurements:
1 jin: 500 grams
1 liang: 50 grams

General Etiquette

Despite rapid modernization, China remains a traditional society governed by strong family values. Beijing and Shanghai give the outward impression of Western modernity, but older generations retain a deep-seated and family-oriented conservatism. Confucian values promote respect for elders and those in positions of authority. Religious observance is not widespread, and is largely separate from mainstream social behavior. The Chinese are, above all, welcoming and generous, and visitors are often amazed at their hospitality. If invited to someone's home, a gift of chocolates, French wine, or some other imported treat will be greatly appreciated.

Worshipers praying at a shrine at one of Beijing's many temples

GREETING PEOPLE

Shaking hands is commonplace in big cities, and certainly considered the norm with foreign visitors. Although the Chinese are not particularly tactile in their greetings, bodily contact is quite common between friends, even of the same sex. Young men often walk arm in arm, or with their arm around another's shoulder. The usual Chinese greeting is "Ni hao" (Hello) or "Nimen hao" in its plural form, to which you reply "Ni hao" or "Nimen hao" – the polite form is "Nin hao".

The Chinese will not blanch at asking how much you earn, your age, or whether you are married. Such questions are seen as nothing more than taking a friendly interest in a new acquaintance. When proffering business cards, the Chinese use the fingertips of both hands, and receive cards in the same manner. For business travelers, cards are essential, preferably with Chinese on one side and English on the other.

DRESS

The improvement in living standards is reflected by people's clothes: where once conservative fashions in black or brown dominated, now anything goes. In cities, people wear what they wear the world over: jeans, T-shirts, and skirts, and many youngsters dress provocatively and dye their hair. Don't worry too much about what you wear, but try to avoid looking scruffy. Shorts are acceptable, but having cleavage on display will attract attention. Both cities are very fashion conscious, but generally Shanghai is considered to be a more dress-oriented society and Beijing a little more casual.

FACE

Reserved in manner and expression, the Chinese also harbor strong feelings of personal pride and respect. The maintenance of pride and the avoidance of shame is known as "face." Loss of face creates great discomfort and major embarrassment for Chinese, so although you may often be frustrated by bureaucracy and delays, or the incompetence of hotel staff, try not to embarrass anybody in public. Be firm but polite, and use confrontation only as a very last resort.

CHINESE HOSPITALITY

If invited out for dinner, expect to see the diners competing to pay the entire bill, rather than dividing it up between them. It is a good idea to join in the scramble for the bill, or at least make an attempt – your gesture will be appreciated, though almost certainly declined. For more on dining etiquette, *see pages 190–91.*

PLACES OF WORSHIP

Although there are no dress codes for Buddhist, Daoist, or Confucian temples, visitors to mosques should dress respectfully – avoid wearing shorts or mini skirts – and cover your upper arms. Buddhist, Daoist, and Confucian temples are relaxed with visitors wandering about, but be considerate toward worshipers. Also, check whether you can take photographs within temple halls, as this is often not permitted. Taking photos in courtyards, however, is usually not a problem. Some Buddhist and Daoist temples are active, such as Beijing's Lama Temple, and you should show respect towards the resident monks.

Advice for burning incense

ANNOYANCES

The Chinese habit of staring, especially in smaller towns and rural areas, can be a little annoying. It can also be encountered in Beijing and Shanghai, since these cities attract a lot of migrant workers and peasant tourists. However, the intent is rarely hostile. Another problem that visitors face are constant calls of "Hellooo!" or "Laowai!" (foreigner). It is best either to ignore them or smile, as replying often results

A busy shopping street, stalking ground for "art student" scamsters

in bursts of laughter. In Beijing and Shanghai, people some-times strike up conversation to practice their English, but caution is necessary as increasingly these approaches are lead-ins to scams. Around Beijing's Wangfujing shopping street, Liulichang, Tian'an Men Square and the Forbidden City, and on Shanghai's main shopping streets, decline to accompany "art students" who in the guise of fund-raising will pressure you to buy hugely overpriced art. Similarly be wary of "language students" who suggest entering a nearby café or bar and who will leave you with a bill for thousands of *renminbi*. Also watch for "accidental" encounters with seemingly friendly and helpful English speakers who eventually suggest partaking in a tea ceremony.

Although more orderly queues are beginning to replace the usual mêlée at ticket offices, you still need to be prepared for a lot of pushing and shoving. Spitting is still widespread, although there is always a crack-down in the run-up to major inter-national events. Despite the best attempts of public educators, spitting is still common on buses and trains, and it is not considered rude to spit in mid-conversation, so do not take offense.

SMOKING AND ALCOHOL

As the world's largest producer and consumer of cigarettes *(xiangyan)*, China is a smoker's paradise. Despite the appearance of no-smoking zones and rudimentary anti-smoking campaigns, Beijing and Shanghai remain shrouded in a haze of nicotine clouds. Smoking is now banned on domestic flights, on trains (except in connecting passages between carriages), and on buses, but unless the latter are air-conditioned, and sometimes even then, the rule is ignored. Smoking during meals is acceptable, especially if there are other smokers present. The Chinese are very generous when it comes to offering cigarettes, so remember to be equally generous in return. They also enjoy drinking alcohol, and there is no taboo against moderate intoxication. The usual accompaniment during a meal is beer *(pijiu)*, or white spirits *(baijiu)*. Wine *(putaojiu)* is increa-singly popular with the middle classes and China now produces its own wine. If someone raises a toast to you ("Ganbei!"), it is good form to return the toast later.

A popular white spirit, or *baijiu*

BARGAINING

As a foreign national in China, it is essential to bargain *(taojia huanjia)*. You may often be overcharged – sometimes by large amounts – in markets and anywhere else where prices are not indicated. Some restaurants charge higher prices on the English menu than on the Chinese one. You should bargain to reduce your hotel room-rate: no one pays rack rate and substantial discounts are almost always available, especially at Chinese-run hotels. Always ask for a discount on airfares, too. Be sure to bargain pleasantly and with a smile. At markets, let the vendor speak first and don't be afraid to counter offer with 10 percent or less.

First prices to foreigners are often as much as 15 times higher than what will eventually be accepted. Your next offer should only be fractionally higher than your first. The prices in large shops and government emporia *(guoying shangdian)* may appear to be fixed, but the Chinese will routinely ask for discounts, and frequently get them, too. Asking is normal practice, so never be afraid.

TIPPING

There is no tipping in China, so do not tip guides, taxi drivers, or anyone else. In China the price you agree for the service is the one you pay, although some restaurants in larger hotels or fine-dining venues now routinely add a service charge. Away from hotels and tourist areas waitresses will pursue you down the street to return the change they think you've forgotten. However, five-star hotel bell boys do now expect tips.

BEGGING

China's imbalanced economic progress and huge population of rural poor have resulted in large numbers of beggars, especially in Beijing and Shanghai. Foreign visitors naturally attract attention, and groups of children are often sent by their parents to extract money. The best strategy is to ignore them and walk away.

A tourist bargaining with a vendor for his purchase

Personal Security & Health

Distinctive green cross of a pharmacy

Compared to many places in the world, China is a very safe place to travel and the vast majority of visitors won't encounter any problems. A small minority may be the victims of petty crime, especially from opportunistic thieves in tourist destinations, so like anywhere, you should protect your valuables and important documents at all times. Health wise, it pays to eat in clean places, and drink only mineral water. If you do want to eat at street stalls, choose the busiest as it will have a high turnover of food and make sure what you eat is piping hot.

POLICE

The police in China, or *jingcha*, are more commonly known to foreigners as the Public Security Bureau (PSB) or *gong'an ju*. However, most visitors to Beijing and Shanghai are unlikely to encounter the PSB, unless extending their visas, or reporting a loss or theft of personal items. Note that only the largest police stations (*jingcha ju*) have English-speaking staff.

Beijing PSB officer

in China are reliably secure, but management will not accept responsibility should anything vanish. If you are staying in a hostel dormitory then be very cautious. Make use of hotel safety deposit boxes and in-room safes.

Be discreet when taking your wallet out. It is best to pocket only as much cash as you need for the day and keep the rest in a money belt under your clothes, along with your passport and other valuable documents.

It is always a good idea to carry photocopies of the personal information and China visa pages of your passport, as well as any other important documents, such as insurance policies. These should be stored separately from the originals in case of theft or loss.

WHAT TO BE AWARE OF

Traveling in China is generally safe, and foreign visitors are unlikely to be the victims of crime, apart from petty theft and occasional scams. Sadly, anyone who approaches looking to speak English with you should be treated with caution: friendly Chinese who suggest a chat over tea, or pretty girls who want to practice English over a drink, may in both cases be in cahoots with a bar or café and looking to leave you with an artificially pumped-up bill for thousands of *renminbi*. Refuse to pay, make plenty of noise, and insist on calling the police. On buses and trains guard your camera and valuables, wear a money belt at all times, and secure your luggage to the rack on overnight train journeys.

At some sights, you will be asked to deposit your bag before making a visit. Hotels

IN AN EMERGENCY

Don't wait for an ambulance: head directly to a hospital by any means possible (taxi is usually best) as ambulances will take too long and there may be communication problems. Enlist the help of your hotel to contact police or emergency healthcare – there are emergency telephone numbers in both cities, but they are Chinese-speaking only. It is vital to have good insurance coverage as healthcare bills can rack up frighteningly quickly.

LOST AND STOLEN PROPERTY

As in all countries, you should keep a close eye on your belongings; although China is in general very safe, there are pickpockets in tourist spots, cafés, and other public spaces. Crowded public transportation like buses and the subway are also prime target areas. If you do have items stolen or lose something, you will need a police report for your insurance claim. Reports can be obtained from your nearest PSB; check if your insurance company requires reports in English.

HOSPITALS AND PHARMACIES

Both Beijing and Shanghai have good public hospitals which have foreigners' wings with English-speaking doctors. Healthcare at public hospitals is cheap, but if you have good insurance, the city's private hospitals and clinics, with great facilities and highly qualified staff, are preferable. Unless you have direct billing with your insurance, you will not be allowed to depart before the bill is settled. Pharmacies (*yaodian*), identified by green crosses, are plentiful and easily found. They stock both Western and Chinese medicine. Many drugs are available over the counter without prescriptions, but there have been a few cases of contaminated drugs, so it is best to take any medication you need with you.

Shu Guang, one of several public hospitals in Shanghai

Street food – only eat it when it is cooked in front of you

STOMACH UPSETS AND DIARRHEA

If you have a stomach upset, stick to plain food, such as rice, until any diarrhea subsides. Most importantly, drink lots of fluids, as diarrhea quickly leads to dehydration, and use oral rehydration salts. Do not eat salads, cut fruit, or cold dishes, or drink fresh juice bought from street stalls. Never drink tap water or brush your teeth with it – use bottled mineral water. Only eat street food that is freshly cooked in front of you.

HEAT, HUMIDITY, AND POLLUTION

In summer, drink plenty of fluids to guard against dehydration. Wear loose-fitting cotton clothing and sandals, a sun-hat and sunglasses, and use plenty of sunscreen. Beijing and Shanghai can see chronic levels of pollution: this aggravates chest infections, and asthmatic travelers should always carry their medication.

SEXUALLY TRANSMITTED AND OTHER INFECTIOUS DISEASES

AIDS is a growing problem in China and more than 700,000 people are believed to have the disease. Hepatitis B, also transmitted through contact with infected blood, is spread through sexual contact, unsterilized needles, tattoos, and shaves from roadside barbers, but unlike AIDS it can be prevented with a vaccine. When visiting a clinic, ensure that the doctor opens a new syringe in front of you, or bring your own disposable syringe. Avoid any other procedure using needles, such as tattooing, ear-piercing, or acupuncture.

WATER-BORNE DISEASES

Visitors should be on their guard against dysentery. Bacillary dysentery is accompanied by severe stomach pains, vomiting, and fever. Amoebic dysentery has similar symptoms but takes longer to manifest. Pre-travel vaccination against hepatitis A, cholera, and typhoid is advisable.

INSECT-BORNE DISEASES

Those planning visits solely to Beijing and Shanghai (and Hangzhou and Suzhou) do not need to take malarial prophylaxis. For trips to rural areas consult a tropical medicine specialist.

TRAVEL AND HEALTH INSURANCE

It is advisable to take out an insurance policy for medical emergencies, preferably including evacuation, trip cancellation, loss of baggage by airlines, and travel delay. Policies covering the theft of valuables need to be carefully examined as exclusions and deductibles often make these worthless, and caution is often both more effective and cheaper. Remember to make sure that any adventure activity or sport that you may undertake during your trip is covered by your policy. In the case of a claim, be aware that your policy may require you to have English language reports from the police or healthcare facilities.

VACCINATIONS

Ensure that all of your routine vaccinations are up to date, such as tetanus, polio, and diphtheria. It is advisable to also get vaccinated against hepatitis A and B, typhoid, meningococcal meningitis, and cholera. Visitors traveling from countries where yellow fever is endemic must provide proof of vaccination against the disease. Malaria medication is essential for those visiting rural areas, as is a Japanese encephalitis vaccination, but neither are necessary for visits to Beijing and Shanghai, nor most other major cities. For up-to-date travel-health information and more advice on immunization visit **MD Travel Health** online.

DIRECTORY

IN AN EMERGENCY

Police
Tel 110.

Fire
Tel 119.

Ambulance
Tel 120.

HOSPITALS AND PHARMACIES

Beijing United Family Hospital
2 Jiangtai Lu, Chaoyang, Beijing. **Tel** (010) 5927 7120 (24-hr).
www.ufh.com.cn

International SOS Pharmacy
Suite 105, Wing 1, Kunsha Building, 16 Xinguanli, Chaoyang, Beijing.
Tel (010) 6462 9112.
www.internationalsos.com/en

Parkway Community Pharmacy
9-B101A, Green Garden, 333 Bi Yun Road, Shanghai.
Tel (021) 3382 1382.
www.parkway-communitypharmacy.com

Parkway Health Shanghai Center
203–4, West Retail Plaza, 1376 Nanjing West Road.
Tel (021) 6445 5999.

Shanghai East International Medical Center
150 Jimo Road, Pudong.
Tel (021) 5879 9999.

TRAVEL HEALTH

Medical Advisory Services for Travelers Abroad
Tel (0113) 238 7575.

MD Travel Health
www.mdtravelhealth.com

Banking and Local Currency

**24-hour
banking sign**

Most foreign exchange transactions take place at major branches of any bank or at foreign exchange counters at airports and in major stores, or are performed by hotels for their residents only. In Beijing and Shanghai there are plenty of ATMs that accept foreign cards, including at both airports, and these are generally the most convenient way of acquiring Chinese currency. You cannot pay for goods or services with foreign cash or traveler's checks. Foreign credit cards are accepted in larger hotels, restaurants, and retail outlets.

BANKS AND EXCHANGING MONEY

The **Bank of China** has the most extensive network in the country, although several other banks, including ICBC and China Construction Bank, also operate nationwide. Some banks are only open 9am–noon and 2pm–4:30pm or 5pm Monday to Friday, but others are open all day, and some on Saturdays. All banks remain closed for at least the first three days of the Chinese New Year, and for three days during the October holidays. For all foreign exchange transactions, you will need to show your passport. While the currency is still officially non-convertible, restrictions are easing and you can buy and sell *renminbi* in more and more countries these days (near neighbors, the UK, Australia, and the US, for example). Exchange rates are decided centrally and distributed nationally on a daily basis. Rates vary very little within banks so there's little point in shopping around. Never

bother with the black market as you run the risk of receiving counterfeit notes. If you wish to convert any left-over *renminbi* back before you leave, do so at the airport.

Hong Kong & Shanghai Banking Corporation (HSBC) ATMs

ATMS

It is now common for ATMs to accept foreign cards. There are many ATMs in banks, shopping malls, and hotels around the centers of Beijing and Shanghai. Those machines that do accept foreign cards are part of the Maestro, Cirrus, JCB, and Visa networks.

Check the back of your card for logos. Both Beijing and Shanghai have branches of **HSBC**, **American Express**, and **Citibank**, whose machines will take almost any card. Most ATMs have a limit of ¥2,500 per transaction, up to ¥20,000 in withdrawals per day. Try to withdraw the maximum amount allowed on your card per transaction to reduce the impact of fees that your bank will charge for each cash withdrawal. Although the vast majority of the time you are unlikely to have a problem, it is best not to rely solely on taking money out at ATMs as cards can occasionally be "swallowed". It is also advisable to notify your bank or credit card provider that you are going abroad ahead of traveling as they may block cards to avoid fraudulent use.

TRAVELERS' CHECKS AND CREDIT CARDS

Some hotel foreign exchange counters will no longer exchange checks, and will send you to a bank. All popular foreign brands are accepted, but occasionally cashiers nervous of responsibility will reject those that look unfamiliar. Keep the proof of purchase slips and a record of the serial numbers in case of loss or theft.

Credit cards are widely accepted in upscale restaurants, shopping malls and hotels, and in large tourist shops, but always check before attempting to make a purchase that your foreign card is accepted.

DIRECTORY

BANK OF CHINA	HSBC	CITIBANK	AMERICAN EXPRESS
Beijing	**Beijing**	**Beijing**	
Asia Pacific Building, 8 Yabao Lu.	Block A, COFCO Plaza 8, Jianguo Men Nei Dajie.	1st floor, Tower 1, Bright China Chang'an Building, 7 Jian Guo Men Nei Dajie.	**Beijing**
ATMs *Oriental Plaza, 1 Dongchang'an Jie.*	**ATMs** *The Place Mall, 9 Guanghan Road.*	**Shanghai**	Room 2313, China World Trade Center, 1 Jianguo Men Wai Dajie.
Shanghai	**Shanghai**	Citigroup Tower, 33 Huayuan Shi Qiao Road, Pudong. **ATMs** *Adjacent to the Peace Hotel, Zhongshan East Road.*	**Shanghai**
Bank of China Tower, 200 Yin Cheng Road, Pudong.	HSBC Tower, Shanghai IFC, 8 Century Ave, Pudong.		Room 455, Shanghai Center, 1376 Nanjing West Road.
ATMs *23 The Bund.*	**ATMs** *Shanghai Center, 1376 Nanjing West Road.*		

Note that there may also be a small surcharge added. The commonly accepted cards are MasterCard, Visa, JCB, Diners Club, and **American Express**. Air tickets can be bought by credit card, but train tickets have to be paid for in cash. Cash advances can be made on credit cards at banks, but it is far cheaper to use a debit card in an ATM.

CURRENCY

The official name of China's currency is the *yuan renminbi*, literally people's currency, but it is also called *kuai* (in Shanghai) or *yuan*. One *yuan* divides into 10 *jiao*, or *mao*, which in turn divides into 10 almost worthless *fen*. The most common coins include 1 *yuan*, and 5 and

1 *jiao*. Bills in circulation are 1, 2, and 5 *jiao*, and 1, 2, 5, 10, 20, 50, and 100 *yuan*. The 1-*yuan* note is being phased out. It has been proposed that there should be a 500-*yuan* note but there is no news of when this will be. Counterfeiting in China is widespread, and it is not unusual for retail outlets to regularly scrutinize notes using a special machine.

Bank Notes
The more recently printed bills have Mao Zedong on one side and a well-known heritage sight on the other. The older bills depict the traditional dress of various ethnic minorities.

1-*yuan* note

5-*yuan* note

10-*yuan* note

20-*yuan* note

50-*yuan* note

100-*yuan* note

Coins
*Chinese coins are not widely circulated. There are a 1-*yuan coin and some* jiao *denominations, as well as tiny and lightweight* fen.

5 *jiao*

1 *jiao*

1 *yuan*

Communications and Media

Sign for a public telephone

China has an efficient postal network with a variety of services, including registered post and express mail. Telecommunication systems are reasonably advanced and international telephone calls can be made from all but the cheapest hotels. The Internet is hugely popular, and access in cafés, bars, restaurants, and hotels is widespread. Broadband and Wi-Fi are available in all but the most modest of hotel rooms. The government, however, scrupulously polices the net, and many websites, including Facebook and Twitter, are blocked, although sometimes not in the best foreign hotels. Foreign newspapers and magazines are sold in five-star hotel bookstores and in some shopping malls.

A wheelchair-accessible phone booth in Beijing

INTERNATIONAL AND LOCAL TELEPHONE CALLS

VoIP services like Skype are freely accessible in China and are the cheapest way to make international calls. International (guo ji) and long-distance (guo nei) calls can also be made from most hotels and public telephones. Hotels are only allowed to add a small service charge to the cost of calls; local calls should be free. Most public phones require an IC (Integrated Circuit) card, sold in shops and kiosks wherever the letters "IC" are seen. These are available in various values up to ¥100. International calls are best made using an IP (Internet Protocol) card; you dial a local access number and enter a code hidden behind a scratch-off panel on the card. Voice instructions are in both Chinese and English. IP cards typically come in ¥50 and ¥100 varieties. If you wish to use one at a payphone, you will still need an IC card to enable you to dial the local access number.

USEFUL DIALING CODES AND NUMBERS

To call China from abroad, dial your international access code, China's country code 86, then 10 for Beijing or 21 for Shanghai, followed by the local number. When dialing long-distance from within China dial 010 and 021 respectively. Other city codes also have a leading zero. To make a local call, omit the area code.

To make an international call from China, dial 00, the country code, the area code omitting any initial 0, and the local number. Country codes include: UK 44; USA and Canada 1; Australia 61; New Zealand 64; and Ireland 353.

MOBILE PHONES

There are four main GSM frequencies (Global System for Mobile Communications) in use around the world, so if you want to guarantee that your phone will work, make sure you have a quad-band phone. You may also need to ask your network operator to enable your phone for roaming. Remember you are charged for the calls you receive as well as the calls you make, and you have to pay a substantial premium for the international leg of the call.

The cheapest option by far – although you must have an unlocked phone – is to buy a local SIM card from any phone shop and use the Chinese mobile phone system. SIM cards cost about ¥60, along with a deposit of ¥1000. China Mobile has the best coverage. Some SIM cards work only in the town in which they were purchased, so if you wish to use the same number in Beijing and Shanghai, make sure you have the right kind of card. Even using a Beijing number in Shanghai is vastly cheaper than using foreign companies' roaming options. ¥100 of phone credit will allow you almost 2 hours of local calls. If, however, your phone is not compatible, you can buy a basic new one for about ¥400.

INTERNET AND EMAIL

China is better connected than the vast majority of western countries with a huge number of cafés, bars, restaurants, and hotels

One of many cafés offering free Wi-Fi access

offering free Wi-Fi access in both Beijing and Shanghai. Unless you need to get online urgently, avoid using hotel business centers or Internet cafés aimed at tourists as they are generally over-priced.

POSTAL SERVICES

The postal service in China is, for the most part, reliable and reasonably fast. It takes a day for mail to reach local destina-tions, two or more days to inland destinations, while the international postal service takes about one to two weeks to send airmail and postcards overseas. Visitors can send mail by standard or registered post, while EMS (Express Mail Service) is a reliable way to send packages and documents abroad and within the country. Note that before you can send a parcel, its contents will have to be examined by post office staff. Most post offices are open all day, seven days a week. Large hotels also usually have post desks. Take your mail to the post office, rather than dropping it in a mail box. It will help postal staff sort your letter if you can write the country's name in Chinese characters as many postal workers do not speak much English. Envelopes and packaging materials are available at post offices.

COURIER SERVICES

Courier services are widely available in both cities. While it is cheaper to send large, bulky items by regular land, sea, or air cargo, important letters, documents, and parcels are best sent through a courier agency. International operatives **UPS**, **Federal Express**, and **DHL** are all present in China.

NEWSPAPERS AND MAGAZINES

China Daily is China's official English-language newspaper.

A choice of Chinese newspapers on display at a newsstand

It is full of propaganda and little else. *Global Times* is better, though not brilliant. In Shanghai, *Shanghai Daily* is the state-run newspaper. An increasingly diverse selection of international papers and magazines can be found at many hotel bookstores and upscale supermarkets, although these are subject to occasional censorship. Beijing and Shanghai have a number of expat-written free entertain-ment and culture magazines, such as *The Beijinger*, *Time Out Beijing*, *Time Out Shanghai*, and *That's Shanghai*. These are published at the begin-ning of each month and are available in most bars, cafés, and hotels.

TELEVISION AND RADIO

The state-run Chinese Central Television (CCTV) has CCTV News as its flagship English station. Despite a style over-haul, content can still be a bit dull, as propaganda and bright-eyed promotion for China travel are the norm. ICS (International Channel Shanghai) has higher production values. Cable and satellite television with BBC and CNN is only available in top-end hotels, although some Hong Kong channels with English programming appear lower down the scale. Chinese programs range from historical costume dramas (with political bias) and tepid soaps (intended to reinforce government social messages)

Mail box, Beijing

to domestic travel (everything is perfect) and heavily biased news programs. Many Beijing and Shanghai bars subscribe to satellite sport channels that broadcast major international games and events. The Chinese radio network has only a few local English-language programs: China Radio International (CRI) is the state-run English language radio service. You will need a short-wave radio to pick up the BBC World Service and other international programs. Voice of America has been blocked.

Shanghai's iconic Oriental Pearl Tower, a TV transmitter

DIRECTORY

USEFUL NUMBERS

DHL Worldwide Express (Beijing only)
Tel (010) 5860 1076 or 800 810 8000, Beijing. (021) 5551 4777 or 800 810 8000, Shanghai.

Federal Express
Tel (010) 6438 5560 or 800 810 2338, Beijing. (021) 5411 8333, Shanghai.

International Post Office
Jianguo Men Bei Dajie, Beijing. Sinan Road (junction with Huaihai Road), Shanghai.

United Parcels Service (UPS)
Tel 800 820 8388 nationwide or 400 820 8388 from a cell phone.
Beijing
Room 1818, China World Tower 1, 1 Jianguomenwai Avenue.
Shanghai
23/F, China Insurance Building, 166 Lujiazui East Road, Pudong.

TRAVEL INFORMATION

Most visitors to China arrive by air, though overland routes exist with train links to neighboring Russia, Mongolia, Kazakhstan, and Vietnam, and bus links to Laos and Pakistan. It is also possible to arrive by sea; there are regular ferries from Japan and South Korea to China. Once you have arrived, flying internally is straightforward. Domestic air tickets are easy to buy, so shop around for discounts on online travel agents. There are scores of flights daily between Beijing and Shanghai Hongqiao Airport, and between Beijing and Shanghai Pudong. China's high-speed rail network is increasingly fast, efficient, and comfortable, although buying tickets can seem daunting. Bus travel is improving with an increasing number of "luxury" and "no smoking" buses. Hiring a self-drive car is not possible, although hiring a car and driver is often the best way to take a trip out of town.

AIR CHINA

Logo of China's national airline, Air China

ARRIVING BY AIR

All major international airlines fly to China. China's own **Air China**, **China Southern**, and **China Eastern** plus Taiwan's **China Airlines** between them cover most of the world's major airports. Hong Kong's **Cathay Pacific** and its Dragon Air affiliate have an extensive international network and service standards considerably higher than those of most other carriers. China's four main international gateways are Hong Kong, Beijing, Shanghai, and Guangzhou, and all are superior in quality to most in Europe and North America.

Beijing Capital International Airport is 12 miles (20 km) northeast of the city center. It has three terminals, with most international flights arriving at terminal 3. A free bus service connects the terminals.

Shanghai Pudong Airport serves international flights and is 30 miles (50 km) southeast of the city center. It has two terminals which are within walking distance of each other. **Shanghai Hongqiao Airport** serves domestic flights, Hong Kong, and some Asian routes and is 6 miles (10 km) from the city center. A second terminal opened in 2010.

ON ARRIVAL

Visitors are given a form to complete for immigration and customs. This is submitted to officials between the plane and the arrivals hall, where there are foreign exchange counters, ATMs, left-luggage services, restaurants, and shops. There's usually someone at airport tourist information counters who can speak some English.

GETTING TO AND FROM THE AIRPORTS

In Beijing there are multiple bus routes into the city, and the ABC high-speed light rail line links the airport with Dong Zhi Men station in the city. Taxis wait for passengers at a marshaled rank outside the arrivals hall. Ignore the touts and insist on the driver using the meter. If you already have a hotel booked, check whether it offers a courtesy airport pick-up. In Shanghai there are bus and taxi services from Hongqiao and Pudong airports and both are connected to Line 2 of the Shanghai Metro System.

INTERNAL FLIGHTS

There are currently some 12 domestic carriers operating in China. In-flight service and on-board food is of average quality. Announcements are in both Chinese and English.

Air flight safety records are excellent now, and most airlines have new fleets. Between Beijing, Shanghai, and other major cities the aircraft are usually brand new Airbus or Boeing planes. The baggage allowance is 44 lbs (20 kg) for economy class and 66 pounds (30 kg) for first and business class. You are also allowed up to 11 pounds (5 kg) of hand luggage, although this is rarely weighed. Excess baggage incurs charges.

The check-in time for internal flights is an hour and a half before departure, although in practice very few passengers ever arrive that early. The ¥50 airport tax for domestic flights is added to the price of the ticket at the time of purchase.

The impressive departure hall at Beijing Capital International Airport

In-flight service on Sichuan Airlines, a domestic Chinese carrier

TICKETS AND FARES

Ticket prices are most expensive between June and September. It can also be harder to find reasonably priced tickets during Chinese holidays: Spring Festival, the first week of May, and the first week of October. While flying indirectly to China via another country is cheaper than flying direct, traveling by a Chinese airline will often be the cheapest option.

International tickets can be booked online through a travel site such as www.travelocity. com or www.orbitz.com. Where possible, book internal flights online before you travel to avoid disappointment. Reservations can be made at www.ctrip.com.cn or www.elong.net, or through ticket offices, travel agents, or the travel desks of some of the better hotels – you should not be charged a booking fee. If using an international credit card, you may be charged a surcharge. Visitors are required to show their passports or give their passport numbers when purchasing tickets.

Domestic ticket prices are calculated according to a one-way fare, and a return-ticket is usually double that. Discounts on official fares are the norm, and whatever price you are first offered you should always ask for a discount. Children over the age of 12 are charged adult fares, but there are cheaper fares for younger children. The departure tax for international flights is ¥90 and is included in the total ticket price.

If you need to change your flight, you can usually get a refund as long as you cancel before the date of departure, and return your ticket to the same agent who sold it to you. Note that discounted tickets usually carry more restrictions so if you are not sure of your dates book a flexible ticket.

PACKAGE DEALS

Travel websites such as www.expedia.com offer flight and hotel packages, as do some airlines such as British Airways – these packages can often work out cheaper than booking separately.

Online travel agents like ctrip.com and elong.net (see above) should be your first port of call for domestic package deals combining flights, hotel stays, and tours. This can be a very cost-efficient way of seeing other parts of China. Be aware though that you will then be part of a Chinese tour group which can be huge in size and you might have to wear something distinctive to indentify you as part of the group. Some youth hostels also offer package deals.

DIRECTORY

AIRPORTS

Beijing Capital International Airport
Tel (010) 96 158.
www.bcia.com.cn

Shanghai Hongqiao Airport
Tel (021) 6268 3659.
www.shanghaiairport.com

Shanghai Pudong Airport
Tel (021) 91 990.
www.shanghaiairport.com

AIRLINES

Air China
Tel 95583, Beijing.
www.airchina.com.cn

British Airways
Tel (010) 800 744 0031, Beijing.
www.britishairways.com

Cathay Pacific
Tel 4008 886 628, Shanghai.
www.cathaypacific.com

China Airlines
Tel (010) 6510 2671, Beijing.
Tel (021) 5237 5269, Shanghai.
www.china-airlines.com

China Eastern Airlines
Tel (010) 8441 5000, Beijing.
(021) 95 808 (domestic), Shanghai.
www.ce-air.com

China Southern Airlines
Tel 4006 695 539, Beijing.

Emirates
Tel 4008 822 380.
www.emirates.com

KLM
Tel 4008 808 222.
852 2808 2168 (overseas).
www.klm.com

Northwest Airlines
Tel (010) 6505 3505, Beijing.
4008 140 081, Shanghai.
www.nwa.com

Qantas
Tel 800 819 0089.
www.qantas.com.au

United Airlines
Tel (0852) 2810 8616, Hong Kong.
1-800-864-8331, US.
www.united.com

Virgin Atlantic
Tel (021) 5353 4600, Shanghai.
0844 209 7777, UK.
1-800-821-5438, US.
1300 727 340, Aus.
www.virgin-atlantic.com

Traveling by Train, Bus & Ferry

The Chinese rail network is extensive, with tracks running over 58,500 miles (91,000 km) and still expanding. It is possible to reach every province of China by rail from Beijing and Shanghai. High-speed bullet trains, capable of traveling at 218 mph (350 km/h), operate between Beijing and the port city of Tianjin, and between Shanghai and the cities of Suzhan, Nanjing, and Hangzhan. Even faster trains began running between Beijing and Shanghai in October 2011, cutting the journey to around five hours. Along the east coast many bus services are efficient, comfortable, and well-regulated. In other areas they vary. Driving is invariably rash, and road conditions can be bad. Only a very limited number of passenger ferries leave Shanghai for Yangzi River destinations, and there are few coastal services.

High-speed train at Beijing South train station

TRAINS & TIMETABLES

Timetables are published in April and October each year, and are available at railway station ticket offices. You can find information and reserve tickets at www.chinatrain tickets.net (note that booking fees are high). An alternative timetable is also published at www.travelchinaguide.com/ china-trains.

Conventional trains with numbers prefixed by the letter "T" or "K" are express *(te kuai)* or fast *(kuai)* trains, and those whose numbers have no prefix are ordinary *(pu kuai)* trains of varying speeds and comfort. "Z" are prestige services, including some running between Beijing and Shanghai. High-speed trains are prefixed by the letter "G." All long-distance trains have sleeper carriages.

There is no smoking permitted except at carriage junctions. Beijing–Shanghai trains have a bar and most trains have dining cars, though the food is poor and over-priced. Staff continually push trolleys through the carriages selling instant noodles, snacks, mineral water, coffee, and newspapers. The noise level in the carriages is often very high, as announcements and music are regularly broadcast over the speakers, although soft sleeper compartments have a volume control.

CLASSES

Chinese trains have four main classes. One of the more comfortable is the Soft Sleeper *(ruan wo)*, with four berths per compartment. It offers more privacy and security than less expensive classes, but is often little cheaper than flying. The most expensive and luxurious is the Deluxe Sleeper *(gaoji ruanwo)* with only two berths and sometimes with shower or private bathroom. This is available on certain routes, including Beijing to Shanghai. The high-speed intercity trains have two classes – first class and economy.

Hard Sleeper *(ying wo)* can be an economical choice when traveling between cities overnight, especially as it also saves the cost of a night in a hotel. Carriages consist of doorless compartments with six bunks in two sets of three. Higher berths are slightly cheaper than the lower and offer more privacy. Pillows, sheets, and blankets are provided, as are flasks of boiling water. Once aboard, the inspector will exchange your ticket for a token, and return the ticket at the end of the journey.

The cheapest class is Hard Seat *(ying zuo)*, with three people side-by-side on lightly cushioned seats. Carriages are usually crowded and dirty, the speakers blare endlessly, lights remain on at night, and compartments are filled with smoke. If you have no reserved seat you'll likely stand for the whole trip.

Available only on certain short daytime routes, Soft Seat *(ruan zuo)* carriages are more comfortable.

Exterior of Beijing Zhan train station

Passengers waiting at one of Beijing's 12 long-distance bus terminals

MAIN STATIONS

Beijing's train stations are spread across the city. The main station, Beijing Zhan, links Beijing with cities in the north and northeast, while Beijing South station services the Tianjin line and the high-speed Beijing–Shanghai route. Beijing West links the capital with Xian and Hong Kong. Shanghai's main station, Shanghai Zhan, is located in the north of the city, while Shanghai Nan Zhan is in Xujiahui. Both stations are connected to Metro line 1.

TRAIN TICKETS, FARES & RESERVATIONS

On most routes, and certainly on those between Beijing and Shanghai, it is vital to buy tickets a few days before you travel. Tickets between these two cities and some other tourist destinations are for sale 20 days before departure and a week before for other destinations. You can now buy return tickets on most high-speed inter-city routes. Train fares are calculated according to the class and the distance traveled. Joining the crowds at station ticket counters can be very trying, so unless the station has a separate ticket office for foreign visitors, which is the case in Beijing and Shanghai, ask your hotel or travel agent to arrange your bookings. They usually charge a fee of ¥20–30 per ticket for this service.

Note that getting hold of tickets during Spring Festival and May and October holiday periods can be difficult.

LONG-DISTANCE BUSES

Beijing and Shanghai both have several long-distance bus stations *(changtu qiche zhan)*, so check carefully which station you want. Destinations are displayed in Chinese characters, and sometimes in Pinyin, on the front of buses.

Long-distance buses vary enormously in quality, age, and comfort. You may find that several buses are running along the same route, so make sure you are sold a ticket for the fastest and most comfortable *(gaoji* or *baohua)* bus – or the cheapest *(zui pianyi)* bus, if you prefer.

Ordinary buses such as those serving rural sights around Beijing, are the cheapest and have basic wooden, or lightly padded, seats. These buses stop often, so progress can be slow. They provide little space for baggage – there's no room under the seats and the luggage racks are minuscule. Backpacks are usually stacked next to the driver, for no additional charge.

Sleeper buses *(wopu che)* speed through the night, so reach their destination in good time. They usually have two tiers of bunks, or seats that recline almost flat. The older models can be quite dirty, but others are so clean you are required to remove your shoes as you board.

Shorter routes are served by rattling minibuses *(xiao ba)*, which depart only when every spare space has been filled by a paying passenger. Crammed to the roof, minibus trips can be uncomfortable.

Express buses *(kuai che)* are the best way to travel. Most have air conditioning, and enforce a no-smoking policy. Receipts are given for luggage stowed in the hold.

BUS TICKETS & FARES

Traveling by road is generally much cheaper than train travel. Tickets are sold at long-distance bus stations but book in advance where possible. Main bus stations invariably have computerized ticket offices with short queues, and tickets are also sold on board.

FERRIES & BOATS

An overnight ferry service runs along the Grand Canal between Suzhou and Hangzhou, and Shanghai also has services to Yangzi River ports including Nanjing and Wuhan. Several lines also link Pudong and Puxi. Note that ferry timetables change frequently and services may have been added or removed. There are also international services from Shanghai to Kobe and Osaka in Japan, and to Incheon in South Korea.

Ferry on the Huangpu River, Shanghai

City Transportation

Beijing traffic sign

Beijing and Shanghai both have expansive subway systems that should be your first choice where possible. Both are in the process of being further expanded. City buses are slow and usually packed, but are very cheap. Taxis (*chuzu che*) are a necessity for most travelers, and, despite the language barrier and misunderstandings with drivers, they remain the most convenient way to get around. Bicycles, which once ruled the roads of China's cities, are another alternative, and those who feel confident can use a rental bike to explore the cities.

GREEN TRAVEL

With China's well-documented environmental problems, it is essential for travelers to do their bit to combat the country's pollution problems. It is relatively easy to travel green in Beijing and Shanghai as the public transportation systems are comprehensive and efficient. From the airports, catching trains – either the Maglev or metro in Shanghai or the light rail in Beijing – into the two cities is very straightforward. Cycling is obviously the greenest way to travel and there are plans for city-wide cycle rental schemes, but for now you can hire bikes from independent stores or from your hotel for very low prices. The subways in both cities are also environmentally friendly and convenient, and some green buses run on hydrogen fuel cells. Online travel agent ctrip (www.ctrip.com.cn) puts some of your fee towards carbon offsetting programs. However, exploring the countryside is more difficult without hiring private transportation.

BEIJING'S SUBWAY

The metro system in Beijing is undergoing development. There are currently ten lines (plus a handful of extension lines in theater suburbs), with 19 lines planned by 2015.

The metro is a swift way to get around. The system is easy to use, although walks between lines at interchange stations can be long. There is a flat rate of ¥2 on all lines except for the airport light rail link, which is ¥25.

Buy your ticket from either a manned booth or a machine (which has an English language option) and then insert your ticket into the automated ticket gates to gain access. Stored-value *yikatong* cards, sold at subway stations, are a good option if you want to make several journeys. They require a ¥20 deposit which is refundable upon return of the card.

Sign for the Beijing subway

SHANGHAI'S SUBWAY

The rapidly growing Shanghai metro system is clean and efficient, with the first line built in 1995. There are now 12 lines and the system is the longest in the world. Lines 1, 2, and 3 are most useful to tourists.

Fares range between ¥3 and ¥10, depending on the number of stops traveled, and tickets can be purchased from ticket booths or machines. Stored-value *jiaotong* cards cost ¥20 and are worth buying for multiple journeys. Put your ticket into the slot at the electronic barrier and the gates will open. Retrieve your ticket on the other side of the gate and hold on to it – you will need it when you exit.

The primarily domestic Hongqiao Airport is on Line 2, and the much touted German-designed high-speed Maglev train (*see p137*) travels from Longyang Road metro station, also on Line 2, to Pudong Airport. It runs daily between 6:45am and 9:30pm.

BUSES

City bus (*gonggong qiche*) networks are extensive and cheap. Most trips within Beijing and Shanghai city centers cost a flat fare (no change given), which is clearly posted on the side of the bus; typically ¥1 or ¥2. Air-conditioned services are usually a little more expensive. Traffic jams tend to last all day in both cities, and no priority is shown to buses, which means journeys can be very slow. The buses are almost always overcrowded and provide good conditions for thieves so keep a watchful eye on your belongings. Consider using buses only for short journeys, or for suburban sightseeing.

Bus routes can also be tricky to navigate, but, increasingly, on-board announcements are made in English as well as Chinese, though destinations and schedules are sometimes listed in Chinese only.

TAXIS

The best way to get to places away from subway stations is by taxi (*chuzu qiche*). Taxis are found in large numbers in both Beijing and Shanghai, and can be hailed easily in the street. When arriving at airports, avoid the touts who

Buses and taxis on a busy Beijing main road

immediately surround you, and head instead to the taxi rank outside where you are less likely to be overcharged. Make sure your taxi uses the meter, which drivers usually only start once the journey is actually under way – so wait a moment, then say, "Dabiao" (start the meter), if necessary. Taxis rarely have rear seat belts *(anquan dai)*, and those in the front may not work, although it is required by law that they be worn. Few taxi drivers speak English, so have your destination written down in Chinese by your hotel staff. Also get into the habit of picking up business cards at places in areas that you might want to return to – such as your hotel.

Fares per half mile (a kilometer) are clearly posted on the side of the car. The minimum charge in Beijing is ¥10, rising ¥2 per half mile. ¥25 should get you anywhere within the city. In Shanghai the minimum charge is ¥14 (¥16 after 11pm) and each additional half mile is ¥2.40. Fares in both cities rise by 20–30 percent between 11pm and 5am. There is no need to tip (the driver will be bewildered if you do).

Most taxi journeys are straightforward and trouble-free, and in general only the run from the airport into town could be problematic, as less scrupulous drivers prey on new arrivals unfamiliar with the city. Note that on the run to and from Beijing's Capital Airport you must pay the driver the road toll of ¥10 on top of the metered fare.

In addition to ignoring touts at airports and train stations, avoid cabs waiting at popular tourist sights and those that call out to you. It is also wise to ask your hotel to

Bicycles – the traditional way to get around the city

call a cab rather than flag down a passing driver, especially in peak hours and during rainstorms.

Taxis can also be hired for the day, a convenient way to see sights just out of town. This is best arranged by your hotel who can negotiate for you. Let hotel staff know the details of what you want, including date, pick-up time and location, and your complete itinerary, and then get them to ask for a price. You should also expect to pay any road, tunnel, or bridge tolls.

Street sign in two scripts

In smaller towns, motorcycle rickshaws *(sanlun motuoche)* and bicycle rickshaws *(sanlun che)* are a fun way to get around. However, be careful in both Beijing and Shanghai as they can often overcharge tourists.

CYCLING

If you are not used to heavy traffic, cycling in the cities can be intimidating. However, hiring a bike is a great way to explore. Bike lanes are common (although usually not respected by drivers) and roadside repair stalls are everywhere. Both Beijing and Shanghai are flat but Beijing is a superior place to cycle as it has more bike lanes and quieter roads, especially in the *hutong* areas. Make sure that any bike you rent has a lock provided. Bike stands are found all over and have an attendant to watch the bikes for a fee, usually ¥0.30.

ROAD NAMES

Main streets, avenues, and thoroughfares are often divided into different sections based on the four cardinal points. For example, Huaihai Lu (Huaihai Road) may be divided into Huaihai *Xi* Lu (West Road), Huaihai *Zhong* Lu (Middle Road), and Huaihai *Dong* Lu (East Road). Similarly, you may also see Zhongshan *Bei* Lu (North Road) and Zhongshan *Nan* Lu (South Road). Road names in Beijing display the Pinyin translation, but in smaller towns and remote places only Chinese is used. Apart from *lu* (road), other key words to look out for in Beijing are *jie* (street), *dajie* (avenue), and the lanes or alleyways called *hutong*.

WALKING

Crossing the road can be perilous in China, so take care. Be aware that even when a "green man" is displayed a pedestrian cannot walk across the road without fear of being hit; cars can still approach from the side or behind – and watch out for bicycles. In Beijing, the *hutongs* are the best place for a walk, while in Shanghai, the pedestrianized Bund area is an excellent place for a stroll, as is the boardwalk on the other side of the Huangpu River in Pudong. People's Square and the French Concession are also good spots for ambling around.

A city taxi, a convenient way of traveling

General Index

Acknowledgments

Dorling Kindersley would like to thank the many people whose help and assistance contributed to the preparation of this book.

Design and Editorial
PUBLISHER: Douglas Amrine
PUBLISHING MANAGERS: Vivien Antwi, Jane Ewart

Proofreader
Ferdie McDonald

Photography Co-ordinator
Amanda Mengpo Li

Map Co-ordinators
Uma Bhattacharya, Casper Morris

Revisions Team
Emma Anacootee, Shruti Bahl, Rachel Barber, Subhashree Bharati, Katie Bradley, Gary Bowerman, Iris Chan, Emer FitzGerald, Anna Freiberger, Rhiannon Furbear, Katharina Hahn, Lydia Halliday, Helena Iveson, Caroline Jackson, Yang Jie, Helen Partington, Marianne Petrou, Rada Radojicic, Marisa Renzullo, Beverly Smart, Ajay Verma, JACKET DESIGN: Tessa Bindloss, Sonal Bhatt

Additional Photography
Max Alexander, Simon Blackall, Demetrio Carrasco, Andy Crawford, Ian Cumming, Tim Draper, Gadi Farfour, Eddie Gerald, Nigel Hicks, Dave King, Stephen Lam, Ian O'Leary, Colin Sinclair, Chris Stowers, Hugh Thompson, Linda Whitwam

Photography Permissions
The Publishers thank all the temples, museums, hotels, restaurants, shops, and other sights for their assistance and kind permission to photograph their establishments.

Picture Credits
Key: a-above; b-below/bottom; c-centre; l-left; r-right; t-top

AKG-IMAGES: Laurent Lacat 41tr; ALAMY IMAGES: Pat Behnke 30br; George Brice 216br; David Crausby 218c; Li Jiangshu/ Panorama Stock 94br; Lou Linwei 222bl; Iain Masterton 221tc; Panorama Media (Beijing) Ltd. / Panorama Stock / 84br; Panorama Stock Photos/Zhang Zhenguang 146tr; Places 224cl; Snap2000 Images /

David Robinson 15c; Alex Segre 122bl, 133 bl; Shayne Tarne 10cla; VisualHongKong 227br; Matthew Wellings 35cra; Ron Yue 34c.APOTHECARY: 106cr; THE ART ARCHIVE: Bibliotheque Nationale, Paris 41cra, 143cr; Bibliotheque Nationale, Paris/Marc Charmet 20tr; British Library 18br, 20bl; British Museum/Eileen Tweedy 30tr; Freer Gallery of Art 26-27; Genius of China Exhibition 26tr, 39bc, 42bl; Musée Thomas Dobrée Nantes / Dagli Orti 49tl; National Palace Museum of Taiwan 22cl.
BIBLIOTHÈQUE NATIONALE DE FRANCE, PARIS: 18tr; BRIDGEMAN ART LIBRARY: 22cr, 23cl, 23cra; after Alexander, William (1767-1816) 48crb; Bibliotheque Nationale, Paris 6-7, 20cl, 23tr; *Portrait of T'ai T'sin Che-Tsou* (1638-61) 48bc; Giraudon 42br; Yu Zhiding (1647-1709) *The Depiction of the Poet Wang Yuang* (1634-1711) water colour 28tr.

©THE TRUSTEES OF THE BRITISH MUSEUM: 21tc, 26clb, 26bc, 26crb, 27bl, 27cb, 27br, 27cra, 27tr.

CHINA SPAN/KEREN SU: 29cl, 143cl; CHINAPIX: 122tr; CORBIS: 49c, 52bl, 53tc; Asian Art & Archaeology, Inc. 39c, 40clb, 42ca, 44ca, 44bc; Tiziana and Gianni Baldizzone 21cr; Dave Bartruff 190cla; Bettmann 51tl, 51br, 52tl, 135br; Bohemian Nomad Picturemakers 189tl; Bohemian Nomad Picturemakers/ Kevin R Morris 143br; Burstein Collection 22br, *The First Emperor of the Han Dynasty Entering Kuan Tung* by Chao Po-chu 30, 41cb, 43t, 46bl; Christie's Images 40tr; ChromoSohmINC/Joseph Sohm 90br; Dean Conger 62cla, 153br, 195c; Ric Ergenbright 143bl; Macduff Everton 53cr, 53bl, 133tc; Free Agents Limited 24tr; Paul Hardy 10cla; Hulton-Deutsch Collection 81tl, 153bc; Robbie Jack 33bl; Jean-Pierre Lescouret 123tl; Kelly-Mooney Photography 75tc; Charles & Josette Lenars 45tr; Liu Liqun 93tr, 133cb, 224br; Carl & Ann Purcell 23crb; Roger Ressmeyer 72cr; Reuters 36bc, 223tl; Royal Ontario Museum 26bl, 27cr, 46t; Sean Sexton Collection 135; Stapleton Collection 31tr; Keren Su 34cr; Julia Waterlow 20br; Michael S. Yamashita 29br; COTTON'S: 165tl; CPA MEDIA: 48ca, 50tr, 135cl, 135tc; Bibliotheque Nationale Paris/Oliver Harvgreave 46clb; Chinese Government (1961)/Meng Qingbiao 51crb.

DK IMAGES: ©The Trustees of the British Museum 26cl, Alan Hills 26tl.

FOTOE: 22tr; Zhang Weiqing 22clb.

GETTY IMAGES: AFP/Frederic J. Brown 220br; AFP/Liu Jin 136tl; Scott E Barbour 5tl, 15b; AWL Images/Christian Kober 66cr; Walter Bibikow 14; China Photos 225br; Hulton 65bc; Jeff Hunter 16t; The Image Bank 54-55; National Geographic 40cla; Photographer's Choice/John Warden 91tl; Stone /D E Cox 86; GRAND HYATT: 137bc, 165br; SALLY & RICHARD GREENHILL: 50tl, 51tr; S.A.C.U. 50br, 50cl.

IMAGINECHINA: 52crb, 93br; Jin Baoyuan 29tr; Adrian Bradshaw 133cla; Wu Changqing 88tr; Jiang Chao 95tl; CNS 31cr; Guo Guangyao 28cr; Jiang Guohong 32crb; Zhang Guosheng 69bl; Long Hai 30bc, 31crb, 125cra; Wu Hong 33br, 61br; Wei Hui 33cr; Li Jiangsong 21crb; Wang Jianxin 31clb; Huang Jinguo 29cr; Kan Kan 22cb; Zhou Kang 126tr; Zhou Kang Pzhk 75cr; Xu Ruikang 29tc; Chen Shuyi 73br; Lin Weijian 28bl, 122cl, 122cr; Shen Yu 28br, 138br, 220br; Fang Zhonglin 130clb; Yi Zhou 123bl; Yin Zi 18-19c; INSTITUTE OF HISTORY & PHILOLOGY: Academia Sinica 18cl, 18cb.

THE KOBAL COLLECTION: Columbia 33tr; Tomson Films 33cla.

PANOS PICTURES: 19cra; PHOTO12.COM: OIPS 96cl; Panorama Stock 78bl, 89tl; Panoramic Stock 90cl; PHOTOLIBRARY: TAO Images Limited 15b; Photographer's Choice/Tom Bonaventure 123tl; POPPERFOTO.COM: 50-51; 135cra, 135cb; Portman Ritz-Carlton: 176br.

RED GATE GALLERY, Beijing: 73; THE RED MANSION LTD.: Fang Lijun 32-33; Zhan Wang 32clb; Cang Xin 32cla; ROBERT HARDING PICTURE LIBRARY: 139tr; PanoramaStock 47tr.

SCIENCE & SOCIETY PICTURE LIBRARY: Science Museum 19bl; SHANGHAI MUSEUM: 126, 126cla, 126c, 126clb, 127, 127t, 127cr, 128tl, 128c, 128br, 129c, 129br; SHANGRI-LA HOTELS AND RESORTS: 106bl; CHINA STOCK: 41bl, 45c, 45clb, 50clb, 51cra; SUPERSTOCK: age fotostock 118-119.

THAMES & HUDSON LTD: Eileen Tweedy 20-21c; TOPFOTO.CO.UK: British Museum 23bc, 49bl; The Museum of East Asian Art / HIP 47bc; TRANSRAPID: 137tr.

WERNER FORMAN ARCHIVE: 43crb; P'yongyang Gallery, North Korea 23cla; Peking Palace Museum 44crb; Private Collection 41br, 47c, 49br; Victoria & Albert Museum 43cb; Yang-Tzu-Shaw 42crb.

JACKET
Front - PHOTOLIBRARY: Michele Falzone.
Back - AWL IMAGES: Christian Kober cla; DORLING KINDERSLEY: Tim Draper bl, c, t.
Spine - PHOTOLIBRARY: Michele Falzone t.

Front Endpapers: GETTY IMAGES: The Image Bank / Andrea Pistolesi Ltr; SUPERSTOCK: age fotostock R br.

All other images © Dorling Kindersley
For further information see:
www.dkimages.com

SPECIAL EDITIONS OF DK TRAVEL GUIDES

DK Travel Guides can be purchased in bulk quantities at discounted prices for use in promotions or as premiums. We are also able to offer special editions and personalized jackets, corporate imprints, and excerpts from all of our books, tailored specifically to meet your own needs.

To find out more, please contact:
(in the United States) **SpecialSales@dk.com**
(in the UK) **TravelSpecialSales@uk.dk.com**
(in Canada) DK Special Sales at **general@tourmaline.ca**
(in Australia) **business.development@pearson.com.au**

Phrase Book

The Chinese language belongs to the Sino-Tibetan family of languages and uses characters which are ideographic – a symbol is used to represent an idea or an object. Mandarin Chinese, known as Putonghua in mainland China, is fairly straightforward as each character is monosyllabic. Traditionally, Chinese is written in vertical columns from top right to bottom left, however the Western style is widely used. There are several romanization systems; the Pinyin system used here is the official system in mainland China.

This phrase book gives the English word or phrase, followed by the Chinese script, then the Pinyin for pronunciation.

Guidelines for Pronunciation

Pronounce vowels as in these English words:

a	as in "father"
e	as in "lurch"
i	as in "see"
o	as in "solid"
u	as in "pooh"
ü	as the French u or German ü (place your lips to say oo and try to say ee)

Most of the consonants are pronounced as in English. As a rough guide, pronounce the following consonants as in these English words:

c	as ts in "hats"
q	as ch in "cheat"
x	as sh in "sheet"
z	as ds in "heads"
zh	as j in "Joe"

Mandarin Chinese is a tonal language with four tones, represented in Pinyin by one of the following marks ˉ ˊ ˇ ˋ above each vowel – the symbol shows whether the tone is flat, rising, falling and rising, or falling. The Chinese characters do not convey this information: tones are learnt when the character is learnt. Teaching tones is beyond the scope of this small phrase book, but a language course book with a cassette or CD will help those who wish to take the language further.

Dialects

There are many Chinese dialects in use. It is hard to guess exactly how many, but they can be roughly classified into one of seven large groups (Mandarin, Cantonese, Hakka, Hui etc.), each group containing a large number of more minor dialects. Although all these dialects are quite different – Cantonese uses six tones instead of four – Mandarin or Putonghua, which is mainly based on the Beijing dialect, is the official language. Despite these differences all Chinese people are more or less able to use the same formal written language so they can understand each other's writing, if not each other's speech.

In Emergency

Help!	请帮忙！	Qing bangmang
Stop!	停住！	Ting zhu
Call a doctor!	叫医生！	Jiao yisheng
Call an ambulance!	叫救护车！	Jiao jiuhuche
Call the police!	叫警察！	Jiao jiingcha
Fire!	火！	Huo
Where is the hospital/police station?	医院/警察分局在哪里？	Yiyuan/jingcha fenju zai nali ?

Communication Essentials

Hello	你好	Nihao
Goodbye	再见	Zaijian
Yes/no	是 / 不是	shi/bushi
... not ...	不是	bushi
I'm from...	我是 ... 人	Wo shi ... ren
I understand	我明白	Wo mingbai
I don't know	我不知道	Wo bu zhidao
Thank you	谢谢你	Xiexie ni
Thank you very much	多谢	Duo xie
Thanks (casual)	谢谢	Xiexie
You're welcome	不用谢	Bu yong xie
No, thank you	不，谢谢你	Bu, xiexie ni
Please (offering)	请	Qing
Please (asking)	请问	Qing wen
I don't understand	我不明白	Wo bu mingbai
Sorry/Excuse me!	抱歉／对不起	Baoqian/duibuqi
Could you help me please? (not emergency)	你能帮助我吗？	Ni neng bang zhu wo ma?

Useful Phrases

My name is	我叫 ...	Wo jiao ...
Goodbye	再见	Zaijian
What is (this)?	（这）是什么？	(zhe) shi shenme?
Could I possibly have ...? (very polite)	能不能请你给我 ...？	Neng buneng qing ni gei wo ...
Is there ... here?	这儿有 ... 吗？	Zhe'r you ... ma?
Where can I get ...?	我在哪里可以得到 ...？	Wo zai na li keyi de dao ...?
How much is it?	它要多少钱？	Ta yao duoshao qian?
What time is ...?	... 什么时间？	... shenme shijian?
Cheers! (toast)	干杯	Ganbei
Where is the restroom/toilet?	卫生间 / 洗手间在哪里？	Weishengjian/ Xishoujian zai nali?

Useful Words

I	我	wo
woman	女人	nüren
man	男人	nanren
wife	妻子	qizi
husband	丈夫	zhangfu
daughter	女儿	nü'er
son	儿子	er'zi
child	小孩	xiaohai
children	儿童	er'tong
student	学生	xuesheng
Mr./Mrs./Ms.	先生／太太／女士	xiansheng/taitai/ nüshi

big/small	大／小	da/xiao
hot/cold	热／凉	re/liang
cold (to touch)	冷	leng
warm	暖	nuan
good/not good/ bad	好／不好／ 坏	hao/buhao/ huai
enough	够了	goule
free (no charge)	免费	mianfei
here	这里	zheli
there	那里	nali
this (nearby)	这个	zhege
that (nearby)	那	na
that (far away)	那个	nage
what?	什么?	Shenme?
when?	什么时候?	Shenme shihou?
why?	为什么?	Wei shenme?
where?	在哪里?	Zai nali?
who?	谁?	Shui?

Signs

open	开	kai
closed	关	guan
entrance	入口	rukou
exit	出口	chukou
danger	危险	weixian
emergency exit	安全门	anquanmen
information	信息	xinxi
restroom/toilet (men) (women)	卫生间／洗手间 （男士）（女士）	Weishengjian/ Xishoujian (nanshi) (nüshi)
men	男士	nanshi
women	女士	nüshi

Money

bank	银行	yinhang
cash	现金	xianjin
credit card	信用卡	xinyongka
currency	外汇兑换处	waihui
exchange office		duihuanchu
dollars	美元	meiyuan
pounds	英镑	yingbang
yuan	元	yuan

Keeping in Touch

Where is a telephone?	电话在哪里?	Dianhua zai nali?
May I use your phone?	我可以用你的 电话吗?	Wo keyi yong nide dianhua ma?
mobile phone	手机	shouji
sim card	卡	sim ka
Hello, this is ...	你好，我是 ...	Nihao, wo shi
airmail	航空	hangkong
e-mail	电子邮件	dianzi youjian
fax	传真	chuanzhen
internet	互联网	hulianwang
postcard	明信片	mingxinpian
post office	邮局	youju
stamp	邮票	youpiao
telephone booth	电话亭	dianhua ting
telephone card	电话卡	dianhua ka

Shopping

Where can I buy ...?	我可以在哪里 买到 ...?	Wo keyi zai nali maidao ...?
How much does this cost?	这要多少钱?	Zhe yao duoshao qian?
Too much!	太贵了!	Tai gui le!
Do you have ...?	你有 ... 吗?	Ni you ...... ma?
May I try this on?	我可以试穿吗?	Wo keyi shi chuan ma?
Please show me that.	请给我看看那 个。	Qing gei wo kankan na ge.
bookstore	书店	shudian
clothes	衣服	yifu
department store	百货商店	baihuo shangdian
electrical store	电器商店	dianqi shangdian

ladies' wear	女式服装	nüshi fuzhuang
market	市场	shichang
men's wear	男式服装	nanshi fuzhuang
pharmacist	药剂师	yaojishi
picture postcard	图片明信片	tupian mingxinpian
souvenir shop	纪念品店	jinianpin dian
supermarket	超市	chaoshi
travel agent	旅行社	lüxing she

Sightseeing

Where is ...?	... 在哪里?	... zai nali?
How do I get to ...?	我怎么到 ...?	Wo zenme dao ...?
Is it far?	远不远?	Yuan bu yuan?
bridge	桥	qiao
city	城市	chengshi
city center	市中心	shi zhongxin
gardens	花园	huayuan
hot spring	温泉	wen quan
island	岛	dao
monastery	寺院	siyuan
mountain	山	shan
museum	博物馆	bowuguan
palace	宫殿	gongdian
park	公园	gongyuan
port	港口	gangkou
river	江，河	jiang, he
ruins	废墟	feixu
shopping area	购物区	gouwu qu
shrine	神殿	shendian
street	街	jie
temple	寺庙	si/miao
town	镇	zhen
village	村	cun
province/county	省／县	sheng/xian
zoo	动物园	dongwuyuan
north	北	bei
south	南	nan
east	东	dong
west	西	xi
left/right	左／右	zuo/you
straight ahead	一直向前	yizhi xiangqian
between	在 ... 之间	zai ... zhijian
near/far	近／远	jin/yuan
up/down	上／下	shang/xia
new	新	xin
old/former	旧	jiu
in	在 ... 里	zai ... li
in front of	在 ... 前面	zai ... qianmian

Getting Around

airport	机场	jichang
bicycle	自行车	zixingche
I want to rent a bicycle	我想租一辆自 行车。	Wo xiang zu yiliang zixingche.
ordinary bus	公共汽车	gonggong qiche
express bus	特快公共汽车	tekuai gonggong qiche
minibus	面包车	mianbaoche
main bus station	公共汽车总站	gonggong qiche zong zhan
Which bus goes to ...?	哪一路公共汽 车到 ... 去?	Nayilu gonggong qiche dao ... qu?
When is the next bus?	下一辆公共汽车 是什么时候?	Xiayiliang gonggong qiche shi shenme shihou?
Please tell me where to get off?	请告诉我在哪 里下车?	Qing gaosu wo zai nali xia che.
car	小汽车	xiaoqiche
ferry	渡船	duchuan
baggage room	行李室	xingli shi
one-way ticket	单程票	dancheng piao
return ticket	往返票	wangfan piao
taxi	出租车	chuzuche
ticket	票	piao
ticket office	售票处	shoupiao chu
timetable	时刻表	shikebiao

Accommodations

air-conditioning	空调	kongtiao
bath	洗澡	xizao
check-out	退房	tui fang
deposit	定金	dingjin
double bed	双人床	shuangren chuang
hair drier	吹风机	chuifeng ji
room	房间	fangjian
economy room	经济房	jingji fang
key	钥匙	yaoshi
front desk	前台	qiantai
single/twin room	单人 / 双人房	danren/shuangren fang
single beds	单人床	danren chuang
shower	淋浴	linyu
standard room	标准房间	biaozhun fangjian
deluxe suite	豪华套房	haohua taofang

Eating Out

May I see the menu?	请给我看看菜单。	Qing gei wo kankan caidan
Is there a set menu?	有没有套餐？	You meiyou taocan?
I'd like ….	我想要 …	Wo xiang yao …
May I have one of those?	请给我这个。	Qing gei wo zhege
I am a vegetarian	我是素食者。	Wo shi sushizhe.
Waiter/waitress!	服务员！	Fuwuyuan!
May I have a fork/knife/spoon	请给我一把叉 / 刀 / 汤匙。	Qing gei wo yiba cha/dao/tangshi
May we have the check please.	请把帐单开给我们。	Qing ba zhangdan kaigei women
breakfast	早餐	zaocan
buffet	自助餐	zizhucan
chopsticks	筷子	kuaizi
dinner	晚餐	wancan
to drink	喝	he
to eat	吃	chi
food	食品	shipin
full (stomach)	饱	bao
hot/cold	热 / 冷	re/leng
hungry	饿	e
lunch	午餐	wucan
set menu	套餐	taocan
spicy	酸辣	suan la
hot (spicy)	辣	la
sweet	甜	tian
mild	淡	dan
Western food	西餐	xi can
restaurant	餐馆	canguan
restaurant (upscale)	饭店	fandian

Food

apple	苹果	pingguo
bacon	咸肉	xianrou
bamboo shoots	笋	sun
beancurd	豆腐	doufu
bean sprouts	豆芽	dou ya
beans	豆	dou
beef	牛肉	niurou
beer	啤酒	pijiu
bread	面包	mianbao
butter	黄油	huangyou
chicken	鸡	ji
crab	蟹	xie
duck	鸭	ya
eel	鳗	man
egg	蛋	dan
eggplant	茄子	qiezi
fermented soybean paste	酱	jiang
fish	鱼	yu
fried egg	炒蛋	chao dan
fried tofu	油豆腐	you doufu
fruit	水果	shuiguo
fruit juice	果汁	guo zhi
ginger	姜	jiang
ice cream	冰淇淋	bingqilin

meat	肉	rou
melon	瓜	gua
noodles	面	mian
egg noodles	鸡蛋面	jidan mian
wheat flour noodles	面粉面	mianfen mian
rice flour noodles	米粉面	mifen mian
omelet	煎蛋饼	jiandanbing
onion	洋葱	yangcong
peach	桃子	taozi
pepper	胡椒粉，辣椒	hujiaofen, lajiao
pickles	泡菜	paocai
pork	猪肉	zhurou
potato	土豆	tudou
rice	米饭	mifan
rice crackers	爆米花饼干	baomihua bing'gan
rice wine	米酒	mi jiu
salad	色拉	sela
salmon	鲑鱼，大马哈鱼	guiyu, damahayu
salt	盐	yan
scallion	韭葱	jiucong
seaweed	海带	haidai
shrimp	虾	xia
soup	汤	tang
soy sauce	酱油	jiangyou
squid	鱿鱼	youyu
steak	牛排	niupai
sugar	糖	tang
vegetables	蔬菜	shucai
yoghurt	酸奶	suannai

Drinks

beer	啤酒	pijiu
black tea	红茶	hong cha
coffee (hot)	（热）咖啡	(re) kafei
green tea	绿茶	lü cha
iced coffee	冰咖啡	bing kafei
milk	牛奶	niunai
mineral water	矿泉水	kuang quanshui
orange juice	橙汁	cheng zhi
wine	葡萄酒	putaojiu

Numbers

0	零	ling
1	一	yi
2	二	er
3	三	san
4	四	si
5	五	wu
6	六	liu
7	七	qi
8	八	ba
9	九	jiu
10	十	shi
11	十一	shiyi
12	十二	shier
20	二十	ershi
21	二十一	ershi yi
22	二十二	ershi er
30	三十	sanshi
40	四十	sishi
100	一百	yi bai
101	一百零一	yi bai ling yi
200	二百	er bai

Time

Monday	星期一	xingqiyi
Tuesday	星期二	xingqi'er
Wednesday	星期三	xingqisan
Thursday	星期四	xingqisi
Friday	星期五	xingqiwu
Saturday	星期六	xingqiliu
Sunday	星期天	xingqitian
today	今天	jintian
yesterday	昨天	zuotian
tomorrow	明天	mingtian

BEIJING SUBWAY

Line 1 crosses central Beijing from east to west, and the circular Line 2 runs around its perimeter, tracing the route once occupied by the walls of the Inner City. Dongzhimen station on Line 2 is the connection point for the ABC Airport Express train. Line 5 splices through the city, running from north to south. The other lines are commuter routes.

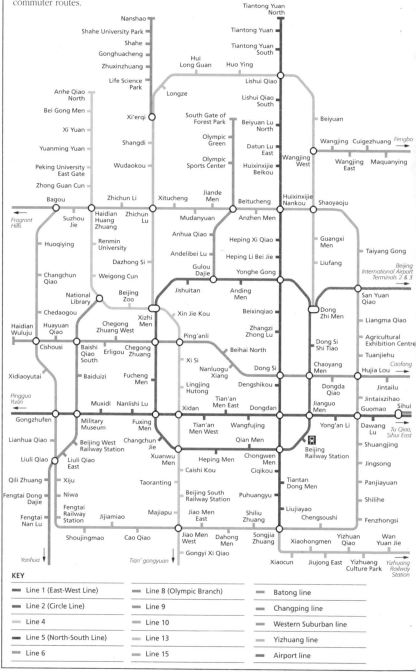

KEY

▬ Line 1 (East-West Line)	▬ Line 8 (Olympic Branch)	▬ Batong line
▬ Line 2 (Circle Line)	▬ Line 9	▬ Changping line
▬ Line 4	▬ Line 10	▬ Western Suburban line
▬ Line 5 (North-South Line)	▬ Line 13	▬ Yizhuang line
▬ Line 6	▬ Line 15	▬ Airport line